T0339666

Selling Sustainability Short?

Can private standards bring about more sustainable production practices? This question is of interest to conscientious consumers, academics studying the effectiveness of private regulation, and corporate social responsibility practitioners alike. Grabs provides an answer by combining an impact evaluation of 1,900 farmers with rich qualitative evidence from the coffee sectors of Honduras, Colombia and Costa Rica. Identifying an institutional design dilemma that private sustainability standards encounter as they scale up, this book shows how this dilemma plays out in the coffee industry. It highlights how the erosion of price premiums and the adaptation to buyers' preferences have curtailed standards' effectiveness in promoting sustainable practices that create economic opportunity costs for farmers, such as agroforestry or agroecology. It also provides a voice for coffee producers and value chain members to explain why the current system is failing in its mission to provide environmental, social, and economic co-benefits, and what changes are necessary to do better.

JANINA GRABS is a postdoctoral researcher at ETH Zurich. She is the recipient of APSA's 2019 Virginia M. Walsh Dissertation Award, the 2018 Giandomenico Majone Prize for the best early career contribution to the ECPR Standing Group on Regulatory Governance, the 2019 Oran R. Young Prize of the Earth System Governance Project, and the 2016 IFAMA Best Paper Award in the category 'relevance for managers'. She also provides strategic advice to the coffee industry, for instance as 2019 SCA Re:Co Speaker.

Organizations and the Natural Environment

Series Editors

Jorge Rivera, *George Washington University*
J. Alberto Aragón-Correa, *University of Surrey*

Editorial Board

The increasing attention given to environmental protection issues has resulted in a growing demand for high-quality, actionable research on sustainability and business environmental management. This new series, published in conjunction with the Group for Research on Organizations and the Natural Environment (GRONEN), presents students, academics, managers, and policy-makers with the latest thinking on key topics influencing business practice today.

Published Titles

Forthcoming Titles

Selling Sustainability Short?

The Private Governance of Labor and the Environment in the Coffee Sector

JANINA GRABS
ETH Zurich

CAMBRIDGE
UNIVERSITY PRESS

University Printing House, Cambridge CB2 8BS, United Kingdom

One Liberty Plaza, 20th Floor, New York, NY 10006, USA

477 Williamstown Road, Port Melbourne, VIC 3207, Australia

314-321, 3rd Floor, Plot 3, Splendor Forum, Jasola District Centre, New Delhi - 110025, India

103 Penang Road, #05-06/07, Visioncrest Commercial, Singapore 238467

Cambridge University Press is part of the University of Cambridge.

It furthers the University's mission by disseminating knowledge in the pursuit of education, learning and research at the highest international levels of excellence.

www.cambridge.org
Information on this title: www.cambridge.org/9781108799508
DOI: 10.1017/9781108875325

First published 2020
First paperback edition 2022

A catalogue record for this publication is available from the British Library

Library of Congress Cataloging in Publication data
Names: Grabs, Janina, 1989– author.
Title: Selling sustainability short? : the private governance of labor and the environment in the coffee sector / Janina Grabs.
Description: Cambridge, United Kingdom ; New York, NY : Cambridge University Press, 2020. | Series: Organizations and the natural environment | Includes bibliographical references and index.
Identifiers: LCCN 2019057537 (print) | LCCN 2019057538 (ebook) | ISBN 9781108835039 (hardback) | ISBN 9781108875325 (ebook)
Subjects: LCSH: Coffee industry – Environmental aspects. | Sustainable development. | Social responsibility of business.
Classification: LCC HD9199.A2 G73 2020 (print) | LCC HD9199.A2 (ebook) | DDC 338.1/7373–dc23
LC record available at https://lccn.loc.gov/2019057537
LC ebook record available at https://lccn.loc.gov/2019057538

ISBN 978-1-108-83503-9 Hardback
ISBN 978-1-108-79950-8 Paperback

D 6 - Dissertation, Westfälische Wilhelms-Universität Münster

Contents

Figures

Tables

Acknowledgments

Early in my PhD journey, I came across a quote (attributed to Thomas Jefferson) that has stayed with me ever since: "If you want something you have never had, you have to do something you have never done." Over the course of this experience, I have indeed done many things I could have scarcely imagined at its outset: I visited the second-most dangerous city in the world (San Pedro Sula in Honduras); traipsed around isolated coffee farms in villages whose only connection to the outside world was one communal jeep and a frequently flooded dirt road; renegotiated contracts over dinner in the middle of a Colombian origin tour; chatted with international traders over the fluctuations of the stock market at prestigious industry conferences; and learned more about coffee agronomy and economics than I thought I would ever need to know. None of it would have been possible without the continuous support of a large number of people who have been exceptionally generous with their time, knowledge, and friendship.

First and foremost, I owe an enormous amount of gratitude to all participants in this research project. To preserve confidentiality, I cannot share names or organizations, but I have enjoyed incredible levels of hospitality and enthusiastic assistance in coffee communities across Honduras, Colombia, and Costa Rica. This ranged from logistical support – being driven around with my suitcase on the back of a motorcycle stands out as a highlight –, invitations for lunch, dinner, and coffee, to participants taking substantial amounts of time out of their busy days to share their insights. *Muchísimas gracias* for inviting a young female German social scientist into your world, and for your patience, respect, and dedication toward making this project succeed. I hope that I can repay a small amount of the debt owed through making your voices heard. Many thanks also to all expert interviewees who connected with me, in person or over Skype, from all over the world to explain their role in the complex coffee value chain, and who responded to my numerous questions with grace and generosity.

The Centro de Inteligencia sobre Mercados Sostenibles (CIMS) team at INCAE Business School under the leadership of Bernard Kilian introduced me both to the practicalities of fieldwork in coffee and life in Costa Rica. Many thanks to Andrés Guevara, Juan Pablo López, Emilie Dardaine, Melissa Menocal, Alejandro Roblero, and Yensy Corella for sharing their expertise and making me feel like an honorary *tica*. I would furthermore like to thank Bernard Kilian for sharing his knowledge on the economic-environmental trade-offs of coffee farming, as well as for helping us solve implementation problems the *tico* way, and Jan Börner from Bonn University for steadfast and reliable advice on the econometrics of impact evaluation. Sharing the ups and downs of fieldwork, data cleaning, and analysis with my colleagues Daniel Calderón and Andrea Estrella was a bonding experience like no other – thank you for the laughs and the venting sessions, both of which greatly enhanced my mental well-being. Many thanks also to my fellow PhD students and the faculty members at the Graduate School of Politics at the University of Münster who welcomed me with open arms during my summer stays in Münster, supported me in my teaching and research activities, and were both understanding and encouraging of my frequent stays abroad.

My academic advisors have been steadfast supporters without whom this journey would have been impossible. Thank you to my *Doktorvater* and primary supervisor, Thomas Dietz, for successfully creating and heading the TRANSSUSTAIN junior researcher group within which this project was carried out; for your advice and guidance in questions large and small on the process of writing a PhD and embarking on an academic career; and especially for the large amount of trust and independence you granted the junior researcher group in designing and implementing this study. Thank you also for continuously helping to refocus my attention and redirect the many early ideas and diversions into a well-specified work program. I furthermore greatly appreciated the financial support of the Ministerium für Kultur und Wissenschaft des Landes Nordrhein-Westfalen (Ministry of Culture and Science of the Federal State of North Rhine-Westphalia) and the University of Münster. Finally, thank you for your generosity in supporting my plans to develop international research experience through academic exchanges with unhesitant enthusiasm.

One of these exchanges was at the School of Public Policy and Administration (SPPA) of Carleton University, Ottawa, under the guidance of my second supervisor, Graeme Auld. I am extremely grateful for this opportunity, which started out from an email exchange and turned into an incredibly enriching experience. It greatly expanded my horizons, allowing me to delve deeper into the theoretical underpinnings of private regulatory governance and develop much of the final framework of this project. Graeme, thank you for dedicating so much of your time and energy to reviewing early drafts of sections of my thesis and related work; and for your boundless generosity in introducing me to your network and providing general advice on future steps to come. I am also greatly appreciative of the hospitality of the SPPA, which hosted me as a visiting academic researcher in the winter of 2017/ 2018 and provided an inspiring and welcoming environment in which I wrote large parts of the thesis this book is based on. The book further benefited from a second research exchange at Yale University's School of Forestry and Environmental Studies in the academic year 2018/2019, where I was hosted by Benjamin Cashore at the Governance, Environment and Markets Initiative. This stay provided an invaluable time to transform my thesis into the present pages and gather feedback from a stellar group of scholars, including Xun Cao, Greg Distelhorst, Stacy VanDeveer, and Yixian Sun. Thank you so much, Ben, for supporting my research through your generosity, hospitality, and incredible creativity – even if "Boom – Roasted!" did not become the final book title after all.

I am also very grateful to the academic editors of the ONE Series, Jorge Rivera and Juan Alberto Aragón-Correa, as well as the staff at Cambridge University Press, first and foremost my editor Valerie Appleby, for believing in this book and making the publication process so smooth. Thank you also to the four anonymous reviewers whose comments improved the final version immensely.

Finally, I am ever so thankful to my friends and family for providing the emotional support and encouragement necessary for this long and strenuous process to come to fruition. Thank you both to old friends around the world, who made these last years special by reconnecting in person and electronically despite the distance separating us, and to new friends in Alajuela, Münster, Ottawa, and New Haven, who invited me into their lives even though I could only stay a short while at a time. To close, I cannot properly express my gratitude to my parents and grandparents for their unwavering belief in me and the path I have chosen. From my first memories onward, you have supported me in more ways than I can count – my grandpa getting the right documents to me in time to sign up for my PhD graduation was only the last in a chain of innumerable large and small ways in which this work would have been impossible to achieve without you. I dedicate this book to you.

The following book is a revised version of the PhD dissertation "The effectiveness of market-driven regulatory sustainability governance. Assessing the design of private sustainability standards and their impacts on Latin American coffee farmers' production practices", successfully defended and accepted on November 9 2018 at the Westfälische Wilhelms-Universität Münster.

1 | *Introduction*

If you ask the question 'if all the coffee in the world were sustainably certified, would that sort out all the environmental problems related to coffee?', the answer is no. Then the next question is 'would it sort out most of the important ones?' and I think there again the answer may be no. So the third question is: 'what is the point?'

(Interview 6, Centre for Agriculture and
Bioscience International, 2015)

Approaching yet another tiny Honduran coffee farm, I marvel at its integration into the mountainous landscape. Tall pine trees rise above the man-high coffee shrubs; orange trees offer a quick snack; a stream snakes its way through the plot; and I hear birds chirping. I am on my way to interview the farm owner, a shy gentleman of about 60 years of age, on the production practices he uses to manage his Fairtrade-/organic-certified farm. About halfway through the conversation, I ask what types of fertilizer he uses – does he apply only organic or also synthetic fertilizer, which would be prohibited according to the certification rules? He hesitates, looks me in the eye, and then says softly, "I use both." After a pause, he adds, "only using organic fertilizer simply does not produce high enough yields."

Back at the cooperative headquarters, the manager sighs.

We converted to organic production because they promised it would give us access to higher prices. But we experienced yield declines so severe that the premiums barely allow us to break even compared to conventional production. To make matters worse, our largest Fairtrade buyer wants to renegotiate our contracts and is asking us for a discounted price. But that would be a noncompliance in our books and could lead to us losing our certification! We are having trouble finding demand for our certified coffee in general. The conscientiousness and reliability of other supply chain actors is a huge problem. (Field notes, 2016)

As our discussion concludes, he sends me off with some cooperative-produced honey, and an associate drives me to the next village in the one Jeep the community owns.

On the way there, and looking out over wide swaths of clear-cut forest that have been planted with interminable rows of coffee saplings, I ponder what I just heard and think back to a conversation I had over breakfast in a luxurious hotel at the Costa Rican Pacific Coast. This is where large coffee buyers, traders, and producing-country actors gather annually for the Semana Internacional del Café, the International Coffee Week. A representative of a multinational trading house had just asked me about my work. As I explained my focus on certifications, he scoffed.

Oh, certifications! What you need to understand is that the coffee trade is about much more than that. I only ever buy Honduran Fairtrade coffee at the fixed minimum price if I get a container of conventional coffee from the same cooperative at a discount. Otherwise, why would I buy Honduran coffee if I can get also get Fairtrade coffee from Peru, which has much higher quality? The problem with Peruvian Fairtrade/organic coffee, however, is that everybody knows there is certificate-trading going on. There are far too many certificates floating around for the amount of coffee they are actually producing. (Field notes, 2015)

As if on cue, that same day the head of another trading house noted in his keynote speech to the assembled representatives of the coffee industry that "unfortunately, as many of us here would be aware, there are loopholes and malpractices in many coffee origins in the sourcing of certified coffee. I feel that each of us has to strongly guard against these. A PR disaster with any one player will hurt the entire industry and will take a long time to recover from" (Verma 2015). The frankness of the statement raised eyebrows and generated meaningful glances between members of the audience, but caused little visible surprise among these leaders of the coffee trade.

As the Jeep continues making its way along the bumpy Honduran mountain roads, my thoughts wander to Germany, my home country, and one of the very first interviews I conducted there before moving to Costa Rica. I had taken the train to Hamburg to talk to the sustainability project manager of a leading coffee importer, who looked at me with genuine exasperation.

I really wonder what impact all the money that the coffee industry spends each year on certifications has in the field. We recently did a back-of-the-envelope calculation and determined that the sector is paying around 250 million dollars in premiums annually. But there seems to be so much red tape and overhead costs that the improvements in the field – from what we can see – are quite moderate compared to these high costs. Could putting this money into results-oriented projects, rather than supporting global certification programs, have a better return on investment?" (Interview 3, importer-affiliated nongovernmental organization [NGO], 2015)

When I put this question to the head of the Corporate Social Responsibility department of a major German roaster, he provided a differentiated answer:

I think we need both. For our specialty segment, we have established our own training program that leads farmers in high-quality regions toward fulfilling NGO-led certification requirements while also advising them in other aspects that are important to us – such as improving quality and yields, or providing for gender equality – that the certifications do not cover. However, we estimate that overall, around 300,000 smallholder farmers are involved in producing the coffee that comes through our supply chain. It would be economically ruinous to roll out such closely accompanied projects to everyone; and this is where baseline industry-led standards such as 4C could allow for at least first steps in – let me put it very carefully – a developmental process toward sustainability. But if I now ask from a managerial perspective: 'do they fulfill that function? Do I get smallholder farmers from the conventional sector onto a pathway toward sustainability?', I have to honestly say that I have increasing doubts. In particular, there appears to be a political opposition by leading global roasters – other than us – to seeing 4C as a first step in a transformational pathway. Instead, they want to settle for the baseline standards alone. And that, for me, is not sustainable. (Interview 20, roaster 3, 2016)

As I approach my destination, a tiny town close to the Salvadoran border where I will spend the night, I wonder: Are these impressions and experiences representative of the way private sustainability standards are implemented in the coffee value chain? How effective are such standards in bringing about the sustainability advances they promote? And can we identify features of such schemes that make them more likely or less to succeed in their mission to simultaneously change production practices and redistribute wealth across the value chain? This book uses research carried out in three countries, interviews with over sixty experts, and surveys of more than 1,900 coffee farmers to answer these questions.

1.1 The Private Governance of Sustainability in the Coffee Sector

Why look at the private governance of coffee rather than another commodity? Arguably, coffee is the lifeblood of modern society. It provides energy in workplaces with ever-increasing demands; it facilitates social encounters in a highly individualized culture; and it delivers new sensatory experiences to consumers seeking out high-quality products. Coffee also connects individuals across the globe through intricate supply chains. This allows us to appreciate the advantages and pitfalls of globalization in a very concrete fashion. For decades, the sustainability of coffee production has therefore carried great weight in the minds of consumers and policymakers. How can we guarantee that our purchasing habits contribute to the socioeconomic advancement of the estimated 25 million smallholder coffee farmers worldwide? And can we do so without destroying the fragile ecosystems of the subtropical regions where coffee is produced?

Thanks to the public interest in these questions, the governance instrument I examine – private sustainability standards such as Fairtrade or Rainforest Alliance certification – has enjoyed a longer existence and greater proliferation in coffee than any other commodity sector. The very idea of using market-based instruments to improve farmer livelihoods by providing 'fair trade' labels arose from a collaboration between Mexican coffee producers and a Dutch civil society organization (Renard 2003). The coffee sector also sports the greatest number of competing schemes. At least seven standards are used in the mainstream market, and new ones continue to emerge. Overall, between 40 and 50 percent of all coffee is produced according to the tenets of some certification or verification scheme (GCP 2015; Lernoud *et al.* 2017). For all these reasons, the coffee sector is a front-runner in global supply chain governance. Lessons learned in this sector also travel to comparable value chains such as the production and trade of cocoa, tea, cotton, or palm oil. Like coffee, these industries are defined by transnational webs of production in which smallholder farmers in the Global South produce a large share of global supply. They also share similar challenges regarding the ethical and environmentally friendly production of commodities in biodiversity hot spots where public governance capacity is frequently limited. The private governance of coffee is thus a test case that can provide insights into the intractable challenge of sustainable commodity production worldwide.

Given its front-runner status, scholars researching the introduction and dissemination of private sustainability standards have shown great interest in coffee as a case study (see, for instance, Giovannucci and Ponte 2005; Muradian and Pelupessy 2005; Raynolds 2009; Auld 2010; Manning *et al.* 2012; Reinecke *et al.* 2012; Levy *et al.* 2016). Similarly, impact evaluation studies have increasingly focused on the coffee sector (see DeFries *et al.* 2017 and Bray and Neilson 2017 for comprehensive meta-reviews), providing us with an ever-growing evidence base on outcomes and impacts of certification. Yet, this evidence continues to be inconclusive, with contradictory findings that appear to be strongly linked to local contexts. Only a subset of studies applies robust counterfactual designs. Many are outdated and refer to certifications when they were just a niche occurrence, not a mainstream strategy. Furthermore, few such studies use a clear theoretical framework of analysis that allows for between-standard differentiation or hypothesis testing on institutional design features. Consequently, there has been little linkage of those results back to the governance literature. This book fills this research gap by adding a novel theoretical approach and unique comparative data, as well as rich contextual information to the existing knowledge.

1.2 Defining Transnational Market-Driven Regulatory Governance

The empirical focus of this analysis are private standards, certification and verification schemes focused on economic, environmental, and social sustainability in the coffee sector. Such schemes create systems of private rules, formalized in standards, according to which sustainable production practices and products arising from such practices are verified and/or certified. These products are then made recognizable to either intermediate buyers (in business-to-business standards) or final consumers (through on-package labeling) in the marketplace (cf. Pattberg 2005a). Importantly, the implementation of these standards is not mandated by governmental authority. Rather, such initiatives use market-based incentives to attract and maintain participating producers (Bernstein and Cashore 2007). Typical market-based incentives are promises of premium pricing and preferential market access, as well as a latent threat of market exclusion if producers decline to take part (Cashore *et al.* 2004).

Others have conceptualized these types of initiatives using a variety of terms: eco-labels (van der Ven 2019), non-state market-driven governance systems (Cashore 2002; Bernstein and Cashore 2007; Auld *et al.* 2009), regulatory standard-setting schemes (Abbott and Snidal 2009), private governance organizations (Fransen 2011), or transnational private regulation (Bartley 2007). Yet, not all initiatives focus mainly on eco(logical) characteristics and not all use front-package labeling – making the term eco-label a misnomer in certain cases (cf. Delmas and Grant 2014). Other terms include only some of the key distinctive features of this governance instrument. Instead, I consider such schemes to be *transnational market-driven regulatory governance initiatives*.

Transnational market-driven regulatory governance exhibits features common to many, but not all, initiatives that have been categorized as 'private governance' to date. First, it is governance that is applied *through or within the marketplace*. It does not include private governance that occurs through standardizing focal institutions such as the International Organization for Standardization (ISO). In such settings, nonmarket negotiations shape standards' content, and network compatibility pressures enable the self-enforcement of standards (Büthe and Mattli 2011). In the absence of a single focal institution, however, multiple standards may emerge that compete for the participation of actors at all levels of the value chain (Cashore *et al.* 2004; Auld 2014). As this book shows, this leads to distinct strategic calculations by both standard-setters and participants. Second, the regulatory aspect focuses our attention on private governance initiatives that set at least some *substantive rules* that participants are subject to and which may affect their core behavior. Purely procedural rule-making (such as, for instance, accounting procedures [e.g., Green 2010]) is therefore not in the purview of this analysis. It may, however, have indirect or secondary effects that spur behavioral changes. Finally, this book focuses on *transnational* governance in which the 'shadow of the state' and the possibility of governmental intervention in standard-setting or enforcement is comparatively less present than in domestic settings (although not completely absent; compare Verbruggen 2013). Still, many of the core insights also apply to domestic market-driven regulatory governance in states that have made credible commitments to relegate certain regulatory tasks to private initiatives and the market.

To avoid excessive wordiness, I occasionally use the term 'private governance' in the following chapters. This should be read, in line with the preceding explanation, as a stand-in for 'market-driven regulatory governance'. Given the empirical focus, I will also intermittently use 'private sustainability standards', 'certification schemes', or similar language in later text. However, the theoretical scope applies to other transnational market-driven regulatory governance initiatives as well.

1.3 Research Questions and Structure of This Book

At its core, this book aims to answer a simple question: does private governance work? Can the use of market-driven, voluntary mechanisms compel value chain actors to change their practices in the direction of greater sustainability? And, if yes, why are some standards more successful in that mission than others?

This book thus evaluates market-driven regulatory governance initiatives' effectiveness in leading to sustained behavioral change in line with the original institutional goals of resolving collective environmental and social problems (cf. Black 2008). It identifies institutional design features that are more likely to contribute to such effectiveness, as well as flaws in regulatory design and implementation that limit the potential of private standards in achieving their mission. With this aim, it connects five elements related to the effectiveness of private governance. First, it defines institutional effectiveness by identifying the *outcome goals* of market-driven sustainability governance. It then assesses the success of such initiatives in passing *market incentives* down through the chain and changing conventional supply chain mechanisms. Third, it studies the impacts of such initiatives in the field on *producer behavior and practices*. Fourth, it evaluates the initiatives' *institutional design* as it relates to these two outcomes. Recognizing that private regulation does not exist in a vacuum, it finally analyzes how private standards *interact with international and national-level institutions* already in place.

I draw on Kiser and Ostrom's (1982) Three Worlds of Action to locate the empirical focus of this research on the operational level of institutional analysis, where "participants interact in light of the internal and external incentives they face to generate outcomes directly in the world" (Ostrom 2005, p. 60). Combining this framework with definitions of institutional effectiveness drawn from the study of international environmental regimes (Bernauer 1995; Young and Levy 1999; Underdal 2002), I proceed as follows.

After this introduction, Chapter 2 presents the theoretical framework underpinning the analysis. It serves two functions. First, it introduces the micro-institutional rational choice approach to evaluating institutional effectiveness used in this book. The chapter explains why I consider producers targeted by market-driven regulatory governance boundedly rational actors, what this characterization entails, and how institutional arrangements can help such actors to overcome coordination problems. It then explains how I leverage Kiser and Ostrom's Three Worlds of Action to link institutional design choices to their outcomes and to operationalize institutional effectiveness. In a second step, Chapter 2 examines market-driven regulatory governance using this approach. It uncovers the institutional design dilemma that standards face as they scale up. It also specifies a number of hypotheses on how these choices (e.g., between binding and flexible standard-setting; strict or flexible oversight mechanisms; and a focus on price premiums or on capacity building) will affect the implementation of standards by drawing on institutional rational choice theory as well as insights from the socio-legal literature.

Chapter 3 then introduces the first piece of the puzzle – the definition of the *institutional goal of a sustainable coffee sector*. In comparison to other foci of private governance, for instance, technological standards (Büthe and Mattli 2011), sustainability is a loaded term whose concrete definition has long been disputed. This is no different in the coffee sector – representing a reality that makes the neutral evaluation of sustainability governance initiatives tricky. I solve the dilemma by identifying, and separately analyzing in the field, different interpretations of 'coffee sector sustainability' put forward by different stakeholders. Each of these interpretations has different implications for the role that private governance is required to play.

Chapter 4 takes a deeper look at the *integration of private sustainability standards in the broader market*. In particular, it analyzes how well economic compensation trickles down to the farm level once standards enter mainstream marketing channels. It further probes how the level of economic incentives corresponds to the practice changes farmers are expected to make.

Chapter 5 presents an overview of the *field-level evidence of producer behavior* gathered in three producing countries across three categories of sustainability practices. In doing so, it summarizes the state of sustainability across 1,900 coffee producers, and provides in-depth information on the agro-ecological and social challenges in coffee production.

As the fourth analytical component, Chapter 6 compares the *institutional design of the seven market-driven regulatory governance initiatives* in the coffee sector. Drawing on a meta-analysis of the indicators from Chapter 5, it assesses whether certain design characteristics of standards make it more likely that farmers change their production practices and adopt more sustainable behavior.

Chapter 7 explains how standards interact with public regulatory frameworks in the three case study countries. Specifically, it asks whether *public and private regulation complement or counteract one another* in the case of socially and environmentally responsible farming practices in Latin America.

Finally, Chapter 8 concludes and provides an outlook for the future of the private governance of the coffee chain and supply chains in general. It furthermore explores what implications the analytical conclusions of this work have for the broader disciplines of regulatory governance and international political economy.

1.4 Theoretical and Empirical Contributions to the Literature

This book's main contribution is a novel theoretical framework for analyzing the large-scale effectiveness of market-driven regulation, one of the most-heralded new forms of global governance. Although a vast literature has examined the development and design of private governance initiatives, such efforts are rarely in conversation with research about their on-the-ground effects. By allowing for the interaction of several private governance schemes, considering sector-wide dynamics, and tracing their effects to the producer level, this theory of private governance effectiveness uncovers the limits of regulating through markets in unprecedented ways. These advances further our knowledge of the likely potential of private regulatory tools to complement or replace state action in attempts at 'smart regulation' (Gunningham and Grabosky 1998). My framework furthermore introduces three innovations: an improved approach to linking institutional design choices to their outcomes; a new conceptualization of effectiveness; and a novel approach to allow for regime complexity and polycentricity. Finally, I employ a rich new data set that draws on both qualitative and quantitative research in a multilevel and comparative triangulation design.

First, contributions from political science and business ethics that study private regulation have to date struggled to provide consistent theoretical frameworks that permit the examination of rule-setting and implementation in the same analysis. In consequence, such work has focused on the behavior of certification organizations (Fransen 2011; Auld 2014), stakeholders (Fransen 2012; Moog *et al.* 2015), or lead firms (Dauvergne and Lister 2012; van der Ven 2014; Levy *et al.* 2016), paying less attention to the choice sets of producers. Impact evaluations and work on the decoupling of rules and practices (Aravind and Christmann 2011; Bray and Neilson 2017; DeFries *et al.* 2017; Giuliani *et al.* 2017), in turn, tend to focus solely on outcomes without analyzing the institutional design choices that led to suboptimal implementation in detail. This book bridges this gap by extending and adapting a micro-institutional rational choice analysis approach (Kiser and Ostrom 1982) to investigate the effectiveness of private regulatory governance. This framework presumes all actors to be boundedly rational, and uses three levels of decision-making (constitutional, collective choice, and operational) to logically connect rule-making to its outcomes. The innovative operationalization of this framework in the present case demonstrates its applicability to the evaluation of both private and public regulatory tools, and provides a blueprint for other scholars to adapt it to their own cases under investigation.

Second, previous efforts at examining the effectiveness of private regulatory governance (Gulbrandsen 2005, 2009; Pattberg 2005b; Espach 2006; Auld *et al.* 2008; Auld 2010; Marx and Cuypers 2010), while valuable in their own right, have used idiosyncratic definitions of effectiveness that – due to their timing and data availability – frequently did not allow for the assessment of on-the-ground impacts. Most focused on certification uptake and – at best – audit reports of required changes in practices, making the a priori assumption that effective monitoring and enforcement of standard rules are universal, and that certifiers' audits reflect the real implementation rates on the ground – which may, but must not, be the case. Finally, few authors (with the notable exception of Gulbrandsen 2004) spell out explicitly the causal mechanisms (and necessary conditions for those mechanisms to work long-term) that connect the institution of private standard-setting to its goal attainment and problem-solving potential. These mechanisms, and their impacts on the ground, are at the central focus of analysis of this book. I incorporate insights on problem solving and goal attainment by political scientists concerned with environmental regime effectiveness (Bernauer 1995; Young 1999, 2011) and take an explicit problem-solving approach, asking sequentially: (1) whether individuals adhered to the rules specified in the private standards; (2) whether institutional change changed their behavior toward more sustainable production behavior; and (3) whether the aggregation of behavioral change leads to different results in line with institutional goals. In line with step 2, a central analytical component of this definition of institutional effectiveness is *outcome additionality*, that is, the extent to which initiatives change the behavior of producers and value chain members from what they would have done otherwise. Comparing seven different standards in how they contribute to outcome additionality allows me to connect the institution of private standard-setting to its goal attainment and problem-solving potential, defined in the words of Young (2001, p. 19854) as "the extent to which regimes contribute to solving or mitigating the problems that motivate those people who create the regimes."

Third, it has been increasingly recognized that private regulation does not exist in a void; instead, it enters a crowded governance arena (Bartley 2018) of preexisting national-level rules, supranational treaties, market relations, and contractual governance (Gulbrandsen 2004; Amengual 2010; Bartley 2011; Verbruggen 2013). My theoretical framework explicitly allows for the coexistence of various institutional arrangements and their results, such as the layering of rules from multiple sources and the provision of competing incentives. By examining coffee production in three national-level jurisdictions, I further show how the existence of differing public rules on the ground affects the supposed equivalence of the certified goods in terms of their credence attributes and reinforces differences in competitive advantage.

Finally, reliable and up-to-date evidence on the field-level adoption and implementation of private governance initiatives is essential for answering academic questions about their effectiveness and helping practitioners improve practices on the ground. While certification schemes have existed for over thirty years, impact evaluations have only recently moved to studying the ways in which they spur practice changes, and resulting micro-level impacts on land-use change, erosion, biodiversity, and other environmental and social consequences of commodity production, in a comparative fashion. I codesigned and led the collection of fine-grained survey data on sustainable farming practices (the questionnaire included 290 partially conditional questions) in over 1,900 farm-level observations in three Latin American countries (Honduras, Colombia, and Costa Rica). The analysis uses a variety of econometric methods, including propensity score matching and linear and logit regression models, to arrive at outcome additionality results that compare certified to noncertified farmers over a wide range of sustainable production practices. My field-level survey results provide novel insights on the state of sustainability of certified products, given that they cover social and environmental sustainability as well as both practices and biophysical impacts on the ground. This allows for the appreciation of the double burden and trade-offs between social and environmental sustainability; the linkage of practices and their biophysical results; and a more comprehensive and fine-grained understanding of the circumstances and choices that small-scale farmers face as they struggle to reach differentiated markets. In addition, I conducted over sixty semi-structured interviews with economic actors along the coffee value chain to understand how certification schemes are implemented in mainstream global value chains, allowing me to fine-tune the interpretation of the survey results and put them in context.

In the remainder of this introduction, I present the theoretical approach and argument, offer a primer on the global coffee sector, introduce the case selection and methods, and summarize my results.

1.5 The Institutional Design Dilemma of Market-Driven Regulatory Governance Initiatives

When using a micro-institutional approach, researchers study individuals' actions in the context of *institutional arrangements*. Institutional arrangements refer to all types of rules that people are subject to and which govern their actions (Kiser and Ostrom 2000). In the case of small-scale coffee farmers, these arrangements include mainstream market pressures as well as national-level regulation. As a novel institutional arrangement, private sustainability standards may introduce new rules, payoffs, incentives, and enforcement pressures into the preexisting decision environment of smallholder producers. Yet, such market-driven regulatory governance initiatives face an inherent institutional design dilemma: that is, they struggle to pursue two simultaneous goals that lead to contradictory implications for optimal

Table 1.1 *The institutional design dilemma of market-driven regulatory governance initiatives*

Goals	Persistent market-based incentives	Upscaling and mainstreaming
Optimal design choices		
Standard-setting	Reasonably high entry barriers	Improvement pathways for lower-performing producers
Standard enforcement	Strict in-group/out-group differentiation	Improvements in capacity to comply
	Legalistic compliance enforcement	Cooperative compliance management
Standard coexistence	Single standard/super-seal	'Co-opetition' by segmenting the market and differentiated targeting

standard-setting, enforcement, and broad-level coexistence (compare Table 1.1).

On the one hand, producers are likely to leave a voluntary scheme that has a net-negative impact on their operation's bottom line. Market-based private governance schemes relying on voluntary participation therefore have to ensure that *persistent market-based incentives* exist that outweigh the compliance costs (including the administrative burden) of participating in the regulatory scheme (Vogel 2009; Carter *et al.* 2018). Maintaining substantive market-based price premiums requires the establishment of quasi-monopoly conditions, for example, through the implementation of strict process rules that can act as effective barriers to entry to a scheme. According to microeconomic theory, if effective entry barriers are in place, price premiums should arrive at an equilibrium where they are equal to the marginal cost of compliance. Such premiums can then compensate participating producers for their increased costs and create alternative institutional arrangements that allow for the pricing of positive externalities. Alternatively, if entry barriers are weakened, premium prices are likely to disappear as competition is unleashed (Guthman 2007, p. 461). To prevent such rent erosion, it is important to design standard rules in a way that minimizes opportunities to free ride and shirk compliance of practices that raise long-run operating costs. This rationale is in line with the 'logic of control' identified by Auld *et al.* (2015, p. 109). It holds that costly beneficial activities require "institutions capable of controlling behaviour," such as prescriptive rules, audits, and effective incentives, to ensure compliance. It has therefore been a relatively unquestioned assumption in the private governance literature (e.g., Cashore *et al.* 2015) that functionally, market-based private governance frequently resembles command-and-control state regulation, where specific rules and regulations are set out and compliance is monitored and enforced.

However, there exists a simultaneous push for certification schemes to reach beyond the 'low-hanging fruit' of relatively advanced, professional producers and enroll lower-performing individuals in a process of *upscaling and mainstreaming* (Dietz and Auffenberg 2014). To reach such producers, who have a lower capacity to comply with strict rules, strict compliance enforcement may be counterproductive. It may also create regulatory unreasonableness, that is, "the imposition of uniform regulatory requirements in situations where they do not make sense" (Bardach and Kagan 1982, p. 58). Since market-driven standards are voluntary, it is likely that producers will opt out of the certification scheme when encountering regulatory unreasonableness. Such producer defection will limit the ultimate reach and effectiveness of private regulation.

Instead, it is preferable for certification schemes to provide low entry barriers in the beginning and successively ratchet up requirements. They should also provide ample opportunities for producers to correct mistakes and help them to understand and implement the standard rules. Such an institutional design approach further takes into account the limited financial resources that small-scale producers have at their disposal to implement upfront infrastructural investments, and spreads such investments across time. Under this logic, compliance needs to be managed rather than enforced (cf. Chayes and Chayes 1995; Downs *et al.* 1996; Young 2011; Bernstein and Cashore 2012) by providing capacity-building and learning activities such as training sessions and incremental goal-setting.

However, allowing for different rules for different subgroups (e.g., first-year vs. third-year producers) creates much more diffuse entry barriers, as first-year producers can sell the same certified product but have lower compliance costs than third-year producers. Furthermore, as the threat of program exit in the case of noncompliance becomes less credible, there is less risk in delaying implementation until an auditor raises the issue. This may also allow lower-cost producers with sub-optimal behavior to access the certification and increase the supply of certified products. In this way, combining the instrument of market-based private regulation with a development-focused mentality may contribute to a long-term dynamic that undermines the very incentive structure market-driven governance is based on.

As an added challenge, the presence of initial price premiums provides an incentive for the competitive market entry of alternative schemes with different interpretations of 'sustainability', creating a dizzying array of options for buyers and sustainable consumers (Auld 2014). Standard-setters in this position have three options: to strive toward strong collaboration and unified efforts toward creating a sustainable market; to compete on the claim of being the best guarantor of sustainability and risk the destruction of a vulnerable movement; or to pursue a 'divide-and-rule' strategy of 'co-opetition' (Ingenbleek and Meulenberg 2006) by divvying up the market and attempting to target different niche producers and consumers. This third strategy, while most promising for fast and relatively 'painless' upscaling, further weakens demand signals. It also contributes to the erosion of a unified definition of sustainable production that could harness the market-based generation of premiums equal to marginal compliance costs.

In this book, I show that a slow but steady shift toward 'upscaling and mainstreaming' design choices has occurred in most standards under analysis. This shift has undermined the ability of private sustainability standards to act as guarantors for environmentally and socially sustainable behavior and as vehicles for the payments of such ecosystem and social services by consumers. Instead, their effectiveness in driving sustainable behavior – especially practices that incur higher costs – is highly contingent on supportive local institutions. Collectively, acquiescing to a 'co-opetition' strategy has weakened the competitive edge of more stringent standards in terms of providing better sustainability credentials, and has contributed to a 'race to the middle' of sustainability definitions and requirements.

This theoretical framework goes beyond previous insights that low standards are likely to lead to broad coverage, but few behavioral changes, while high standards are more likely to lead to large improvements in a small number of producers (Gulbrandsen 2005; Bernstein and Cashore 2007; Auld 2010). My findings in the coffee sector show that when standard organizations interact in the marketplace, the need to remain competitive in the 'standards market' by attracting large roasters leads organizations with initially high standards to make trade-offs that lower their problem-solving effectiveness. In this fashion, the experiences of the coffee sector – the recognized front-runner regarding sustainable commodity governance – represent a cautionary tale of good intentions gone awry in the marketplace. It may also inform improvements in the sustainability strategies of other sectors.

Before turning to the case study selection, analytical methods, and a summary of findings, the next section provides an initial overview of the coffee sector and the most important steps in the production chain.

1.6 Overview of the Global Coffee Sector and Its Players

Prima facie, coffee is a consumer good with a straightforward production process. In its most simple form, the main commodity product – the coffee bean – only needs to be roasted, ground, and steeped in water to be ready for final consumption. Nevertheless, its supply chain is surprisingly complex, with a multitude of actors that are involved at each processing stage. By some estimates, a coffee bean may change hands 150 times before reaching the end consumer (Milford 2004).

The coffee bean is in effect the seed of a fruit, the coffee cherry, which needs to be grown, peeled, fermented (at which point it is called 'wet parchment'), dried (becoming 'dry parchment' coffee), and hulled before reaching the stage of green coffee ready for export (see Figure 1.1). These primary processing steps are located in the coffee-producing countries, a group that is defined by the subtropical climate necessary for coffee growing. They cluster around the equator between the Tropic of Cancer and the Tropic of Capricorn (ICO 2014) (compare Figure 1.2). By virtue of their subtropical location, many coffee-producing countries are important biodiversity hot spots (Myers *et al.* 2000).

As Figure 1.2 shows, the coffee market is subdivided in two main crop varieties: Arabica (*Coffea arabica*) and Robusta (*Coffea canephora*). Arabica coffee originated in southern Ethiopia and Sudan,

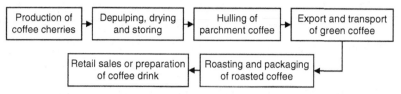

Figure 1.1 Steps in the coffee value chain. Source: Own illustration

and spread over Yemen (in the ninth century) to India, Sri Lanka, Java, and Réunion as well as the rest of Latin America in the seventeenth and eighteenth centuries (Teketay 1999). Today, it makes up around 60 percent of global coffee supply (ITC 2011a). Robusta is native to central and western Africa and emerged commercially in the late nineteenth century as a variety that was more resistant to coffee leaf rust (*Hemileia vastatrix*), a fungal disease that can decimate Arabica coffee farms (Teketay 1999). Nowadays, Robusta coffee is mainly produced in Asia (e.g., Vietnam) and West Africa, while Arabica coffee is mainly grown in East Africa (e.g., Ethiopia) and Latin America. Brazil as well as several African nations produce both Robusta and Arabica. In general, Arabica beans are perceived to have a higher-quality taste profile and sell at a higher price point than Robusta coffee. While over eighty countries export coffee, only three – Brazil, Vietnam, and Colombia – are responsible for the grand share of coffee traded in the world market (compare Table 1.2).

Coffee production can occur on both large-scale plantations and small family farms, with a trend to the latter. The Fairtrade Foundation estimates that 70–80 percent of the global coffee volume is produced by 25 million smallholder farmers, and that 125 million people globally depend on coffee for their livelihoods (Fairtrade Foundation 2012). In most countries, the majority of smallholders do not belong to producer organizations. Rather, they use intermediaries to bring their product to market. Around 55 percent of all global coffee producers are independent smallholder farmers, 25 percent are organized smallholders, and 20 percent are larger farms (Zamora 2013). Independent small-scale farmers are particularly vulnerable in the marketplace. They often only have limited processing equipment at hand, leading to a lower-quality final product, and rely on one or two intermediaries to purchase their coffee, which creates unequal bargaining power. In Latin America, intermediaries are frequently called

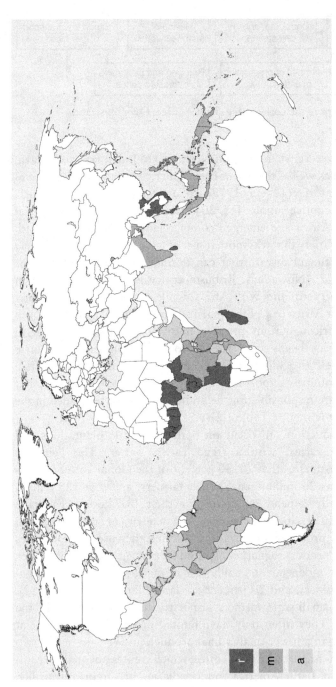

Figure 1.2 The 'bean belt' of countries that produce Robusta (r), Arabica (a), and both types of coffee (m). Source: Image "Carte Coffea robusta Arabic," Wikimedia Commons, in public domain. Available at: https://commons.wikimedia.org/wiki/File:Carte_Coffea_robusta_arabic.png (accessed: November 12, 2017)

Table 1.2 *Top coffee-producing countries in 2017/2018 and their share of world production. Case study countries are bolded. Source: ICO (2019a)*

Country	Share of world production (%)
(1) Brazil	32
(2) Vietnam	19
(3) **Colombia**	9
(4) Indonesia	7
(5) **Honduras**	5
(6) Ethiopia	5
(7) India	4
(8) Uganda	3
(9) Peru	3
… (13) **Costa Rica**	1

'coyotes' for their perceived tendency to defraud isolated small-scale producers (Milford 2014). Well-managed producer organizations can thus bring great advantages to coffee farmers, including access to information, cheaper inputs and credit, processing equipment, quality control, market access, and – in the most advanced cases – price risk management (Rice and McLean 1999; Zamora 2013).

National and multinational coffee traders are responsible for buying green coffee in origin countries, exporting it, shipping it overseas, and importing it in order to sell it to roasters. The market concentration of green coffee traders is considerable. Four globally operating companies each move around 10 percent of the world's green coffee, often through an intricate network of partners and subsidiary companies (Grabs 2017). Most leading coffee traders are also engaged in trading other commodities such as sugar, cocoa, cotton, and grains, which insulates them to a certain extent from price and contract risk in the coffee sector (Newman 2009). The increasing financialization of the sector and the market's volatility has further expanded traders' portfolios: many offer price risk management services and are active in the commodity derivatives market by hedging and speculating on the movement of the coffee price (Newman 2009).

These leading traders also dominate the coffee landscape on the ground in growing communities. Not only do they own a large part of the processing and storage infrastructure, and in some cases even coffee farms, in most coffee-producing countries they are the focal point of interaction between farmers and the downstream supply chain (interviews with traders, 2016). They engage in data gathering to construct harvest estimations, provide processing services and trainings, and relay demand information to farmers, including the demand for sustainably certified coffee (Grabs *et al.* 2016). This growing responsibility makes them lead actors for the implementation of sustainability projects and certification of producers (interview 41, multinational exporter 2, 2016). This includes both the collaboration with coffee cooperatives, if they exist, as well as the direct uptake of group administrator responsibilities.

After producers sell their green coffee, it is transported to the consuming country, roasted, possibly freeze-dried (in the case of instant coffee) or ground, packaged, and distributed to retailers and cafés, where final consumers purchase it in packages or as a drink. Finland and other Scandinavian countries lead in the per capita consumption of coffee by country, consuming up to 12 kg per person per year. As Table 1.3 shows, coffee consumption is still concentrated in the Global North, with the European Union, the United States, Japan, and Australia leading in per capita and total consumption (ICO 2017a). In the United States and Europe, per capita coffee consumption is stabilizing at a high level, with growth opportunities mainly present in the specialty and novelty coffee segment.

On the other hand, the last years have also seen the expansion of coffee consumption in coffee-producing countries such as Brazil, increasing internal demand, as well as the slow introduction of coffee in societies that traditionally prefer tea, such as China or India. China had an annual consumption growth rate of 16 percent over the past decade, for instance, and now consumes as much coffee as Australia (ICO 2015), while consumption in origin countries such as Brazil or Indonesia has increased by more than 5 percent per annum (Verma 2015). Extrapolating existing consumption trends, experts expect the world to need an additional 40 million bags of coffee per annum in ten years' time – almost the production of Brazil, which produced 51 million bags in 2017/18 (Verma 2015; ICO 2019a). If this forecasted rise in demand materializes, it will produce pressure on either

Table 1.3 *Top-ten coffee-consuming countries (or country groups) in 2017/2018 and their share of world consumption. Source: ICO (ICO 2019b)*

Country	Share of world consumption (%)
(1) European Union	27
(2) United States	16
(3) Brazil	14
(4) Japan	5
(5) Indonesia	3
(6) Russian Federation	3
(7) Canada	2
(8) Ethiopia	2
(9) Philippines	2
(10) Vietnam	2

land use, intensification, or both, as coffee producers will need to increase their yields or production surface to meet demand.

Consumer demand is served by coffee roasters, which range in size from tiny start-ups to huge multinational corporations. In 2014, two roasting companies, Nestlé and Jacobs Douwe Egberts, each controlled over 15 percent of the coffee retail market, with Keurig Green Mountain a strong contender for third place (Grabs and Ponte 2019). The segmentation of the coffee market (beyond roasted and ground coffee, there now exist subsegments for freeze-dried and soluble, single-serve capsule, traditional espresso, and out-of-home specialty, as well as Third Wave coffee) allows for high profit margins[1] and amplifies roasters' regional market power, since consuming countries follow different patterns of consumption. For instance, since single-serve coffee is now the most popular form of coffee consumption in the United States, Keurig Green Mountain is the strongest roaster in that market, with 18.4 percent of the market share. In the rest of the world, the

---

[1] Nestlé's powdered and liquid beverage category had trading operating profit margins of 21.3 percent in 2015 (Nestlé 2016), while its single-serve categories such as Dolce Gusto and Nespresso are estimated to have operating margins of 25 percent (Gretler 2015). Smucker's retail coffee segment profit margin was 29.9 percent in 2016 (The J. M. Smucker Company 2016); and Keurig's single-serve packs had a gross margin of 38.6 percent in 2015 (Statista 2016).

popularity of soluble coffee and Nestlé's monopoly position in that sector make it the market leader, with 35.2 percent of market share in Asia-Pacific (Nisen 2014).

For each of their brands, these roasters create a characteristic taste profile based on a blend of coffees from different origins. In many cases, they mix Arabica and Robusta coffees. Due to improvements in processing technology, over the years roasters have been able to add greater shares of less expensive Robusta coffee into the blend while keeping the flavor profile constant. This dynamic switching behavior between origins and types of coffee based on market conditions links global coffee markets and lowers the price spread between Arabica and Robusta coffee in situations of supply shortage. It also creates highly volatile demand conditions for exporting countries, which see themselves locked in a price-value competition (ITC 2011a).

In recent years, a countervailing movement of high-end specialty roasters has sprung up that celebrates the consumption of high-quality 'single-origin coffee' with distinguishing flavor characteristics from specific micro-regions (Wilson and Wilson 2014). While this niche market holds significant appeal for individual coffee farmers, it still only represents around 1 percent of overall coffee volume. This market is also entering into a period of roaster consolidation and increasing competition between boutique origins (Cohen 2015, 2016; Chamlee 2016). From 2012 onward, industry leaders such as Nestlé and the holding company JAB have bought up small specialty roasters at a breakneck pace and imposed ever more stringent contract terms on their suppliers. This further curtails producers' ability to extract a greater share of the product value from the chain (Grabs and Ponte 2019).

The economic, social, and environmental sustainability of the industry is a key issue in both the mainstream and the specialty coffee sector, as Chapter 3 will show. The chapter highlights that the definition of sustainability in the coffee sector is subject to a contentious debate that crucially influences the institutional goals that market-driven sustainability schemes set out to attain. In the chapter, I also present coffee farmers' agronomic and environmental production choices in more detail and situate these choices in the sectoral sustainability discourse. I further describe the rise of private governance schemes as well as the trend of private sustainability standards to engage in mainstreaming in order to gain influence beyond small niche sectors. Chapters 4–7 then delve to the field level and connect it with the broader institutions in the coffee sector to understand how those different definitions of sustainability play out on the ground.

1.7 Selection of Sustainability Standards and Country Cases

For a comprehensive analysis of the private regulatory governance of coffee-sector sustainability, I chose to compare the major sustainability standards implemented in the coffee sector and review their impact and effectiveness in three different country contexts. According to Pierrot and Panhuysen (2014), in 2014, seven voluntary sustainable standards had broad uptake in the market: Fairtrade (now differentiated between Fair Trade USA and FLO), UTZ Certified,[2] Rainforest Alliance/Sustainable Agriculture Network (SAN),[3] the Common Code for the Coffee Community (4C), Starbucks C.A.F.E. Practices, Nespresso AAA, and organic. The first three are third-party certification schemes, 4C is a multi-stakeholder standard, and the latter two are company-led verification initiatives that were developed in collaboration with major NGOs. Somewhat of an outlier, the organic standard is a hybrid public–private standard since it has been regulated through the state in the majority of consuming countries (Arcuri 2015), and only covers environmental criteria. To provide a comprehensive analysis of the impacts of private governance on the environmental and social sustainability of coffee, I decided to focus on its combination with Fairtrade certification. This combination enjoys great popularity in the field; in fact, around 57 percent of Fairtrade coffee is also certified organic (FLO 2017a). My final sample thus includes farmers producing coffee under seven different

---

[2] In 2016, the organization dropped the 'Certified' and changed its name to only 'UTZ'. In line with this change, in the remainder of the book I will refer to 'UTZ', although at the time of data collection it was still known as 'UTZ Certified'.

[3] In 2017, the Rainforest Alliance and UTZ standard-setting organizations announced that they intended to merge, and the merger has been official from January 8, 2018 (Rainforest Alliance 2018a). The organizations have subsequently developed a joint standard that is expected to be published in June 2020, rolled out in 2020–2021, and become mandatory by mid-2021. However, this recent development had no bearing on the empirical analysis and results reported in this book, given that data collection concluded before the merger occurred. The binding standards in force during the time of data collection were the Rainforest Alliance/SAN 2010 standard and the UTZ Certified 2014 Group Certification standard.

standards: Fairtrade/organic, Fairtrade/conventional, Rainforest Alliance, UTZ, 4C, Nespresso AAA, and Starbucks C.A.F.E. Practices.

Certification with most of these standards is more prevalent in Arabica than Robusta coffee due to Arabica's higher consumer price point. I thus limited my comparative case study set to three Latin American Arabica-producing countries. By production volume, the main countries growing Arabica coffee are Brazil, Colombia, Honduras, Mexico, Guatemala, Peru, Nicaragua, and Costa Rica (Index Mundi 2015). My goal was to construct a representative sample of coffee-producing regions that allowed me to shed light on sustainable coffee production under different levels of development of the coffee sector, as well as different underlying public governance conditions. I compared countries based on related variables such as good governance indicators (e.g., the World Bank's World Governance Indicators), strength of (coffee) institutions (Lora 2013), and provision of services and level of development (using the Social Progress Index; compare Table 1.4 for an overview of all three indicators). In addition, I included practical considerations such as levels of security and costs of data collection. This process led me to choose Costa Rica, Honduras, and Colombia as my three case studies for the following reasons.

Costa Rica: I included Costa Rica in the comparison both for pragmatic reasons, since our research team was based in the country and had good connections to the local coffee institutions, and because of its unique position in the national governance ranking. As seen in Table 1.4, it is the country with the best governance indicators, a relatively high level of development, and a strong institutional setting and relatively democratically organized coffee system. Due to the crop's historical importance, the coffee sector is highly regulated in Costa Rica. Its coffee law limits the profit margins for exporters and processors, which guarantees that a large share of the coffee price paid at port reaches farmers (ICAFE 2015a). Other national laws govern land use, protect forests, mandate water use efficiency and waste management in the coffee sector, and set high minimum wages compared to the Central American average (ICAFE 2015b). Costa Rica is thus an institutional setting where many private regulations may be mirrored by public standards, making compliance easier, but potentially providing limits in additionality.

On the other hand, Costa Rica's coffee sector is relatively small and continues to shrink. The country's economy is dominated by the service

Table 1.4 *Overview of country-level indicators in 2015 (World Governance Indicators reported in percentile rank) (Lora 2013; Porter et al. 2015; World Bank 2017)*

Country	Control of corruption	Government effectiveness	Political stability	Regulatory quality	Rule of law	Voice and accountability	Mean World Governance Indicator	Strong coffee institutions	Social Progress Index score
High level of governance									
Costa Rica	75.96	66.83	67.62	69.71	69.71	86.21	72.67	Yes	77.88
Medium level of governance									
Brazil	42.79	48.08	34.29	48.08	51.44	62.07	47.79	Yes	70.89
Colombia	47.60	52.40	12.86	68.75	46.63	47.78	46.00	Yes	68.85
Peru	34.62	44.23	32.38	69.23	37.50	54.68	45.44	No	67.23
Mexico	23.56	61.54	21.43	64.90	38.46	44.33	42.37	No	67.50
Low level of governance									
Nicaragua	18.75	20.67	43.33	39.42	26.44	32.51	30.19	No	62.20
Guatemala	25.00	24.52	22.86	47.12	16.35	35.96	28.63	Maybe	62.19
Honduras	32.69	20.19	29.05	38.94	16.83	31.53	28.20	Maybe	61.44

sector and there is increasing competition both for land and labor. Costa Rica can compete neither on quantity nor comparative costs on the international coffee market, which is why it has focused on quality and the access to niche markets. This strategy has been so successful that in 2008 it ranked as the fourth largest producer of specialty coffee after Colombia, Guatemala, and Brazil, with 80 percent of its production targeting the specialty sector (Bamber *et al.* 2014). Nevertheless, the number of coffee farmers is steadily dropping (by almost one-third between 2000 and 2010) as lower-altitude farms that cannot reach peak quality succumb to urbanization pressures. Thus, the pressure to reach maximum productivity – occasionally at the expense of environmentally friendly practices – is high due to the comparatively high opportunity costs, which might make certification compliance particularly costly.

Overall, Costa Rica is among the countries with the highest share (32 percent) of certified national production (Potts *et al.* 2014). According to the ITC, in 2015, 30.7 percent of Costa Rica's total coffee production area was Fairtrade certified, while 23 percent of coffee lands were cultivated under the Rainforest Alliance certification (Lernoud *et al.* 2017).[4] On this land, Costa Ricans produce 6 percent of global Rainforest Alliance-certified coffee and 5.4 percent of Fairtrade volumes (Lernoud *et al.* 2017). The country is also an important sourcing origin for Nespresso and Starbucks; thus, the respective company-specific verification schemes are also widespread. UTZ and 4C certification, in turn, are less common.

Honduras: Second, I sought to find a counterexemplary case with relatively low levels of good governance and service provision. From the indicators in Table 1.4, this was the case for Guatemala, Nicaragua, and Honduras. Of these options, Honduras is the country with the largest and fastest-growing coffee production, targeting mainly mainstream commercial quality, and simultaneously the lowest development indicators. Honduras is the largest coffee producer of Central America, third in Latin America and sixth globally (USDA FAS 2016; ICO 2017b). Coffee is an important crop for rural development: the coffee sector represents 26 percent of the country's agricultural GDP

---

[4] Most of the certification organizations do not have data on double- or triple-certified products; thus, overlap between, for instance, Fairtrade- and Rainforest Alliance-certified products is possible.

(LeSage 2015), and, overall, around 1 million Hondurans (or one-eighth of the population) depend on coffee for their livelihoods (USDA FAS 2016), with another million joining them for harvest (interview 17, Honduran exporter 1, 2015). The low labor and land costs, along with the relative lack of alternative employment options and land-use legislation, make Honduras a strong competitor in the international coffee marketplace, and a rapid expansion of the Honduran coffee production has been predicted (LeSage 2015). This expansion would be largely feasible through deforestation of wooded areas in a highly biodiverse region that acts as a vital biological corridor and carbon dioxide sink (Tucker 2008).

Honduras shows a country-wide mean education level of 5.5 years of schooling (UNDP 2017), a decentralized rural production infrastructure that is heavily reliant on intermediaries, and low levels of public extension services that have only occasionally been supplemented by commercial or NGO actors (LeSage 2015). Hence, small-scale coffee farmers are highly vulnerable to price, disease, and production shocks. Many have never received extension assistance (field notes, Honduran extension agent, 2015). Around 56.1 percent of rural Hondurans lived in extreme poverty in 2016 (INE 2017). Regarding the presence of private sustainability schemes, Honduras is the fourth-largest source of UTZ coffee, the fifth-largest producer of 4C-verified coffee (with 16 and 18 percent of total production surface certified/verified, respectively), and the eighth-largest producer of Fairtrade coffee globally (Lernoud *et al.* 2017).

Located at the opposite end of the governance spectrum as well as in the first stage of the sectoral evolution toward quality differentiation, this country thus provides an ideal foil for the conditions in Costa Rica. Furthermore, it represents a country context that is emblematic of the global economic, social, and environmental challenges facing sustainable, long-term coffee production – as well as a case where private sustainability governance is direly needed due to the comparative lack of state presence. Its low levels of preexisting institutional support, legislation, and education provide a 'hard test' for the effectiveness of mainstreamed private governance: If participating farmers show significant sustainability improvements, we can likely attribute them to private regulation and rely on private sustainability standards to regulate the future expansion of coffee in countries with little state capacity. If few notable improvements are visible, we should be more skeptical regarding the effectiveness and transformative power of private governance institutions.

Colombia: Third, I aimed to include one country with medium levels of governance and development and high levels of coffee production. Brazil, Colombia, Peru, and Mexico all fell into this category. Of these options, Colombia provided a particularly attractive case due to its comparative geographical and linguistic proximity while expanding my analysis beyond Central America. Furthermore, the presence of a strong coffee institution in a country with notorious challenges to effectively govern rural regions provides interesting insights on institutional dynamics.

Long the second-largest coffee producer worldwide, Colombia was recently overtaken by Vietnam, but remains in third place with an output ten times the production of Costa Rica. Although the coffee sector has shrunken in its economic significance (making up 7.7 percent of exports in 2016 compared to 60 percent in 1970), it provides employment to more than half a million households and is vital for rural development. In Colombia, rural areas still contend with a poverty rate of 46 percent (CIMS 2013). As Chapter 7 will explore in more detail, the Federación Nacional de Cafeteros de Colombia, the national coffee growers' federation, is one of the world's best-organized coffee institutions and provides an array of services to its members. In addition, coffee producers have extensive experience in organizing and lobbying the government for support in times of low harvests and/or prices (Roldán-Pérez *et al.* 2009). Historically, direct income support and renovation subsidy schemes have been common. The most recent and expansive wave of support occurred during the outbreak of coffee rust in 2012/2013, when more than US$300 million were spent on direct transfers to coffee farmers alone (Contraloría General 2013).

Thanks to its high level of organization, Colombia is an attractive country of origin for sustainably certified products. It has the largest Fairtrade International coffee area globally (213,000 hectares), the second-largest 4C-verified area after Brazil (more than 330,000 ha), and the third-largest Rainforest Alliance (39,000 ha) and UTZ (50,000 ha) areas. However, after Peru, Colombia is the country with the second-largest share of multiple-certified farms. Multiple certification has led to a significant oversupply, especially of UTZ-certified coffee, of which only 12 percent is sold as certified

(Potts *et al.* 2014). Colombia thus provides a setting where institutional support for participation in private governance initiatives through standards has been widespread. Yet, the need to seek double and triple certifications may mean that expected economic payoffs may not have materialized. On the other hand, the presence of multiple sources of institutional support and incentives toward more sustainable production may have initiated deep and sustained behavior changes of a broad share of the rural population. Such evidence could demonstrate the effectiveness of the interplay of public and private institutional arrangements.

Comparing the three country cases – Costa Rica, Honduras, and Colombia – and the implementation of seven different standards hence provides me with a high level of variation between national-level institutional preconditions and implementation modalities. This research design allows me to shed light on the context-specificity of standards' effectiveness in a structured fashion.

1.8 Data and Methods Used

To understand both the implementation of market-driven incentive structures (which are defined at the supply chain level) and the impact of regulatory strategies (which are visible at the farm level), I chose a multilevel model variant of the triangulation research design (Tashakkori and Teddlie 1998, p. 48; Creswell and Clark 2007). In this design, "different methods (quantitative and qualitative) are used to address different levels within the system" (Creswell and Clark 2007, p. 65). It is stylized in Figure 1.3.

In a first step, I conducted a multidisciplinary literature review and gathered secondary data such as standard documents, roasting company websites, and published industry records. In addition, I collected primary qualitative data stemming from expert interviews as well as participant observation during fieldwork in Latin America (Costa Rica, Colombia, Guatemala, and Honduras) between 2015 and 2017. I conducted over sixty semi-structured interviews with coffee producers, cooperative managers, exporters, traders, roasters and café owners, members of coffee institutions, NGOs, and researchers, fifty-four of which were recorded with an audio recorder and twelve of which were in writing or recorded by hand. Table 1.5 shows the distribution of the different value chain actors. An overview list of interviewed organizations and interview dates

Table 1.5 *Overview of expert interviews*

Interviewee type	Roasters	Traders	Producer organizations	Institutions	NGOs	Fellow researchers
Number of interviews	15	17	11	8	9	6

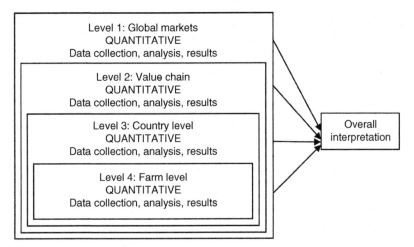

Figure 1.3 The multilevel triangulation research design used in this study. Source: own illustration

can be found in Appendix 1. All experts were assured individual anonymity to improve the veracity of their statements. I also anonymized the organizational identity of all commercial value chain actors (roasters, traders, and producer organizations).

Furthermore, I attended nine coffee industry events at various levels of organization: the Semana Internacional del Café (Sintercafe), a meeting point for large-scale coffee stakeholders, roasters, and traders, in 2015 and 2016; the 2016 Forum of the Specialty Coffee Association of America, a gathering of specialty coffee actors; the first General Assembly of the Global Coffee Platform, an incipient platform aiming to become the central unifying force for large-scale sustainability efforts (attended virtually); the first World Coffee Producers' Forum, organized in 2017 in Medellin, Colombia (attended virtually); and three producer forums in Costa Rica and Honduras focused on coffee quality and sustainability; as well as a local consultation regarding the new Rainforest Alliance standard in Honduras. These events allowed me to observe the intra-industry conversation regarding sustainability and provided many opportunities for additional informal dialogue with industry members. They were part of the larger data collection effort on field-level impacts of sustainability certifications in Colombia, Honduras, and Costa Rica. In this process, I was also able to speak with many coffee farmers about their views of the industry and to test my analytical conclusions through continuous feedback processes and triangulation. I kept a field journal during all instances of participant observation and fieldwork in which I transcribed quotes gathered during conversations. I summarized conversations and observations immediately or, if immediate capture was impossible, at the end of the day. Relevant transcribed interview quotes as well as field notes and secondary literature were then sorted into subthemes in a recursive process (akin to the method of constant comparison [Glaser and Strauss 2000]) to identify and triangulate the main findings.

I combined this information with quantitative questionnaire data on the production practices of over 1,900 coffee farmers in three Latin American countries (Honduras, Colombia, and Costa Rica) that are subject to various private sustainability schemes and their regulatory strategies. To allow for internal validity, in my sampling strategy I focused on regions that had the highest density of certified producers by building on previous work (Grabs *et al.* 2016). For even greater within-country validity, I reached out to work with two types of intermediaries: producer cooperatives as well as traders that organize their own certification groups, depending on country circumstance. While large parts of the coffee sector are organized through cooperatives in Colombia and Costa Rica, this avenue is less common in Honduras, where private traders dominate the coffee infrastructure. To be able to account for cooperative-specific organizational capacity that may influence producer behavior, I thus chose to collaborate with only cooperatives in both Colombia and Costa Rica, and to analyze both cooperatives (in the cases of Fairtrade and Fairtrade/organic) and trader-led certification groups (in the cases of Rainforest Alliance, UTZ, and 4C) in Honduras.

Using full lists of producers provided by my collaboration partners, I randomly selected certified farmers from each cooperative/certification group, and I sampled in several cooperatives/certification groups simultaneously to control for cooperative/group effects.[5] These precautions contributed to ensuring that the interviewed producers resemble other certified farmers in the study countries. Given the lower marginal cost of certification for larger, better organized, and better situated farms, it is likely that certified farmers are not representative of the average farmer. To address this challenge, whenever possible I used data from existing farmer lists (including, for instance, farm size, produced coffee volume, gender, and education levels of farmers) for a preliminary propensity scoring analysis to construct a population of control group farmers that are as similar as possible to the treatment farmer sample group. During the initial sampling I also created a list of possible replacements for farmers in the original sampling list that were unavailable or that refused to participate, which mirrored the originally sampled farmers in underlying characteristics.

On the basis of a comprehensive review of sustainability standard documents, previous impact evaluation literature, as well as the recommended indicators of the Committee on Sustainability Assessment (COSA 2018), I designed a survey of 290 (partly conditional) questions on socioeconomic and environmental indicators. I field-tested the questionnaire in an iterative process to ensure that questions were appropriate, intuitive, and well-understood by both data collectors and survey participants. The survey included both reported (interview-based) as well as observational data. The observational data mainly related to the ecological condition of the coffee farm, which data collectors reported by visiting the coffee field. The tablet-based data collection allowed the inclusion of corroborating photos taken of local production conditions as well as assets such as first aid kits and agrochemical storage rooms. Data collection was implemented with the assistance of local agronomists and extension agents, which my colleague and I trained in full-day workshops as well as through supervised field tests. All data collectors furthermore received a manual that provided explanatory information on the survey along with sample pictures for observational indicators to ensure consistency in data collection.

Prior and informed consent was assured twofold: on an institutional level, our research group convened Memoranda of Understanding with all cooperatives and producer organizations specifying the data

---

[5] In the cases of Colombia and Costa Rica, my colleague Andrea Estrella from the TRANSSUSTAIN junior researcher group supported this process.

collection process and academic use of information. On the individual level, we elicited the consent of participating farmers prior to the interview on the basis of a description of the research project and its context. If farmers were unwilling to participate, data collectors politely ended the interaction and moved on to request the participation of alternative producers. For privacy reasons, no farmer was asked to be present in the pictures used as corroborating evidence. During data analysis, all information was anonymized and only aggregated results are reported.

To analyze this data, I chose to use a propensity score matching model, supplemented by logit and linear regression models, to calculate the outcome additionality of the indicators under analysis. I supplement these with within-group t-tests when accounting for the effectiveness of capacity-building activities and the importance of rule knowledge. My control variables include farm size, farmer's gender, farmer's age, farmer's level of education, household size, land tenure, association membership status, location information (time to school, clinic, and market), and altitude, as well as region (where applicable). Appendix 2 describes the quantitative data analysis methods applied in detail.

The wealth of indicators gathered in this study further provides an opportunity to quantitatively test my hypotheses on the most important institutional design choices for effective market-based regulatory governance. To do so, I constructed a meta-data set by logging the standardized effect size for thirty-two outcome additionality indicators separately by certification group, for up to fourteen certification groups per indicator (and a total of 435 observations). The standardized effect size is defined as the mean difference in outcomes between the treated and matched control groups divided by their pooled standard deviation. It thus takes into account both the size of the effect and its significance, and allows for both negative and positive effects. I used the standardized effect size as dependent variable, and coded indicator- and standard-specific institutional design choices that might affect outcome additionality, alongside control variables. I describe this approach in more detail in Chapter 6.

1.9 A Wide Variation between Types of 'Sustainable' Coffee and Effective Outcomes

The results of this micro-level impact evaluation can be leveraged to gain valuable insights on the question: How effective are transnational

market-driven regulatory governance initiatives in improving environmental and social practices of Latin American smallholder coffee farmers? They are especially powerful once they are combined with the
qualitative findings and compared across indicators, certifications,
and countries.

Chapter 4 reviews the effectiveness of market-based regulatory governance in changing *economic incentive structures* by analyzing the
development of price premiums provided by the major market-driven
regulatory governance initiatives in the coffee value chain. It shows that
the upscaling of private sustainability schemes into mainstream markets has made it difficult for them to protect the financial incentive
mechanisms that they set out to establish. The coexistence of other
sourcing characteristics – especially quality, but also volume, origin,
and consistency – that are highly valued by buyers leads to a weakening
of the link between sustainability standards and the market differentiation that they can provide. Furthermore, information asymmetries,
particularly regarding future demand for sustainably certified coffee,
make it more difficult for these markets to work as intended.

Next, Chapter 5 provides a comprehensive answer to the central
question confronting conscientious consumers – *how sustainable is
my sustainably labeled coffee?* Through the exploration of a wide
array of farm-level environmental and social sustainability indicators,
this analysis moves beyond the current literature's prevalent focus on
economic outcomes of certified coffee production and engages deeply
with the complex question of how to define and ensure environmental
sustainability and social well-being in intensive cash crop sectors.

Analyzing a wide-ranging number of indicators from an agro-
economic perspective allowed me to inductively group them into three
categories according to their definition and theory of change with regard
to sustainability. Tier I holds indicators that fall into a *sustainable
intensification* definition of agricultural sustainability. Production practice changes in this category constitute win-win outcomes for both
environmental and economic outcomes, such as yield increases and
input use optimization. Tier II indicators are those that may induce
producers to *shift their time horizons backward* and accept incurring
short-term costs to gain longer-term beneficial outcomes. Examples
include worker health and safety, erosion prevention, and climate
change resilience practices. Finally, Tier III indicators constitute zero-
sum trade-offs between economic and social or environmental outcomes

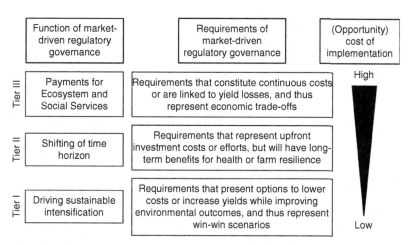

Figure 1.4 Three categories of sustainable agricultural practices. Source: own illustration

and would require *payments for social and ecosystem services* to recompense farmers for their losses. This includes the payment of higher wages, the setting aside of production areas for biodiversity conservation zones, or the voluntary implementation of agroforestry systems. Figure 1.4 shows this categorization in a visual form. To my knowledge, this is the first impact evaluation study that uses a theoretically robust typology of sustainability outcomes which can be linked back to different expectations of field-level behaviors and feed into concurrent regulatory governance debates.

In general, I find that win-win Tier I indicators show greater impacts in the field than the higher-cost Tier III indicators. However, I further find large between-country differences that make it difficult for most standards to work as a signaling mechanism for a specific type of resource-efficient production. For instance, Costa Rican farmers in the most stringent private sustainability standard (Rainforest Alliance) showed pesticide and fertilizer use at much higher rates than even noncertified farmers in Honduras.

For Tier II indicators, local-level institutional support in the provision of financing or infrastructure is a crucial predictor of behavioral outcomes. Such institutional support in turn may be, but is not always, given to farmers subscribed to certification schemes, which can limit standards' outcome additionality. Second, the rules' clarity and level of obligation influence whether we see outcome additionality. Less specific rules provide more ample opportunity to defend status quo practices as standard-compliant and may lower the motivation to adopt new, unfamiliar practices, even if they would have beneficial long-term impacts for a farm's environmental resilience.

Tier III indicators have the highest potential to benefit social welfare and environmental outcomes such as biodiversity, but also impose the highest, ongoing costs for farmers. For such practices, standards could function as payments for social or ecosystem services, which compensate producers for higher production costs, foregone yields, and lower incomes due to their adoption of sustainable practices. However, this book finds that most market-driven regulatory governance schemes have not been able to take on such a function, leading to limited outcome additionality and a reversion to national-level best practices that tend to support 'technified', yield-maximizing forms of production. On the social side, it finds that private regulatory governance may present producers with a motivation to abide by regulations that are cumbersome, but not costly. Yet, such governance provides little additionality in many instances where standards refer to public labor law such as minimum wages, which producers either universally comply with or universally disregard, possibly due to their lack of financial capacity to comply.

Chapter 5 furthermore moves from individual behavior all the way up to the highest level of aggregation by comparing the relative implementation of sustainability standards in the leading coffee-producing countries with their market share, yield levels, and presence of environmentally beneficial types of coffee farming. It finds that, counterintuitively, the implementation of sustainability standards has reinforced the dominance of productivist, intensified production origins, while marginalizing regions that have prioritized more ecologically sustainable ways of growing coffee.

1.10 The Use of Comparative Micro-level Analysis to Examine the Institutional Effectiveness of Market-Driven Regulatory Governance

Comparing the field-level results across the three indicator categories, seven sustainability standards, and three case study countries allows me to answer several novel questions on drivers of private institutional effectiveness. For instance, are requirements that constitute high opportunity costs for farmers typically binding, making them more difficult to implement, or are they formulated in a flexible manner that allows for step-by-step improvements? Is the risk of being audited and found noncompliant a better motivation for farmers to comply than the positive inducement of capacity building? Are the global certification rules and their regional adaptations sufficiently clear in their formulation to allow for universally similar implementation, or are there large differences between country contexts in the on-the-ground interpretation of the rules? The present data can enhance our understanding of these and other questions in exceptionally rich ways since the same indicators are compared across standard systems, leveraging variability both in rule-setting and implementation.

Chapter 6 summarizes the insights gained by comparing the outcome additionality of thirty-two indicators in a quantitative meta-analysis, and testing hypotheses derived from an inductive theoretical analysis of micro-institutional dynamics. It examines the comparative impact of regulatory clarity and stringency; effective training and capacity-building; the existence of significant, individualized price premiums; the presence of investment and opportunity costs; restrictive auditor oversight policies; and the coexistence of public regulation on the likelihood that a requirement will show outcome additionality in matched farmers. The results show that regulatory clarity and stringency, along with the provision of substantive price premiums, have the most significant positive correlation with outcome additionality (i.e., likely behavior changes); while the coexistence of public regulations and the presence of high opportunity costs have a significant negative impact on additionality. These results are striking, as the majority of standards are currently moving away from a stringent regulatory approach and toward a developmental, compliance management perspective (Fransen 2018). However, this approach is unlikely to allow for the creation of price premiums that could compensate farmers for high-cost practices.

Finally, the different national institutional preconditions in which this study is embedded allow for new and exciting discoveries on the effectiveness of *transnational* private sustainability governance, especially as it interacts with public regulation and institutional strategies. Chapter 7 exploits two types of country-level differences: first, the overall legislative structure that private regulatory arrangements frequently default to (in the case of, for instance, minimum wages or minimum worker age); and second, the institutional structures specific to the coffee sector that may define and circumscribe producer-level options both in the production as well as the marketing process. The chapter arrives at three main conclusions. One, standards perform poorly when they aim to reinforce public regulation, with little difference between certified and noncertified groups' compliance with national-level rules. Two, national-level institutions may constitute powerful barriers to the effectiveness of private regulation when they pursue goals orthogonal to those of certification schemes – which is frequently the case in the coffee sector, as I show. Three, even when national institutions align on the goals for a sustainable coffee sector, the greater insulation they provide from the mainstream market – with its price volatility and bargaining power disparities – the more difficult it is for private sustainability standards to work as intended. Here we find a hitherto underappreciated trade-off between public and private regulation.

1.11 Ways Forward for Sustainability in Coffee, Transnational Market-Driven Regulatory Governance, and Operational-Level Regulatory Governance Research

What conclusions can we draw from this analysis, and what takeaway messages are we left with? There are several ways to interpret the findings and conceive of calls for action, depending on whether we see policymakers, consumers, or researchers as our main addressees.

From an institutional and political perspective, this analysis showcases the challenges associated with deferring to market instruments to solve sustainability problems, particularly those that represent economic-environmental trade-offs. These challenges are embedded in the broader problems of commodity production and trade in globalized markets, where origins with fundamentally different productive circumstances compete against each and face collective action problems. However, the tide may be turning, with producing-country governments reconsidering more national-level market intervention as well as novel forms of collaboration across origins. Chapter 8 provides an overview of some first steps in that direction. It will be an interesting area of future research to understand how private regulatory instruments interact with such renewed state-level efforts to govern trade and sustainable development, and in which ways they may be harnessed by states for improved problem solving.

From a consumer perspective, the results of this analysis may appear disheartening. Coffee is a commodity that has made important strides in mainstreaming ethical consumerism. Many individual consumers are familiar with Fairtrade, organic, or Rainforest Alliance certifications and purposefully seek out coffee with such labels. Yet, the way the value chain is set up does not allow much of the added price paid in retail to trickle down to the producer. The flexible amendments and interpretations to existing standards may lead to on-the-ground rules and requirements that are at a considerable distance from the image of sustainability projected to consumers by the certification organizations. Furthermore, the considerable market power of roasters and retailers in influencing the products on offer places doubts on the efficacy of ethical consumerism as a mechanism to steer global production processes. Indeed, Ingenbleek and Reinders (2013, p. 466) quote the founder of the Dutch Fairtrade initiative reflecting the following: "I was convinced that power would be with the consumers, but it turned out otherwise. Even taking into account the socially-desirable responses in the market research, consumers are agenda-setting to a very small extent, a very small push factor. The market is made by the choices that producers and retailers make."

Under such circumstances, what is the appropriate consumer response? Do we just need an even greater share of consumer-citizens that 'vote with their dollars' and consistently punish companies for insufficient performance, regardless of brand preference or sales incentives? Or should consumers take greater organized action and pressure companies to make long-term commitments to the purchase of one particular standard whose rules are in line with the effectiveness characteristics already explored? A third alternative is to analyze the concept of demand-side solutions even more critically, and question industry assumptions about steep demand increases for coffee in the next decades. After all, coffee is not strictly a necessary consumption good (even if it frequently feels that way to many individuals, including the author of this work). What if we reconsider coffee as a luxury good, and become willing to pay higher prices per unit while limiting our individual consumption? This could be a demand-driven solution that addresses both producer livelihoods and ecosystem preservation. Such 'strong sustainability' solutions are of even greater relevance when considering global population growth and the emergence of a middle-class in highly populous countries such as India and China that may contribute to worldwide demand in the coming decades.

Finally, from an analytical perspective, this book demonstrates the importance of focusing on the on-the-ground implementation of any institutional arrangement, particularly those aspiring to have regulatory effects. At its core, most political science research aims to make credible policy recommendations with regard to solving pressing global issues, be they environmental degradation, human development, climate change, resource scarcity, or even issues further removed from the present topical focus such as security or migration. For any of these issues, it is crucial to closely study Ostrom's operational level of on-the-ground implementation and enforcement, since it is "the only level of analysis where an action in the physical world flows directly from a decision" (Kiser and Ostrom 2000, pp. 77–78). Reflecting closely on how institutional arrangements and rules will influence individual and collective actions, interact with preexisting behavioral incentives and simultaneously emerging competing institutions, and finally change our physical environment and social relations is thus a crucial part of political science and governance research. It is of particular relevance given that the environmental and social problems to be solved are becoming more acute. It is my hope that this book's approach of connecting field-level findings to the differentiated hypothesis testing of governance theories will join a growing number of works that do the same on other pressing global matters.

2 | *The Dilemma of Effective Private Governance*

The worst coffee disease is the price. The price is killing us.

(Interview 58, Costa Rican
cooperative 1, 2017)

Amongst our members, there is a recognition that at scale, [price] premiums are unlikely, but that the standard systems need to be very focused on delivering value to all users of the supply chain.

(Karin Kreider, Executive Director of the International
Social and Environmental Accreditation and
Labelling [ISEAL] Alliance [ISEAL 2016])

As these introductory quotes illustrate, the market-driven governance of commodity production is contentious. One main point of disagreement among stakeholders is the importance of price premiums as incentives to motivate behavior changes among producers. For many farmers, gaining access to such premiums is the central purpose of implementing sustainability standards, at least in the short term. Yet, as standards scale up, they lose their ability to provide such premiums within the marketplace. This endangers the effectiveness of private governance initiatives in two ways. First, they may have a lower impact on producer livelihoods than expected; and, second, they lose the 'carrot' that animates producers to bear the opportunity costs of sustainable production.

This chapter makes this argument more formally. In it, I use a micro-institutional rational choice framework to examine the effectiveness of market-driven regulatory governance of sustainability in the coffee sector. My framework draws on the early work of Elinor Ostrom and the Indiana Workshop in Political Theory and Policy Analysis as summarized in Kiser and Ostrom (1982, 2000).[1] It is micro-institutional in

---

[1] This approach shares most of the basic tenets of Ostrom's subsequently elaborated Institutional Analysis and Development (IAD) framework (Ostrom

scope; that is, it takes *individual agents* as its main unit of analysis. It then analyzes the decision-making processes of these individual agents, as well as aggregate outcomes, in the context of *institutional arrangements* that "individuals use to affect the incentive system of a social order and the impact of incentive systems on human behavior" (Kiser and Ostrom 2000, p. 57).

One main strength of this approach lies in its differentiation between three levels of micro-institutional analysis. The constitutional level explains the design of collective-choice mechanisms; the collective-choice level explains the world of authoritative decision-making; and the operational level explains the world of action, where actual change occurs on the ground. Focusing on the operational level within this framework has two benefits. First, it allows me to harness analytical tools and insights provided both by the institutional rational choice framework and by the socio-legal literature on compliance enforcement and management. Second, it enables me to connect on-the-ground effectiveness with regulatory design and implementation choices, and with preexisting public and market institutions that simultaneously shape individual actors' choices. In doing so, this work connects the micro- with the macro-level analysis of private governance, and it generates concrete policy recommendations to improve the efficacy of private regulation.

This chapter first reviews existing work on the effectiveness of private regulation and certification schemes to date. It identifies a persistent research gap in conceptually connecting the design of private governance arrangements with their problem-solving potential and effectiveness. It then presents the basic assumptions of the conceptual framework in the context of private regulation. I argue that the micro-institutional rational choice framework is a hitherto underused but immensely powerful approach to studying the effectiveness of private sustainability governance. Finally, I present the institutional design dilemma at the core of market-driven regulatory governance, and derive theoretical expectations to be tested using the data at hand.

2005). Yet, I decided not to engage in a traditional fully fledged IAD analysis and refrained from using the concomitant vocabulary that has since developed – arguably making the framework "quite complicated" (McGinnis 2011, p. 169) – in an effort to make the work more readable and relevant to scholars from multiple disciplines. I will however refer to later work of Ostrom and her coauthors in this chapter whenever applicable.

2.1 Theoretical and Practical Antecedents

International institutions and regimes' effectiveness in solving collective problems has been an important analytical focus of political scientists, most of whom study international environmental treaties and agreements (Bernauer 1995; Young and Levy 1999; Underdal 2002). In the view of these scholars, "successful institutions, in a very comprehensive sense of success, are those that (1) change the behavior of states and other actors in the direction intended by the cooperating parties, (2) solve the environmental problems they are supposed to solve, and (3) do so in an efficient and equitable manner" (Bernauer 1995, p. 358). This definition encompasses three approaches toward conceptualizing effectiveness that have alternatively been used in the past decade. The first is mainly concerned with *compliance* – that is, do participating actors hold themselves to the collectively agreed rules. The second, going further, looks into *goal attainment* or *problem-solving potential*; that is, do the institutions contribute toward behavioral change or changes in the biophysical environment that are in line with their stated objectives. I follow Bernauer (1995, p. 354) in defining goal attainment as "the difference over time or across cases between actor behavior – or the state of the natural environment – along dimensions . . . and end points defined by institutional goals." Problem-solving potential can be defined in the words of Young (2011, p. 19854) as "the extent to which regimes contribute to solving or mitigating the problems that motivate those people who create the regimes." The third approach incorporates elements of *efficiency* or *equity* (Bernauer 1995; Young 2011). Scholars in this last tradition, for instance, have attempted to calculate an ideal outcome (the so-called collective optimum or Pareto frontier). They then conceptualized the effectiveness of a regime as the location of actual performance on the spectrum ranging between the no-regime counterfactual and the collective optimum (Helm and Sprinz 2000).

Past assessments of the comparative effectiveness of public environmental regimes (Young 1999, 2011; Miles *et al.* 2002; Breitmeier *et al.* 2011) have highlighted the importance of carefully defining dependent and independent variables, explaining causal pathways, and properly attributing behavioral change (Bernauer 1995; Young 1999, 2011). Moreover, both Young (2011) and Mitchell (2002) draw attention to the desirability of triangulating between qualitative and quantitative evidence. To date, conclusions regarding the effectiveness of regimes frequently depend on the operationalization and methods used, with qualitative case studies (typically carried out by political scientists) reporting more optimistic results than quantitative assessments (which are most often undertaken by economists). In response, Young (2011, p. 19858) issues a call to future scientists "to build up the stock of large N quantitative studies to facilitate triangulation in efforts to enhance our understanding of the determinants of effectiveness." However, there are underlying methodological limitations. The use of advanced quantitative methods in the study of international treaty effectiveness is often curtailed by the small number of observations at hand when states are the unit of analysis (Mitchell 2002). This makes the study of private institutional arrangements comparatively attractive: since not states but private actors are the target of private governance regimes, it is possible to use large-N quantitative methods to carefully construct counterfactuals, as well as to account for alternative institutional and circumstantial influences on behavior. This advantage has not been fully exploited in the private governance literature to date.

Most private governance scholars studying effectiveness draw on the work of Young and Levy (1999) and Underdal (2002) and apply a problem-solving approach in which "an institution is effective if it solves or alleviates the problem that motivated its creation" (Gulbrandsen 2005, p. 128). This view is in line with a rational choice, or functional, approach to institutions that focuses on "purposive, intentional, or instrumental explanation[s]" for social institutions (Yarbrough and Yarbrough 1990, p. 253). In this approach, "institutions are functional if reasonable men might create and maintain them in order to meet social needs or achieve social goals" (Simon 1978, p. 3) – a point of view that is also adopted in this book. However, the operationalization of this definition and related methods of analysis have hitherto come in a variety of forms when applied to transnational market-driven regulatory governance through private standard-setting and certification. Many contributions are thus subject to similar limits in research design and operationalization as previously cited studies on public environmental regimes (Young 2001, 2011).

In particular, governance analyses have seldom integrated quantitative field-level results. Instead, authors either take multidimensional perspectives on effectiveness that rely on qualitative assessments (Giovannucci and Ponte 2005; Pattberg 2005b), or focus on certification uptake, patterns of adoption, and possible spillover effects (Gulbrandsen

2005, 2009; Espach 2006; Auld *et al.* 2008; Auld 2010; Marx and Cuypers 2010). When studies do draw on field-level evidence, they mostly rely on secondary literature that is either constituted of qualitative case studies (in the case of coffee) or audit documents and "corrective action requirements" issued by certifiers (in the case of forestry and fisheries) (Newsom *et al.* 2006). While providing important insights, this latter method assumes a priori that effective monitoring and enforcement of standard rules are universal, and that certifiers' audits reflect the real implementation rates on the ground – which may, but must not, be the case. Furthermore, there has been an empirical overemphasis on forest certification schemes, possibly because forest standards developed early on and have been a focal case study for scholars interested in private governance (cf. Cashore *et al.* 2004). Finally, few authors (with the notable exception of Gulbrandsen 2004) spell out explicitly the causal mechanisms (and necessary conditions for those mechanisms to work long-term) that connect the institution of private standard-setting to its goal attainment and problem-solving potential. These mechanisms, and their impacts on the ground, will be the central focus of analysis of this book.

There has been greater engagement with field-level implementation and the effects of private agri-food standard systems in other disciplines such as rural sociology, development studies, and impact evaluation. However, these streams have engaged little with the previous group of private regulation scholars.

The focus of sociological and political economy analyses, which use concepts such as global value chain analysis and convention theory, tends to be on relational and structural aspects of the economic institutions that producers are subjected to (Ponte 2002, 2008; Guthman 2004; Raynolds *et al.* 2004; Gereffi *et al.* 2005; Bacon 2010). Hence, themes of dependency and power imbalances are highlighted, with a number of scholars using a neo-Gramscian lens on transnational economic relations (Bloomfield 2012; Graz and Nölke 2012; Levy *et al.* 2016). In contrast, this literature puts less emphasis on producers' individual choices within these institutions, making feedback into private regulation and governance studies more challenging.

The impact evaluation literature, in turn, first focused mainly on certification systems' on-the-ground effects on producer incomes and poverty reduction. It has only recently pivoted toward analyzing their effects on environmental and social practices in more detail (ITC 2011b; Kuit and

Waarts 2014; Lambin *et al.* 2014; Petrokovsky and Jennings 2018). Kuit and Waarts (2014), DeFries *et al.* (2017), and Bray and Neilson (2017) provide exhaustive meta-analyses of the existing literature to date in the agricultural sector, while the RESOLVE report summarizes impacts across agriculture, wild-caught fisheries, and forestry (Steering Committee of the State-of-Knowledge Assessment of Standards and Certification 2012). The ISEAL-commissioned State of Knowledge Review on the effectiveness of standards in driving adoption of sustainability practices by Petrokofsky and Jennings (2018) covers all private sustainability standards. Although they all acknowledge a recent rise in scholarly attention to certification impacts, they also identify a number of unanswered research gaps as these standards move from a niche to a mainstream phenomenon.

First, only a fraction of existing studies have used (at least partially) credible counterfactuals and robust econometric techniques (Blackman and Rivera 2011; Steering Committee of the State-of-Knowledge Assessment of Standards and Certification 2012; Kuit and Waarts 2014; DeFries *et al.* 2017; Petrokovsky and Jennings 2018). Without a trustworthy measure of the counterfactual – that is, what would have happened to a similar producer in the absence of certification – it is difficult to draw conclusions on the effectiveness of standard-setting and adoption (Blackman and Rivera 2011). As regards coffee certifications, the literature also shows a clear bias toward Fairtrade and organic certifications, with less attention to younger labels such as Rainforest Alliance and UTZ (Blackman and Rivera 2011; Bray and Neilson 2017). Although the Common Code for the Coffee Community (4C) is the most widespread sustainability scheme in the coffee sector, almost no robust peer-reviewed research on its impacts exists. Firm-owned standards such as Nespresso AAA or Starbucks C. A.F.E. Practices are equally understudied (Bray and Neilson 2017; DeFries *et al.* 2017; Petrokovsky and Jennings 2018). Finally, only a handful of studies (Beuchelt and Zeller 2011; Ruben and Zuniga 2011; Chiputwa *et al.* 2015; van Rijsbergen *et al.* 2016; Mitiku *et al.* 2017) use the same evaluation methodology across certifications. Even fewer explicitly compare the underlying rules, regulations, and incentive mechanisms when reporting their results, or link field-level findings to features of the standards under analysis.

Yet, it is impossible to draw conclusions on the impact of institutional design features (for instance regarding decision rules, membership conditions, and compliance systems [Bernauer 1995]) on institutions' effectiveness without comparative data that uses the same measurements across a variety of institutional arrangements and contexts (Mitchell 2002; Young 2011). Petrokovsky and Jennings (2018) further identify a persistent need to include insights from behavioral psychology and economics to better understand the drivers of behavior change. Thus, the (by now considerable) impact evaluation literature tends to be again isolated from the private governance and regulation scholarship. This bifurcation of research efforts limits our understanding of how to create institutions with rules that have greater on-the-ground impact. It also ignores real-world dynamic interactions between the making of rules and their implementation. In the following, I outline an alternative conceptual approach that allows for clearer theoretical and practical linkages between institutional design and on-the-ground changes in human behavior and the natural environment – a micro-institutional rational choice framework.

2.2 A Micro-institutional Rational Choice Approach to Institutional Effectiveness

The micro-institutional rational choice framework views market-driven regulatory governance initiatives such as sustainability standards as changes in the institutional arrangements that influence individual producers' behavioral choices (Kiser and Ostrom 1982). The effects of these behavioral changes, in the aggregate, will then constitute the problem-solving potential (and effectiveness) of this particular institution. This section presents the framework's focal actors, boundedly rational individuals; introduces the conceptualization of market-driven regulatory governance as changes in institutional arrangements; and highlights the power of focusing micro-institutional analysis on the operational level of action, while linking it to the collective-choice level of institutional design. It closes by summarizing the micro-institutional rational choice perspective of the effectiveness of market-driven regulatory governance.

The Choices of Individual Actors in Complex Environments

How do individual actors make choices? This question is at the heart of any inquiry in social processes. It is especially relevant when trying to understand the potential for changing individuals' behavioral patterns toward outcomes that are more environmentally friendly or socially preferable. The institutional rational choice approach used in this book builds on a political economy model of individual behavior characterized by *bounded rationality*. In this view, individuals seek to make optimal choices based on how they perceive and weigh the costs and benefits of different strategies and their likely outcomes. However, they are constrained in that aim by considerable uncertainty about both the outcomes and alternatives available to them, risk attached to more uncertain strategies, and the general complexity of the environment in which they make such choices (Simon 1972, 1990; Williamson 1975; Ostrom 1998). This characterization shows a great empirical fit for individual agricultural smallholder producers who depend on their farms for their families' livelihoods. Such producers can be assumed to want to maximize net earnings from their cash crop production, especially if it is their main source of income. However, their levels of education, atomization, and position in the commodity market may prevent them from making optimal decisions (Rice and McLean 1999).

This is not to say that profit maximization is their only objective. Following Braithwaite (1985), Ayres and Braithwaite (1987), and Gunningham and Grabosky (1998), I see farmers as economic actors that can sometimes be motivated by their business interests and at other times choose their actions based on normative beliefs of social or ecological responsibility (cf. Granovetter 1985; Margolis 1991; Ostrom 2005). However, their tenuous economic situation makes it likely that some sort of "lexical ordering of money and responsibility" (Ayres and Braithwaite 1987, p. 27) occurs in which the first principle in the ordering must be satisfied before being able to move on to the next. Ayres and Braithwaite (1987, p. 27) give the example of regulated economic actors who aim to "list their priorities under the following headings: 'Must do. Should do. Could do. Won't do.' Then they … start at the top of the list and work down until the money runs out." In this sense, the implementation of socially or ecologically responsible practices may form part of farmers' objectives, but is circumscribed by the first ordering principle – which is to guarantee their family's livelihood through their farm's production.

In theories of bounded rationality, a major source of uncertainty is incomplete information. It can stem from three basic sources: not having access to information (i.e., the information exists but is unavailable to the decision maker); random or unpredictable external variables that cause constant shifts of both outcomes and alternatives; and the existence of interdependent decision-making where individual-level outcomes depend not only on a single individual but also on the conglomerate of choices by others (Simon 1990). This, again, is empirically valid for small-scale agricultural producers. First, many farmers live in rural contexts without access to knowledge about larger market or price movements, opportunities for differentiation, risk-management options (e.g., price hedging), or sustainable production practices, although such information exists. Second, agriculture is one of the professions with the greatest number of external, unpredictable risk factors. These range from weather anomalies (both short-term extremes such as heat spikes, frosts, droughts, and floods, and long-term shifts in weather patterns due to climate change) to price volatility due to exchange rate fluctuations and commodity speculation (Ayres and Braithwaite 1987). Third, the position of atomized smallholder farmers in a global commodity market means that the aggregation of individually optimal strategies may have perverse collective outcomes. For instance, it is individually rational to plant more crops in response to price increases. However, in the aggregate, global increases in output may lead to oversupply when facing stable demand, causing prices to drop and individual income to fall. Optimal strategies would need to take the interdependence of decision-making into account and anticipate the choices of other actors as well as one's own – a probabilistic calculation that quickly becomes overwhelming for a single decision maker.

The presence of such uncertainty, or in contrast an overwhelming amount of information that is difficult to process, may influence the decision strategy of individuals as well. Perfectly rational economic actors are assumed to maximize their utility at all times; that is, they make the optimal choices based on their preferences. In contrast, individuals that are intendedly rational may use shortcuts and choice rules (so-called heuristics), such as choosing the first option that they find that satisfies some minimum threshold of expected outcome (Simon 1972), or copying successful strategies from their neighbors. The use of such choice heuristics themselves, however, can lead to inaccurate evaluations of likely outcomes ('cognitive biases'), as behavioral economists have explored at length (Thaler and Sunstein 2009; Kahneman 2013). Institutional arrangements, on the other hand, may alleviate information asymmetries and uncertainty, or fundamentally change the perceived costs and benefits of alternative outcomes.

Institutional Arrangements and Their Way of Shaping Preferences and Choices

Institutional arrangements are understood in this volume (following Kiser and Ostrom 2000, p. 65) as "sets of rules governing the number of decision makers, allowable actions and strategies, authorized results, transformations internal to decision situations, and linkages among decision situations." Such arrangements may have a strong influence on the choice set of possible actions, the perceived benefits and costs of individual decision makers' strategies, and their likely outcomes. On the one hand, they can be seen as restricting the freedom for individual action. On the other, they may expand such freedom by increasing the predictability of outcomes and lowering uncertainty (Kiser and Ostrom 1982). Thus, in business, the establishment of markets and contract law allows for mutually beneficial trade relationships (Williamson 1975; Cutler 2017). Agenda-setting, committee membership, and voting rules define the strategic space of intendedly rationally acting political actors (Shepsle 1989). In this context, Shepsle (1989) speaks of structure-induced equilibria, in which optimal outcomes (equilibria) are no longer just a feature of agents' preferences, as in early rational choice and game theory models, but are also crucially shaped by the 'rules of the game' played – that is, the institutional arrangements underpinning social or political interaction.

The role of institutional arrangements is of particular importance in collective action problems where the optimal outcome for a group depends on all participants voluntarily and collectively restraining their own individual actions (Hardin 1968; Ostrom 1990, 1998; Abbott and Snidal 2001). This frequently occurs in the protection of common-pool goods from which all individuals benefit and exclusion is costly, such that overuse is likely (e.g., fisheries), or in the prevention of externalities (e.g., pollution) that produce common costs but individual cost-saving benefits (Ostrom and Ostrom 1971). Elinor Ostrom (1990) famously showcased that self-organization may lead to a large variety of institutional arrangements, all based on jointly agreed and enforced rules, which lead to collectively beneficial outcomes.

This understanding of institutions allows for the presence of multiple, overlapping institutional arrangements that individuals are subject to: some of which they may choose to join voluntarily, others that they are subject to by virtue of their economic position, and yet again others based on national or regional legislation that may or may not be enforced. In the example of smallholder coffee farmers, individual producers may sell some of their cash crop in specialty channels that have strict quality rules, and the rest on the conventional commodity market where large volumes of standardized goods are traded at the lowest possible price. Simultaneously, by virtue of their nationality, they are bound by rules regarding the inputs they are allowed to use and the wage they are required to pay out.

To locate private governance arrangements in this framework, I follow Pattberg (2005b, p. 359), who conceptualizes private standard-setting as "the act of agreeing on regulative rules, which, although being voluntary in nature, require some degree of compliance to qualify as private regulation." I thus view private regulation as a *system of private rules through which sustainable production practices and products arising from such practices are verified and/or certified and made recognizable to both intermediate buyers and final consumers in the marketplace* (cf. Pattberg, 2005b, p. 362). From a micro-institutional perspective, the establishment and implementation of private sustainability standards is then conceptualized as the introduction of new institutional arrangements for participating producers. For such producers, the rules they are subject to, the enforcement procedures to ensure compliance with those rules, and the incentives they receive are fundamentally altered from the counterfactual situation of being immersed in a mainstream commodity market.

The Three Levels of Action and the Power of the Operational Level

According to Elinor Ostrom (2005), micro-institutional analysis based on individual actions defined by bounded rationality can be applied at three levels of analysis: the constitutional level, which explains the design of collective-choice mechanisms; the collective-choice level, which explains the world of authoritative decision-making; and the operational level, which explains the world of action (Kiser and Ostrom 1982). The constitutional level is "where decisions are made about who is eligible to participate in policymaking and the rules that will be used to undertake policymaking" (Ostrom 2005, pp. 60–61). In the context of private standard-setting, it represents the arena where decisions on standard-setting forums (e.g., multi-stakeholder round-tables or nongovernment organization [NGO]–firm bilateral partner-ships) and procedures (e.g., allowing for public comments or requiring unanimity) take place. At the collective-choice level (where "policy making (or governance) regarding the rules that will be used to regulate operational-level choices is carried out" [Ostrom, 2005, p. 61]), the analysis focuses on the rules embodied in the sustainability standard that market actors have to respect in order to be certified or trade certified products. It also examines procedural choices regarding the implementation, monitoring, and enforcement of such rules. Finally, the operational level (where "participants interact in light of the inter-nal and external incentives they face to generate outcomes directly in the world" [Ostrom 2005, p. 60]) focuses on the 'real-world' impact of rules on behavioral decisions. This may include the adoption and use of sustainability standards by supply chain actors, their compliance with the standards, standards' additionality (i.e., whether the adoption of voluntary rules actually lead to behavioral change, or whether only already compliant producers self-select into a program), and impacts of behavioral changes on biophysical or social outcomes.

Figure 2.1 provides a visual representation of the three levels of analysis, along with their main analytical foci. The private governance literature to date has focused greatly on Elinor Ostrom's constitutional and collective-choice levels, by analyzing the establishment of private governance systems, their set-up, and the rules they embody. While a growing number of contributions (in addition to the effectiveness literature already referenced, one could mention Lenox and Nash 2003; Marx 2008; or Fransen and Burgoon 2012) have also touched on the operational level, few of these use primary data on behavioral changes or differentiate between types of rules and their implementa-tion in much detail.

All three levels are needed to understand final decision-making out-comes, especially when we recall Shepsle's (1989) notion that structural equilibria are defined by the institutional arrangements underpinning social or political interaction. For instance, decisions made at the con-stitutional level about the membership, agenda-setting, and voting pro-cedures at the collective-choice level influence the process through which

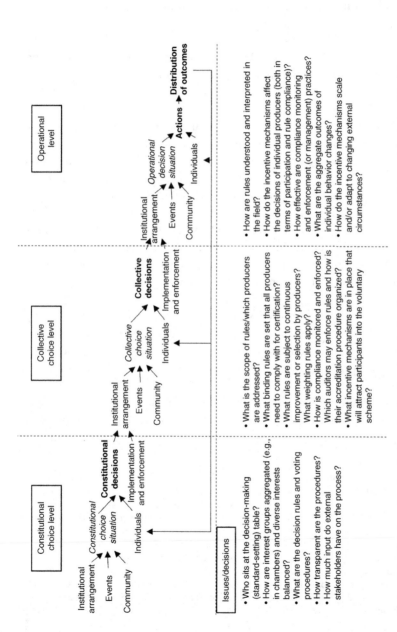

Constitutional choice level

Institutional
arrangement →
Events → *Constitutional choice situation* → **Constitutional decisions** → Institutional
Community → Individuals → Implementation and enforcement → arrangement

Collective choice level

Events → *Collective choice situation* → **Collective decisions** → Institutional
Community → Individuals → Implementation and enforcement → arrangement

Operational level

Events → *Operational decision situation* → **Actions** → **Distribution of outcomes**
Community → Individuals

Issues/decisions

- Who sits at the decision-making (standard-setting) table?
- How are interest groups aggregated (e.g., in chambers) and diverse interests balanced?
- What are the decision rules and voting procedures?
- How transparent are the procedures?
- How much input do external stakeholders have on the process?

- What is the scope of rules/which producers are addressed?
- What binding rules are set that all producers need to comply with for certification?
- What rules are subject to continuous improvement or selection by producers? What weighting rules apply?
- How is compliance monitored and enforced? Which auditors may enforce rules and how is their accreditation procedure organized?
- What incentive mechanisms are in place that will attract participants into the voluntary scheme?

- How are rules understood and interpreted in the field?
- How do the incentive mechanisms affect the decisions of individual producers (both in terms of participation and rule compliance)?
- How effective are compliance monitoring and enforcement (or management) practices?
- What are the aggregate outcomes of individual behavior changes?
- How do the incentive mechanisms scale and/or adapt to changing external circumstances?

Figure 2.1 The three levels of micro-institutional analysis of private governance. Adapted and simplified from Kiser and Ostrom (2000, p. 60)

operational rules are decided. These will then be the rules on paper, or in the books, that govern individual agents' decision-making at the operational level. Following Kiser and Ostrom, I will also denote these as rules-in-form, as opposed to the rules-in-practice actors in the field perceive to be true. Kiser and Ostrom (2000, pp. 77–78) are clear that although institutional scholars have analyzed the constitutional, collective choice, and operational levels in a similar fashion, the operational level is fundamentally different from the other two, since "the operational level is the only level of analysis where an action in the physical world flows directly from a decision."[2]

Drawing attention to the limited focus on implementation, monitoring, and enforcement in the policy analysis literature compared to agenda setting and the negotiation of agreements, they highlight "the folly" of assuming that implementation and enforcement automatically flow from rule formulation. This is particularly the case since rules may be ambiguous or open for interpretation at the operational level (cf. Driver 1989). As "rules are not self-formulating, self-determining, or self-enforcing" (Ostrom 1999, p. 383), human action is necessary at every step of the way. The on-the-ground impact of institutional change thus depends on how the formulation, interpretation, and enforcement of rules occurs in practice. Changing circumstances of the event the rules apply to (due to transformations in technology, shared norms, or other external factors) may further affect the way the previously agreed-upon rules are used and what effect they have, making appropriate rule formulation even trickier (Ostrom 2005, p. 172).

Closely examining rule implementation is all the more important when the individuals making collective-choice decisions are not those who implement the agreed-upon rules. The likelihood of implementation

---

[2] We should note that Kiser and Ostrom's focus is on actions governed by the institutional framework in place. Clearly, the meetings and decision-making processes at the constitutional and collective-choice level also occur 'in the physical world' (and may even have add-on effects on the problem at hand; think for instance of greenhouse gas emissions generated by delegates flying to climate change mitigation conferences). Yet, their point is this: however many discussions on optimal rules on paper and enforcement mechanisms happen and however intricate the governance framework is set up in theory, its ultimate usefulness will only be seen on the ground where it is implemented – and where one cannot presuppose a priori that all rules-in-form will be adopted as rules-in-practice.

gaps arising from such a separation led Ostrom (1990) to identify the close correspondence between rule makers and rule users as one central design principle for successful local common-pool resource management. In contrast, most market-driven regulatory governance arrangements through sustainability standards are global in scope, potentially covering millions of producers, while the standard-setting process is highly centralized, often located in the Global North, and producers are represented by (often Northern) NGOs, if they are represented at all (Rice and McLean 1999; Bennett 2017). In such cases, rule changes at the collective-choice level may be disconnected from the productive reality and real-world constraints of producers. Yet, collective-choice decisions will only have an effect in so far as they are implemented on the ground in the manner intended by rule makers. In addition, feedback mechanisms may well flow back from the operational level to the collective-choice level if, for instance, there is high pressure from actors in the field to abolish rules they find troublesome. Indeed, Cashore *et al.* (2004, pp. 206–210) identify several examples of such feedback processes in the case of forestry certification, such as changes to chain-of-custody rules made to accommodate wood-sharing arrangements between Swedish forest products companies that complicated traceability and 100 percent certified on-product claims.

To assess the problem-solving effectiveness of specific institutional arrangements, it is therefore paramount to pay close attention to the operational level, how decisions made at higher levels influence it, as well as potential feedback processes toward rule-making. For these reasons, this book combines the collective choice-level analysis of the sustainability standards' problem definition, goal definition, and institutional design choices with an empirical focus on Ostrom's operational level.

A Micro-institutional Rational Choice Perspective of Market-Driven Regulatory Governance Effectiveness

Changing the institutional arrangements that govern boundedly rational individuals' actions through the introduction of market-based regulatory governance may be an effective way to create behavioral change if it is successful in combining the introduction of new rules on the ground with an adjustment of the costs and benefits of different choice alternatives. The use of a micro-institutional approach allows me to examine both of these necessary conditions for success in turn by analyzing the effectiveness of the *market incentives* market-driven regulatory governance initiatives have put into place, as well as the effectiveness of the *rules and compliance mechanisms* they have established.

Kiser and Ostrom (2000, p. 56) point out that there are three steps for the effects of institutional change to be felt in the real world: "First, the individuals affected by a change in rules must be cognizant of and abide by the rule change. Second, institutional change has to affect the strategies they adopt. Third, the aggregation of changed individuals must lead to different results." There are obvious parallels between this definition and the conceptualizations of institutional effectiveness discussed in Section 2.1. Kiser and Ostrom's first step involves *compliance* with the rules put forward by the institutional arrangement (which in turn presupposes individuals' awareness and understanding of these rules – a nontrivial step that I separately take into consideration). Here, compliance can be understood in two ways – in a legalistic, binary way of deviance or nondeviance; or, in the socio-legal tradition, as a fluid process "that involves negotiated interpretations of both rules and facts" (Hawkins 1984; Reichman 1992, p. 257). For normative and pragmatic reasons, this book tends toward the second interpretation. At the time of the survey, all sampled farmers were in a certification group that had been audited and found in compliance with the certification norm according to the respective oversight procedures put in place by certification organizations. Since in most cases only a small proportion of farmers are audited during group certification processes, my results do not duplicate the auditing process either regarding the sample or the procedures, which are more in-depth than the present questionnaires allowed. Although I may report farming practices that contradict the rules-in-form (i.e., the rules-in-the-books) of the standard documents, it is not my aim to prove or disprove farmers' deviance from the relevant standard. When farmers report results that are clearly counter to specific requirements of private standards, I categorize this as occurrences where they did not seem to follow the on-paper rule, which would affect the effectiveness of the rule in question. Yet, this gap between paper and practice could be due to several reasons: maybe they consciously decided to shirk the rule, but possibly it was renegotiated, got 'lost in translation' on the way to the field, or was never introduced on the ground due to a lack of awareness raising.

Kiser and Ostrom's (2000, p. 56) second step – "institutional change has to affect the strategies they adopt" – is closely linked to *additionality*, in that behavioral change is produced beyond maintenance of the status quo. Empirically, this requires the existence of a comparable group that models the counterfactual (what would have happened in the absence of the institutional change), which is at the core of the impact evaluation reported in Chapter 5. The third step, finally, points to the need for individual behavior change to have *tangible consequences* (or results) in outcomes in line with the intentions that initiated the institutional change. This micro-institutional rational choice framing of effectiveness thus explicitly adopts a *problem-solving approach*, in which rule compliance is a necessary, but not sufficient, indication of effectiveness.[3]

Assessing the problem-solving effectiveness, or goal attainment, of institutional arrangements requires us to closely understand the *goal*, or *ideal intended outcome*, of the institution in question. This, in turn, relies strongly on the subjective *problem definition*, which frames the way the problem is seen by stakeholders (Mitchell 2006; Young 2011; Auld *et al.* 2015). Depending on the alignment of stakeholders, a single institution may also have more than one goal – and those goals may even be contradictory (Bernauer 1995). This possibility is all the more likely when comparing the effectiveness of different institutional arrangements targeting a single problem, and when their common stated objective is a concept open to wide interpretation, such as is the case with 'sustainability'. Consequently, Chapter 3 will present an overview of historical and contemporary definitions of sustainability, with a special focus on the coffee sector, and discuss differences in problem definitions that may have had direct impacts on the institutional design, and subsequent effectiveness, of some of the standards in question (Mitchell 2006). Identifying and analyzing outcome indicators that represent each of these problem definitions then allows me to comprehensively assess whether market-driven regulatory governance institutions are effective in attaining their goals by deductively applying Kiser and Ostrom's (2000, p. 56) tripartite definition.

---

[3] In turn, while notions of efficiency or equity may be discussed in due course, they are not the primary object of inquiry of this book; nor does it have the ambition to define and operationalize a socially optimal solution and measure private standards' distance to this normative optimum.

2.3 The Institutional Design Dilemma of Market-Driven Regulatory Governance

With its grounding in institutional rational choice theory, the micro-institutional approach provides a solid theoretical basis to analyze the linkage between the collective-choice level – regarding institutional design choices on rules, incentives, and enforcement – and its expected outcomes at the operational level. In doing so, it is possible to identify a central tension in designing market-driven regulatory governance institutions that is crucial to understand field-level outcomes: the tension between *stringency* (concerning both rule development and enforcement) and *inclusivity* (by providing more flexibility to enter and remain in schemes). This tension grows as standards exit their respective niche markets and aim to attract a larger share of the commodity market.

A broad trade-off between standards' strictness and their likely over-all coverage and impacts has been noted by a number of previous authors (cf. Cashore *et al.* 2007; Prakash and Potoski 2007; Dietz and Auffenberg 2014). However, the present data allow me to go one step further in analyzing how this dilemma affects the dynamic design of standards and their implementation in the field, and test resulting hypotheses in a quantitative fashion. This section first presents two broad choices concerning institutional design that will shape both incentive-setting and compliance management. It then goes into detail how standard-setters encounter dilemmas – driven by both market-driven and regulatory tensions – when choosing between these two options. It does so by applying institutional rational choice theory, complemented by insights from the socio-legal literature, which has a long tradition of studying how the design of administrative laws and regulations influence their implementation and enforcement in practice. Finally, it introduces competing hypotheses of how these design choices will influence standard effectiveness that will be tested in Chapter 6.

Stringency versus Inclusivity in Standard-Setting and Enforcement

Market-driven regulatory systems encounter two contrary imperatives that they need to consider during standard-setting and enforcement, especially as they aim to scale up their operations. On the one hand, market-based private governance relying on voluntary participation stands and falls by one basic premise: that market incentives exist that outweigh the compliance costs (including the administrative burden) of participating in the regulatory scheme (Vogel 2009; Dietz and Auffenberg 2014; Carter *et al.* 2018). From an economic and club good perspective (Guthman 2004; Potoski and Prakash 2009), private regulation's main function is therefore the definition, implementation, monitoring, and enforcement of specific sustainability requirements that are transformed into approximations of private law for participating producers. These requirements define the in-group, or club, that will gain access to market premiums for the differentiated good, and set it apart from conventional producers. If the private regulatory standard is well designed, the adoption and enforcement of a standard should be sufficient for it to induce positive changes in behaviors and outcomes. From this perspective, it is crucial that all important sustainability criteria are made into *binding compliance requirements* in order for the standard to be able to monitor and enforce their implementation. Also, the *enforcement capacity* of standard-setters and certification bodies needs to be strong to reliably exclude noncompliant actors from the system. Finally, the voluntary nature of private governance efforts makes opt-out and switching systems deceptively easy; in consequence, standards need to provide strong and *persistent market-based incentives* for continued participation such as high price premiums or credible market-access barriers.

On the other hand, in recognition of the high initial compliance costs, the complexity of market structures, and the limited capacity of smallholder farmers in many tropical value chains, alternative voices have called for a move away from a purely in-group/out-group-driven perspective. This has included producer organizations that have vocally asserted that setting unattainably high environmental or social standards is counterproductive to the aim of creating widespread change. In line with their goal of mainstreaming private governance across entire sectors of smallholder farmers, many certification schemes thus operate under or have moved to '*continuous improvement*' models, in which requirements are relatively low at entry into the scheme and are raised year by year (Sizer and de Freitas 2016). In this continuous improvement model, certified farms need to comply with a core set of 'critical' criteria (by eliminating 'unacceptable' or 'zero tolerance' practices) from the beginning in order to attain initial certification. Thereafter, additional requirements are added year by year, with farms giving different amounts of leeway to choose between criteria. This approach underlines the importance of training and learning opportunities in order to change practices, and the sequencing of requirements, starting with more easily achievable indicators and moving onto more demanding ones. It furthermore allows for greater flexibility in enforcement, where complying with the spirit of the standard is more important than checking every single box. This perspective also provides auditors with greater autonomy in making on-the-ground compliance decisions.

Private standard-setters hence need to decide between institutional design choices that represent greater stringency and those that allow for more inclusivity. This choice plays out on several levels. On a standard-setting level, private standards have a broad choice between being in-group/out-group differentiators and using a continuous improvement approach. Regarding the enforcement approach, standard-setters can maintain a higher grade of oversight or decentralize their enforcement strategy. On the ground, they can support legalistic or cooperative compliance enforcement. And when interacting, they can attempt to strive toward super-seals or toward greater market segmentation. This choices are summarized in Table 2.1. Table 2.1 also shows that there

Table 2.1 *The institutional design dilemma of market-driven regulatory governance initiatives*

Design choices	Stringency	Inclusivity
Primary economic goal	Maintain persistent market-based incentives	Attract higher roaster demand
Primary implementation goal	Facilitate equivalence and compliance enforcement through clear rules	Facilitate upscaling and mainstreaming through flexibility
Design features		
Standard-setting	Reasonably high entry barriers	Improvement pathways for lower-performing producers
Standard enforcement	Strict in-group/out-group differentiation	Improvements in capacity to comply
	Legalistic compliance enforcement	Cooperative compliance management
Standard coexistence	Single standard/super-seal	'Co-opetition' by segmenting the market and differentiated targeting

are both economic and practical rationales for either approach. These dilemmas are explained in the next sections.

Designing Market-Driven Regulatory Institutions: The Market-Driven Tension

From an economic perspective, standards deciding between stringency and inclusivity are in effect choosing between appealing to boundedly rational producers, by maintaining persistent market-based incentives, and appealing to buyers, by providing affordable certified products. Let us consider each in turn.

In the theory of change of many certification organizations, external incentives that can make up for the implementation of costly practices are usually divided in two: price premiums and market access. The promise of price premiums for certified goods is a straightforward incentive mechanism for producers, as it fits well into the profit maximization framework of firms and agricultural producers. Such premiums may either constitute part of the regulatory framework – that is, participating buyers are required to pay a specified premium in order to comply with the standard – or they can be determined by the market through negotiations between buyers and sellers of the certified good (which I will denote as market-based premiums).

The market access incentive, in turn, can work in two ways: either, what is really meant is access to *differentiated* markets with higher prices; that is, it translates to an implicit price premium. Or else, certification may also be treated as a requirement for accessing mainstream markets (i.e., similar to a private nontariff trade barrier). However, this incentive only works if there are virtually no alternative markets to sell in (or, alternatively, if the switching costs to find other buyers are perceived to be higher than compliance with the voluntary regulation[4]). Given that this incentive mechanism transfers the costs of compliance to producers, the rational producer choice would be to sell in any other channel before submitting to the voluntary regulation

---

[4] An example of such high perceived switching costs can be found in the case of British Columbian forestry companies, which supported and complied with Forest Stewardship Council standards after their UK buyers threatened to cancel their contracts (and in some cases terminated business relationships due to the lack of certification) (Cashore *et al.* 2004).

(unless, of course, the regulation is so lax that it does not create any additional costs because it sets the bar below the current implemented practices). In the absence of exceptional market control (e.g., small oligopsonies, highly vertically integrated supply chains, or internationally coordinated import restrictions), price premiums are thus likely to be the main economic incentive for producers to participate in private sustainability schemes that raise the bar beyond the status quo.

However, the implementation of market-driven standards in transnational markets creates a high threat of premium erosion, especially if premiums are market-based. Producers certified with a private sustainability standard who wish to benefit from higher prices are faced with the collective action problem typical to many cartels. Since the premium is paid out on a per-unit basis, there exist strong incentives for participating farmers to produce greater quantities of products (in an agricultural context, either by increasing their yields or by expanding their production surface) to derive a greater overall income from premiums. Additionally, the higher-than-average prices will attract non-participating producers, who will want to enter the scheme in order to gain access to the price premium. Both of these trends will lead to rises in supply irrespective of demand, and shrinking premium prices unless demand increases at an equal pace with supply. Indeed, de Janvry *et al.* (2015) show both conceptually and empirically that in a disequilibrium market without either strong process rules or formal limits to entry, the expected net benefit of certified producers is close to zero because of the overproduction of certified goods.

Hence, as Guthman (2004, 2007) notes, maintaining substantive market-based price premiums requires the creation of effective barriers to entry to a scheme (i.e., strict process rules) and the establishment of quasi-monopoly conditions. Otherwise, "competition is unleashed and the incentive disappears" (Guthman 2007, p. 461). Indeed, she highlights that consumption-based rents almost always disappear, following the same pattern: "at first, firms with a novel, valorized commodity see premium prices; new firms are attracted to the above-normal price as they enter into production of that commodity; thereafter, scarcity diminishes, prices fall, and rent is eroded" (Guthman 2004, p. 520). To prevent such rent erosion in the context of sustainability certifications, rules need to be designed such that there are few opportunities to shirk. This is especially important regarding requirements that raise long-run operating costs.

This rationale also applies to institutional design choices regarding compliance enforcement. A credible exclusionary threat (and thus strict enforcement of regulation) is critical for the protection of the barriers to entry that allow market incentives to accrue in the face of uncertain or incremental demand (Williamson 1975; North 1990; Potoski and Prakash 2009). Greater flexibility in enforcement, in turn, erodes the market entry barriers that protect the price premium that the differentiated product obtains over the mainstream commodity price (Guthman 2004). Indeed, the less stringently the strategy of market exclusion is used, the lower its threat potential that could motivate participating producers to comply with the provided regulation, since producers will not feel a significant economic difference when the price premium they are foregoing is inconsequential to begin with. In contrast, if entry barriers can be maintained, economic theory predicts that price premiums would arrive at an equilibrium where they are equal to the marginal cost of compliance.[5] In this way, certification schemes could compensate participating producers for their increased costs and create alternative institutional arrangements that allow for the pricing of positive externalities.

Yet, if we widen our scope of analysis to allow for the coexistence of various competing certification organizations, the picture becomes more complex. As the first standard-setting organization discovers that ethical consumers show a willingness to pay higher prices for differentiated products in a certain sector, it will work on expanding that niche market further by engaging in outreach and consumer education activities. Alternative initiatives aiming for market transformation will then face strong incentives to try accessing that same niche (Auld 2014). This situation may lead to the rapid proliferation of standards that now compete for uptake at the consumer level. Many times, this access to final consumers is mediated by the companies producing the consumer good (Bartley *et al.* 2015). Standard organizations thus face an increasing pressure to appeal to such buyers of raw materials. In this case, market pressures may encourage standard-

---

[5] It should be noted that this theoretical expectation also presupposes the existence of perfect information, such that producers are able to anticipate future demand with enough certainty to make adequate decisions on entering or exiting the scheme. We will critically evaluate this assumption in the case of coffee certification schemes where producers instead are boundedly rational and faced with considerable information asymmetries.

setters to move toward greater flexibility in standard-setting and enforcement. This introduces institutional design incentives contrary to those described earlier, which presupposes that schemes would aim for strict rules and strong enforcement in order to protect price premiums.

Rather than modeling the choices of rational producers, this perspective focuses on the boundedly rational choices of raw material purchasers. In the case of coffee, this means roasters in consuming countries such as Nestlé and Jacobs Douwe Egberts. Given the high concentration among roasters, they are in a position of strong market power in determining the relative demand for various types of sustainable and nonsustainable coffee (Fitter and Kaplinsky 2001; Ponte 2002; Bitzer *et al.* 2008; Bamber *et al.* 2014; Grabs 2017, 2018). As any boundedly rational market actor, these buying firms will strive toward maximizing their business benefits and minimizing costs. Given that their costs are in effect the *price premium paid to certified producers above the current market price*, they will do so using two strategies. First, when premiums are market-based, they will aim to source the least costly certified product in order to minimize their additional cost and improve their margins at the point of sale. If consumers continue to pay the same premium prices, roasters can then capture an increasing share of the retail premium for themselves. Hence, Guthman (2004, p. 520) notes the danger of rent appropriation, such that even more durable rents "eventually may be redistributed to other actors in the chain of provision, especially those who can exercise some monopoly control." This strategy further pits certified producers against each other in a competition for the lowest-cost offer possible while fulfilling the certification requirements, opening up incentives for cutting corners and a minimalist implementation strategy.

Second, as certification schemes proliferate, buying firms are given an increasing array of options of 'sustainable coffee' they may purchase, and will choose participation based on the relative costs of participation (the premium to be paid) in relation to the reputational benefits received. Hence, even if premiums are fixed in a regulatory framework, as is the case for the fair trade labels, competition between labels may erode the volume of sales of such certified goods, particularly if they are seen as equivalent to alternative schemes. This danger is compounded if certification organizations take a 'live-and-let-live' approach that curtails their ability to criticize other initiatives and clearly delineate their own approach as 'the best' ethical solution. In this case, market forces will strongly favor less ambitious initiatives (Raynolds *et al.* 2007; Dietz and Auffenberg 2014) and oppose approaches that go 'against market principles' such as minimum pricing (Bitzer *et al.* 2013). Given certification organizations' goal to expand demand for certified products at the same time as supply, their need to appeal to buyers who value low price premiums may lead to their tolerance of, or indeed, support for 'competitive' market-based premiums. This, however, lowers the incentives for producers to comply with high-cost requirements that have the greatest likelihood of internalizing environmental and social externalities, leading to difficult trade-offs at the point of rule formulation and enforcement.

The business reality of large-scale buyers and their status as profit-maximizing corporations further leads to them having additional requirements for certification organizations. Beyond providing certified products at competitive prices, standard-setting initiatives also need to guarantee buyers the ability to source high volumes of the respective product. At the same time, buyers often demand high flexibility in sourcing origins that allows them to adjust their relative volumes at short notice based on key variables such as taste and baseline market prices. Certification organizations thus have substantial market-based incentives to lower the stringency of their requirements and enforcement strategies to allow for a faster and easier roll-out to producers, particularly as they reach out to more marginal producers that had not yet been included in the more advanced schemes to date (Dietz and Auffenberg 2014). This dilemma is linked to the "contradiction of concentrated retailing" (Bartley *et al.* 2015, p. 216). The market power of large, well-known buying firms creates attractive conditions for civil society-led efforts to engage in 'naming-and-shaming' campaigns with the goal of efficiently changing industry standards, given that such standards can be dictated by concentrated buyers (cf. Dauvergne and Lister 2010, 2012; Elder *et al.* 2014). Yet, the dominance of concentrated buyers simultaneously contributes to threats to the independence of certification initiatives and a latent danger of cooptation and a move toward business-friendly solutions (Burchell and Cook 2013; Bartley *et al.* 2015; Levy *et al.* 2016).

What role does consumer pressure play in this scenario? In this model, consumers are equally assumed to be boundedly rational actors for whom searching for full information on a particular consumption good is costly. Sustainability attributes are only one of many attributes consumers focus on, with brand and price frequently more important for the average consumer than sustainability considerations (Moser *et al.* 2011; Wirth *et al.* 2011). Confronted with label proliferation, the average consumer may find it difficult to differentiate between credible and lax schemes, and use 'satisficing' techniques by indiscriminately choosing products that bear any sustainability seal (Harbaugh *et al.* 2011). In a market characterized by consumers' label fatigue and information overload (Harbaugh *et al.* 2011), it is thus very difficult for voluntary programs to exclude free riders from taking advantage of the 'warm glow' benefits of ethical marketing. Indeed, the institution of third-party–verified certification schemes had been devised to overcome this problem of the unobservability of so-called credence goods. Yet, the proliferation of labels and dependence of such schemes on the participation of large market actors may reproduce many of the same shortcomings they were designed to address.

Designing Market-Driven Regulatory Institutions: The Regulatory Tension

A closely related tension highlighted by the socio-legal literature is the trade-off between regulatory precision and discretion, both when setting rules and standards (Driver 1989) and when enforcing them (Bardach and Kagan 1982), regarding their likely on-the-ground implementation effectiveness. If regulatory requirements and penalties are prescribed in detail, they are likely to be overinclusive and insensitive to local circumstance. If they are flexible and discretionary, under-regulation, regulatory capture by the regulated, and regulatory ineffectiveness may be the result (Bardach and Kagan 1982; Hawkins 1984; Hawkins and Thomas 1989). This dilemma is heightened for private regulatory standards that have a global scope, span producers of various sizes in different country settings, and rely on a decentralized enforcement infrastructure through for-profit auditing firms that may exhibit substantial conflicts of interest (Grabosky 1991, 1995; Meidinger 2003, 2006; Newsom *et al.* 2006; Auld *et al.* 2015).

As Bardach and Kagan (1982) explore in detail, in public policy, there are strong legal, political, and pragmatic reasons to make rules precise at the regulatory design stage. Specific, objective rules fulfill the requirement for equal treatment before the law, bolster politicians' and agencies' image of 'addressing the problem' in an impartial way, and make enforcement faster and more efficient since they facilitate proof of violations. As discussed earlier, in a market setting, the need to protect rents by erecting nontrivial entry barriers adds a strong commercial argument for precise, objective, and universally applicable rules, such as 'zero tolerance' requirements, that differentiate a certain category of goods from others.

However, setting uniform substantive standards that are applied in vastly diverse and individual contexts inevitably creates friction at the time of implementation. Here, Bardach and Kagan (1982, p. 58) argue that an overly legalistic approach to regulatory enforcement can lead to increasing "regulatory unreasonableness (the imposition of uniform regulatory requirements in situations where they do not make sense) and unresponsiveness (the failure to consider arguments by regulated enterprises that exceptions should be made)" when the 'official perspective' clashes with the 'civilian perspective'. This may lead to economic inefficiencies and backlash by the regulated. In the case of market-driven private standards, such backlash can lead to producers choosing to forego the market benefits of participation and opting out of the certification scheme, decreasing the ultimate reach of and effectiveness of private regulation. The option of exiting – or switching to an alternative scheme – furthermore lowers the likelihood of producers mobilizing and demanding change in a concerted fashion, especially if the rule-setting arena is perceived to be hard to access and not very responsive to producer input.[6]

Regulatory unreasonableness is particularly problematic when noncompliance stems not from willful deviance, but from a lack of capacity to comply, as well as "instances of ignorance, incompetence, or inadequate supervision" (Bardach and Kagan 1982, p. 62) . In such cases, social utility (i.e., that sanctions should provide a net social benefit) would speak for regulators acting "more like a 'persuader' or educator than a rule-bound bureaucrat" (Bardach and Kagan 1982, p. 38). Regarding compliance enforcement, Bardach and Kagan (1982) thus

---

[6] Although there exist exceptions in practice. For instance, regional Fairtrade producer organizations such as CLAC (the Coordinadora Latinoamericana y del Caribe de Pequeños Productores y Trabajadores de Comercio Justo) are very active in co-constructing standards.

champion the 'good inspector' who applies rules flexibly, cooperatively, and with an eye to problem solving rather than prosecution. Supporting this theoretical insight with practical evidence, Hawkins finds that in environmental pollution control, "standards are by no means treated as absolute proscriptions inexorably enforced. The agencies display a sometimes considerable flexibility both in the standards set and in the enforcement policy adopted, in recognition of the technical difficulties and costs of complying, the potential for error, and the stigmatizing effect of strict legal enforcement ... Non-compliance with standards is thus organizationally sanctioned" (Hawkins 1984, p. 27) and compliance is seen as a process, rather than a condition.

There are strong arguments why we might expect to find a similar, flexible approach in the enforcement of private regulatory governance. First, such programs were designed as mechanisms to induce better behavior, rather than to punish misconduct. This may contribute to psychological barriers to pursuing a strict, punitive compliance approach. One also needs to consider the practical threat of producer flight if the approach taken is too stringent, particularly in the case of multiple competing certification schemes (Reinecke *et al.* 2012). Furthermore, private standards face the same problems regarding compliance enforcement as public regulations. These are heightened in the agricultural sector due to a frequently low educational or financial capacity to comply, an independent political culture that resists regulation, the spatial distribution that leads to low visibility of noncompliance, and the surrounding institutional context that rewards rationalization and profit-maximizing practices (Gunningham and Grabosky 1998). The lack of legal recourse further means that the highest potential level of 'regulatory escalation' for enforcers is the refusal to certify producers, thereby excluding them from access to potential market benefits. This highest point of 'escalation', however, also excludes these 'noncompliant' producers from future beneficial interaction with regulators and may not be socially optimal if the goal of regulatory implementation and enforcement is the overall improvement of practices (Bardach and Kagan 1982).

The voluntary nature of private regulation, along with its multiplicity and the nonmonopoly status of each private standard in turn, further poses constraints on these regulators in their ability to exclude producers from 'green market benefits'. Such producers may easily turn to a different label – or even create their own – in an effort to 'change jurisdiction' and maintain access to lucrative markets. Moreover, certification organizations only have incomplete control over the threat of exclusion from market benefits. They may revoke the certification itself, but the corresponding access to premium markets will need to be revoked by the business partner of the previously certified enterprise, who may decide that the quality, provenance, or other attributes of the final product continue to justify the enterprise's place in the high-end value chain even without a sustainability certification.

Finally, private regulatory governance schemes also have a more decentralized enforcement infrastructure than most public regulatory agencies. Standard-setting organizations can delegate enforcement authority to auditing organizations in a number of ways, but virtually any variant showcases principal-agent dilemmas and conflict-of-interest problems (Meidinger 2003). On the one hand, if standard-setting organizations maintain close control of their auditing procedures (i.e., through a subsidiary body with an auditing monopoly) they are in danger of influencing the auditing procedure with their own preference for a rapid growth in the number of certified users (which increases the standard's market share and the organization's reputation and influence). This may lower the credibility and legitimacy of the process. On the other hand, if they take a highly hands-off approach in selecting auditors and allow for a high level of competition, auditing firms may opportunistically pursue their primary interest of having long-term certifiable clients (e.g., by providing low-cost, lenient audits) over the principal's interest of a stringent and credible process (Calegari *et al.* 1998; Barrett *et al.* 2002; Makkawi and Schick 2003; Pierce and Sweeney 2004; Jahn *et al.* 2005; Albersmeier *et al.* 2009).

In this context, Calegari *et al.* (1998) and Makkawi and Schick (2003) describe the phenomenon of 'low-balling', wherein competing auditors set the fee for the first audit below the calculated real costs to win a specific contract. In this model, profits only arise in an ongoing business relationship, transforming auditing fees from subsequent inspections into quasi-rents that depend on customer loyalty. This creates high levels of dependence of the auditors on their clients, which may lead to principal-agent conflicts. In turn, Jahn *et al.* (2005) note that profit-maximizing producers have the incentive to select auditors known to employ low standards (given the higher probability of successful certification), while auditors are under pressure to provide cost-effective auditing services, which may affect the quality of their inspections (Pierce and Sweeney 2004). The agreed-on best practice to date has coalesced around requiring auditing bodies to be accredited according to the specific standard in question, which inserts an additional layer of oversight by national or international accreditation bodies. This practice, however, often leads to regional auditing monopolies and high prices for services, which goes against the aim of lowering entry barriers for participation for smaller-scale or poorer farmers. There thus exist both normative arguments against stringent rule-setting and compliance enforcement in the private regulatory arena as well as numerous practical hurdles.

So what institutional design choices do market-driven regulatory governance initiatives make, and how does this shape their effectiveness in driving behavioral change on the ground? The coffee sector provides a unique setting to apply this research agenda due to the possibility of comparing both different private governance institutions as well as different underlying country contexts.

Designing Effective Market-Driven Regulatory Governance Institutions: Hypotheses Predicting Outcome Additionality

Taking account of the literature already presented, I construct nine hypotheses regarding the institutional design choices of market-driven regulatory governance institutions that will be tested through a meta-analysis of a subset of the analyzed indicators and their group-wise results regarding outcome additionality. I take outcome additionality, as measured by *differences in practice implementation compared to matched control observations*, as my central dependent variable. This allows me to isolate design choices that, to the best of our knowledge, affect producer behavior, which is a key characteristic of institutional effectiveness as defined in the micro-institutional perspective (which requires that change in institutional arrangements affects the strategies that affected individuals adopt). This approach further allows me to account for selection effects (wherein private regulatory governance is only adopted by individuals whose practices are already in line with the requirements), which are frequently observed in the literature, but limit the transformative power of market-driven regulatory governance initiatives (Marx and Cuypers 2010; Auld *et al.* 2015). The derived hypotheses are as follows.

Following a prescriptive approach to compliance enforcement, we may expect the following:

H1: Critical requirements (those that are mandatory for certification attainment) are **more likely** to show outcome additionality than noncritical requirements because they do not allow for cost-minimizing choices between alternative options and provide clarity on obligations for both auditor and auditee, leading to low amounts of on-the-ground variability.

On the other hand, and following the compliance management approach, we may find the alternative hypothesis to be true:

H2: Critical requirements are **less likely** to show outcome additionality than noncritical requirements because they do not account for producers' capacity to comply and do not give auditors leeway to aid participants toward compliance.

Following this argument, it could be that capacity building is the key criterion that leads to outcome additionality:

H3: Requirements in groups that had received effective training on the practice in question are **more likely** to show outcome additionality due to participants' improvements in their capacity to comply.

Regarding market benefits, I expect that the provision of individualized, significant price premiums will have a positive effect on the outcome additionality of practices, given the incentive to remain in the program:

H4: Programs that offer individualized, significant price premiums (>20 percent over noncertified price) to producers are **more likely** to show outcome additionality due to their provision of a financial disincentive for noncompliance.

Along the same lines, combining rational choice arguments with socio-legal concerns over producers' financial capacity to comply, we may find that the associated upfront or continuous compliance costs decreases producers' likelihood to improve practices beyond their current status quo:

H5: Requirements that necessitate significant upfront investment costs are **less likely** to show outcome additionality due to limits in regulatees' capacity to comply and their likelihood to opt out of or evade such requirements.

H6: Requirements that represent significant continuous opportunity costs are **less likely** to show outcome additionality due to limits in regulatees' financial capacity to comply and their likelihood to opt out of or evade such requirements.

Building on the discussion on conflicts of interest and principal-agent problems during auditing, the following might be true on the program level:

H7: Programs that only allow for one monopoly auditing organization or that require accreditation to their standard are **more likely** to show outcome additionality than programs that allow for a large group of proxy-accredited or desk-approved auditing organizations due to higher familiarity with the relevant standards and the reduction of adverse incentives and conflicts of interest.

Finally, Chapter 7 examines the interactions between private regulation and national-level incentives and regulations. Theoretically, the presence of equivalent public regulation may either *increase* outcome additionality, by providing private enforcement capacity of public regulation that represents no cost beyond legal compliance, or *decrease* such additionality due to the fact that such regulation already exists and is enforced in the country setting in question.

H8: Private regulation requirements that mirror public regulation are **more likely** to show outcome additionality due to the provision of enforcement capability for clear rules on the ground.

H9: Private regulatory requirements that mirror public regulation are **less likely** to show outcome additionality due to regulatory duplication.

By harnessing the large-N data set at the core of this study, and exploiting the variability across standards and country contexts while keeping the sectoral and market context constant, I aim to contribute to broader-level insights on behavioral change that may be fostered through private regulation, and the best way to go about it.

In sum, Chapter 2 has shown that the micro-institutional rational choice approach fits my context of analysis, where boundedly rational smallholder farmers make decisions embedded in a web of various institutional arrangements. I have argued that private sustainability standards can be seen as additional institutional arrangements that introduce new rules, enforcement mechanisms, and incentives for compliance to participating farmers. As standards aim to expand their reach, they run into the institutional design dilemma of market-driven regulatory governance: it is impossible to maintain the existing level of market incentives, which are based on differentiation, if standard-setting organizations simultaneously try to bring the largest possible number of farmers into their systems. Theoretically, it is unclear what consequences this state of affairs will have for the effectiveness of market-driven regulatory governance, as we can identify arguments both for and against more flexible rule definition and inclusive compliance management. On the one hand, strict rules may prevent regulatory capture, shirking, and under-regulation, while the provision of market incentives motivates participation. On the other, it is possible that a trend toward more flexible compliance management can prevent regulatory unreasonableness, over-regulation, and result in greater outcome additionality, especially among more marginalized farmers. The rest of this book will investigate these questions in greater detail. But first, in order to assess the goal attainment of private governance, we need to define the goal of a sustainable coffee sector. This is done in the following chapter.

3 | Defining the Goal of a Sustainable Coffee Sector

There is an advantage in leaving the definition of 'sustainability' imprecise. As soon as something can be defined the discussion stops. You have to keep people in the game.

(Specialty Coffee Association of America, cited in Rice and McLean [1999, p. 89])

The production of coffee occurs under fragile ecological and socio-economic conditions in some of the most biodiverse regions of the world (Mittermeier *et al.* 1998; de Beenhouwer *et al.* 2013). As production volume and demand continue to rise, it is of high priority to identify the ways in which coffee production can impede or contribute to ecosystem conservation and sustainable livelihoods, as well as how private governance mechanisms can help to address such issues. Defining what a sustainable coffee sector should look like is also paramount to evaluate the effectiveness of private regulatory initiatives in moving the sector into that direction.

After a short introduction to the concept of sustainability and select controversies, this chapter presents an overview of the difficulty of achieving a sustainable market price for coffee in the mainstream market. It then relates these market signals to different agronomic modes of coffee production and their environmental and social consequences. Building on these insights, it provides an overview of the emergence of sustainability as a collective concern in the coffee sector, and examines the concurrent rise of private sustainability standards and their entry into mainstream markets. I further discuss how the definition of 'sustainable coffee', and appropriate solution pathways through private standards have evolved in this field of tension between producers, roasters, and nonprofit groups.

3.1 Defining Sustainability: Concepts and Controversies

For a concept that is ubiquitous in academia, business, and policy-making, defining 'sustainability' is an unexpectedly tricky endeavor. As the epigraph of this chapter illustrates, the complex and contested nature of the concept may be one reason for its rapid ascendance: in this way, many actors can commit to the same nominal goal while using fundamentally different interpretations of the ideal outcome. For instance, environmentalists may view a sustainable system as one that keeps natural resources and ecosystems intact, disregarding issues of economic growth or development. On the other hand, businesses and economists might see a sustainable economy as one with solid growth rates that exploits resources at a rate that optimizes their long-term production potential. These two juxtaposed views defined the nascent environmentalist debates in the 1960s and 1970s. They have so little common ground that collective action was close to impossible. Confrontations between businesses and civil society were the norm, with calls for limits to growth coming from groups of scientists such as the Club of Rome (Mebratu 1998).

Beginning with the 1972 United Nations (UN) Conference on the Human Environment in Stockholm, gradually it became clear that sustainability and economic development had to be thought together. This realization was also reflected in international discourse, most notably in the shift from a focus on 'sustainability' toward 'sustainable development' as the main goal of global collaborative efforts (Mebratu 1998). The definition of *sustainable development* that has gained the greatest international acceptance is that of the UN World Commission on Environment and Development (also known as the Brundtland Commission). It was introduced in the 1987 Report "Our Common Future" and reads as follows:

Sustainable development is development that meets the needs of the present without compromising the ability of future generations to meet their own needs. It contains within it two key concepts: the concept of needs, in particular the essential needs of the world's poor, to which overriding priority should be given; and the idea of limitations imposed by the state of technology and social organization on the environment's ability to meet present and future needs. (World Commission on Environment and Development 1987, p. 43)

Going beyond the Brundtland Commission's bifurcation of sustainability into development concerns and environmental limits, later definitions frequently separated development issues into economic and social features. This resulted in a tripartite definition that encompasses the three categories (or 'pillars') of *economic, social, and environmental sustainability* (Viederman 1994; Pope *et al.* 2004; Kuhlman and Farrington 2010). This framing is mirrored in the business ethics literature by the 'triple bottom line' approach, where environmental and social bottom lines are added to the (primary) financial one (Elkington 1997). However, there is considerable dispute over the appropriate prioritization when trade-offs between these pillars emerge (Gibson 2006; Kuhlman and Farrington 2010): how far should human economic activity be constrained in order to protect the environment, particularly in areas where there are still high rates of poverty and underdevelopment? Many political solutions, including the Brundtland definition (Gowdy and Walton 2010), remain agnostic about this question.

For a single smallholder producer of commodity crops, these abstract questions become pressing, given that the cash crop income generally sustains the livelihoods of all household members. The primacy of survival means that economic sustainability – that is, making sufficient profits to meet household needs – is often farmers' primary concern. Yet, this concern is closely interwoven with the environmental and social sustainability of commodity production, depending on farmers' production choices. Farming profits follow the general economic formula of Profit = Price*Quantity – Costs. A farm's profit thus relies on three factors: farm-gate prices, production volume (determined by both yields and production surface), and production costs. Increasing economic sustainability – and, relatedly, the social welfare of the household – may then derive from four sources: *higher prices*, a higher production volume through either *higher yields* and/or a *larger production surface*, or *lower production costs*.

Manipulating these factors to pursue greater economic sustainability will have direct effects on the farm's environmental or social sustainability. For instance, if farmers focus on lowering production costs by paying low wages to their workers, this has a negative impact on the community's social sustainability. High tensions between different pillars of sustainability also exist in the case of expanding one's production surface to attain greater output. This strategy may contribute to ecosystem destruction if agricultural expansion encroaches upon primary forests or other vital ecosystems. In many cases, it is small-scale or hitherto landless farmers that move into forests out of economic necessity to make a living by farming. In this case, the sustainability goals of protecting the ecosystem and improving farmer livelihoods appear in direct conflict. Two schools of thought attempt to reconcile them.

The *land sparing* hypothesis argues that it is more efficient to set land with high ecological value aside and to maximize yields on the currently farmed land (Balmford *et al.* 2005; Phalan *et al.* 2011). Land sparing proponents are more often found in the development or agriculture literature, and the concept is more aligned with the principle of sustainable intensification (Green *et al.* 2005). Under *sustainable intensification*, farmers are encouraged to adopt best agricultural practices to achieve the highest output-to-input conversion ratio. That is, the goal is to maximize productivity while minimizing the amounts of fertilizer, pesticides, agrochemical inputs, labor, and land used (Tilman *et al.* 2011; Garnett *et al.* 2013). Land sparing advocates see the central purpose of sustainable agriculture as achieving the goal of meeting growing consumption demands with as little expansion of existing farmland as possible, especially in areas with high existing biodiversity (Borlaug 2000; Balmford *et al.* 2005; Green *et al.* 2005). This practice thus aims to *increase yields* and *lower input costs* while restricting increases in production surface – focusing on two of the four economic criteria, while holding the other two constant.

However, a number of commentators are skeptical of the long-term viability of the land sparing approach, given the Jevons paradox: the more productive one's production surface becomes, the greater the economic incentive to expand this intensified type of production further, including into protected areas. Land sparing approaches thus rely on strong and well-enforced land-use regulations, which may be a challenge even in well-governed states (Perfecto and Vandermeer 2010; Ceddia *et al.* 2013; Byerlee *et al.* 2014). Furthermore, if intensification of production is the primary goal (because farmers focus on higher yields on the same land), there needs to be heightened attention that such intensification is indeed sustainable. Traditionally, productivity increases occur by using higher amounts of fertilizers and pesticides, and planting more of the same crop on one's land. Such monoculture practices, however, are linked to disease susceptibility, a decline of soil quality, and a loss of diversification, which makes farmers more dependent on commodity price development.

On the other hand, the *land sharing* argument proposes that food production is compatible with biodiversity protection if wildlife-friendly production practices such as organic farming or agroforestry are applied (Green *et al.* 2005; Perfecto and Vandermeer 2008; Gabriel *et al.* 2009; Vandermeer and Perfecto 2012; Fischer and Victor 2014). Land sharing is generally advocated by conservationists and is closely related to the concept of agroecology, wherein sustainable agriculture is based on a deep understanding of ecological processes and a mimicking of such processes in the production landscape (Green *et al.* 2005). Agroecology as a production practice advocates for systemic approaches to whole-farm management that integrate crops and livestock, crop rotation, diversification, the use of complementary crops that allow for natural pest management methods, and an approximation of natural growing conditions for each plant variety[1] (Altieri 1995; Duru *et al.* 2015; Gliessman 2015). Land sharing advocates argue that the creation of farmed biodiversity corridors that continue to provide habitats for birds, insects, and mammals is a more holistic management option than land sparing, as it simultaneously minimizes the ecological impacts on the farmed land (Bosselmann 2012). While this production system relies on low chemical input costs, it generally requires more labor than a monoculture system. Thus, *production costs* are likely to remain the same or increase. It is furthermore likely to *decrease the yield potential* of the production surface in question. Thus, in this type of production, a *sustainable price level* plays a critical role for a farm's overall survival and economic sustainability.

The economic, social, and environmental sustainability of agricultural production thus depends on two broad factors: overall price levels and individual-level production decisions. The next section will apply these insights to the coffee sector by first looking at the development of coffee prices over time and point out key sustainability issues. Afterward, it will highlight agronomic choices regarding a farm's

---

[1] Sustainable intensification and agroecology, in turn, have an uneasy relationship: while agroecological practices can form part of the sustainable intensification paradigm, given their common aim to minimize the use of external inputs (Lampkin *et al.* 2015), sustainable intensification's ultimate aim of yield maximization on a given production area runs counter to many agroecological principles. The discursive conflation of the two approaches has become a point of contention in the community of agroecology practitioners, who stress the concept's central focus on food sovereignty and farmer empowerment (Anderson *et al.* 2015).

production volume and input costs that will affect coffee's environmental and social sustainability.

3.2 Finding a Sustainable Price in the World Coffee Market

As typical in commodity markets, single farmers are price-takers without considerable clout to individually influence market prices. However, they tend to adjust their production behavior based on market conditions by expanding their coffee plots when prices are high or future shortfalls are expected, and limiting inputs and efforts when prices are low or there is evidence of oversupply. As a perennial crop, coffee plants require 3–4 years of maturation to generate fruit, and do not fully mature until 9–12 years of age (Rising *et al.* 2016). This combination of factors contributes to boom and bust cycles where high prices in one year are met with expanded supply several years later, deflating prices and leading in the worst case to the abandonment of coffee for other crops until prices rise again.

Figures 3.1 and 3.2 show an overview of coffee price development from 1965 to 2017, using the FOB indicator prices of the International Coffee Organization (ICO). FOB stands for 'free on board', and is the price paid for coffee already loaded onto a ship in the export harbor. It thus also needs to include processing and transportation costs from the farm to the ship, which means that farm-gate prices going into the

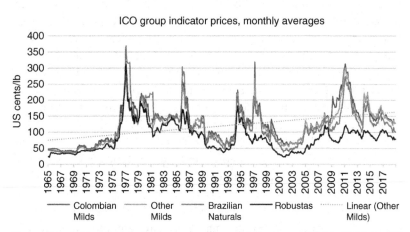

Figure 3.1 ICO group indicator prices, monthly averages 1965–2019 (in US cents/lb). Source: ICO (personal communication, 2019)

Figure 3.2 ICO group indicator prices, monthly averages 1965–2019 (in US cents/lb), adjusted for inflation using the US Consumer Price Index (base year 1990), and International Coffee Agreement quota system in place (arrows). Source: ICO (personal communication, 2019)/US Bureau of Labor Statistics (2019)

pockets of farmers can be substantially lower. Still, FOB prices can give us a first idea of overall price movement. They are specified in US dollars per pound of green coffee.

As Figure 3.1 shows, green coffee prices have shown wild swings over the last five decades, ranging from US$0.50 to US$3.70 per pound, with an average of around US$1.10 per pound. We also see that in the market, Arabica coffee scores higher prices than Robusta due to its perceived higher cup quality. In the group of Arabica coffees, the ICO makes three further subdivisions that group countries based on the main processing method used (Brazilian Naturals, Colombian Milds, and Other Milds) in order to calculate indicator prices. Colombian and other Milds, which are washed Arabicas (i.e., depulped through fermentation), receive higher prices than Brazilian Naturals. Finally, nominal prices trend upward over the depicted period. However, when adjusting them for inflation, as done in Figure 3.2, prices show a clear downward trend. Indeed, the adjusted trend line in 2017 arrives at less than half the price paid in the 1960s. As coffee prices did not keep pace with living expenses or input costs, today's coffee producers need to put significantly more coffee into the market to maintain the same standard of living as their brethren in the 1960s.

How are these prices determined? Although most green coffee is traded directly between farmers, intermediaries, exporters, and roasters, the prices agreed in these transactions are based in large part on the futures commodity market. In the futures market, coffee-related derivative contracts are traded in order to determine appropriate price levels. Such trade tends to reflect global demand and supply for green coffee in a simplified way. The futures market thus generates world market baseline prices, which are then corrected upward or downward by a small margin depending on coffee origin or quality.

The derivatives market works as follows: futures contracts for coffee are traded on the international stock exchanges in New York (Arabica contracts) and London (Robusta contracts). Such contracts represent a standardized quantity and quality of coffee from a given country that will be delivered to a given port at a certain date in the future. Based on the average coffee quality, countries are assigned differentials above or below the baseline stock market price (the so-called C-price for Arabica, for instance). As the delivery date approaches, the price for the futures contract and the price in the physical (or 'spot') market converge.[2] Thus, the futures market is used as a convenient tool for price discovery, and many spot market contracts tend to use the futures price as a reference point for negotiation. In the case of 'price-to-be-fixed' contracts, for instance, buyers and sellers only agree on quantities of coffee delivered, while the final price of the good depends on the price of a relevant futures contract at the time of delivery (Newman 2009).[3] However, the incursion of speculative traders has also added considerable volatility in commodity derivatives markets (Fickling 2016). Price volatility on the futures market is then passed on to farmers in the spot market as well. As we see in Figure 3.1, not only may

[2] This is because otherwise traders could exploit differences between the futures and spot markets and make a profit. For instance, if the futures price were higher than the spot price, they could sell a futures contract, committing themselves to delivering the coffee, buy coffee of the respective specification, and make delivery. When aggregated, such 'arbitrage' would lower the futures price (by adding a greater supply of contracts) and raise the spot price (by adding more demand for physical coffee), leading the prices to inch toward each other. If the spot price were higher than the futures price, the opposite (traders buying futures contracts, accepting delivery, and then selling physical coffee) would occur.

[3] For example, such a contract may stipulate the price as "New York 'C' December plus 10 cents/lb." If the coffee is delivered in November, it will be paid at whatever the price of a New York 'C' December futures contract is in November of that year plus the differential.

coffee prices vary by 30–40 percent year to year, they can fluctuate significantly even between individual months in the same growing season.

Under these conditions, only sophisticated knowledge of and access to hedging instruments in the futures market can ensure that profitable prices reach the producer level. 'Hedging' is a strategy that locks in a target price by taking opposite positions in the physical and futures markets. Indeed, the skill sets of managing price risk and using hedging instruments is seen as indispensable for coffee-selling cooperatives and is being taught in a growing number of international development initiatives (Kraft 2015). Yet, the absence of the necessary business acumen, as well as their limited financial capital and small organizational size, limits many producer groups' access to such activities, exposing them to significant price volatility and shifting the balance of power in favor of large traders.

Low and volatile prices resulting from a combination of the boom and bust cycles and the structural oversupply seen in the coffee marketplace have been an enduring problem for coffee farmers. In response, multiple interventions by public actors have aimed to stabilize prices at a sustainable level. The most promising has been a series of 'International Coffee Agreements' (ICAs), agreed upon by producing and consuming country members of the ICO. The first ICA was concluded in 1962, with subsequent treaties negotiated in 1968, 1976, and 1983.[4] Quota systems were used on and off to raise and maintain coffee prices in an agreed-upon price band, with moderate success (Ponte 2002), as can be seen in Figure 3.2. Quotas were in place from 1963 to 1972 and from 1980 to 1989 (with an intermittent breakdown of negotiations caused by high prices in 1973) (ICO 2017c). Yet, the rigid quota system came under criticism as consumption patterns changed in the 1980s, and free riding as well as trade with nonmember importing countries increased (Auld *et al.* 2009). Simultaneously, US geopolitical priorities shifted with the winding-down of the Cold War, because less importance was placed on supporting Latin American coffee-producing countries to prevent communist incursions (Luttinger and Dicum 2011). This confluence of factors created an impasse as

---

[4] Although there have been subsequent ICAs (in 1994, 2001, and 2007), these have not included binding restrictions on members and thus fall into a somewhat different category.

producing and consuming countries' interests (especially those of the United States and Brazil) continued to diverge, causing the ICA to lapse in 1989 (Ponte 2002; Auld *et al.* 2009).

The resulting return to a free market system and its structural conditions makes the long-term economic sustainability of coffee production a complex problem. The World Bank already observed in 2004 that

[t]he economic causes of these [boom and bust] cycles suggest that they are likely to continue to repeat themselves regardless of the actual levels at which supply and demand would actually converge. Price recovery then, given the inherently cyclical nature of current coffee markets, is likely to be only temporary, while other issues of social, environmental, and economic sustainability will remain. (Lewin *et al.* 2004, p. xiv)

Bernstein and Campling (2006) similarly observe that the overproduction of tropical export crops is structurally enhanced as a systemic effect of neoliberal free trade competition for comparative advantage. They judge it "most unlikely, then, that the economic and income 'sustainability' of the vast majority of smallholder producers of tropical export crops could be effectively protected as an exception to the force of such tendencies" (Bernstein and Campling 2006, p. 442). Indeed, this impression is borne out by the most recent data: a recent study from the ICO concluded that from 2006 to 2015, producers in Colombia, Costa Rica, and El Salvador frequently realized very low operating profits or even losses (ICO 2016), endangering the long-term viability of coffee farming.

3.3 Making Sustainable Production Decisions

In this macroeconomic context, what is the best management style that will allow smallholder coffee farmers to stay afloat? These producers face a number of complex decisions and trade-offs regarding the management of their coffee farm and its surrounding environment. This concerns both the choice between their preferred farm management style – on a continuum between shaded agroforestry and technified sun production – as well as a consideration of interactive effects with external influences such as climate change. To understand these choices, this section introduces the botany and agronomy of coffee farming.

Canopy layer

Shrub layer (<5m)

Herbaceous layer (<1.5m)

Forest floor

Figure 3.3 The stratification of a forest or agroforestry system. Source: Image "Stockwerke wald.png," Wikimedia Commons, in public domain. Available at: https://en.wikipedia.org/wiki/Stratification_(vegetation)#/media/File:Stock werke_wald.png (accessed: February 20, 2018)

The Arabica coffee tree originated in the montane regions of southern Ethiopia, where wild coffee can still be found growing in forests (Hylander *et al.* 2013). In its native habitat, it makes up the shrub layer of a multistrata ecosystem, with large trees rising above it and herbaceous layers underneath it (see Figure 3.3). These properties make coffee uniquely suitable to be grown in a diversified agroforestry system – the ideal case of a *land sharing approach* mentioned earlier. Farmers that grow coffee plants underneath multistrata shade trees can simulate the conditions of subtropical forests and provide habitat for birds, mammals, and insects (Perfecto *et al.* 1996), while also insulating coffee from extreme weather (DaMatta 2004). This system is known as 'shade coffee production'. It is often combined with organic input regimes, integrated pest management (IPM), and efforts to establish healthy, nutrient-rich soils from leaf litter under shade (Haggar *et al.* 2011). Legume shade trees may also bind nitrogen (contributing to fertilization), while timber or fruit trees provide secondary products that can provide farmers with additional income (de Beenhouwer *et al.* 2013).

However, shade production also has drawbacks. Up to a certain point, coffee cherries ripen faster and grow bigger when exposed to more solar radiation. In higher altitudes, where the average temperature is lower and cloud cover is more common, shade production may thus be detrimental to yields (and lead to lower net profits) (DaMatta 2004; Perfecto *et al.* 2005). Unless well managed, shade trees may also compete with coffee plants for nutrients. Furthermore, shaded coffee farms often have more humid conditions, which may encourage the spread of fungal diseases such as coffee rust (Perfecto *et al.* 1996; López-Bravo *et al.* 2012) and pests such as the coffee berry borer (Mariño *et al.* 2016).

The first major coffee rust outbreaks in Latin America in the 1970s contributed to the creation of an alternative production paradigm: technified, or sun coffee production (McCook 2008). Here, coffee is grown in intensified monoculture farms without shade cover. Growing conditions are enhanced by considerable fertilizer input and the use of pesticides to clear weeds and fight diseases. The sun coffee system is perceived to produce higher yields than shaded coffee, although the evidence – above all the relative contribution of input regimes and shade presence – is still inconclusive (Soto-Pinto *et al.* 2000; Haggar *et al.* 2011). Full sun production also leads to more unstable yield levels (often in biennial cycles), puts more stress on the coffee plants, requires more frequent replanting, and is more vulnerable to climatic shock (DaMatta 2004). Yet, from 1970 to 1990, this alternative production system was heavily supported by governments, national coffee institutions, technical assistance and input providers, and development organizations such as USAID, as well as national banks (McCook 2008; Jha *et al.* 2014). In consequence, almost 50 percent of Latin American shade coffee farms were converted to low-shade systems during this time period (Perfecto *et al.* 2005). Leading countries included Colombia (where 69 percent of farms were 'technified' and adopted input-intensive, monoculture management systems in full sun), Costa Rica (with 40 percent technification), and Honduras (with 35 percent of adaption of technified procedures) (McCook 2008).

In a subsequent paradigm shift, another category – sparse shade – arose as a de-facto compromise mode of production when the co-benefits of shade trees became more prominent (McCook 2008). In this approach, specific shade trees are reintroduced onto formerly monoculture farms and managed closely to prevent coffee yield trade-offs (Rice and McLean 1999). Opinions are split on the ecosystem benefits of sparse shade production (Perfecto *et al.* 1996). For instance, some producers distribute banana or plantain palm trees on their farms, which are good water reservoirs but do not provide considerable shade or bird habitat (Borkhataria *et al.* 2012). Others grow one particular species of nonnative shade trees and plan to sell the timber once the tree has matured, which is a good economic choice but again may disrupt the ecosystem. 'Shade management' also includes allowing fast-growing shade trees to develop a canopy during the coffee flowering period, but radically trimming back branches during the bean maturation period in order to benefit from full solar radiation. Here, again, the ecosystem will bear little resemblance to the original native forest habitat, although co-benefits such as soil cover and temperature insulation may still exist.

The spectrum of coffee management techniques hence ranges from an agroforestry approach, with a diverse canopy of native forest trees, high to medium shade and low chemical input use; over intensified shade production, with lower canopy cover, fewer shade trees, fewer shade tree species, and fewer epiphytes; to technified production, the most intensified mode of cultivation in full sun with high planting densities, pruning, and chemical input use (Perfecto *et al.* 1996; Jha *et al.* 2014). This range of production styles goes beyond the choice between sun and shade production and includes the decision on which and what quantity of pesticides to apply; whether to use organic and IPM methods; how to deal with waste products on the farm; and other decisions that will be discussed in further detail in Chapter 5.

Under mainstream market conditions with low and volatile prices, the most rational choice for individual producers who cannot influence prices has long been seen to maximize yields on their production surface. This creates rightward pressure in Table 3.1, with intensified shade and/or technified production seen as the more commercially viable management styles of coffee production. Indeed, although the global coffee production surface declined by 9 percent between 1990 and 2010 (to 10.2 million ha), output increased by 36 percent – an indication of substantial intensification (mainly in Asia and Latin America) and the abandonment of less productive areas (mainly in Africa) (Jha *et al.* 2014). This trend puts considerable price pressure on less productive origins such as Central America, where most coffee is planted on steep slopes and has to be tended and picked by hand. Furthermore, the intensification of production may have negative environmental consequences, including ecosystem

Table 3.1 *Types of coffee plantation management styles*

Agroforestry	Intensified shade	Technified production
Diverse, native canopy	Dispersed shade trees	Little shade
Lower planting density; diversification	Medium planting density	High planting density
Organic inputs and IPM	Mix of chemical inputs, some organic inputs and IPM	High levels of chemical inputs
Lower yields (although more stable)	Medium yields	Highest yields (although variable)

degradation, erosion, and the runoff of fertilizers and pesticides into waterways.

As noted in Section 3.1, besides price and production volume, production cost is the third variable needed to assess net income. Therefore, in theory, this calculation should be subject to input costs. However, many farmers do not know their production costs in detail and are compelled by both coffee institutions, their producer organizations, and many development initiatives to optimize productivity (i.e., yields) on the land they have available. If farmers have insufficient upfront capital to purchase inputs, in many cases they have the option of getting informal loans by input suppliers against the promise of future coffee sales. This, however, also means that they are tied into one particular sales channel at the time of harvest and have little negotiating power over the final sales price. The reliance on costly petroleum-based fertilizers and pesticides in high-input coffee production, combined with volatile coffee prices, may thus increase producers' economic vulnerability (Perfecto *et al.* 1996; Haggar *et al.* 2011). A recent study concluded that rather than improving farm profitability, input-driven yield improvements lowered short-term profitability due to the higher per-unit input costs (Montagnon 2017). Here, the option to switch to IPM or low-input methods, in line with a sustainable intensification philosophy, may be one way to move toward more sustainability without altering the broad production system all too much.

In thinking about production costs, there is another difficult trade-off to make: the largest category by far is constituted by labor costs, which represents around 70 percent of total production costs (SCAA

2016). Trying to minimizing production costs in this category runs in conflict with the social sustainability of the hired farm workers, many of which are paid below minimum wage (which itself may only amount to several US dollars a day). It is also possible to hire cheaper, underage workers – which however may amount to child labor under several international provisions. Furthermore, many environmentally or socially sustainable practices – including, for instance, the use of personal protection equipment when applying agrochemicals or filtering polluted water before leading it back to the river – increase production costs compared to the status quo. Here again, bringing production in line with economic sustainability would require high (enough) prices to warrant switching to higher production costs.

Finally, coffee producers also need to consider the already existing and impeding climatic changes when making agronomic choices. The expected impact of climate change is particularly dire for vulnerable populations in the tropics and subtropics, including coffee farmers. Changes in mean and maximum temperatures, rainfall patterns, and global weather phenomenon such as the El Niño and La Niña cycles all constitute threats for a predictable, consistent coffee harvest (Rising *et al.* 2016). Arabica coffee is very sensitive to climate extremes and tends to react more negatively than Robusta coffee plants, although both may be affected (Coffee & Climate 2015). Warmer, more humid conditions also facilitate outbreaks of coffee rust and other diseases in regions that previously had not been affected (Coffee & Climate 2015; Rising *et al.* 2016). Technified, monoculture coffee farms that are exposed to the elements tend to be more vulnerable to such variable conditions, making climate change adaptation a major priority to ensure the long-term survival of coffee production (Coffee & Climate 2015). Shade trees on farms can provide insulation from wind gusts and strong rainfall, maintain higher water content in soils, lower and stabilize soil and air temperatures, and provide alternative incomes from fruits and timber, making sun-to-shade conversions an important climate adaptation strategy in many regions (Coffee & Climate 2015). Agroforestry systems have also shown lower erosion rates due to their canopy cover's contribution to the litter layer covering the soil (Blanco Sepúlveda and Aguilar Carrillo 2015).

Climate change is also likely to dramatically change land-use patterns for coffee production. A recent study estimates that by 2050, on a global scale suitable coffee-growing regions will decrease by 56 percent for

Arabica coffee, including 24 percent of current cultivation, with nineteen countries that could lose more than half of their currently harvested land to losses in suitability (Rising *et al.* 2016). If average temperatures rise by 2–2.5°C, for instance, in Central America and Kenya the minimum altitude suitable for coffee production is expected to increase by around 400 m (Rising *et al.* 2016). Conversely, areas in higher altitudes or those located further away from the equator that henceforth had been considered too cold for coffee growing may become more attractive. This could lead to more rapid deforestation in mountainous areas along the coffee belt that have so far avoided ecosystem destruction (Bunn *et al.* 2015; Conservation International 2016; Rising *et al.* 2016).

This short overview shows that mainstream coffee farmers encounter a plethora of production choices that may affect the short-term profit and long-term survival and sustainability of their farm and the coffee sector in general. They need to make many of these under conditions of uncertainty, incomplete information, and unpredictable biophysical and market changes. The next sections will examine how the concept of sustainable coffee production emerged in this environment, and describe the rise of private sustainability governance and their challenge of existing institutional arrangements.

3.4 Defining and Regulating Sustainability in the Coffee Sector

The emergence of private sustainability standards in the mainstream coffee market is closely intertwined with the development of a working definition of 'sustainable coffee'. This process is characterized by considerable contestation and power struggles between civil society and industry actors (Levy *et al.* 2016). It also has important historical antecedents, since civil society initiatives have challenged mainstream market structures even before the goal of sustainability moved into the focus of analysis.

Historical Antecedents Creating Alternative Trade Arrangements

Alternative trade organizations and 'third world shops' had existed in the United States and Europe since the 1950s to provide small coffee-producer organizations with better access to markets. In many coffee-producing countries, local elites had captured the institutions that governed exports to adhere to ICA quotas. In consequence, small-holder farmers struggled to gain access to export permits and the world market. Trust-based collaborations between cooperatives, small Northern roasters, and specialized retailers aimed to establish more direct connections and circumvent these institutionalized barriers to entry. For instance, the first fair trade[5] label, Max Havelaar, was created in the Netherlands in 1988 to assist a Mexican cooperative in marketing their products in Europe (Renard 2003). Other initiatives politicized coffee, using it as a means to support leftist revolutionary governments that had been embargoed by their former trading partners (e.g., in the case of Nicaraguan Sandinistas or Castro's Cuba) (Renard 2003), or punish right-wing autocratic regimes (e.g., the boycott of Salvadoran 'death squad' coffee) (Garcia-Johnson 2003).

These independent and largely uncoordinated initiatives focusing on smallholder welfare and social justice received a new raison d'être when the ICA collapsed in 1989. Green coffee prices dropped to less than half of the ICA target range within weeks of the failed talks, as the de facto price floor disappeared and price volatility rose (Green and Auld 2017). A long period of low prices in the 1990s and early 2000s followed. This period, known as the 'coffee crisis', spurred an outcry by nongovernmental organizations (NGOs) such as Oxfam, who raised the awareness of mainstream consumers about the plight of coffee farmers (Gresser and Tickell 2002). Simultaneously, and in direct reaction to the ICA's demise, reestablishing a price floor as producer protection mechanism became a defining characteristic of Max Havelaar and other national **fair trade movements** (Auld *et al.* 2009). In this way, private initiatives positioned themselves as a pragmatic alternative that would allow conscientious consumers to combat unfair trading relationships and lift producers out of poverty through their purchasing choices. As their markets grew, fair trade initiatives soon realized that some type of verification would be needed to ensure that fair trade coffee sold in stores really provided the promised support to producer groups (Bird and Hughes 1997). This requirement led to the establishment of certification and auditing processes and infrastructure that culminated in the 1997 creation of the Fairtrade Labelling

---

[5] Here and subsequently, I use 'fair trade' to denote the broader civil society movement for more just and egalitarian North–South trading relationships, and 'Fairtrade' to refer to the leading standard-setting umbrella organization, FLO, as well as its members.

Organizations International (Fairtrade International or FLO) umbrella association (Auld 2010). Comprised of three producer networks, nineteen national labeling initiatives and three marketing organizations, FLO aims to be the global fair trade standard-setting and certification organization that ensures consistency in the certification of fair trade producers (Auld *et al.* 2009).

Around the same time, international civil society movements also became alerted to the worsening degradation of ecosystems due to widespread industrialized coffee production (Auld *et al.* 2009). The first line of response was a push to support the broad adoption of organic farming practices in coffee-growing regions. The **organic movement** had followed a similar path to that of fair trade, originating in independent civil society initiatives that joined forces in an effort to control and unify the definition of organic agriculture. The International Federation of Organic Agriculture Movements (IFOAM) was established in 1972 and released first guidelines for coffee production in 1976 (Auld *et al.* 2009). Subsequently, it adopted a standard for organic coffee in 1995 (Auld 2010). Under its umbrella, a multitude of private national labels, many of which had slightly different requirements, attempted to ensure that agricultural goods produced according to their guidelines preserved soil fertility and that production followed natural biophysical processes.

Finally, in the mid-1990s, many Latin American origins had experienced two decades' worth of coffee technification and shade-to-sun transformation. Vast swaths of subtropical forest had been replaced by uniform, regimented rows of coffee bushes. At the same time, North American birders noticed a curious decline of migratory birds whose traditional wintering habitats had been those same forests. This confluence of events brought the preservation of subtropical forests and shaded coffee agroforestry systems to the forefront of the conservationist agenda. **Shade coffee** advocates thus joined the existing fair trade and organic movements to create a trifecta of early coffee sustainability concepts. Most shade coffee was sold without third-party certification, meaning that consumers had to trust roasters' word on the ecosystem benefits of the coffee they were purchasing (Rice and McLean 1999). In contrast, by this time fair trade and organic standards were well-established; baseline organic standards were being developed by the US and European Union authorities (Arcuri 2015); and preparations for the establishment of FLO were underway. Still, the three initiatives were only in the early stages of institutionalization when the idea of uniting the sustainable coffee community emerged.

Efforts at Unification and the First Sustainable Coffee Congress

In a first such effort, from 1993 to 1995 a group of US nonprofits and coffee companies held a series of strategic discussions over the potential development of common standards for 'sustainable coffee' (Rice and McLean 1999). NGOs represented around the table included Conservation International, the Smithsonian Migratory Bird Center (SMBC), the Institute for Agriculture and Trade Policy, Oxfam America, and the Rainforest Alliance. Equal Exchange and Thanksgiving Coffee represented the roasters' side. However, disagreements surrounding attribution, identity, leadership, and strategic focus, as well as participants' "strong personalities," ultimately led to the unraveling of this informal coalition. Participants were left with "feelings of distrust and disillusionment with the coalition approach, prompting a few to unilaterally launch their own guidelines and labels shortly thereafter" (Rice and McLean 1999, p. 113).

A second attempt at unification was started in 1996, when scientists from the SMBC convened the First Sustainable Coffee Congress to raise awareness about the importance of shade coffee production for biodiversity protection. The SMBC also lobbied for a certification program with strong shade cover requirements for that purpose. The congress was the first formal event that brought a considerable number of stakeholders – researchers, growers, importers, exporters, and nonprofits – around one table to discuss sustainability in coffee. However, the SMBC's hopes that the conference would lead to a set of common principles and a new certification regime for sustainable coffee were disappointed: despite multiple attempts, both at the conference and afterward, stakeholders were unable to arrive even at a joint mission statement. According to observers at the time, "the attendees were apparently too diverse in their interests and strategies to come to agreement on the definition of sustainable coffee, let alone criteria on which to build a certification regime" (Rice and McLean 1999, p. 113). The definition and criteria for 'shade coffee' were particularly contested: roasters that used the phrase on their products clashed over what constituted 'shade-grown' in their view. Conservationists in turn advocated for criteria that according to coffee growers were overly complex and not universally applicable.

There was also strong competitive pressure between the initiatives. Many had invested years in creating their brand and customer base, and were unwilling to put these achievements on the table to support a new initiative such as a super-seal. A lack of leadership – both ideational and financial – that would have supported such a unitary effort further prevented progress. Under these conditions, neither a second Sustainable Coffee Congress nor the establishment of a planned Sustainable Coffee Foundation succeeded. The SMBC decided to pursue labeling efforts independently, and established its own **SMBC Bird Friendly** label the following year (Auld *et al.* 2009). Simultaneously, the **Rainforest Alliance**, a US-based NGO focusing on tropical forest conservation, certified its first coffee plantation (with the then so-called Eco-OK standard) in an effort to address the negative effects of tropical commodity production by encouraging better land stewardship and watershed protection.

It took another number of years until a coalition of sustainability actors in the coffee sector finally emerged. One piece of evidence of such rapprochement was the elaboration of the Conservation Principles for Coffee Production in 2001 by a consortium of environmental NGOs, such as Conservation International, the Rainforest Alliance, the SMBC, the Consumer's Choice Council, and the Summit Foundation. A number of industry partners provided an advisory role in the developmental process. The principles (reprinted in Appendix 3) focus on aligning coffee production with biodiversity conservation while improving the social and economic livelihoods of producers and providing economic benefits to local communities. They include ecosystem and wildlife protection through the protection of areas of high conservation value and the use of a canopy cover of diverse native tree species; soil, water, and energy conservation; water protection and waste management; and pest and disease management (aiming for the elimination of all inputs of chemical pesticides, fungicides, herbicides, and synthetic fertilizers). Sustainable livelihoods are addressed by encouraging income diversification, adherence to minimum wage laws, adequate health and safety practices, and workers' access to potable water, housing, education, and health services (Conservation International *et al.* 2001). Finally, according to the principles, both long-term trading relationships with buyers and equitable prices for producers should be a primary consideration in all marketing agreements. These principles thus address both land sparing (limiting expansion to natural forests and areas of high ecological value) and land sharing (emphasizing a multi-species canopy cover as essential wherever coffee is grown in originally forested areas, alongside equitable prices).

The language of these principles is present in a number of private sustainability standards. This shows the influence they had on the definition of environmental and social sustainability in coffee production. On the other hand, the principles only emerged once a number of competing standards were firmly entrenched; have no binding power; and are infrequently referenced even by the original contributing organizations. Consequently, no one standard fully adopts the principles in their original strength. However, they provide a good approximation of the general agreement over what sustainable coffee meant to conservationists and nonprofit organizations before the concept entered the mainstream.

The Emergence of Industry- and Company-Led Sustainability Standards and Definitions

Soon, a number of firm-led and multi-stakeholder standards emerged as alternatives, and in response to, these primarily civil society-led efforts. First, in 1997, the Dutch roasting firm Ahold conceived the **Utz Kapeh** (later UTZ) certification in collaboration with a Belgian-Guatemalan producer (Manning *et al.* 2012). Utz Kapeh derived its name from the translation of 'good coffee' in the Mayan language Quiché. The program's code of conduct was based on the Euro-Retailer Produce Working Group's 1997 initiative EurepGAP. It aimed to encourage generalized good agricultural practices among suppliers, while being accessible to a larger number of producers due to its mainstream appeal. Coffee roasters also established their own internal verification systems that included both quality and sustainability requirements and offered compliant producers preferential supplier status and/or price differentials over the mainstream market price. Two of the first and most widespread verification systems are **Starbucks C.A.F.E. Practices** and **Nespresso AAA**, both of which were put into place in 2004. The most recent standard to date, the **Common Code for the Coffee Community (4C)**, emerged from a multi-stakeholder initiative supported by the German development agency GTZ in 2007 (Kolk 2005; Auld 2010; Manning *et al.* 2012). The stated aim of 4C was to develop a business-to-business standard that could constitute the first rung of the ladder toward sustainability. It aimed to do so by focusing on the elimination of worst practices while providing a first benchmark of sustainable practices that farmers could pursue in order to later access more demanding certifications (GCP 2015). This brought the available sustainability standards present in the market up to eight: Fairtrade, organic, SMBC Bird Friendly, Rainforest Alliance (the former Eco-OK), UTZ, 4C, Starbucks C.A.F.E. Practices, and Nespresso AAA. In the following chapters, I will evaluate all of these apart from SMBC Bird Friendly due to its small volume.[6]

The rising industry involvement in the sustainability discourse through company-led initiatives as well as multi-stakeholder platforms such as the 4C Association also generated new contenders for a definition of sustainable coffee production. Two industry associations that are driving such alignment are the Sustainable Coffee Challenge and the Global Coffee Platform. The Sustainable Coffee Challenge was launched by Starbucks in 2015 in collaboration with the NGO Conservation International. Its stated aim is to "transition the coffee sector towards becoming the first sustainable agricultural product" (SCC 2016, p. 13). One year later, the former 4C Association dissolved and reconstituted as the Global Coffee Platform, having spun off its 4C standard-setting and verification operations. The Global Coffee Platform is the preferred platform of large coffee buyers such as Nestlé and Jacobs Douwe Egberts (interview 20, roaster 3, 2016).

[6] Of all the certifications that emerged in the coffee sector, the SMBC's Bird Friendly label has the most stringent criteria regarding multi-strata, native, and diverse forest cover. All farms have to be certified organic, as well as undergo additional certification to show that their production methods are in line with agroforestry principles and ensure the protection of bird habitats and tropical ecosystems on an ongoing basis. Bird Friendly certified farms are likely to show high levels of environmental conservation contributions as well as climate change resilience. Yet, the Bird Friendly standard is not included in the following assessment for a simple reason: unlike the others, it has not engaged in any mainstreaming efforts. Despite existing an equal amount of time as many of the other labels, the SMBC Bird Friendly label still occupies a comparatively tiny niche of the coffee market. In total, 33 farms and farmer groups were certified in 2017, representing a little over 2,000 farmers and around 8,000 hectares of production surface. They produced 93,000 bags of bird-friendly coffee annually, compared to 2.6 million bags of organic coffee, for instance (Smithsonian Institute 2017). Thus, this label's transformative power for the coffee sector seems limited; however, I will refer back to its criteria when critically evaluating the other private sustainability initiatives.

According to the Sustainable Coffee Challenge's Sustainability Framework, "sustainable practices will ensure coffee contributes to economic prosperity and improved well-being for the 25 million coffee growers, workers and their families." This will be achieved "by implementing sustainable agricultural practices to *improve productivity on the existing 10 million hectares of coffee* to sustain supply and enable the sector to meet rising consumption and the growing demand for coffee in a socially and environmentally responsible way." Importantly, such rising demand will be met "*without clearing one additional hectare* of high conservation value forest or depleting other natural resources for enhanced coffee production" (SCC 2016, p. 17; emphasis added). We can observe that in this definition, land sparing is a major focus of conservation efforts, while land sharing techniques move to the background. A large emphasis is put on productivity enhancements, given the assumption that "meeting future demand for coffee could require tripling production by 2050" (SCC 2016, p. 16). Changes to price levels or contract lengths, in contrast, are not mentioned.

For the Global Coffee Platform, economic sustainability and farmer income improvements will be fostered through "*optimum productivity*, improved quality, improved supply chain efficiency and increasing demand for sustainable coffee" (GCP 2017a; emphasis added). Environmental sustainability encompasses climate change adaptation, reductions in water use, soil protection, and reductions in deforestation (GCP 2017a). Finally, social sustainability means "improving opportunities for all people participating in the coffee sector, including young people and women, better working conditions and improved access to health and education" (GCP 2017a). Again, productivity and quality improvements stand at the center of focus of this definition, while climate change adaptation is added to the environmental category.

When comparing civil society and industry-led definitions, we find that sustainability in coffee is an elusive concept. The best way to overcome trade-off between environmental and economic criteria continues to be contested. While the Conservation Principles for Coffee Production advocate for a number of land sharing techniques such as agroforestry and organic input use, and highlight the importance of changes to mainstream marketing structures such as contract length and price levels, later multi-stakeholder definitions show an increasing focus on land sparing and productivity improvements. This relates to our earlier insight that higher coffee incomes may come from different sources: improving prices achieved (through, for instance, certification premiums) while holding yields and inputs constant; decreasing input use while holding yields constant; improving quality (and associated prices) while holding yields and inputs constant; or increasing yields with less-than-proportional increases in input use (Montagnon 2017). A combination of the last two strategies is most in line with industry priorities, as they directly contribute to the provision of larger amounts of higher-quality coffee at competitive prices, which is necessary for industry to satisfy future demand. In consequence, they are increasingly present in sustainability definitions.

We can furthermore observe a shift from focusing on improving systemic market conditions (as framed by the original fair trade idea) to a more individualistic framing. In this new way of approaching economic sustainability, farms need to become small businesses and farmers need to become entrepreneurs by maximizing output and minimizing production costs. Low economic sustainability then is a result of farmers not knowing their production costs or making suboptimal production decisions that limits their output capacity, rather than of unfair market conditions. This shift in framing is also in favor of large-scale market actors such as traders and roasters, as it limits contentious debates over the proportional distribution of value along the supply chain.

3.5 Convergence and Co-opetition of Private Sustainability Standards

Such shifts within the sustainability discourse have important consequences for private governance initiatives. On the one hand, they might change the ideal-case scenario that stakeholders would consider a success. On the other, they may affect standards' presumed theory of change by limiting governance options, such as financial incentives, that were available previously. We can expect to see changes over time in the definitions and requirements of standards that interact with the market environment that they need to operate in. This is because market-driven regulatory governance systems such as private sustainability standards constitute dynamic governing arenas "in which adaptation, inclusion, and learning occur over time and across a wide range of stakeholders" (Bernstein and Cashore 2007, p. 349). In refining their respective missions, standard-setting organizations interact both with each other as well as with other market actors such as powerful corporations who can shape demand through their sourcing strategies. In consequence, standard-setting organizations regularly revise their core standards and adapt them to the market features at hand, which in turn increases or lowers the barriers to entry and burdens placed on compliant producers. This is especially true when standards start to scale up.

Indeed, having emerged at different times and in different contexts, coffee sustainability standards suddenly found themselves competing against each other in a 'standards market' (Fridell 2007; Reinecke *et al.* 2012; Dietz and Auffenberg 2014; Levy *et al.* 2016; Dietz *et al.* 2018). Once these standard-setting organizations had established their own offices, infrastructures, and bureaucracies, they were often highly resistant to give up their own identities and engage in consolidation (Fransen 2011; Reinecke *et al.* 2012). Instead, they focused on gaining higher market shares within the sustainable coffee segment by convincing producers and buyers to enter their scheme. Since all promised 'sustainability', they needed to find a way to acknowledge that they were working toward the same goal, while showcasing that their organization was uniquely equipped to partner with specific buyers or producers (Ingenbleek and Meulenberg 2006; Kolk 2013). This happened through the simultaneous convergence of key criteria, and 'co-opetition' with regard to specific focal areas.

On the one hand, the different backgrounds of standard-setters, corresponding to their initial focal areas, allowed for considerable dialogue and mutual learning. This interaction has culminated in a shared sustainability vocabulary that emphasizes the three pillars of economic prosperity, social equity, and environmental quality. Manning and Reinecke (2016) speak of a 'modular governance architecture' for private sustainability standards, within which different sustainability governance modules are developed through niche experimentation and negotiated with peers. Some elements are then institutionalized in principle (while implemented flexibly in practice), widening the scope of existing standards, while others remain 'add-on' modules. For instance, the Fairtrade standard began to incorporate environmental aspects in 2007, while the Rainforest Alliance expanded their social requirements (Reinecke *et al.* 2012; Manning and Reinecke 2016; Dietz *et al.* 2018). As one interviewee explained, such shifts were often part of a competitive strategy to attract more buyers: "You probably make those kinds of drastic changes [to include environmental criteria] not just to strengthen your standard and be a goal standard but also in the understanding that buyers, brands, they are looking for a universal solution. If you cover economic, social and environmental [criteria], in theory that would be the total solution" (interview 5, former employee of Fair Trade USA, 2015).

The growing professionalization of standards in coffee and other commodities also led to efforts at the meta-standardization of good practices in standard-setting, impact evaluation and assurance. For instance, the International Social and Environmental Accreditation and Labelling Alliance (ISEAL Alliance) was founded in 2002 (Reinecke *et al.* 2012; Fransen 2015; Paiement 2016). This umbrella organization defines itself as uniting "leaders in their fields, committed to creating solid and credible standard systems" (Reinecke *et al.* 2012, p. 804). Its members use the ISEAL Alliance as a legitimizing agent that allows them to differentiate themselves from less credible sustainability schemes on procedural elements while continuing to compete based on their specialized attributes and 'add-on modules' (Dingwerth and Pattberg 2009; Reinecke *et al.* 2012).

With regard to this latter competitive element, agricultural standards have pursued a 'divide-and-rule', 'agree-to-disagree', or 'co-opetition' process (Ingenbleek and Meulenberg 2006). In this approach, they target separate groups of adopters by positioning themselves as either a baseline or a 'premium' solution, or emphasizing specific features of the standard's definition and implementation of sustainable coffee production (Reinecke *et al.* 2012; Levy *et al.* 2016). In 2011, the members of the ISEAL Alliance that focus on agricultural standard-setting (Rainforest Alliance, UTZ, and Fairtrade) formalized this 'co-opetition' approach. After tensions had been rising for several years, they made a joint statement that "a variety of complimentary approaches gives producers and buyers alternatives and the opportunity to select the system – or combination of systems – that best suits their interests and needs" (ISEAL Alliance 2011). They also agreed not to criticize each other publicly anymore (Fransen 2015).

Another example of attempted co-opetition is the 2012 decision of the US Fairtrade chapter, Fair Trade USA, to split from the FLO umbrella group over a continuous and contentious disagreement over the decision not to certify plantations. The leader of Fair Trade USA argued that the insistence on limiting the Fairtrade seal to smallholder producer cooperatives stymied the growth potential and possible impact Fairtrade could have in the mainstream market. After many unsuccessful years of lobbying FLO to change its approach, he took the unilateral decision to leave FLO (Jaffee and Howard 2016). Today, two mainstream Fairtrade groups (Fair Trade USA and Fairtrade America, which remained under the FLO umbrella) are present in the US market, in addition to two further, more marginal seals – Fair for Life and the Small Producer Symbol (Renard and Loconto 2013; Jaffee and Howard 2016). This, however, contributes to even greater label proliferation and potential consumer confusion over what 'fair trade' really means (Renard and Loconto 2013).

'Co-opetition' also undermines the competitive position of standards that may provide a comparatively higher value added to producers, such as Fairtrade, or the environment, such as shade standards (Mutersbaugh 2005; Fridell 2007; Raynolds 2009; Solér *et al.* 2017). Fridell (2007, p. 78) points out that "most ethical consumers make little distinction between various 'sustainability' initiatives, which gives corporations considerable flexibility in determining their strategies to carve out territory in niche markets." If standards are then unable to defend their unique attributes by arguing that they are the only standard that really provides sustainability, the rise of business-driven initiatives with lower price premiums and producer benefits is likely to crowd out the higher-priced initiatives (Fridell 2007). It is furthermore likely, as Mutersbaugh (2005, p. 2033) argues, to "transform ... rent relations in ways that benefit certain actors (that is, retailers) and imperil the earnings of others."

When relating these insights to the institutional design dilemma shown in Table 3.2, we can see that private sustainability standards have chosen the strategy of coexistence that is most in line with upscaling and mainstreaming, namely co-opetition. Despite early attempts to unify the sustainability movement, they ultimately rejected the idea of a single standard or super-seal. Such a super-seal, however, would have been more in line with creating persistent market-based incentives. It would prevent competition between standards on pricing in order to appeal to roasters, and instead give the relevant standard a bargaining position that might allow it to force roasters or traders to pass a larger share of the final consumer value down the supply chain. In the absence of such a super-seal, the micro-institutional rational choice model would predict that price premiums paid to producers will likely decline

Table 3.2 *Choices of standard coexistence*

Goals	Persistent market-based incentives	Upscaling and mainstreaming
Optimal design choices		
Standard coexistence	Single standard/super-seal	'Co-opetition' by segmenting the market and differentiated targeting

in a standards market dominated by large roasters. This may affect farmers' motivation to implement sustainable production practices. The next two chapters will test these assumptions.

Chapter 3 has shown the difficulty of agreeing on the optimal goal of 'sustainability' that should be attained by private sustainability standards. While many stakeholders agree on the tripartite definition of economic, environmental, and social sustainability, the chapter has uncovered tensions between these dimensions that may lead to implementation challenges on the ground. It has further highlighted that the coffee sector has made large strides forward in its goal to mainstream private regulatory sustainability governance across its supply chain. On the one hand, multi-stakeholder platforms have started to make subtle but unmistakable changes to the definition of what a sustainable coffee sector should look like, bringing it more in line with industry priorities. On the other, private sustainability standards have engaged in their own process of mainstreaming, including by adapting to buyers' demands and pursuing a 'co-opetition' strategy of targeting different producer and consumer segments. This raises the question: How have standards in practice managed to change the marketing relations between different value chain members, as well as the production conditions of coffee production in the field? Chapter 4 of this book first analyzes how current standards' approach to setting sustainable prices has developed in this mainstreaming environment. Chapter 5 then dives down to the farm level.

4 | Changing the Market

Our mantra is that sustainable coffees should no longer be considered specialty coffees because the increase in supply has limited their added value.

(Interview 48, Federación Nacional de Cafeteros de Colombia [FNC], 2016)

Drawing on our understanding of the challenges in achieving a sustainable coffee price in the mainstream market presented in Chapter 3, this chapter evaluates the market-driven aspect of market-driven regulatory governance in the coffee sector. It first presents the importance of price premiums in the view of producers, supply chain members, and sustainability standards. It then reviews the development of demand and supply for sustainable coffees, showing consistent and considerable oversupply. Following that, it analyzes the development of two types of incentive models – the market-based price premiums and fixed price premium model – over time in this context of oversupply, and puts a special emphasis on how such premiums interact with mainstream market incentives.

4.1 The Role of Price Premiums in Private Sustainability Standards

We have seen that the economic sustainability of their farming activities is of key importance to producers. Since mainstream coffee prices are volatile and often fail to cover the cost of production, farmers make great efforts to achieve a higher price for their output. In a competitive market, producers have long treated certification as one differentiation criterion among many that may allow them to access a higher willingness to pay. The price premium is therefore undoubtedly the main incentive for engaging in sustainability certifications for coffee farmers, producer organizations, and traders. Both a rational market logic as

102

well as a keen understanding of the short-term decision horizon and opportunity costs of the average coffee farmer drive this prioritization. As one coffee processor explains,

> I understand all the long-term benefits that certifications may have, but the producers do not care. What does the producer see? 'Will I eat tomorrow?' ... I say that the best certification is to pay a good price. With a good price, you can become conscientious. And there is money to do things. If the farmer receives a good price, he can say, 'All right, I will move away another meter from the river, who cares – now I have more money and can move away and plant trees', but if I take away this meter right now, I will not have coffee to sell. (Interview 7, Costa Rican processor 1, 2015)

When engaging with smallholder farmers, the price premium is thus treated both as a short-term incentive for participation, leading producers to the long-term benefits certifications may provide, and as a compensation for the lost income from improving the sustainability of production. At a minimum, the trade-offs that will have to be made long-term to become and stay certified need to be covered in order to make certification a decent business case (Kuit and Waarts 2014). However, if farmers are only breaking even, they will most likely pursue other differentiation strategies that allow them to make a positive profit, such as quality improvements, regional denominations, or novelty products (interview 52, Costa Rican exporter 3, 2016). When considering the future of coffee production and the movements of prices in the commodity market, one market analyst was clear: "Premiumisation, that's the only way to provide a living for the farmers" (Financial Times 2016). The differentiation potential of sustainability certifications is thus a key element in encouraging improved environmental and social performance alongside better economic outcomes for participating producers (Rivera 2002; Rivera and Roeschmann 2019).

Paradoxically, most certification organizations have limited the importance they place on pricing as a decisive factor in their theory of change toward improving the coffee sector's sustainability. The only schemes that include price setting in their regulatory requirements are the Fairtrade and Fairtrade/organic standards, which specify both a minimum price and a set price premium (a social premium that flows to the cooperative for Fairtrade participation, and an individual-level premium for organic production practices). How these minimum price requirements have changed over the years is explored in the following sections. In contrast, while Starbucks C.A.F.E. Practices and Nespresso AAA require pricing transparency of their suppliers, and Nespresso mentions that a price premium is paid out to producers, none of them make binding reference to premiums or their amount in the standard documents. Of the remaining standards, UTZ requires buyers to pay out some price premium for certified products, but does not specify an amount. 4C requires price to reflect quality (after three years) and relegates the recognition of sustainable production practices in price-setting to a 'green' (optimal, but not required) level of compliance. The Rainforest Alliance makes no mention of product pricing whatsoever in their standard, leaving the generation of premiums to the market alone.

Certification organizations justify this approach by referring to market preferences – specifically, the lack of buyers' demand – as limiting their options. During the 2017 World Coffee Producers' Forum, UTZ program director Britta Wyss Bisang noted in response to producer complaints that "[w]e would love to say 'this is the price you have to pay' but then we just lose the market. We don't want to be niche, we want to provide change at scale. It's a difficult discussion" (field notes, 2017). In a similar argument, the Rainforest Alliance points out that

a system that focuses primarily on pricing misses out on a number of other critical elements that influence whether or not a farmer can lift himself out of poverty. For example, price-based systems depend on the willingness of customers to pay premiums for certified products. But this approach is of little use to farmers who are not lucky enough to have such customers. (Rainforest Alliance 2010)

In addition, when asked, many industry experts argue that sustained changes of certified producers' farming practices (i.e., through productivity increases) have a greater impact on their bottom line than price premiums. One interviewed nongovernmental organization representative was adamant: "Price premiums won't lift small farmers out of poverty" (interview 55, Catholic Relief Services, 2017). A United Nations Development Programme (UNDP) representative agreed, explaining that "improving the livelihoods of smallholders is a development issue: neither supply chain nor demand-driven initiatives can fulfil their needs. The key is technical assistance and training to farmers to support them in improving their production practices" (interview 26, UNDP, 2016). As stated by a representative of a large roaster, beyond the promise of higher prices, "the greatest benefit of producers of belonging to the [in-house] program is the consulting and support we give them through the technical assistance" (interview 11, roaster 2, 2015).

4.2 The Development of Price Premiums Over Time

The last section has shown that with the exception of the Fairtrade models, most private governance schemes delegate the compensation for certification to the marketplace. Considering the primacy of the price premium for the appropriate working of market-based regulatory governance in the field, how did the different strategies – market-based premiums and fixed price premiums – play out in reality? This section first gives an overview of the growth of both demand and supply for sustainable coffee, given its importance for market-based premiums, before presenting the development of market-based and Fairtrade premiums in this context.

Certification Uptake in the Marketplace

When we examine the rate of adoption of private sustainability standards in the coffee sector, it is apparent that certification organizations have had considerable success in accessing the mainstream market. As of 2017, around 55 percent of coffee was produced under the purview of a verification or certification (Panhuysen and Pierrot 2018). This makes coffee the commodity that has seen the greatest mainstreaming of nonstate market-driven governance by far (Lernoud *et al.* 2017). Figure 4.1 shows that all major schemes have expanded their production base and sales markets in the recent years. In line with Fridell's (2007) predictions, it is apparent that the schemes with closer links to industry (4C and UTZ) account for the highest growth rates of both production and sales of certified products. 4C alone represents 39 percent of all sustainable coffee sold and 55 percent of coffee produced under one of these standards.

However, Figure 4.1 also show that uptake – that is, sales – of certified or verified coffee is considerably lower than production for all labels under investigation. In 2017, only 23 (4C) to 43 percent (organic) of produced sustainable coffee was also sold under the corresponding label. The rest was sold into the mainstream market with no special

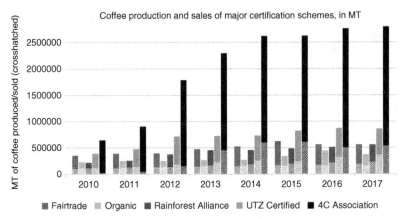

Figure 4.1 Coffee production and sales of the major sustainability standards (in metric tons). Source: GCP (2015), Pierrot (2016), Lernoud *et al.* (2017, 2018), Morgan (2017), UTZ (2017), Panhuysen and Pierrot (2018)

recognition or price advantage. This oversupply of sustainable coffee has severe consequences on the economic viability of sustainable coffee. It creates further pressure on intra-certification competition, especially as firm-led schemes enter the market. It also contributes to the multiple certification of the same farms with several sustainability standards as they aim to access more sales channels. Yet, for each standard, such multiple certification further boosts the available supply.[1] How does this affect pricing in the marketplace?

Decline of Market-Based Price Premiums Due to Information Asymmetry and Coordination Problems

While market-based price premiums show regional and context-specific differences, given that they are negotiated separately for each coffee contract, the trend is clear: market-based premiums for certified coffee have markedly decreased over the last decade. Take the example of Honduras: in 2007, on an average baseline price of US$1.20 per pound, it was possible to receive premiums of around US$0.20 per pound of Rainforest Alliance coffee, US$0.10 per pound of UTZ Certified coffee, and US$0.03–0.04 per pound of 4C-verified

---

[1]   Due to a general lack of information of certification overlap, Figure 4.1 does not take multiple certification into account.

coffee (interview 21, Honduran exporter 1, 2016). In 2016, the price premiums paid FOB (i.e., for coffee loaded on board of the exporting ship) were US$0.06–0.08 per pound for Rainforest Alliance, US$0.03–0.04 for UTZ certification, and at most US$0.01 for 4C verification. Many buyers even refused to pay a premium for 4C, but required it for market entry (interview 21, Honduran exporter 1, 2016). This downward trend was confirmed by numerous interview partners, and is also acknowledged by certification organizations such as UTZ (UTZ Certified 2016a). Even in the rare context where the premium remained rather stable, such as Costa Rica, the associated compliance costs (e.g., paying the minimum wage, which is adjusted to inflation and increases year by year) have markedly increased (interview 7, Costa Rican processor 1, 2015).

One main factor contributing to this drop in premiums is the oversupply of certified coffee introduced in Figure 4.1. As shown in Table 4.1, between 57 and 77 percent of certified coffee is even sold as conventional coffee with no premium at all.[2] These numbers have been stable over the last decade of the development of sustainable

Table 4.1 *Share of coffee produced under sustainability schemes that is sold under the same scheme. Source: GCP (2015), Pierrot (2016), Lernoud et al. (2017, 2018), Morgan (2017), UTZ (2017), Panhuysen and Pierrot (2018)*

Certification	Product sold as certified (%)			
	2010	2013	2015	2017
Fairtrade	29	30	30	34
Organic	50	54	45	43
UTZ	30	31	29	42
Rainforest Alliance	52	37	40	41
4C	4	19	23	23

[2] The presence of multiple certification complicates this picture a bit – in such cases, a double certified coffee could have also been sold into a different certification scheme, rather than into the mainstream market. Still, this inefficient system pushes down prices for each certification scheme, while farmers have to incur multiple auditing and compliance costs.

coffee markets, with only minute improvements in the uptake of certified products.

This oversupply has several reasons. On the one hand, as coffee
estates, coffee cooperatives, traders, and institutions aimed to take
advantage of this new marketing opportunity, many decided to pursue
certification and incur the start-up costs without lining up final buyers
in advance, following the siren call of a promised access to differentiated markets. However, in reality, this is a common misconception,
according to a certification expert:

they hope that when they are certified, that they will meet the other requirements. I don't think that all producers understand frankly that getting
certified is really just the first step if you are trying to build new relationships.
If you already have your relationship and you already understand quality and
delivery requirements, you are already one step ahead. In some cases, they
really don't. (Interview 5, former employee of Fair Trade USA, 2015)

Another importer explained that

in Colombia, unfortunately, I have seen the case that organizations incur all
the costs of investing resources, time, and effort, and after two or three years
of working toward achieving the certification they do not manage to find
a client that is willing to pay for the label and buy the certified coffee. That is
the worst-case scenario and unfortunately, it happens. (Interview 10, importer 2, 2015)[3]

On the other hand, according to one industry expert, "the adoption of
sustainability standards has been much slower than anticipated ...
Companies with strong sourcing commitments [were] at a disadvantage
in the marketplace around 2010, which led to a softening of commitments" (interview 27, Colombian exporter 1, 2016). It is important to

---

[3] Some certification organizations have reacted and try to raise awareness to the
marketing challenge. When prospective producers access the Fairtrade
International (FLO) website, for instance, one of the first pieces of advice they
receive is "[a]s part of this decision [to become certified], you should find out if
there are any buyers who want to buy your products under Fairtrade terms in the
countries you want to sell to. Being certified does not guarantee that you will sell
your product to the Fairtrade market on Fairtrade terms"; furthermore, they are
told that "[d]eciding whether to get certified is an important business decision.
Your organization will have to pay for the annual audits at the actual costs. Once
certified, you'll need to invest in improvements each year and in accessing
Fairtrade markets. You should decide whether you think the costs are going to be
worth the expected benefits" (FLO 2017b).

understand that a time lag between the production and sale of certified products exists. At the very least, since products need to be certified or verified before entering the supply chain, a one-year lag between the certification decision and sale applies. However, many times this lag is even longer if the transition toward sustainable production practices is more time consuming. This means that producers make forward-looking decisions and upfront investments based on their anticipation of future demand and price premiums. This time lag contributes to uncertainty regarding the real benefits of engaging in private regulatory schemes (interview 27, Colombian exporter 1, 2016). Coffee traders may also contribute to the oversupply, as they recruit producers and support their certification process in anticipation of future demand for certified products (which they will compete for against other traders) (interview 8, importer 1, 2015).

In general, the uncertainty related to the demand for certified products – and, in particular, which certification will be favored over another in a given year – causes considerable information asymmetry, since roasters are hesitant to commit to one particular origin or certification and switch relatively easily between certification schemes. Thus, premiums are unpredictable, making farmers invest without having a good estimate of their return on investment. Finally, none of the certification schemes put supply management regulations in place. The Fairtrade movement was the only scheme that considered administering a capped list of Fairtrade producers, but decided that it would be unfair to those left out of the scheme (Rice and McLean 1999). In consequence, a typical coordination problem emerged, mirroring the challenges of maintaining high prices in the mainstream market. In the race to access more profitable markets, individual producers attained certification without considering how their additional supply would affect certification premiums. This flooded the market for certified products, providing a choice for coffee buyers to take their pick of certified supply, and ultimately lead to a narrowing of the gap between sustainable and conventional prices.

Consequently, producers have become disenchanted with the promise of private sustainability standards to improve market conditions. At the World Coffee Producers' Forum in Colombia in 2017, one farmer addressed representatives from Walmart and Starbucks, stating:

we have waited for many years to see the meaning for growers of sustain-ability seals. The truth is, the prices do not compensate for the investments we have done to comply with social or environmental sustainability prac-tices. Two cents of price premium does not make a huge difference from the production point of view ... What you are saying is not changing our productive reality. (Field notes, 2017)

Another chimed in:

We engage in sustainability certifications, more because of our responsibility, but not because it gives us economic benefits. And that is not the fault of the certification organizations, they just provide the codes. But we get the impression that the multinationals that use these labels are doing it more as a marketing tool than to benefit coffee producers, because we do not see the benefits. (Field notes, 2017)

These quotes provide a good example of the 'lexical ordering of money and responsibility' in individual coffee farmers. They may have joined the certification scheme because of a perceived alignment between their economic outcomes and their social responsibility and made the requisite changes both due to an intrinsic motivation as well as in anticipation of a later payoff. However, when this payoff does not materialize, they face clear economic penalties that create disillusion-ment and may lead to their dropping out of the program. Indeed, a growing number of group certification holders, for instance, in Costa Rica, have had to drop out when maintaining the certification became a negative cost–benefit analysis (interview 7, Costa Rican processor 1, 2015). One way to safeguard against this disillusionment is to specify both minimum prices and price premiums, as done in the Fairtrade system. The next section examines the implementation and effects of this institutional design choice on market incentives.

Evolution and Implementation of the Fairtrade Minimum Price

The Fairtrade price governance system consists of two elements: first, a minimum price applies to all sales contracts of Fairtrade-certified goods as soon as the international stock market price falls under a specified price floor. As noted, this policy was put into place specifi-cally to replace the International Coffee Agreement price band after it was disbanded. Second, a specified 'social premium' is always paid to the selling cooperative on top of the applicable price (either the floor price or, when stock market prices rise above the price floor, the market price). The social premium may be used in a number of ways, dependent on a general assembly vote of member producers. Some cooperatives choose to pass most of the premium down to individual farmers; some make communal infrastructure or social service investments (e.g., building a drying patio or a school, or funding pension schemes); and some use it to cofinance international development projects (Snider *et al.* 2017). Since 2011, the Fairtrade guidelines stipulate that 25 percent of the social premium needs to be used for 'productivity and quality improvements' in some form (FLO 2015).

A central policy choice in such a system is where to peg the minimum prices and premiums. It becomes especially delicate considering the standard is in constant competition with other standards that use the market-driven premium approach. Accordingly, the appropriate level of the fair trade minimum price has been fiercely debated since the establishment of the first minimum fair trade price scheme in 1988 by Max Havelaar (Reinecke 2010). It was originally set at US$1.26/lb for washed Arabica coffee (including the social premium), and it remained at that level throughout the 1990s and early 2000s, being adopted as the global reference price once Fairtrade International (FLO) was established. As input and labor costs increased, the regional producer organizations belonging to FLO – in particular, the Latin American branch (Coordinadora Latinoamericana y del Caribe de Comercio Justo, or CLAC) – began lobbying for an increase based on an independent estimate of the 'sustainable cost of production' of coffee (Reinecke 2010). The academic tasked with the appraisal, Christopher Bacon, noted that the Fairtrade minimum prices had lost 41 percent of their value from 1988 to 2008 due to inflation. Had prices been pegged to a cost of living adjustment based on the US consumer price index, the original 1988 price would have risen to US$2.29/lb in 2008 (Bacon 2010).

In response to the producers' pressure, the price was first raised successively to US$1.35/lb in 2007/2008 (US$1.25 floor price plus US$0.10 social premium) (Bacon 2010; Reinecke 2010). Bacon (2010) and Reinecke (2010) provide first-hand accounts of the political and tactical decision-making involved in negotiating this compromise. A larger price jump was possible in 2011 when world market prices soared to over US$2.50/lb. Under cover of this momentary price hike, board members of FLO decided on a new floor price of US$1.40/lb plus a social premium of US$0.20. This brought the minimum fair trade price payable to exporters at the harbor of the originating country (FOB) to US$1.60 (FLO 2018a). The additional organic differential currently lies at US$0.30, making Fairtrade/organic the label with the highest required price premium (US$0.20 + US$0.30 = US$0.50) and minimum price (US$1.90 FOB) (FLO 2018a). This second price rise created considerable concern by some producers and national labeling organizations over the possibility of declining demand (interview 57, Costa Rican cooperative 3, 2017).

Losing the market was also at the forefront of the Fairtrade price setting decision, as one former employee explains:

It's a price-sensitive market. I think that anybody who would say that there aren't any price pressures wouldn't be telling the truth. Definitely, when the decision was initially made, the market price was high and no one was even looking at the minimum price since it didn't apply. But I know that there were a lot of internal discussions regarding the timing of the price change and whether or not it was the right time, considering that the market was so high and we were thinking about what would happen if the market drops. But the idea was to stick to what the cost of sustainable production is; if that is what the system is supposed to support, you do that and make a tough decision, even if there will be temporary shocks to the system. (Interview 5, former employee of Fairtrade USA, 2015)

At first glance (see Figure 4.2), there is no discernible difference in the growth in global sales year over year, leading us to believe that the moment for the price increase was well chosen.[4] Yet, since the price increase, the (higher) minimum price has had very limited applicability. It only applied in select months of 2013 as well as during 2018, for

---

[4] On the other hand – and as an aside – the simultaneous split of Fair Trade USA from FLO considerably impacted the amount of product sold under an FLO license in consuming countries. Here, we can observe a 36 percent decline in certified coffee sales volume – and, relatedly, licensing fee income – from FLO Annual Reports, which is likely to reflect the share of US sales of Fairtrade products. Fair Trade USA has been slow to develop its own certification system – which was in a pilot testing phase in 2016 – and mainly works through unilateral recognition of the FLO certification; thus, to date, little has changed for Fairtrade producers on the ground that sold mainly to the United States. However, once Fair Trade USA starts to certify large plantations, coffee cooperatives in the Fairtrade system may have to deal with considerable competition from larger actors.

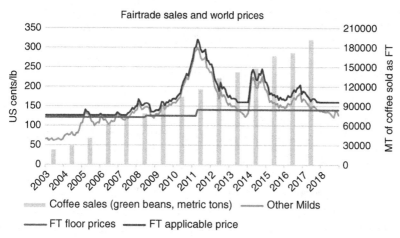

Figure 4.2 Fairtrade sales and world prices. Source: Bacon (2010), GCP (2015), FLO (2018b), Panhuysen and Pierrot (2018), ICO (2019c)

which no sales data were available at the time of publication. Interestingly, despite the encouraging global figures in Figure 4.2, most Fairtrade cooperatives interviewed for this study perceived a distinct decline in their buyers' interest in the Fairtrade label in recent years. According to a regional CLAC representative, some roasters such as Dunkin' Donuts completely stopped buying Fairtrade coffee and switched to other certifications (such as the Rainforest Alliance), citing excessive costs. Others, including Keurig Green Mountain – traditionally one of the largest Fairtrade buyers – shifted away from a 100 percent Fairtrade approach and stopped purchasing Fairtrade coffee in certain countries (field notes, 2017). This occurred, for instance, in Honduras, where several Fairtrade cooperatives were informed during the 2016 crop year that any coffee purchased would be treated as conventional coffee, leaving them scrambling for alternative Fairtrade buyers at the last minute (field notes, 2016). Starbucks, also, reportedly purchased greater amounts of Fairtrade-certified products before the economic crisis, but now focuses mainly on their own certification (which in most cases does not provide a price premium, but only preferred supplier status) (interview 57, Costa Rican cooperative 3, 2017).

Producers cited the premium increase in 2011, as well as the split of Fair Trade USA from Fairtrade International (FLO), as main reasons

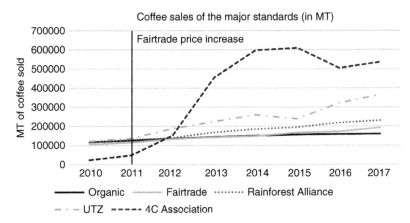

Figure 4.3 Coffee sales of the major sustainability standards (in MT). Source: GCP (2015), Pierrot (2016), Lernoud *et al.* (2017), Panhuysen and Pierrot (2018)

that decreased the comparative attractiveness of the Fairtrade label for buyers. According to one Costa Rican cooperative manager, "Fairtrade dropped the ball when agreeing to increase the price premium without taking into account market demand – they pushed buyers right into the arms of alternative certifications" (interview 57, Costa Rican cooperative 3, 2017). In his perspective, the premium increase in 2011 had a direct impact on the rise in popularity of the Rainforest Alliance and Nespresso AAA schemes. Indeed, if we zoom out and look at overall demand for private sustainability standards (see Figure 4.3), we see a notable change of certification demand trends after 2011 for the certifications with market-based premiums. The change in trends is most strongly perceivable in the commercially driven UTZ and 4C standards.

The growing uncertainty of Fairtrade sales puts cooperatives at a strategic disadvantage if their extended search for buyers delays the payments that they can make to member farmers. Such members may prefer to sell their coffee immediately to intermediaries on the spot market despite the lower prices received, as one Honduran cooperative described (field notes, 2016; see also Pedini *et al.* 2017). Alternatively, in high-quality regions of Costa Rica, the prices that cash-strapped cooperatives can offer to farmers can frequently only compete with quality-related prices offered by multinational traders if they can add the Fairtrade premium (interview 58, Costa Rican cooperative 1, 2017). The second case may be a more innocuous 'problem' to have for local farmers if regional coffee prices are driven up due to competition between different intermediaries. In both cases, however, as the demand for Fairtrade coffee becomes more uncertain and cooperatives provide less attractive purchasing conditions, the self-organized service provision to member farmers, and the marketing infrastructure present in cooperatives, is likely to suffer as a result. As a number of cooperative representatives have argued during interviews, it is questionable whether it would be in the interest of private entities such as intermediaries or traders to provide the same amount of long-term services as cooperatives currently offer (e.g., education funds, inputs, or credit), particularly if roaster demand shifts occur again to a different region.

4.3 The Interaction of Price Premiums with Mainstream Market Institutions

In addition to the baseline challenges of operating the certification schemes in the niche market of sustainable coffee, these new institutional arrangements are superimposed on a number of preexisting mainstream market institutions along with their rationales and incentives. The next sections look at a number of value chain interactions that raise questions about the effectiveness of private regulatory institutions in providing appropriate market incentives to participating producers.

Lock-ins, Dependencies, and Price Premium as Cost of Operating Standards

Given the atomistic structure of coffee production, the certification premium provided to growers is often considerably smaller than the FOB premium that is paid by roasters. Since most smallholder farms are too small or have insufficient resources to become individually certified, higher-level organizations – cooperatives, processors, or traders – tend to organize group certification and pay for the auditing process as well as certain compliance costs, such as the provision of training or the subsidization of personal protection equipment (Grabs *et al.* 2016). Depending on how much assistance is provided, most of the premium received is subsumed in paying for the added coordination costs. For example, in our case study in Honduras, about half of the paid premium – US$0.04 per pound in the case of Rainforest Alliance and US$0.02 for UTZ – was passed along to the farmer (interview 21, Honduran exporter 1, 2016). This was already considered generous, as reportedly many exporters recruited farmers into certification programs and never paid a premium over market price (field notes, Honduran extension agent, 2016). This is at least in part due to the costs of implementing the standard.

In many circumstances, at the current price premium level, it is not even worthwhile for exporters to engage with smallholders. One multinational exporter detailed:

to be honest, for me to certify any small producer who is producing 20 bags is a huge [task] where I have to hire people and my costs will increase even more because I am already paying the certification … Most of the time it's not within the possible extra margin you can make on this coffee to make such an investment. (Interview 9, multinational exporter 1, 2015)

A recent industry consultation led to the conclusion that "certification has led to a business model for sustainability based on *premiums which are commonly used to maintain existing programs*. Traders indicate that declining premiums are insufficient to implement and maintain outreach" (Steemers 2016, p. 45; emphasis added). In a similar vein, a representative of a leading roaster noted that "it will be a challenge to maintain 100% [own verification scheme] in the future if everybody is buying more coffee" due to the costs of reaching out to increasingly marginal producers (interview 51, roaster 8, 2016).

The management of certification groups by traders can further create significant dependencies, since in the group certification setting, the group administrator becomes the certificate holder and thereby the only actor that can sell the coffee with a certificate. If farmers choose to sell their coffee to another buyer, they will forego the certification premium (interview 10, importer 2, 2015). A similar situation of supply chain dependency occurs in the case of Nespresso AAA exports in some countries. In Costa Rica, for instance, the export of Nespresso AAA coffee is in the hands of two large multinational traders that have divvied up the regional Nespresso 'clusters'. Access to this exporting channel then relies on cooperatives' relationships with these traders – who in many cases are also their direct competitors in buying coffee from smallholders. This competition prevented one cooperative in our sample from accessing the valuable Nespresso AAA market, while another one was able to work out a tenuous arrangement with the other multinational trader.

Finally, even when farmers gain access to a label independently or as a self-organized producer group, they may suffer from their weak bargaining position in selling their certified coffee. In Colombia, exporters are known to cancel the price premium if there is a lot of certified coffee available in a particular region (interview 44, Colombian cooperative 3, 2016). Here, institutional support may help. As will be explored in Chapter 7, the Colombian coffee growers' federation FNC has supported both the establishment of certification groups and purchases sustainable coffee while offering a reliable premium throughout the entire crop year. This reliability is key to allow farmers to plan their expenses. Yet, this more stable premium tends to be lower than the sporadic payments of private exporters (interview 44, Colombian cooperative 3, 2016).

Sustainability as One of Many Issues Affecting Price

By how much did the coffee market price increase today? By $6.40 [per 100 pounds of green coffee]. What is the Rainforest Alliance premium [in Costa Rica]? $8–$10. As a processor, I decide when to sell the coffee for the producer. If I sell my coffee today and my Rainforest Alliance competitor sold it yesterday, he is only $2 better off than me. If tomorrow it increases by $3, I sold it $1 better than him. I did not do Rainforest Alliance. So if I calculate my average price and give it to the producer, my average is better than the Nespresso or Rainforest average. So they say "what happened? Why did I go through the effort to get Rainforest and the other guy who didn't gets more money?" Because it has nothing to do with the premium, it's due to the volatility. It is much more important when I sell than what the premium is. (Interview 7, Costa Rican processor 1, 2015)

As noted by the exporter in this quote, the price volatility of the mainstream coffee market complicates the picture. In fact, consider in Figure 4.4 the example of farm-gate prices of a prominent and successful coffee cooperative in Colombia that engages in multiple certification schemes and adjusts its buying prices weekly according to global market conditions (Ovando Palacio 2016).

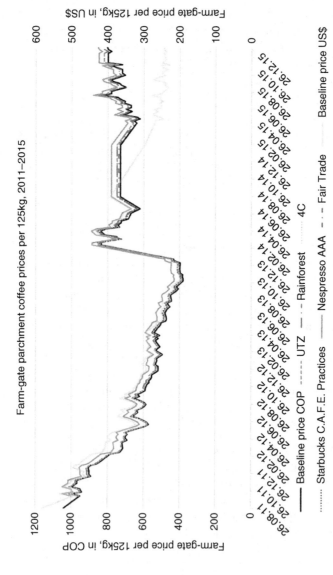

Figure 4.4 Parchment coffee prices of a representative cooperative in Colombia. Source: Ovando Palacio (2016)

It is clear that the price premiums of certification and verification schemes are negligible compared to the intertemporal volatility of the price and changes in the exchange rate between the US dollar, in which coffee is traded on the world market, and the local currency. For farmers, selling at the right moment or locking in a price through hedging instruments is likely to have a much greater effect on economic sustainability than participating in a certification scheme. The only exception is Nespresso AAA, which, however, has very strict quality requirements, meaning that most farmers are unable to sell the majority of their harvest through these channels.

An added complication is that the certification premium is only one of many factors that flow into the final price for a container of coffee (compare Figure 4.5). While the negotiated sales price is mainly based

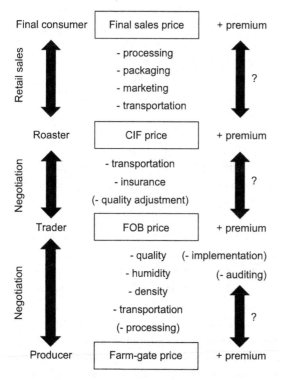

Figure 4.5 Price transmission and added costs from producer to final consumer. FOB = free on board; CIF = cost, insurance, freight. Source: own illustration

on the current stock market price (C-price) of the particular coffee variety in question, it also depends on the coffee's final quality characteristics, humidity, and density levels, as well as the certification premium. It is possible that the buyer acknowledges the certification premium – let us say US$0.02 per pound – but upon delivery determines a higher-than-average humidity level, or is dissatisfied with the density of the delivered beans, and subtracts US$0.02 from the final sales price. This leaves the exporter with the same price as for conventional coffee, but with a sustainable 'price premium' in the books that satisfies the certification agency (if it demands a premium is paid).

While there have been reports that this technique is used deliberately to get around paying a sustainability premium (interview 15, Honduran exporter 1, 2015), it is certain that quality characteristics play a decisive role in determining final sales prices. As one coffee trader explained,

> most of the time, as the price is always higher than the commercial qualities, the requirement from the client at least, at least is this normal commercial quality and on top the certification. But many times they also have a higher quality expectation because they pay a higher price. [O]fficially it's not linked to each other – quality and certification – but most of the time as the price is significantly higher, quality is also a topic. (Interview 9, multinational trader 1, 2015)

Other times, of course, as with the Nespresso AAA and Starbucks C.A. F.E. Practices verifications, quality is a prerequisite for participation in the scheme and is the main driver for the price premium paid out to buyers.

In a price-sensitive market environment, buyers also look at the price of coffee – sustainable or not – from a holistic perspective and pursue strategies that maximize their return. This manifests itself in different ways. For one, it seems that there exists a fixed price ceiling that mainstream buyers refuse to go above. Thus, as one agronomist explained, "when the price of coffee increases, the premiums decrease. It is very tied to the market in this way" (interview 11, roaster 2, 2015). Coffee origins that already have a comparatively high price level due to their country's reputation or coffee quality, such as Costa Rica, may see lower price premiums offered to them in the market due to this implicit price ceiling. In the words of one processor, "what happens with Costa Rica is that the coffee is rather expensive. So, if it is rather expensive, the buyers abroad do not want to pay more, but each certification has its additional cost" (interview 7, Costa Rican processor 1, 2015).

Finally, as explained in Chapter 1, roasters are at considerable liberty to switch their coffee-buying strategy from one origin to another, especially as the quality of lower-priced countries begins to improve. One telling example is that of Starbucks. Coffee producers in Costa Rica spoke with great admiration of Starbucks' sourcing strategy before the economic crisis, when Howard Schultz was at the helm of the company:

Until 2008, they were the best company, helping everybody. They bought a ton from Costa Rica, it was a sustainable price, people were able to stay in business. Then the bottom line became more important, and they began to buy lower quality, and not pay as much. They went to other countries [such as Colombia and Brazil]. And abandoned us here. (Interview 7, Costa Rican processor 1, 2015)

This shift in sourcing strategy was particularly painful to producers since they had invested in the in-house C.A.F.E. Practices verification at large expense, but now had no final buyer that recognized its value.

When Starbucks recovered from the recession and moved back into origins such as Guatemala and Costa Rica, many producers were reluctant to reengage, as one exporter recounted: "to convince farmers now to get back to the certificate is very difficult, obviously. Because there were two or three years where they had the certificate but they could not get any additional margin for it, and therefore most of them stepped away and are not interested in Starbucks anymore" (interview 9, multinational exporter 1, 2015). Yet, new producers without previous experience with the verification, or those in neighboring countries, were recruited to fill the gap. Due to the market concentration of buyers, the issue of supply strategies rapidly shifting certification demand in a particular origin applies also to schemes that are not company-owned. For instance, the market dominance of Nestlé means that it is the main buyer of 4C-verified coffee. As Guatemalan price differentials rose, and the country lost its competitive edge to Honduras and Colombia, Nestlé left the Guatemalan market for the meantime – "so there is almost no demand for 4C. So obviously [exporters] are not pushing on it, there is no farmer that is interested in it because there is no demand," as the same exporter explained (interview 9, multinational exporter 1, 2015). Furthermore, if in 2008 Colombia was the optimal replacement option for Costa Rican coffee, now times have already changed. As one Colombian coffee grower observed at the World Coffee Producers' Forum, "today coffee from Nariño [a coffee growing region in the South of Colombia] is no longer profitable because the same quality is now possible in Honduras. [Focusing on competitive advantage] is a bad strategy since we end up fighting against each other" (field notes, 2017). As the next section will show, this competitive spirit is difficult to overcome, even in the case of Fairtrade-stipulated minimum prices.

Undercutting of Fairtrade Prices

The fact that there is a set premium that can't be negotiated does create problems and I know that there are situations where producers have said 'wait – what if I cut the premium in half? I would still be better off than I would be otherwise but it would give me a competitive advantage or would help me sell more coffee if I could do that.' I can't tell you how many conversations we had over eight years about allowing that possibility. But at the end of the day, thinking about how to create this level playing field and making sure that we are being consistent as to what we are communicating what Fairtrade means, it just never happened. We had many conversations about doing that. But I mean if you start to entertain or allow that, it is a really slippery slope back to 'well then let's just go back to pure market-based.'

(Interview 5, former employee
of Fairtrade USA, 2015)

As this quote illustrates, pursuing a fixed price premium in a market-driven context where buyers have their pick of certifications results in a strong risk of not finding a buyer willing to purchase the coffee under the certification framework. As a rational reaction, producers without stable, long-term relationships with their buyers have lobbied for more flexibility in negotiating the price premium.

While the Fairtrade leadership so far has resisted these changes, there is on-the-ground evidence that negotiating the price premium indeed occurs in practice. At a meeting of the Latin American Fairtrade producers' organizations (CLAC) in 2013, attendees brought up the fact that "producers are still selling their coffee under the Fairtrade minimum price and that destroys the system . . . We need to proceed carefully and with the aim to find solutions" (Simonneau 2013). Similarly, as noted in the opening vignette of this book, one Honduran cooperative described how their buyer of Fairtrade coffee was currently trying to negotiate the price down from the applicable minimum price – which would represent a nonconformity for this cooperative if they agreed (field notes, 2016). As described by a trader, one way to get around that problem is to buy one container of Fairtrade coffee under the condition of buying a second container of conventional coffee at a substantial discount – effectively transferring the price decrease to the nonregulated lot. For this trader, that was the only rational way to purchase Fairtrade coffee in the presence of country-related quality differences: "Otherwise, why would I buy from Honduras if I can get better-quality Fairtrade coffee from Peru?" (field notes, 2015). If this is a commonly accepted industry practice, this may reconcile the apparent juxtaposition of a continued increase in globally sold Fairtrade volumes at a high fixed price premium with high levels of producer disenchantment and lower per cooperative sales volumes.

This chapter has shown that in the minds of most producing-country actors, achieving a price premium is the main motivation for engaging in sustainability certifications – both to finance necessary activities such as training and audits, as well as to equilibrate yield losses and motivate farmers to participate. Fairtrade's cooperative-specific social premium is furthermore seen as an important community investment fund that allows producer organizations to engage in strategic upgrading activities or expand their service provision (interview 44, Colombian cooperative 3, 2016). However, as was predicted by a number of actors, price premiums have dropped precipitously and in many instances tend to cover supply chain implementation costs but not farmer expenses. Looking into the future, there is little evidence of strong purchasing commitments from roasters that would hint at an uptick of price premiums (Pierrot 2016). This suggests that the financial incentive structures put into place to motivate adherence to the private standards under investigation are not scalable when integrating market-driven sustainability governance arrangements into mainstream market institutions. This decrease in economic incentives constitutes a severe misalignment with farmers' motivations to implement expected behavioral changes, especially those that create additional costs for them. What does this mean for farmers' performance regarding sustainability strategies? The next chapter will dive down to the field to answer these questions. It will first introduce three types of sustainability practices that hold different opportunity costs, before describing the sampled groups and discussing how these farmers implemented the three types of practices under investigation.

5 | *Changing Farming Practices*

In Indonesia, Honduras, especially, there is a large problem with deforestation … People say that Peru and Honduras are the new Colombia, and the whole industry is there, and in China as well. So unless there is a real change in leadership in the coffee industry, we are all playing this little game. To an extent you could end up by saying that sustainable coffee certifications could actually be a bad thing – because everybody thinks that it's being taken care of, all these wonderful people certifying coffee and therefore things are ok, but they are not.

(Interview 6, Centre for Agriculture and Bioscience International, 2015)

At their core, all private standards analyzed here see it as their goal to further the sustainability of the sectors they target. According to their official communication strategies, for instance, the Rainforest Alliance criteria "promote sustainability on farms around the world" (Rainforest Alliance 2017a). UTZ is "the label and program for sustainable farming" (UTZ Certified 2018a). 4C is "a set of baseline sustainable practices and principles" (CAS 2018a). Fairtrade standards encourage the "sustainable, social, economic and environmental development of producers and their organizations" (FLO 2018c). Nespresso AAA supports farmers "to grow the highest quality coffee more sustainably" (Nestlé-Nespresso 2018), and Starbucks C.A.F.E. Practices helps farmers "grow coffee in a way that's better for both people and the planet" (Starbucks 2018). However, as noted in Chapter 3, the concept of 'sustainability' – or a 'sustainable coffee sector' – is extraordinarily complex.

In addition, the previous chapter has shown that the financial benefit of certification is becoming increasingly uncertain. The agronomic reality of coffee production means that some sustainable practices are more in line with the mainstream production systems that coffee institutions and private-market actors have fostered in recent decades, and could be considered 'win-win' practices, while others (e.g., diverse agroforestry) create clear economic opportunity costs. Under these conditions, how is environmental and social sustainability defined in private sustainability standards, and how much explicit trade-off with economic factors is expected of farmers? This chapter presents results for three broad types of coffee-sector sustainability found in private regulatory governance schemes that constitute different levels of opportunity costs for implementing farmers. It is based on the field-level results of over 1,900 farmers, distributed across three production countries and seven certification standards. It first introduces the typology of practices analyzed before turning to farmers and their outcomes.

5.1 Three Tiers of Sustainable Agricultural Practices

Viewed from a micro-institutional rational choice perspective, it is clear that not all definitions and components of 'sustainability' in coffee production will have the same reception at the farm level. In particular, there will be vast differences between practices that allow farmers to save production costs, and those that actually create opportunity costs compared to the noncertified status quo. Such opportunity costs may exist either because farmers incur greater expenses, or because they lose income due to lower yields or a smaller available production surface. As Gunningham and Grabosky (1998) point out, the higher the implementation and opportunity cost of a given practice (and the less convergence exists between the regulatory aim and the interests of producers), the less likely it is that farmers will adopt them out of their own volition. It follows that the higher implementation or opportunity costs of a practice are, the more likely it is that stringent enforcement mechanisms and/or strong market incentives will be necessary to ensure compliance. Gunningham and Grabosky (1998, p. 297) illustrate this distinction by juxtaposing two environmentally beneficial agricultural practices: using fewer agricultural chemicals and biodiversity protection. In the first case, "where the producer is aware that input costs can be reduced without detracting from quality and yield, everyone benefits, without recourse to threat or inducement. Here, it is sufficient for a producer to recognize that excessive chemical input is economically inefficient, and that a reduction in chemical use can improve profit." On the other hand, "where, as is most often the case, voluntarism entails financial sacrifice, and commercial influences in furtherance of biodiversity are insufficient to prevail, some degree of incentive instruments may be necessary. Where these, in turn, fail to deliver preferred outcomes, a degree of regulatory intervention may be appropriate" (Gunningham and Grabosky 1998, p. 305). Hence, different types of practices will likely have different implementation outcomes based on their opportunity costs for farmers, the necessary trade-offs with the goal of profit maximization, and the presence of the 'carrots and sticks' of market incentives and regulatory enforcement. Following this logic, this section introduces the theoretical systematization of indicators used in the following chapter to examine how environmental and social sustainability is defined on paper and implemented in practice on certified farms.

I based my empirical selection of indicators on the definitions of sustainability discussed in Chapter 3, as well as inductively on the seven standards under investigation. While the analysis does not cover all standards exhaustively – some have over 200 criteria – it includes the major environmental and social sustainability requirements of all standards that are relevant to smallholders and were raised in the sustainability definitions of Section 3.4. I put special emphasis on environmental conservation, climate change adaptation, and safe and fair working conditions. On the other hand, I excluded criteria that are more applicable to plantations with a large workforce (e.g., freedom of association and of forming unions). After reviewing the relevant environmental and social requirements across standards, I found that they could be grouped into three categories, as illustrated in Figure 5.1.

Each group of indicators is based primarily on the extent to which relevant practices represent opportunity costs for farmers, and what type of costs those are. This also entails that different incentive structures and enforcement strategies might be necessary to induce coffee producers to adopt the practices. The three identified categories are the following.

Tier I – Sustainable intensification co-benefits: Tier I represents practices related to productivity and input efficiency improvements. As explained in Chapter 3, yield increases may play an important role in attaining higher household incomes. Sustainable intensification – increasing yields while decreasing the proportional amount of synthetic fertilizers and pesticides used per unit of output – then holds important economic and environmental co-benefits. In this case, farmers may increase their output, save money on external inputs, and lower their environmental impacts at the same time. For instance, integrated pest management (IPM) techniques can provide lower-cost alternatives to

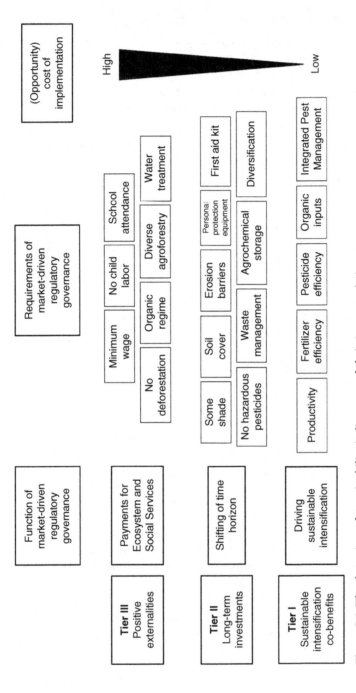

Figure 5.1 The three tiers of sustainability indicators and their (opportunity) costs

chemical pesticides, while the use of organic compost may replace expensive synthetic fertilizer. Such practices thus link the improvement of livelihood conditions with the industry priority of sustainably assuring supply in the future. This aligns with the Sustainable Coffee Challenge's goal to "enable the sector to meet rising consumption and the growing demand for coffee in a socially and environmentally responsible way" (SCC 2016). As these steps – in theory – improve the financial bottom line of farmers immediately, there should be no need for premiums to incentivize the farmer to comply with such best practices once their benefit has been demonstrated. Instead, standards may serve as *continuous best-practice reminders* and be used by field staff for enforcement reasons. Training still needs to be financed, though, requiring a minimum injection of industry finance into such systems.

Tier II – Long-term investments: Tier II holds practices – for instance, related to occupational health as well as climate change resilience – that are aligned with farmers' long-term interests, but might require up-front investments or behavior changes. The certification may thus be an important factor that encourages farmers to *shift their time horizons backward* and accept short-term costs in exchange for long-term gains. In this way, "the creation or evolution of an international regime can provide the impetus for participants in the behavioral complex to undertake measures that will enhance their welfare in the long run but that for one reason or another they find difficult to initiate in the short run" (Young 1999, p. 252). Given that these practices are not directly linked to productivity improvements, and will increase production costs in the short run, a stable price premium may be needed as incentive to shift from short- to long-term thinking. Such financial resources may also be necessary to cofinance investments such as first aid kits or personal protection equipment (PPE).

Tier III – Positive externalities: Finally, Tier III holds environmental and social sustainability components that show great and continuous trade-offs with economic sustainability (limiting the yield maximization potential or continuously increasing production costs). This is particularly the case for the land sharing practices described earlier, but also includes other types of social sustainability measures. For instance, the payment of minimum wages to one's farm workers contributes to the social good of raising the regional standard of living. However, such a practice directly cuts into a smallholder farmers' profits, which may not even amount to the equivalent of paying out a minimum wage to themselves. In a parallel logic, the conservation of forests and biodiversity through set-asides and rustic agroforestry, as well as the protection of water resources, are clearly beneficial for the general population and thereby constitute ecosystem services. However, farmers face nontrivial increases in fixed, variable, and opportunity costs if they undertake such conservation efforts. They will have to build and maintain water treatment systems; buffer zones around aquatic and terrestrial ecosystems reduce the possible production surface; and shade trees compete with coffee plants for nutrients. Profit-maximizing, boundedly rational producers would thus require strict compliance indicators, alongside high and stable price premiums (as a form of social sustainability or agri-environmental payments for the positive externalities created), to be convinced to adhere to such requirements of voluntary standards (cf. Gunningham and Grabosky 1998).[1] In that sense, private sustainability standards could facilitate the *provision of payments for ecosystem and social services*.

To serve this role, the compliance criteria embedded in the standard have to reflect services that buyers (either roasters or final consumers) are willing to pay for, and the premiums have to be set at a level that adequately reflects the opportunity cost of the service provided. This is not a new insight: Perfecto *et al.* (2005, p. 443) already noted more than a decade ago that "transforming a farm from conventional (whether unshaded monoculture or shaded monoculture) to shade coffee will most likely result in yield declines. Under these circumstances the premium incentives will have to be high to convince farmers to change to a shaded system that is certifiable." Yet, it is of continued relevance in the context of the rapid mainstreaming of private sustainability standards in coffee.

From a micro-institutional rational choice viewpoint, I expect that the strict enforcement of 'costly' rules in Tier III would require the provision of substantial price premiums to allow producers to be competitive with the institutional arrangements of the mainstream

---

[1] We can make a further distinction between those two examples: while the first case of minimum wage law represent national-level legislation that is referred to and enforced by private regulatory mechanisms, the second case of conservation efforts are high-cost practices imposed by the private standard itself. Whether the presence of a similar or equivalent public regulation affects rule compliance or additionality is an important question that will be analyzed in Chapter 7.

market model and avoid producer dropout. In the absence of such premiums, I expect that more costly compliance indicators will either be weakened on paper, reinterpreted on the ground during the auditing phase, or 'opted out' from (if a standard provides a level of flexibility in which 100 percent of auditing criteria does not need to be fulfilled). I also expect a higher level of implementation of indicators in Tier I, with both rule stringency and compliance dropping as we move up levels and as we move from standards with higher price premiums to those with lower price premiums.

5.2 Baseline Characteristics of Surveyed Farmers

Using a quasi-experimental research design meant that my ability to observe producer behavior under a variety of standards was constrained by the prior existence of certified farmers in the field. Table 5.1 shows that in my sample, not all standards are used in all case study countries. This mirrors trends in the broader population of certified farmers, where standards with low price premiums (4C and UTZ) as well as the organic standard are less prevalent in Colombia and Costa Rica. Conversely, high-quality standards (Starbucks C.A. F.E. Practices and Nespresso AAA) are not yet prevalent in Honduras. In the other countries, these standards are often combined with the Rainforest Alliance certification, for a variety of

Table 5.1 *Total number of collected observations by country and certification scheme*

	Honduras	Colombia	Costa Rica	Total
Fairtrade	48	250	94	392
Fairtrade/organic	47	0	0	47
4C	135	86	0	221
UTZ	94	0	0	94
Rainforest Alliance	76	81 (+AAA)	71 (+AAA) + 81 (+ C.A.F.E.)	309
Starbucks C.A.F.E.	0	84	118	202
Nespresso AAA	0	144	0	144
Noncertified	259	97	139	495
Total	659	742	503	**1,904**

reasons. On the one hand, the Nespresso AAA standard was developed in collaboration with the Rainforest Alliance and is built in tiers, where the highest level of achievement corresponds to Rainforest Alliance certification. On the other, the trend toward holding multiple certifications as a diversification strategy is particularly pronounced in higher-quality areas. Also, in Colombia and Costa Rica, most cooperatives that engage in private sustainability standards hold both cooperative-wide Fairtrade certification and certification with additional standards for specific subgroups. Indeed, the Fairtrade social premium frequently constitutes a prerequisite to finance investments and capacity building for the subsequent standards. In these countries, I first compared farmers that were only Fairtrade certified with a noncertified control group. The subgroups with additional standards (e.g., Nespresso AAA), in turn, were compared to matched farmers that were only engaged in Fairtrade certification, given that the subgroups were subject to additional rules, trainings, and incentives above and beyond the Fairtrade baseline.

The following overview describes the baseline characteristics of Honduran, Colombian, and Costa Rican farmers, before Sections 5.3–5.5 describe practices on the ground. For better readability, I present the comparative analyses in the following text as vignettes that illustrate and put the underlying quantitative results into context. Readers interested in the specific standard requirements for each category and full econometric results are referred to the accompanying 'Data in Brief', which is freely accessible on the author's website.[2] Also in the interest of readability, I use the present tense throughout this chapter when describing coffee farmers and their practices. Please note, however, that all observations and statements describe the state of affairs in 2016, when data was collected.

Baseline Characteristics of the Groups under Analysis: Honduras

The most common way for producers to access private sustainability standards in Honduras is for a larger trader to recruit them, or – in the case of the Fairtrade certification – to be a member of a cooperative. Thus, this sample includes three groups of farmers (Rainforest Alliance,

---

[2] https://janinagrabs.com/selling-sustainability-short/.

UTZ, and 4C) that have been organized through a large national coffee trader, as well as observations from two individual cooperatives (certified with Fairtrade and Fairtrade/organic, respectively), both of which have been recipients of international development assistance in addition to their certification efforts.

The surveyed Honduran farmers are, on average, between 45 and 50 years old and overwhelmingly male – with, at best, 20 percent of female-headed farms, and shares as low as 2 percent of female farmers in the Fairtrade/organic group. Important educational differences exist in the sample. Farmers in the Rainforest Alliance, Fairtrade/organic, and Fairtrade groups have reached higher levels of education (between seven and eight years of schooling), while the other sampled groups only show an average of five years of schooling. This speaks for a degree of self-selection into the former certified groups. The farmers have between 2 and 3 ha of coffee land under cultivation, and fit squarely into the smallholder category – with the exception of the Rainforest Alliance group, where the average coffee land in production reaches 8 ha. All are at similar levels of altitude between 1,000 and 1,200 m.a.s.l., which does not, usually, allow for high-quality coffee. Farmers need to transport their coffee for 30–50 minutes before being able to sell it, on roads that are not always accessible, especially during the rainy season. According to the Poverty Probability Index (Schreiner 2010), most farmers have a likelihood of over 50 percent of living under the national poverty line, with only Rainforest Alliance farmers showing a notably higher standard of living (38 percent likelihood of poverty). The Fairtrade group has the highest likelihood of living under the national poverty line (69 percent).

Baseline Characteristics of the Groups under Analysis: Colombia

In Colombia, the strong institutional infrastructure through the Federación Nacional de Cafeteros de Colombia (FNC)-cooperative network has meant that the majority of certified producers live in the *eje cafetero*, the coffee belt, and belong to mid-sized to large cooperatives (Grabs *et al.* 2016). My sample thus includes three cooperatives in this region, two of which were Fairtrade-certified, and one which did not hold a certification in 2016, although at the time it was in the process of researching how to access certification.[3] All have made various efforts to access differentiated markets. One cooperative has entered into collaborations with several organizations, such as the UK-based Fairtrade Foundation, and hosted a pilot project to establish producer pensions that is jointly supported by Nespresso and Fairtrade. Another is a regional frontrunner that has pursued a sophisticated differentiation strategy and participates regularly in international coffee events. It engages in a number of quality-focused collaborations with international trading partners, and has received assistance from microlending programs such as Oikocredit and the Grameen Bank. A third has focused its efforts on quality differentiation by investing in a cupping laboratory and supporting microlots and producer-driven brands and labels.

When comparing the Honduran baseline characteristics with those of the Colombian farmers, we can identify some differences, but also many similarities. Colombian farmers tend to be between 55 and 57 years of age, almost ten years older on average than their Honduran counterparts. This illustrates that the Honduran coffee sector is still attractive to younger generations (LeSage 2015), while Colombian farmers' children prefer to find other employment opportunities. Perhaps due to the higher average age, Colombian farmers' educational levels tend to be equal to those of Honduran producers, if not lower. Farmer groups show an average of four to five years of schooling. Anecdotal evidence suggests that the educational infrastructure during the youth of today's coffee farmers was quite poor. Some villages only taught a first- and second-grade class, and children attended both grades several times before leaving school and working on the farm (field notes, Colombian producer, 2016). In this sample, Colombian farmers have fewer children than Hondurans – an average of 3 compared with a Honduran average of 3.5–4 – and slightly smaller coffee areas in production (between 2 and 3 ha on average, although the control cooperative shows an average of 4 ha). They have a similar distance to market, although their roads tend to be better maintained. One important difference is the altitude of this Colombian sample group: most farmers are located at 1,600–1,700 m.a.s.l., a prime altitude for optimal Arabica quality and one reason why private labels

---

[3] Select farmers in this cooperative had been certified with 4C, Rainforest Alliance, or UTZ through the FNC program. However, in this sample I excluded these farmers and only surveyed farmers that were not members of any certification scheme.

such as Nespresso AAA and Starbucks C.A.F.E. Practices source from these regions. The Colombian farmers in this sample tend to have higher standards of living, with better amenities and lower likelihoods (18–29 percent) of living under the national poverty line according to the Poverty Probability Index.

Baseline Characteristics of the Groups under Analysis: Costa Rica

In Costa Rica, both private mills and cooperatives lead certification groups of smallholder farmers (Grabs *et al.* 2016). To ensure comparability, and due to questions of access, we chose to focus on cooperatives, and worked with five different cooperatives due to the smaller size of certified groups compared to groups found in Colombia. In addition to using third-party certifications, many of the Costa Rican cooperatives have developed creative ways to attempt to access higher-value markets. One has created its own in-house sustainability certification scheme to motivate farmers to adopt better practices. Another is pursuing a 'community coffee' certification that will distinguish coffees by their micro-origins and focuses on quality, exclusivity, and culture. A third has been a pioneer of developing 'carbon-neutral coffee' through greenhouse gas mitigation practices. Furthermore, a number collaborate with universities, research centers, development agencies, and government-run programs. Some have access to microloans through international lending organizations, and some have diversified into other crops (e.g., sugarcane) or activities (e.g., the running of supermarkets to subsidize their coffee-marketing activities). For many organized farmer groups, both in Colombia and Costa Rica, the use of private sustainability standards is thus one strategy among many to distinguish their coffees. The improvement of farm-gate prices is at the forefront of these efforts due to the difficult economic situation of their members.

Costa Rican producers again have a higher average age than the farmers in the Colombian or Honduran samples, with the mean age reaching 58–60 years in some groups. The sample includes a similar share of female farmers (13–20 percent), although here again groupwise differences exist, with the Rainforest Alliance/AAA group being almost entirely male (4 percent women). The mean education level is much higher than in the two other countries, with most producers having completed at least the six grades of primary school. Interestingly, the

Fairtrade group shows lower levels of education (seven years) than either the noncertified farmers (nine years) or the groups belonging to more advanced standards (eight to ten years). This pattern is repeated in the total area and coffee area under production – the Costa Rican producers plant almost twice as much land as do the Colombian and several Honduran groups (5–6 ha), but Fairtrade farmers again come in at the bottom (3.5 ha). Similarly, they report much lower altitudes than either noncertified farmers or those that form part of quality-driven certification initiatives. This micro-data provides quantitative evidence for interview-based reports that in Costa Rica, the Fairtrade certification tends to be used by lower-quality or lower-capacity cooperatives in order to gain access to additional financial resources. Such resources allow them to compete in two regards: on a national level with high-quality challenger cooperatives, and on a local level with multinational private exporters who may lure their members away with more attractive prefinancing and price offers. It will remain to be seen whether Fairtrade's regulatory framework empowers producers to overcome these socioeconomic differences and adopt best agricultural practices.

The smaller country size and centralized milling infrastructure mean that Costa Ricans only need around one-third of the time of Colombian or Honduran producers to bring their product to market, significantly cutting down on their transportation costs. Finally, the higher stage of the country's development is also visible in individual-level indicators. Although the low levels of absolute poverty mean that there is no Poverty Probability Index methodology available for Costa Rica, the disaggregated indicators show large differences from the other countries. For instance, between 95 and 100 percent of all farmers report having access to potable water and bathrooms, and most own at least one car. Within-country differences in wealth levels are visible when asking whether households own a television, which shows the higher levels of disposable income of the higher-quality groups, particularly Rainforest Alliance/AAA (where 71 percent own a TV), over the Fairtrade and noncertified farmers (where 12 percent do).

5.3 Standards as Drivers of Sustainable Intensification

This section focuses on the goal of improving productivity in environmentally sound ways; that is, 'sustainable intensification' (Tilman *et al.* 2011; Garnett *et al.* 2013). Through the lens of ecological modernization (Buttel

2000; York and Rosa 2003), this goal can be seen as a technology- and knowledge-driven solution that provides win-wins for both the environmental and economic bottom line. Increasing productivity while minimizing input costs, the goal of sustainable intensification, may provide higher net incomes while decreasing possible adverse environmental effects from an overuse of agrochemicals. Indicators that represent this approach occupy the first level of the pyramid laid out in Section 5.1. I first discuss how such indicators are included 'in the books', that is, in the standard documents of the schemes under analysis; and then turn to evidence on how they are implemented in practice.

Sustainable Intensification in the Books

From a strategic perspective, the alignment of sustainability standards with the industry preference for productivity and quality[4] improvements greatly improves certification uptake and dissemination in the market. The 2016 UTZ impact report is explicit in this respect, noting that "this alignment [of the UTZ code with an industry focus on increasing productivity] has greatly facilitated the strong uptake of UTZ certification by the industry. Certification is considered a logical component of sustainability initiatives, as it combines market incentives with the assurance of good practice" (UTZ Certified 2016b, p. 36). Thus, including productivity and quality requirements in sustainability standards may have functional as well as strategic reasons. Some standards such as UTZ, 4C, and Starbucks C.A.F.E. Practices make explicit mention of productivity improvements and related practices as a desired outcome, while others like the Nespresso AAA standard mention productivity in general, but in nonspecific terms.

---

[4] As noted, achieving quality standards is a prerequisite for participation in the Nespresso AAA and Starbucks C.A.F.E. Practices standards. Meeting quality standards during harvest is furthermore a critical requirement of the UTZ standard, while broader attention to general quality characteristics is required after three years by the UTZ, the 2017 Rainforest Alliance, and the 4C standards and is encouraged through the aforementioned investment in the Fairtrade standards. It is thus one of the few indicators that enjoys broad applicability through the board. However, it is not explicitly linked to environmental or social sustainability and will for that reason not be taken up in detail in the following sections. Also, most detailed quality-related information is only available at the point of sale and did not become part of our sampled data, while producers showed few differences regarding production and harvesting quality standards.

Fairtrade International (FLO) has relatively recently adapted its theory of change to this concern by specifying in 2011 that one-quarter of the social premium paid shall be invested in productivity or quality improvements. The Rainforest Alliance was the last standard to make this shift, as the 2017 standard requires group administrators to "optimize productivity" in their farm management plan (SAN 2017, p. 34).[5]

However, yield increases alone are not necessarily a pathway to short-term income increases if farmers simultaneously have higher per-hectare costs due to high input use (Montagnon 2017). Thus, improving the input efficiency of production (the amounts of inputs used per unit of output) is also a crucial contribution to farm sustainability. This can be achieved, for instance, through implementing IPM (using natural traps and techniques rather than pesticides; mentioned in all standards) or the use of organic inputs such as compost (mentioned in all standards). Procedural elements that may improve input efficiency includes tracking production costs through record keeping (covered by 4C, UTZ, Rainforest Alliance, and Nespresso AAA), and using soil analyses and expert advice to optimize fertilizer use (mentioned in all standards). Improving input use efficiency is explicitly covered by UTZ and the 2017 Rainforest Alliance standard, although not in its 2010 version.

Sustainable Intensification in Practice

I report the productivity of coffee production through the indicator of yields of green coffee (i.e., coffee that has been depulped, washed, and dried) in 100 pounds (which, in Central America, is referred to as one *quintal* or qq) per hectare of coffee area in production.[6] Input efficiency, in

---

[5] For this and all subsequent categories, I include the 2017 Rainforest Alliance standard in the descriptive analysis of standard-setting where appropriate. It should however be noted that the surveyed farmers were operating under the 2010 Rainforest Alliance standard and 2011 group certification standard; compliance results will thus be measured against those criteria, and the 'Rainforest Alliance' standard refers to the 2010/2011 versions unless specified.

[6] I do not take into account area that is currently fallow. I made this choice because my primary aim is to analyze the ecological and economic trade-offs, rather than the economic outcomes alone. For that purpose, it is important to understand the true intensity of production on those areas that are currently in rotation, as well as the amount of inputs used on that area. Using the total coffee area including currently fallow land for these calculations would in effect dilute the intensity of production across a larger area than was being farmed. This choice means that the values I calculate are slightly higher than national yield averages reported in

turn, is calculated as liters of pesticides, or bags of synthetic fertilizer, applied per 100 pounds of green coffee output.[7] For this indicator, lower numbers are better, as it means that a farmer uses fewer inputs for the same amount of green coffee. I further report data on the use of organic fertilizers (including composted coffee pulp) on the farms, as well as two IPM techniques (the use of coffee berry borer traps, and the postharvest collection of leftover coffee cherries to eliminate the breeding grounds for new pests).

In Honduras, only the Rainforest Alliance-certified farmers have significantly higher yields than matched noncertified farmers (by 17 percent, with 43.4 qq/ha versus 37.0). This, however, also necessitates a higher use of synthetic fertilizer per hectare, since the fertilizer efficiency does not differ between groups except in the organic sample. None of the other groups shows significantly higher productivity than their matched controls. However, in addition to the Rainforest Alliance group, the UTZ and Fairtrade groups also show better pesticide efficiency, distributing about half as many pesticides per 100 pounds of output as their control groups (0.03 l/qq versus 0.07). This can be explained by the fact that the Rainforest Alliance and Fairtrade groups use fewer herbicides (with 11 percent of Rainforest Alliance farmers using weed killers, versus 42 percent of controls) and make better use of organic inputs (which one-third of farmers in both groups use, compared with 10–17 percent in the control groups). Encouragingly, even noncertified farmers use IPM practices such as collecting leftover coffee cherries and using coffee berry borer traps, while certification boosts the use of insect traps in all groups. Here, economic and ecological co-benefits appear possible through certification. On the other hand, despite a clear leadership position regarding sustainable input use for

Section 5.6. This is likely due to a combination of the choice to focus on area in production rather than total coffee area as well as the specific circumstances of both treatment and the matched control groups. Inferences derived from these results should therefore be limited to the specific purposes of this chapter.

[7] I decided to report input use/output rather than the inverse in order to allow for the use of no synthetic pesticides or fertilizers while still generating output, as is the case, for instance, in organic production. Those observations would have otherwise been divided by zero and dropped out of the analysis. In general, fertilizer is sold in uniformly sized 50 kg bags. While the concentration of the active ingredient in pesticide preparations may vary, it was impossible to gather more precise data considering the volume of data collected. These numbers should thus be seen as a rough estimate of input efficiency to illustrate the underlying argument.

the Fairtrade/organic group – these farmers almost all (96 percent) use organic inputs on their farms and refrain from using herbicides and other toxic products on their soils – they show significantly lower yields (by 35 percent, at 20.8 qq/ha) compared to noncertified farmers. This may explain why, similar to the farmer in the opening vignette of this book, around one-third of organic farmers reported using synthetic fertilizers, in violation of the organic code.

In the Rainforest Alliance group, input efficiency is partially driven by the introduction of record keeping. This group has a significantly greater share of producers that keeps records than the control group (62 versus 33 percent), these producers spend more time on records (5.5 versus 2 hours per week), and those Rainforest Alliance-certified producers that do keep records show better yields and pesticide efficiency than those that do not. Indeed, as one Rainforest Alliance group coordinator in Honduras reported, "record keeping is helpful for producers and all get capacity building in keeping records. But only for certified producers is there follow-up that makes them actually keep them" (field notes, Honduran extension agent, 2016). Extension agents thus use the certification requirement strategically to support adoption by reluctant producers who feel that being a farmer does not entail 'office work' (field notes, extension agents, 2016–2017).

In Colombia, the Fairtrade cooperatives along with their sub-groups show significantly higher yields than the noncertified group (by almost 50 percent, with 37.2 versus 24.9 qq/ha). All certified groups also demonstrate better fertilizer-use efficiency, with the Rainforest Alliance/AAA group performing significantly better than its Fairtrade baseline. A total of 87 percent of Fairtrade producers use organic fertilizers – over twice the share of comparable noncertified farmers (40 percent). This is mainly driven by the use of composted coffee pulp, a best practice that combines improved waste management (coffee pulp is otherwise routinely dumped into riverbeds and can lead to eutrophication and the decline of aquatic ecosystems) with nutrient recycling and soil enrichment (field notes, extension agents, 2016).

The use of insect traps as an IPM technique is significantly higher in the Fairtrade-certified cooperatives (43 versus 18 percent), showing that a combination of their availability and cooperative-level encouragement may have popularized the practice. Conversely, collecting leftover coffee cherries from the ground and bushes is uniformly practiced by all producers and has a long history of being a best practice in Colombia (field notes, Colombian extension agent, 2016). In addition, the Rainforest Alliance/AAA and AAA groups show lower shares of farmers that apply herbicides. Yet, when tallying total input use, all certified groups have a considerably higher proportional use of pesticides (between 0.07 and 0.11 versus 0.03 l/qq), and are unable to show better pesticide efficiency than the control group. Also, the 4C group appears to backslide in all practices under analysis when compared with its Fairtrade control group. Here, further efficiency improvements may be possible that improve both the environmental and economic bottom line of farmers.

In Costa Rica, finally, Fairtrade farmers' yields equal those of noncertified farmers. On the other hand, all groups that implement additional standards beyond Fairtrade – the Rainforest Alliance/AAA, Rainforest Alliance/C.A.F.E. Practices, and C.A.F.E. Practices farmers – have higher yields (37–39 versus 25–30 qq/ha) with basically the same fertilizer input. They therefore show slightly better fertilizer efficiency than the Fairtrade farmers. The average fertilizer efficiency (0.75–1.00 bags/qq) approaches that of Colombian farmers, with Honduran farmers showing notable improvements over the two other countries with averages of 0.55–0.60 bags/qq. The Costa Rican Rainforest Alliance/AAA group is one rare example where soil analyses seem to contribute to fertilizer efficiency – 92 percent of producers receive such analyses (as opposed to 34 percent in the matched control group), 87 percent use it for their decision-making, and using soil analyses leads to a 40 percent reduction in fertilizer use for the same amount of output.

On the other hand, Costa Rica shows the highest pesticide use of all countries under analysis, with few differences in pesticide efficiency (at around 0.20–0.30 l/qq) between sustainably certified farmers and those without a certification. Although fewer Fairtrade farmers use herbicides compared to noncertified farmers, their total share is still at astonishingly high levels, with 75–80 percent of farmers using weed killers in the certified groups versus 91 percent in the control group. Furthermore, the Fairtrade group shows worse results than the noncertified farmers regarding the two IPM techniques that I analyzed. While the use of insect traps is more common in the Rainforest Alliance/AAA and C.A.F.E. Practices programs, the share of farmers that do postharvest clean-up rounds decreases when moving from uncertified farmers to more strict standards, showing that this practice had not caught on significantly despite the Rainforest Alliance's requirement to phase in IPM methods.

In sum, certification under private sustainability standards *may* result in productivity and input efficiency improvements of farmers, which would provide win-win gains for both economic and environmental sustainability. Rainforest Alliance certification is associated with higher yields, showing significant improvements over the control group in the Honduran Rainforest Alliance group and the Costa Rican Rainforest Alliance/AAA and Rainforest Alliance/C.A.F.E. Practices groups, and showing the highest yields in the Colombian Rainforest Alliance/AAA group. In Colombia, all Fairtrade-certified cooperatives show higher yields than the noncertified control cooperative. Fertilizer efficiency on average improves or remains steady with these increases, showcasing eco-efficiency gains. Overall, fertilizer efficiency shows a low amount of variability, with optimal levels of around 0.6 bags of fertilizer per 100 pounds of coffee output present in most Honduran groups, and Colombian and Costa Rican producers hovering between 0.75 and 1.00 bag per 100 pounds.

On the other hand, pesticide efficiency is much more variable across country contexts. Colombians use around twice as many liters of pesticide per 100 pounds of coffee (around 0.10 l/qq) as Hondurans (with an average of 0.05 l/qq). Costa Ricans (around 0.25 l/qq) again more than double that volume. This is independent of the certification in question, with Costa Rican Rainforest Alliance/AAA farmers using 0.28 l/qq, while Honduran noncertified farmers use 0.07 l/qq. While pesticide efficiency increased across the board in Honduran certified groups – possibly due to their lower labor costs and intrinsic motivation to save input costs – few changes were visible in the Colombian certified groups. Costa Rica, with the highest level of pesticide use by far, showed no significant differences between certified and noncertified groups. Much of the additional use of pesticides is due to the application of herbicides such as glyphosate, rather than employing workers to weed by hand. Indeed, phasing out weed killers requires farmers to allot more manual labor – either their own or their workers' – to pull out weeds by hand. Depending on labor costs, this practice may thus increase, rather than decrease, production costs. In addition, Costa Rican farmers tend to be less resource-constrained than Colombian and Honduran farmers and can afford preventative, rather than reactive, pesticide use. Costa Rica and its coffee sector's level of development therefore result in a greater environmental burden in the pursuit of maximum yields, although they do not end up achieving much greater yield results than Colombian farmers. When farmers make choices between maintaining the status quo and changing their behavior, knowledge concerning best management practices thus interacts with local culture and relative production costs.

These results align well with the existing literature. It is notable that the literature converges upon higher yield levels in farms participating in the Rainforest Alliance certification (Guhl 2009; Ruben and Zuniga 2011; Barham and Weber 2012; Hughell and Newsom 2013; Akoyi and Maertens 2017; Mitiku *et al.* 2018) and private labels (Ruben and Zuniga 2011; Vellema *et al.* 2015). This might be due to an efficiency-driven strategic choice by buyers to push sustainably certified farmers toward higher output levels. As noted by one buyer, "once a certain number of farms is certified, it is much more efficient for us to increase sourcing volumes by increases in yield rather than by going out and certifying more farms" (interview 11, roaster 2, 2015). While certification may thus become a driver for intensification on sustainably certified farms, this strategy can in the worst-case scenario lead to side-trading when farmers that are given highly optimistic quotas that they cannot fill start to buy coffee from their neighbors, which then flow into the sustainably certified value chain (field notes, multinational trader, 2015).

Although the evidence is less established, it also seems that the dissemination of best agricultural management practices can in the best cases lead to eco-efficient win-win scenarios when adequate and sufficient capacity building is conducted. My data shows that pathways do exist that enable producers to increase their yields in environmentally sustainable ways, and that participation in private sustainability standards may provide them greater access to these types of pathways. Record keeping and, more rarely, the use of soil analyses are correlated with improved input efficiency (frequently while increasing or maintaining yields). However, this is only the case when farmers show high rates of implementation and engagement with the learned practices. Many other groups, which report lower enthusiasm for the practices even when confirming that they were exposed to them, show few differences when comparing participating and nonparticipating farmers.

Furthermore, the pathways investigated are far from being uniformly applied in groups that are part of private sustainability standards.

Here, more efforts could be taken if sustainable intensification is a central goal of private sustainability standards. Finally, certain practices that could at face value be considered to improve input costs – such as phasing out the use of herbicides or synthetic fertilizer – in effect do generate considerable opportunity costs. In the case of Costa Rican farmers, this is due to the high cost of the substitute, weeding by hand; in the case of Honduran organic farmers, due to the resulting yield losses. As a result, we see much lower implementation rates for such practices. This leads us to analyze the next set of indicators: those that present upfront costs but potential long-term benefits.

5.4 Standards as Shifters of Time Horizons

When making farm management decisions, boundedly rational agricultural producers need to balance short- and long-term plans. In particular, they have to weigh whether practices that incur short-term costs but promise long-term rewards (with a certain measure of uncertainty) are worthwhile alternatives to the short-term profit maximization route that in most cases constitutes the status quo. If producers live on the edge of poverty, short-term losses or investments may be impossible to sustain financially unless they receive external assistance, effectively barring the way for the gain of long-term benefits. In such cases, private sustainability standards may be an avenue to shift the time horizon backward for short-term–oriented producers by providing concrete short-term benefits (price premiums) or lowering short-term costs (by providing investment or implementation assistance) to pursue the practices that in the long run promise to provide economic, environmental, and social rewards. This chapter analyzes the effectiveness of such time horizon shifting practices using two examples: the assurance of safe working conditions, especially regarding agrochemical use, and long-term farm resilience against climate change and erosion.

Safe Working Conditions in the Books

One of the greatest health risks on coffee farms is the frequent handling of potentially toxic agrochemicals. Pesticides, fungicides, and herbicides used to prevent and combat coffee diseases and weeds contain potent agents that may cause acute pesticide poisoning when they are accidentally ingested, inhaled, or come into contact with skin (Konradsen *et al.*

2003). These risks sink when sufficient safety precautions are taken (Damalas and Koutroubas 2016). On the one hand, the most hazardous pesticides with high levels of toxicity should be avoided entirely. All private sustainability standards use a list of prohibited pesticides, and build on international accords as well as the legislation of the producing country to populate this list, although some go beyond that.[8] Yet, other than the organic label, none of the standards ban chlorpyrifos or glyphosate.[9] However, these substances are hotly contested for their toxicity: prenatal and postnatal chlorpyrifos exposure has been linked to neurodevelopmental issues (Rauh *et al.* 2006, 2015; Marks *et al.* 2010), while the WHO has classified glyphosate as a probable human carcinogen (Guyton *et al.* 2015; Myers *et al.* 2016).

Farmers can further prevent intoxication through skin contact or inhalation if they use appropriate personal protection equipment (PPE). In its most advanced form, this equipment consists of long-sleeved clothing, safety goggles, a mask with respirator, rubber gloves, boots, and a rubber apron that protects the front of the body from possible spillage when mixing agrochemicals. However, the use of this type of equipment is cumbersome in subtropical climates and rather unpopular among farmers (Konradsen *et al.* 2003). It is also a significant expense if farmers have to purchase or replace their own PPE. UTZ, Rainforest Alliance, and Nespresso AAA all mandate the use of full PPE as critical criterion from

---

[8] Relevant international accords include the Montreal Protocol on ozone-depleting substances, the Rotterdam Convention on hazardous pesticides, and the Stockholm Convention on persistent organic pollutants. To these and locally prohibited substances, Fairtrade adds pesticides mentioned in the World Health Organization (WHO) class Ia and Ib and the Pesticide Action Network (PAN) Dirty Dozen list; and UTZ further adds pesticides not approved by the United States, European Union, and Japan. As of their 2017 standard, the Rainforest Alliance and Nespresso AAA used the broadest categorization by referring to the categorization of Highly Hazardous Pesticides according to the Food and Agriculture Organization of the United Nations/WHO Panel of Experts on Pesticide Management. However, in evaluating compliance, I refer back to the 2011 SAN List of Prohibited Pesticides since that one was operative at the time of data collection. This list includes prohibited pesticides listed in the international accords and the PAN Dirty Dozen, as well as those not approved by the United States and the European Union and not registered in the producing country. They further required producers to phase out WHO class Ia and Ib pesticides, but they did not prohibit them. The organic standard prohibits the use of all synthetic pesticides.

[9] Although both of these substances are on the 'vigilance' lists of UTZ and the Rainforest Alliance.

the beginning of the certification period, while it is a continuous improvement indicator for the other standards.

It is important to protect workers' and farmers' families, particularly children, from potential health risks due to agrochemicals (Garry 2004; Rao *et al.* 2006). Recommended measures that prevent children coming into contact with agrochemicals include disposing of agrochemical containers in a safe way and storing agrochemicals in a dedicated shed out of reach of children (Rao *et al.* 2006). The installation of such sheds require significant capital investments for farmers. Storing agrochemicals in a separate, locked storage facility and safely disposing of pesticide containers is only deemed a critical criteria in the UTZ standard, although it is mentioned in all others.

Workers and farmers also use other potentially dangerous equipment such as machetes, grass cutters, or (in some cases) tractors. It is critical that they can receive medical attention if accidents occur, either through the use of a first aid kit (in case of minor injuries) or through access to a medical clinic or hospital. This is a particular challenge for coffee farmers that live far away from urban centers in isolated conditions. Access to medical attention and first aid kits is most prioritized by Fairtrade, where it is a critical condition for certification. It is mentioned in the UTZ, Rainforest Alliance, and Nespresso AAA standards; and not required for 4C and C.A.F.E. Practice certification. Finally, providing farmers, family members, and workers with access to potable water on the farm is a critical requirement for all standards other than the Rainforest Alliance (where it is, however, part of the standard catalog), Nespresso AAA, and C.A.F.E. Practices.

Safe Working Conditions in Practice

The Honduran Rainforest Alliance, Fairtrade/organic, and Fairtrade groups show significantly better occupational health data than matched noncertified farmers, while the UTZ and 4C groups remain closer to the noncertified farmers' averages. The share of farmers with complete first aid kits is very limited, with 20–30 percent of farmers who own a complete kit in the three leading groups, compared to 2–7 percent in the other groups. Due to the Honduran farmers' low use rates of agrochemicals, the sample size for the indicators on PPE and storage facilities is quite small except for the Rainforest Alliance farmers. These farmers have significantly higher but by no means universal adoption rates of safe agrochemical practices: 71 percent for PPE use, almost triple the rates of their controls (24 percent); and 63 percent for orderly storage facilities, compared to around 10 percent of the matched control group. They also show significantly higher rates of safe pesticide disposal (69 versus 17 percent). Furthermore, Rainforest Alliance (80 percent) and Fairtrade/organic farmers (91 percent) report significantly higher rates of access to potable water,[10] while in Fairtrade, UTZ, and 4C groups, up to one-half of farmers do not report having such access, despite it being a critical criterion for certification. On noncertified farms, only 34 percent of producers have access to potable water.

In the Colombian case, certification is also linked to significantly better occupational health behavior. Fairtrade cooperative members show higher rates in their use of PPE (67 versus 40 percent) and the existence of first aid kits (45 versus 7 percent) than the matched, noncertified farmers. Participation in some higher-level standard programs (Rainforest Alliance/AAA and C.A.F.E. Practices) significantly improves farmers' upkeep of orderly storage facilities for agrochemicals (with rates from 45 to 63 percent, versus 20–30 percent among only Fairtrade farmers). The use of complete protection equipment is also higher in these groups, although the difference is not statistically significant – speaking for the fact that other factors, such as wealth or education, may be contributing causes. The availability of potable water is vastly different between the sampled cooperatives. One Fairtrade cooperative shows full access for all producers, while the other two report access rates between 14 and 34 percent, with certification schemes making little difference (with the exception of the Nespresso AAA group, where 67 percent of producers have access to potable water).

The Colombian sample also draws our attention to local infrastructural and institutional differences compared with the Honduran producers. In Honduras, pesticide container disposal by returning them to the original vendors is notably rare in all producers but the Rainforest Alliance (39 percent) and Fairtrade (27 percent) groups, indicating that other producers may not have access to such recycling programs.

---

[10] Potable water was defined as "purified, filtered or coming from a municipal treatment plant" in the questionnaire, since otherwise respondents interpreted it as 'drinkable' – and all did drink the water they had access to, even if this had negative health consequences.

Instead, they pursue the second-best practice of washing pesticide containers three times, puncturing them to avoid their future use for food or water storage, and burying them. In Colombia, virtually everybody that safely disposed of their pesticide containers does so through cooperative-provided recycling programs, in both certified and noncertified cooperatives. Here, farmer organization is key to support sustainable practices.

In the Costa Rican sample, around 50 percent of noncertified and Fairtrade farmers use PPE, and around 20–30 percent have an agrochemical storage shed, with no significant differences between the two groups. In contrast, 80–86 percent of farmers in the three more advanced certification groups use PPE (showing increases of 23 percent over their matched controls) and 91 percent of the Rainforest Alliance/AAA farmers keep their agrochemicals in a separate shed. In the Rainforest Alliance/C.A.F.E group, I find strong cooperative effects, with one cooperative showing high levels of compliance (100 percent implementation of using PPE and 69 percent of using storage facilities), while the lower rates of the other cooperative (69 percent for PPE and 2 percent for orderly storage facilities) attenuates the overall group effects. Regarding first aid kits, the Costa Rican farmers are more similar to the Honduran producers – while around 54 percent of noncertified farmers reported having a first aid kit, but keeping it off-farm, in the other groups, 52–82 percent of farmers reported having no first aid kit at hand whatsoever. Yet, these farmers are on average only 7–11 minutes away from medical attention, and the twenty accidents reported in the previous year were all treated in clinics or hospitals, making the first aid kit less necessary than in the case of Honduras. Finally, the Costa Rican Fairtrade cooperatives show worse results in pesticide container disposal practices than the noncertified cooperatives (66 versus 88 percent in the matched control group). However, all three certification groups that go beyond Fairtrade make important improvements in their disposal practices (with levels of 89–97 percent). Inclusion in the company-driven standard schemes may thus significantly increase the normative pressure to appropriately dispose of hazardous waste. It is also possible that additional pick-up services are organized in these groups as opposed to the larger group of Fairtrade farmers.

Generally, the use of prohibited pesticides is uncommon in the cases of Honduras and Colombia, with only isolated instances in either certified or noncertified groups. However, the situation is different in

Costa Rica, where 22 percent of farmers in one of the control cooperatives use paraquat. Paraquat is a substance that is not covered by international agreements, but is included in the authoritative list of the nongovernmental organization (NGO) Pesticide Action Network (the PAN Dirty Dozen list) and is thus prohibited by the Fairtrade, UTZ, Rainforest Alliance, and Nespresso AAA standards. The use of paraquat is highly controversial in Costa Rica. Its high level of toxicity has been a cause of workers' pesticide intoxication and has also contributed to a number of suicides, particularly in rural youth (InformaTico 2017). Yet, due to its importance for the pineapple sector (Costa Rica is the largest pineapple exporter in the world), paraquat continues to be legal and widely available (Aronne 2017). This is a case where private regulation may fill a regulatory void at the national level. As observed during field work, the regulation of pesticide use through the certification of cooperatives is highly effective since cooperatives often own stores that sell inputs to member farmers. A phase-out of prohibited substances and the provision of alternatives may lead to rapid improvements, especially in rural settings where farmers have little other access to inputs. On the other hand, chlorpyrifos and glyphosate, not banned by any private standards, although potentially dangerous, are extremely popular in producing countries: in Honduras, 23 percent of producers (almost all producers that use chemical herbicides) use glyphosate and 17 percent use chlorpyrifos; in Colombia, 15 percent use glyphosate and 40 percent use chlorpyrifos; and in Costa Rica, 59 percent of producers use glyphosate.

This section has shown that the strict compliance rules of the Rainforest Alliance and Nespresso AAA programs regarding the use of PPE bear fruit in all three country samples. Given that this is a self-reported indicator, I cannot fully exclude the possibility that it is biased upward due to farmers' knowledge of the rules and desire to appear rule-compliant. Even so, clear differences exist between Rainforest Alliance, Nespresso AAA, and C.A.F.E. Practices groups and the rest of the farmers, with all of these groups showcasing 70–85 percent compliance with the use of PPE. Interestingly, this includes the C.A.F.E. Practices farmers in Colombia and Costa Rica, although Starbucks does not make PPE use a critical requirement. Possibly, either the incentive of moving up in the 'preferred supplier' category motivates farmers to go beyond minimum compliance, or PPE use is treated by the cooperative leadership and extension agents as such a strong preference that farmers understand it to be mandatory.

Honduras, in turn, shows the limits of strict compliance requirements to ensure behavioral change: although the UTZ standard mandates that PPE is used and agrochemicals are stored safely in separate
sheds, in practice, producers struggle to meet these standards. Similar
shortfalls are visible in the provision of first aid kits among Fairtrade
farmers in all three countries. This may be due to the clear economic
outlays necessary to achieve compliance. Farmers report that building
agrochemical storage sheds costs them on average from US$500
(Honduras) to US$1,300 (Colombia); purchasing and replacing PPE
ranges from US$45 (Colombia) over US$79 (Honduras) to US$150
(Costa Rica); and purchasing first aid kits is reported to cost between
US$18 (Honduras) and US$45 (Costa Rica). For cash-strapped smallholder farmers, such outlays are not trivial, and frequently impossible
to achieve in their overall farm economy. In Honduras, certification
group coordinators related that investment-intensive continuous
improvement steps are only financially possible once the certification
premium is paid out. They further told of the difficulty when such
payment was delayed or nonexistent, and the need to push an audit
back in time because farmers had not had the possibility to make the
necessary changes (field notes, Honduran extension agents, 2016).
Relatedly, of all certified farmers that had managed their farms during
the certification process, only 5 percent report spending money on
a storage shed in Honduras, and only 9 percent purchased PPE; while
37 and 38 percent of Costa Rican certified farmers, respectively, did
so – possibly because they could afford to. Only 3 percent and less than
1 percent of Colombian farmers, respectively, report making such
investments out of pocket – leading us to the assumption that institutional support was present to help them in achieving compliance.

The existing literature substantiates the insight that improvements in
working conditions rely heavily on the possible outlays that farmers
can afford. Supporting the results found in Honduras, Elder *et al.*
(2013, p. 272) highlight that in Rwandan Fairtrade cooperatives, the
use of face masks when spraying depends both on farmers' experience
(with older farmers showing more resistance) and on their financial
capacity. They cite one farmer who sees universal use as fiscally unrea-
listic: "if [you] take the number of farmers for that number of masks the
cooperative would have to spend millions [of Rwandan Francs]. The
cooperative tells farmers to buy a mask but the farmers sprayed before
without [a mask] so [they] don't want to spend that money."

Factors that are less in the control of farmers, such as the availability of potable water, also show less consistent outcomes. This result is confirmed by van Rijsbergen *et al.* (2016), who find that in Kenya, UTZ certification has no impact on potable water availability, while Fairtrade cooperatives may invest in piped water infrastructure that then benefit all (certified and uncertified) farmers in the vicinity. This mirrors the case of Fairtrade cooperatives in Colombia, where access to potable water is ubiquitous for both 'basic' and higher-level certified farmers in one cooperative, while the other cooperative shows poor results across the board, and potable water access only significantly improved in the Nespresso AAA cluster.

Long-Term Farm Resilience in the Books

Ensuring the long-term health of coffee farms is paramount to make farming viable as a multigenerational business. It is particularly important to guard against two threats that may affect the long-term productive capacity: climate change and erosion. With global warming, it is anticipated that coffee-growing regions are likely to experience increases in the mean temperature, extreme temperature spikes and dips, more heavy and unpredictable rainfall patterns, more frequent droughts and floods, and possibly the shifting of suitable coffee production regions away from today's regions. Exposure to elements such as wind and strong rain, in turn, can cause erosion and the runoff of valuable topsoil (Perfecto *et al.* 1996; Ramos-Scharrón and Thomaz 2017).

UTZ is the only private sustainability standard that explicitly addresses climate change adaptation. It promotes concrete practices such as the use of coffee varietals resistant against diseases predicted to increase in prevalence, such as coffee rust, and the diversification of farm earnings away from coffee entirely by pursuing alternative forms of income generation (Läderach *et al.* 2017). The 2017 Rainforest Alliance[11] and C.A.F.E. Practices standards do encourage farmer

---

[11] Although the press release announcing the 2017 Rainforest Alliance standard revision explicitly mentions the aim to support farmers to become more resilient to climate change, the "climate-smart agriculture" practices included (soil conservation, water use efficiency, and the conservation and restoration of natural ecosystems) are only imperfectly aligned with the struggles of the smallholder farmers in this sample, since they include neither a preference for

groups to include climate change impacts in their farm management plan and training activities, but do not include any specific adaptation measures. As for other specific practices, the use of some shade cover,[12] which may be beneficial to protect crops from climatic variation, is encouraged by some standards, but there are no binding criteria in any standard requiring farmers to maintain a specific number of trees on their farm. Section 5.5 will go into more detail regarding shade production rules in private sustainability standards. Many other climate change resilience practices, such as windbreaks – which can act as buffers against wind gusts that may wreak havoc on coffee farms and also act as erosion prevention practices (Rahn *et al.* 2014; Coffee & Climate 2017) – or soil cover[13] – which lowers the ground temperature, protecting tree roots from overheating due to solar radiation (Coffee & Climate 2017) – are only mentioned as examples of erosion prevention. The use of these and other erosion prevention methods that improve soil health and retention (e.g., installing stone barriers or farming steep slopes through terracing systems) is central only to the organic standard. They are mentioned as continuous improvement criteria in the 4C, UTZ, and Fairtrade standards, and can be opted out from the Rainforest Alliance, C.A.F.E., and AAA standards.

Long-Term Farm Resilience in Practice

In Honduras, a country-wide replanting campaign has contributed to the fact that 95 percent of the sampled farmers' plants are rust-resistant, irrespective of certification group. The only exception is the Fairtrade/organic group, where 80 percent of plants are resistant. Windbreaks are present on 36–76 percent of farms, with the lowest rates in the organic (36 percent) and UTZ (43 percent) groups. The use of shade cover is widespread across all producers, with the highest levels reached (96–98 percent) in the Fairtrade and Fairtrade/organic

---

disease-resistant varieties, diversification, or strong shade criteria. As will be discussed in Section 5.5, the shade criteria are effectively weakened in the new standard revision.

[12] For the purposes of defining 'some shade' in this section, I record the use of shade trees that protect at least 25 percent of the coffee plants from direct solar radiation.

[13] I measure the use of soil cover on over 50 percent of the total production surface (either through cover crops, mulching, or other dead organic matter; as corroborated through photos).

groups. Ironically, the producers certified with the Rainforest Alliance standard – a label that in its name carries it central aim to protect rainforests and subtropical ecosystems – show statistically significant lower rates of the use of shade cover (at 70 versus 86 percent) than their matched controls. In this group, 30 percent of producers are practicing sun coffee production and exposing their coffee to increasingly extreme climatic conditions. This may be a result of their professionalization, since these producers also show higher yields per hectare – however, this choice may have long-term trade-offs. Still, the combination of using rust-resistant varietals, windbreaks, and shade trees show that Honduran coffee farmers have taken first steps toward climate change resilience.

On the other hand, in the UTZ, 4C, and noncertified groups, over half of farmers show signs of erosion. Of these farmers, only around 15 percent use organic inputs and sufficient soil cover. The Rainforest Alliance and Fairtrade farmers show moderately better results, and the Fairtrade/organic farmers stand out as leaders with 96 percent of producers using organic fertilizers and 47 percent using soil cover that protects their soil from erosion. Erosion barriers and terraces are more well-known practices that are adopted by 30–40 percent of farmers. Yet, the high rates of erosion presence and little efforts at preventative practices by nonorganic farmers are highly concerning for the long-term viability of the Honduran coffee sector, given that the country is expanding its coffee output under increasingly extreme climatic conditions.

Most worryingly, only 10–20 percent of farmers produce any other crop but coffee. This means that 80–90 percent of farmers are fully reliant on coffee incomes for their livelihoods (although some had off-farm employment, on average, 90–95 percent of their income came from coffee), and cannot even rely on subsistence crops to fulfill their nutritional needs. This not only leaves them vulnerable to future climate change and other sources of volatility in the market, it also has very real short-term consequences. Between one-third and half of all producers experienced a shortage of food supplies in the previous year, with the highest levels of food scarcity (73 percent) reported in the Fairtrade cooperative. The case of the Honduran Fairtrade/organic cooperative is a clear best-practice example in this regard. In addition to pursuing certification, it is involved in an NGO-led livestock distribution project and a diversification project that teaches farmers how to grow vegetables, supported by an international aid agency. Despite their comparatively low coffee yields and difficult financial situation (73 percent of their income is still coffee-related), of these farmers, only 4 percent report having experienced food insecurity.

Colombia shows similar levels of disease resistance, with an average of 90 percent of rust-resistant plants. In turn, it has the lowest shares of farms with at least 25 percent shade cover from all three countries: only around half of Fairtrade-, Rainforest Alliance/AAA-, Nespresso AAA-, and C.A.F.E.-certified producers and 68 percent of noncertified farmers pursue shade production. Interestingly, the 4C group stands out with a reported 80 percent share of producers using shade. Further, the Fairtrade cooperatives are leading a slow process of soil management improvement, with significant differences to their control group at the level of soil cover (18 versus 6 percent) and erosion barriers (34 versus 12 percent), as well as in the use of organic inputs. The use of wind-breaks is more prominent in the noncertified control group than in certified farmers. Between 10 and 20 percent of farms showed signs of erosion, with no significant differences between the groups.

Regarding diversification, around 70 percent of Colombian farmers produce other crops or hold livestock. The overwhelming majority produce fruits that were sold on local markets. In particular, it is common to intersperse banana and plantain palms between coffee as shade trees and sell the resulting harvest. The Rainforest Alliance/AAA and AAA groups also show shares of 15 and 10 percent farmers, respectively, that grow subsistence crops such as corn and beans. Between 25 and 30 percent of producers in each group further own livestock such as cows, pigs, and chicken. This may contribute to their food security, given that they report lower levels of food scarcity than the Honduran groups, with Fairtrade and the higher-level groups performing better (0–10 percent) than the control group (14 percent). Yet, Colombian farmers still get an average 95 percent of their cash income from their coffee receipts, with the exception of the noncertified group (77 percent).

Costa Rican producers, in turn, show an average of only 23 percent of rust-resistant crops, with two groups reporting even lower averages (the noncertified group, with 10 percent, and the Rainforest Alliance/C. A.F.E. group, with 17 percent). Costa Rica's quality-focused preference for traditional varietals, combined with ageing farms, contributes to the fact that coffee rust susceptibility, the need for disease prevention, and response through fungicides is much higher. This also explains why organic coffee production is almost nonexistent in Costa Rica's main coffee-producing regions – as one previously organic farmer explained, their proximity to strongly affected conventional plots meant that during the last coffee rust outbreak, they had the choice between spraying fungicides (and losing their certification) or watching their fields die off. They chose the former (field notes, Costa Rican coffee producer, 2015).

Costa Rican farmers use at least some shade cover to the same extent as the Honduran sample (72–84 percent), with a slight improvement over the control group in the Rainforest Alliance/C.A.F.E. group (at 95 percent). The use of windbreaks does not significantly change through participating in a certification program; the Fairtrade group even shows worse results than the noncertified farmers. On the other hand, the high levels of intensification pursued in the past may have had long-term consequences on soil health. Erosion presence is even higher than in Honduras, hovering at around 50–60 percent of all sampled farms. Simultaneously, only 20–23 percent of farmers show substantial soil cover levels in the Fairtrade, C.A.F.E. Practices, and Rainforest Alliance/C.A.F.E. groups. In groups where levels of soil cover are higher – the Rainforest Alliance/AAA and noncertified groups, with around 45 percent with significant soil cover – accordingly fewer farms show signs of erosion. Terracing and the use of erosion barriers again is well established, mirroring the Honduran case.

The Fairtrade farmers show greater diversification than their non-certified controls, with 81 percent (versus 46 percent) of farmers producing some other crop than coffee or raising livestock. Some farmers grow sugarcane on lower-lying land that is unsuitable for high-quality coffee, which is a transition that could be expanded as one possible climate change adaptation strategy. Others strike a balance between fruit, vegetable, and bean cultivation and keeping livestock. Yet, these diversification rates decrease as farmers participate in a quality-oriented scheme, such as the C.A.F.E. Practices (69 percent) or Rainforest Alliance/Nespresso AAA (49 percent) programs. In the case of both groups, this decrease in diversification coincides with a higher share of farmers that reported food insecurity, although from a low baseline level. Finally, despite the growing opportunities for off-farm labor in Costa Rica, only around 50 percent of all certified farmers, irrespective of their certification status, and 29 percent of noncertified farmers report having other income sources than coffee –

showcasing their high reliance on coffee to guarantee their livelihoods despite their high production costs compared internationally.

On balance, this section demonstrates that farmers in each country showed nascent climate change resilience and erosion prevention strategies, but also that each country group had major vulnerabilities that could be better addressed. In Honduras, producers should be encouraged to diversify their production strategies better; in Colombia, increased shade cover could help producers in the long-term regulation of temperatures and the mitigation of extreme weather events; and in Costa Rica, increasing the amount of soil cover could prevent further erosion in already highly affected areas. Private sustainability standards showed only limited effectiveness in addressing these country-level shortcomings. Despite individual success stories (e.g., the improved diversification patterns of the Fairtrade/organic cooperative in Honduras; the higher shares of shade production in 4C producers in Colombia; or the improvement in soil cover in the Costa Rican Rainforest Alliance/AAA group), in the majority of indicators, we can observe few patterns of positive change stemming from certification. This aligns with the results of previous studies (Elder *et al.* 2013; Rueda and Lambin 2013; Haggar *et al.* 2017). In some instances, the pursuit of access to differentiated markets through private sustainability standards even stands in the way of increasing long-term resilience. Such examples include the case of lower shade cover presence on Rainforest Alliance-certified farms in Honduras or the trend toward specialization over diversification in Costa Rican Rainforest Alliance/AAA and C.A. F.E. Practices groups (cf. Vellema *et al.*, 2015; van Rijsbergen *et al.* 2016). Here, other incentives – for instance, those related to sustainable intensification, as described in the previous section – may have had a greater impact on producers. Although the UTZ standard is the most progressive in addressing climate change adaptation practices on paper, in the field there is not (yet) a noticeable effect on the Honduran UTZ farmers, demonstrating the gap between rules-in-form and rules-in-practice.

Second, it is evident that, apart from the Fairtrade/organic group in Honduras, all coffee producers under analysis still have significant room for improvement in adopting erosion prevention practices. While certification schemes have accelerated the rate of progress of several beneficial practices – notably the use of composted coffee pulp in Colombia and the use of organic fertilizers in Costa Rica and some

Honduran groups – gaps in the implementation of wide-ranging soil cover persist. Although according to the questionnaire data, an average of 20–30 percent of producers across all groups and country contexts use cover crops, a subsequent analysis of the corroborating pictures showed that the concept of purposefully planted, potentially nitrogen-fixing crops is still exceedingly rare, with only a handful of cases recorded in Costa Rica. More commonly, what was denoted as 'cover crop' were patches of grass or other weeds that seemed to have sprung up independently and were not eliminated by farmers. Yet, this approach did not appear to yield the continuous coverage that a cover crop would need to achieve to provide resilience-enhancing co-benefits. Here, more outreach may be necessary, especially when considering the limited total soil cover results.

Furthermore, in Costa Rica, the use of herbicides such as glyphosate that may adversely affect soil health by decreasing soil organic matter (Casabé *et al.* 2007) and have been linked to increased rates of erosion (Blavet *et al.* 2009; Sabatier *et al.* 2014) continues to be widespread. No standard apart from the organic certification bans glyphosate and other preemergence herbicides or discusses this issue in relation to soil health and erosion prevention. Where the long-term benefits of improved soil health are directly opposed to the short-term cost savings of applying herbicides rather than weeding by hand, most private sustainability standards thus appear unable or unwilling to change the institutional framework and incentives facing coffee farmers.

Reviewing the results of Section 5.4, we find the strongest changes in those issues that are nonnegotiable criteria of the standards under analysis: the use of PPE, the safe disposal of hazardous waste such as pesticide containers, and – in select cases – the construction of agrochemical storage facilities. In addition to being strict compliance criteria that can easily be checked by auditors, these criteria have in common that they can be relatively easily changed through local institutional changes (e.g., the organization of a pesticide container recycling center or the sale of small lockable storage units through the cooperative or trader). They also do not necessitate profound changes to the production system or mentality such as, for instance, the use of cover crops or the diversification of the agroecological landscape. However, where implementation is constrained for financial reasons – such as in the case of Honduras, where many farmers do not have the cash flow or the institutional support for the requisite investments –

investments will not occur, and the short-term barriers to longer-term beneficial practices remain.

Furthermore, this section showed us that a number of ecological best practices (i.e., erosion prevention or climate change resilience) are described in very broad terms in private sustainability standards, which gives both farmer groups as well as auditors considerable leeway in how to interpret the requirements and their compliance. One reason for this variability is the recognition that micro-regional ecological conditions are vastly different and require locally adapted best-practice management. It should be acknowledged that the method presented here of identifying key best practices and comparing their application across cases is, in itself, an exercise that collapses subregional variation and individual-level circumstances. However, by collecting evidence on both best practices and related outcomes (e.g., the presence of erosion or food insecurity), the preceding section also shows that many best practices have beneficial outcomes across the board – but are not universally adopted, even in certified farm groups. It is likely that the short-term costs in combination with the perceived nonbinding nature of individual criteria from a basket of options leads to rationalist cost–benefit calculations where the least costly option will be chosen and, at the moment of the audit, argued to constitute compliance. Thus, farmers that already use shade trees may argue that this constitutes a soil health as well as a climate change resilience practice, while innovative shifts such as purposefully implementing cover crops are unlikely to occur unless the certification group leader strongly pushes for such practices. Here, a focus on low-cost 'low-hanging fruit' may overlook the potential of private sustainability standards to "provide the impetus for participants in the behavioral complex to undertake measures that will enhance their welfare in the long run but that for one reason or another they find difficult to initiate in the short run" (Young 1999, p. 252). The next section turns to even more difficult changes: those that create long-term costs for farmers but social or environmental benefits for society as a whole.

5.5 Standards as Payments for Social and Ecosystem Services

This section examines practices that can be categorized as 'win-lose' scenarios in the trade-off between social and environmental protection and farm output (Gunningham and Grabosky 1998). The implementation of such practices provides public benefits in terms of safeguarding workers' rights, forests, biodiversity, and the integrity of terrestrial and aquatic ecosystems, but creates real and lasting opportunity costs for farmers who limit their production surface, eliminate synthetic input use, and increase their production costs. Microeconomic theory would suggest that the inclusion of such requirements into voluntary standards requires that farmers are compensated for the concomitant loss of income through substantial price premiums, in effect turning such standards into payment for social or ecosystem services mechanisms. These costly requirements are also the ones most likely to be opted out from or evaded if farmers find a possibility to do so. In this section, I test these theoretical assumptions by examining two categories: upholding high labor protection standards by complying with minimum wage law and eliminating child labor; and protecting ecosystems by practicing land sparing and/or land sharing.

Labor Protection in the Books

They throw us in the same category as slave labor conditions in Africa, but one shouldn't generalize. Here, nobody is forced to work, kids go to school and work on Saturdays and the holidays. Some kids don't want to go on and study further – you can't prevent them from seeking work.

(Field notes, Honduran coffee farmer, 2016)

The social sustainability of coffee relies critically on the social welfare of all actors involved in coffee production. This includes workers and pickers who work on a permanent or occasional basis on small-scale coffee farms. However, for smallholder farmers that are strapped for cash, contributing to this bigger-picture social welfare may conversely amount to constraining their own livelihood strategies if they pay higher wages out of their own profits. In the context of low and variable commodity prices, this represents a direct trade-off between private interests and socially optimal solutions. Private sustainability standards defer to national legislation – where it exists – as minimum criterion for compliance. Thus, wage payments greater or equal to official minimum wage (or the regional average, whichever is higher) are zero tolerance requirements for all certifications except for 4C, where it is required after three years. This leniency of 4C – allowing producers to gain baseline 'sustainability' verification while they continue to ignore local law – caused the Institute for Multi-Stakeholder

Initiative Integrity to conclude that "4C's standards do not impose stringent enough obligations to resolve the human rights concerns they seek to address," warning that "a baseline standard should not permit violations of domestic law or international standards" (MSI Integrity 2013, pp. 5–6).

A similar trade-off between the private interest and the public good exists regarding child labor. Many coffee farmers have grown up helping out on the family farm and consider it advisable to introduce their children to the practice of farming at a young age, both to train them and foster an emotional connection to the crop, and to keep them out of trouble (field notes, Honduran coffee farmers, 2016). Furthermore, migrant coffee pickers who move from farm to farm during harvest time frequently arrive as a family. If no childcare services are available in the coffee-growing communities, many pickers refuse to work unless they can take their children onto the coffee farm to keep an eye on them. As one interviewee noted, "if you consider the presence of children on the farm during harvest child labor, then you will find child labor on 90% of farms" (field notes, Costa Rican extension agent, 2017). On the other hand, in many cases, pickers are paid by coffee volume picked instead of on an hourly basis. Enlisting the help of family members – both women and children – may then be a successful strategy to improve their earnings, moving the issue of child labor back into the spotlight. This brings coffee growers into complicated situations, as the following example from a Honduran cooperative manager shows: "Sometimes farmers want to do the right thing, and refuse to let children collect their coffee – but then only four pickers would go with them. The others would say 'if you don't let them come, I will go to another farm.' This is mainly an economic decision – if the kids help picking, they will receive more money for the family, which will be used for nutrition and school supplies" (field notes, Honduran coffee cooperative, 2016). From the farmer's perspective, resolving child labor issues in a strict manner, that is, disallowing their own and pickers' children from working on the farm, could hence create higher labor costs if they have to replace their own family labor with hired labor or provide higher per-volume prices in order to attract pickers willing to forego the added family labor.

On child labor, private sustainability standards also align with international (e.g., International Labor Organization [ILO] Conventions) and national legislation. 4C refers only to the prohibition of the worst forms of child labor (i.e., dangerous working conditions such as the use of agrochemicals or bearing heavy loads). All others prohibit the direct or indirect hiring of workers under the age of 14 (C.A.F.E. Practices; Rainforest Alliance and UTZ if that is the national minimum) or 15 years of age (Fairtrade, Fairtrade/organic, and Nespresso AAA), in line with both international and national laws. Surprisingly, Starbucks C. A.F.E. Practices is the strictest standard on mandatory school attendance. It sets the zero tolerance requirement that "children of legal school age attend school and do not work during school hours" (Starbucks 2014, p. 4), while other standards use more flexible phrasing to encourage educational efforts. For instance, UTZ asks that "actions are taken to encourage compulsory school attendance of children of group staff, group members, and group member workers" (UTZ Certified 2014a, p. 26) as of year 4 of certification.

Labor Protection in Practice

Paying adequate minimum wages is frequently challenging for small farmers, particularly if coffee prices and associated incomes are so low that they are unable to pay themselves an equivalent profit. All groups of Honduran farmers have trouble paying the agricultural minimum daily salary of US$8.30[14] to day workers. Of the entire sample of 659 farmers, only 10 producers (8 of which are in the Fairtrade/organic group) report paying daily wages above the minimum salary. The Rainforest Alliance farmers are the only group that pays significantly more for day laborers than the control group. Coffee pickers, in turn, are paid per volume; and Fairtrade farmers pay slightly more (around 7 percent) per basket than comparable control farmers. When calculating the average daily income based on estimated baskets picked per day, coffee pickers have mean daily earnings that come close to or exceeded the Honduran daily agricultural minimum wage on all farms except in the UTZ group. This divergence between daily laborers' and pickers' salaries could be caused by different labor market dynamics during the year as opposed to during the harvest season. Alternatively, day workers may work less than the standard eight hours, or benefit from a quid pro quo arrangement in the case of neighboring farmers that supersedes legal wage

---

[14] 179.52 Lempiras at the 2015 exchange rate of 21.67 Lempiras/US$ (WageIndicator 2018a).

requirements. Yet, at least in the books, many certified farmers do not comply with the legal framework.

Since the issue of child labor is a sensitive topic, I operationalized it in a number of indirect ways in the farm survey. First, I asked whether school-age children attend school, if they help on the farm, and, if yes, what activities they perform, to gauge whether they include dangerous activities. I report whether they were engaged in pesticide application, which is considered dangerous child labor according to the ILO. Further, I also asked for the age of the youngest worker hired on the farm, and subsequently compare whether this age is below the legal minimum (14 in Honduras and 15 in Colombia and Costa Rica, as specified in their ILO ratifications and enshrined in national law [ILO 2018]). As noted earlier, including children present on the farm during harvest would have shown almost-universal presence of child labor. When asked how certification organizations deal with this potential controversy, the answer from multiple sources was clear: "they almost never schedule audits during the harvest season" (field notes, producer organizations, 2015/ 16) – enabling them to not find any noncompliances.

Still, even using this more narrow definition of child labor, I find evidence that it continues to be a widespread problem in Honduras. With the exception of the Fairtrade cooperatives (2–4 percent), in most groups between 13 and 30 percent of farmers hire underage workers. I do find significant differences to their control groups in the Rainforest Alliance (13 versus 23 percent), Fairtrade/organic (4 versus 26 percent), and UTZ groups (28 versus 40 percent). School attendance is widespread – between 73 and 90 percent of children go to school – but children also routinely help out on the farm, although infrequently in dangerous activities. Rainforest Alliance is the only certification that shows significantly different behavior in this regard when compared to the control group (with 7 versus 32 percent of school-age children that help on the farm).

When adding the data from Colombia, we can take note of three insights: first, Colombian farmers pay twice as much for their labor as their Honduran competitors (with daily wages between US$10 and US$12, compared to US$5–6 in Honduras), and yet compete on the same world market for coffee. Given that labor amounts to around 70 percent of production costs (ICO 2016), this discrepancy illustrates the underlying challenges of sustainable globalized commodity production in diverse production locations. Second, the competitive labor market contributes to the fact that most farmers – whether certified or noncertified – pay more than the minimum wage of US$9.82 per day.[15] The thirty-five observations that are barely below minimum wage are evenly divided between the groups of one Fairtrade certified and the noncertified cooperative. On the other hand, although not regulated explicitly by either national law or private sustainability standards, the certified cooperatives all differentiate between nonhazardous and hazardous work (i.e., applying agrochemicals), and remunerate hazardous work at a higher rate (by almost 40 percent, at around US$16). This differentiation does not take place in the noncertified cooperative. Here, normative understandings about the dangers associated with agrochemical use may have contributed to a more differentiated labor market.

In contrast to Honduras, the data from Colombia show few problems with child labor, as both the hiring of underage workers and the participation of school-age children in farm activities is close to zero (although the presence of workers' children in coffee farms during harvest is also common here). Yet, members of one cooperative appear to have greater problems to send their children to school, as school attendance hovers between 59 and 72 percent in these groups (including the C.A.F.E. Practice group, for whom this is a zero tolerance requirement), with slightly higher values in groups with additional certification. This disparity cannot be explained simply by their remoteness, since respondents report to require only between 17 and 20 minutes to reach the next school. They are also not significantly smaller farmers than the rest. While difficult to verify ex post, it is possible that there were problems with lesson availability that caused children to stay at home. If so, this again raises the issue of structural problems that prevent producers from complying with private regulations.

Finally, Costa Rica sets the minimum daily wage for a nonqualified agricultural worker at US$17.60.[16] Smallholder farmers in this sample struggle to implement these wage levels, both when paying daily as well as monthly wages, although they pay higher per-unit labor costs than any other farmers in our sample (between US$15 and US$16.80). In the field, a representative of a private mill commented that the wage levels

---

[15] 644,350.00 COP/24 = 26,847.91 COP at the 2015 exchange rate of 2,734 COP/
     US$ (WageIndicator 2018b).
[16] 9,509.34 CRC at the 2015 exchange rate of 540.07 CRC/US$ (WageIndicator
     2018c).

had to be seen in regional comparison, noting that "earning $15 per day here with secure work is better than earning $4 in Nicaragua with high unemployment" (field notes, Costa Rican processor, 2015). However, I find sizeable between-cooperative differences in wage levels that cannot readily be explained by regional labor market differences. In particular, members of one Fairtrade cooperative pay significantly higher wages than the rest (an average of almost US$17). Yet, this difference does not seem to be driven by private regulation alone, since other cooperatives that equally have Fairtrade certification, as well as the Rainforest Alliance/C.A.F.E. group, show some of the lowest wages paid (US$14.90 on average).

As in Honduras, coffee pickers' daily wage lies widely above the daily laborers' wage, although it is possible that optimistic overestimations of the picked quantities are skewing this data upward. Costa Rica also has a minimum wage per basket of picked coffee of US$1.67;[17] all producers in our sample pay more than that, and often significantly above this minimum. Here, again, local labor dynamics are at work, as Costa Rican farmers have suffered from a shortage of domestic workers willing to spend their time in the coffee fields during harvest, and the country has made increasing efforts to attract migrant workers from Nicaragua and Panama (Bravo 2016).

On the other hand, despite strict labor laws in Costa Rica that prohibit the employment of any minor below the age of 15 (MTSS 2018), I find high levels of such employment on noncertified coffee farms (29 percent). There is also a significant share of underage labor in the Rainforest Alliance/AAA group (11 percent), in sharp contrast with Fairtrade (0 percent), Rainforest Alliance/C.A.F.E. (5 percent), and C.A.F.E. (0 percent) groups. In most such cases, the youngest employees are between 12 and 14 years old, although some instances of 10-year-old employees were also noted. School attendance, again, is mixed among producers with school-age children, but generally higher in certified groups (80–87 percent) than in the noncertified controls (71 percent). No school-age children of smallholder families are reported to work in any capacity on the Costa Rican farms. It should however be noted that the share of farmers with school-age children in general is lower in Colombia and Costa Rica, as the farm population is

[17]   905 CRC at the 2015 exchange rate of 540.07 CRC/US$ (Bravo 2015).

ageing and many coffee farmers are nearing retirement age, such that these means are based on relatively small subsample groups.

We see that a theoretically simple requirement of private sustainability standards – respecting national minimum wage law – in practice becomes much more complex. Farmers face widely differing goalposts and possibilities to comply with this requirement, while at the same time competing in the same market for conventional and certified coffee alike. De facto, small-scale agricultural production is in somewhat of a gray zone regarding labor law, with high levels of informal labor off the books that is difficult to verify. Furthermore, the definition of a work day, the type of labor, and the possibility of providing nonmonetary remuneration (e.g., food or housing) would have to be taken into account for a comprehensive analysis of legal compliance or noncompliance. Still, on-farm auditors most likely run into the same structural problems of noncompliance due to the lack of financial ability of farmers to follow the standard. In interviews, at least one case was raised where an audited farmer in Costa Rica was paying "cents below the minimum wage" and this was considered a major noncompliance (interview 57, Costa Rican cooperative 3, 2017). To resolve this issue, the cooperative was required to distribute flyers informing their members of their legal obligations. Yet, if the underlying issue is financial capacity rather than ignorance or unwillingness to pay, there is little else either auditors, group leaders, or individual farmers can do to improve compliance.

This section has further shown that child labor concerns continue to be a reality in Central America, spanning countries with both weak (Honduras) and strong (Costa Rica) institutional settings. Private regulation works moderately well in reinforcing public legislation regarding working age by providing additional enforcement capacity on the ground, although pockets of noncompliance exist even in certified farmer groups. The worst forms of child labor, on the other hand, are barely present in this sample of farmers – with the notable exception of the Honduran Fairtrade cooperative, in which 17 percent of farmers with school-age children that work on the farm note that these children performed dangerous activities such as spraying pesticides.

Similar patterns persist in other regions of the world. Citing the excess rural labor supply, and mirroring my results in Honduras, Ruben and Zuniga (2011) find no impact of Fairtrade, C.A.F.E. Practices, or Rainforest Alliance certification on remuneration rates for on-farm labor in the Nicaraguan coffee sector, although they do not specify whether the remuneration rates met the legal minimum wage or not. Kuit *et al.* (2010, 2016), in turn, find mixed results regarding the impact of 4C on child labor prevalence in Vietnam, Uganda, and Nicaragua: only in the case of Uganda was there a notable reduction in the amount of child labor used on farms compared to the control group. Worryingly, even explicitly forbidden practices by the 4C standard (children's involvement in heavy lifting or dangerous activities) occurred on select 4C-verified farms in Vietnam and Uganda. The same research group looked at Vietnamese UTZ-certified farmers, finding similar fallacies in compliance with the UTZ certification: "On some mandatory control points, such as not using child labor for heavy and dangerous work a few isolated farmers are not compliant. For other aspects [e.g., the use of PPE] non-compliance can reach 30% of the UTZ certified producers" (Kuit *et al.* 2013, p. xiii). They conclude that their findings "could endanger the credibility of UTZ Certified's assurance" (Kuit *et al.* 2013, p. xiii).

Ecosystem Protection in the Books

The protection of forests and aquatic ecosystems is a further high-cost sustainability practice to consider. Tropical and subtropical forests act as essential carbon sinks and contain around two-thirds of all species (Pimm and Raven 2000), making them priority regions for conservation (Myers *et al.* 2000). Agriculture is considered the principal cause for deforestation in the tropics (Jurjonas *et al.* 2016). In regions with unclear or private land tenure rights, high commodity prices are strongly correlated with an expansion of the crop land dedicated to cash crops such as coffee (O'Brien and Kinnaird 2003; Gaveau *et al.* 2009; Schlesinger *et al.* 2017). The projected increases in demand coupled with changes in coffee growing conditions due to climate change are further likely to contribute to significant deforestation. A recent modeling analysis found considerable risks for deforestation in Central America and the Andes. Here, rising temperatures will move the ideal production conditions for Arabica coffee into higher altitudes and regions that currently still have forest cover (Conservation International 2016).

Deforestation can occur directly through the conversion of forests to coffee farms (O'Brien and Kinnaird 2003), or indirectly when cultivation patterns shift. In the Central Highlands of Vietnam, for instance,

Meyfroidt *et al.* (2013) observed that the expansion of coffee on traditional agricultural lands pushed the cultivation of annual subsistence crops by local ethnic minorities into the forest margins, causing deforestation. As noted in Chapter 3, to prevent such substitution, two regulatory options exist:[18] land sparing or land sharing.

Using a land-sparing argument, one could prohibit the establishment of coffee fields on forest land, while simultaneously stressing the necessity to optimize productivity and yield levels in order to minimize the production surface necessary to fulfill demand. Yet, if local laws do not already regulate land use, strong economic incentives will be necessary to persuade coffee farmers to forego possible incomes from expanding their land into forested areas and riverbanks, especially if their current land is becoming less suitable due to climate change.

Land sparing is widely present in private sustainability standards. Indeed, the destruction of primary forest, protected areas, and/or areas with high conservation value (HCV) is an unacceptable requirement for all schemes with the exception of the organic standard. Fairtrade prohibits negative impacts on protected areas and HCV areas from the beginning of certification, while the rest choose a reference point in the past. C.A.F.E. Practices is the strictest, prohibiting the conversion of all natural forest from 2004 onward. The Rainforest Alliance forbids the destruction of HCV area from 2005 and the conversion of other forests from the date of application onward. Nespresso AAA focuses on HCV areas and prohibits cutting forest to prepare land, also from 2005 onward. 4C refers only to primary forest and protected areas and takes 2006 as cut-off, and UTZ limits itself to primary forest and the cut-off date of 2008. These definitional details matter, as not all countries have the same approach to protected areas; primary forest is not the same as natural forest; and the identification of areas of HCV is a complex endeavor, requiring broad knowledge of ecology and the local context that may be out of the reach of smallholders (Brown *et al.*

---

[18] Actually, there is a third option: one could advocate for limiting the expansion of coffee production by curbing demand and advocating for consumption patterns that prioritize quality over quantity, thereby halting or reversing the growth trend in total required output. Coffee is a luxury product and not an essential agricultural commodity. If consumers paid more for smaller amounts of higher-quality coffee, farmers could benefit from its production within the current confines of their natural environment. As the private regulation options under analysis focus on the supply side, not the demand side, I leave this option aside for now, but will come back to it during the conclusions.

2013). None of the standard stipulations account for secondary displacement activities such as the ones observed in Vietnam by Meyfroidt *et al.* (2013).

The other regulatory option is to pursue a land sharing approach through the protection and expansion of diverse agroforestry and shade production systems. There is increasing evidence that the negative impacts on biodiversity and climate mitigation of replacing natural forest with coffee production can be minimized in such systems. For instance, Schlesinger *et al.* (2017) find that conversion from sun to shaded coffee may have led to increases in forest cover in El Salvador and Honduras, and Hylander *et al.* (2013) find lower deforestation rates in areas with traditional shade coffee production in Ethiopia. Here, land sharing may have been an effective technique to prevent clear-cutting. In this fashion, coffee production may increase while maintaining the vital ecosystem services provided by the forested areas.

In contrast to the land sparing approaches of HCV forest protection and yield intensification, the use of shade trees and agroforestry methods to provide alternative ecosystem services on coffee plots is less widely encouraged in private standards. Fairtrade, Fairtrade/organic, and 4C do refer to agroforestry when providing guiding examples on how to improve biodiversity or reuse organic matter, but do not make it a specific requirement. UTZ calls for an "adequate" amount of shade trees planted by year 3 of certification (UTZ Certified 2014b, p. 2), leaving it up to producers to determine what the adequate number should be. C.A.F.E. Practices and Nespresso AAA share a similar definition of adequate shade cover that was derived from the Rainforest Alliance's canopy cover parameters: a minimum of 40 percent canopy cover of the productive areas, made up by a large number (12 per hectare in the case of AAA) of diverse, native tree species. Yet, it is not a critical requirement, meaning that no farm needs to comply with this definition to become part of these programs.

Most surprising of all, considering its historic focus, the Rainforest Alliance's standard has ended up specifying very low requirements regarding agroforestry and shade cover. Indeed, the Rainforest Alliance is an interesting case study of weakening shade and agroforestry requirements. The original 2005 standard considered the establishment and maintenance of permanent shade cover a critical requirement for traditional agroforestry crops such as coffee. The initial shade requirements, which were mandatory for all farms located in areas where the original natural vegetative cover was forest, could be found in a separate coffee-specific standard. They were as follows: (a) a minimum of seventy individual trees per hectare that must include at least twelve native species per hectare; (b) a shade density of at least 40 percent at all times; and (c) the tree crowns must comprise at least two strata or stories. In 2008, when a generic standard was issued and crop-specific standards disappeared, these criteria were adapted for all agroforestry crops, but became a noncritical criterion, and could be opted out from by participating producers. In 2009, the requirement of seventy trees per hectare was dropped in favor of the following language: (a) the tree community on the cultivated land consists of minimum twelve native species per hectare on average; (b) the tree canopy comprises at least two strata or stories; and (c) the overall canopy density on the cultivated land is at least 40 percent. This language was kept in the 2010 standard.

In addition, the interpretation guide recognized that "the requirement of 40% density of the canopy is optimal for some areas, but not for all. Shade density on production plots are managed to optimize agronomic and conservation values, considering local production systems, climate, altitude, soil characteristics, and slope levels. SAN local interpretation guides provide further recommendations on adequate shade levels" (SAN 2014, p. 13). When these country-specific interpretations were published, many added economically driven exemptions to the shade criteria. The Honduran guidelines, for instance, allow agricultural professionals to exempt farms located higher than 1,200 m from the shade criteria because they may be at higher risk of disease (SAN 2009). In Colombia, the shade level "shall not be detrimental to production or the economic well-being of the family" (SAN 2012, p. 17). With the newest 2017 revision, the shade requirement has moved to being evaluated after six years at the earliest. It is also part of a less stringent category (only 50 percent of level 'A' criteria are required for continued certification, rather than the 80 percent of the old standard) and no longer includes the specification of two or more tree strata. Furthermore, it measures foliage cover when it is most dense (as opposed to requiring 40 percent cover 'at all times'), and allows for the substitution of shade canopy if 15 percent of the total farm or farm group area is covered by native vegetation.[19] With each of these steps,

---

[19] For the purposes of this study, the producers however still operated under the 2010 standard, which had the previously mentioned shade cover definitions

the comparative advantage of rustic agroforests is weakened, as competitors with nonshaded farms are able to produce Rainforest Alliance-certified coffee at lower costs. This effectively leaves no mainstream private sustainability standard (other than the niche SMBC Bird Friendly Coffee) that reliably provides consumers with the assurance that their coffee was produced under shade cover (Craves 2017). Given this lack of binding criteria, the next section will explore whether producers still maintain diverse agroforestry systems. In particular, the section analyzes how far voluntary or semivoluntary measures (e.g., the UTZ or Rainforest Alliance shade requirements) will be implemented if they create real costs for farmers.

In addition, the processing of coffee can cause considerable pollution of natural waterways when the processing water is led back into streams without having filtered out the organic components. These components cause high biological oxygen demands, leading to eutrophication and 'dead zones' (Beyene *et al.* 2014; Rattan *et al.* 2015; Awoke *et al.* 2016). The water used for fermentation is furthermore highly acidic, upsetting the pH levels of streams (Rattan *et al.* 2015). Best practices thus call for the treatment of processing water through dedicated systems.[20] Such treatment systems can be a considerable investment for small-scale farmers, with UTZ estimating material costs ranging from US$300 (for a controlled surface runoff system) to US$1,000 (for a biodigestor), in addition to labor and maintenance costs (Sánchez Hernández *et al.* 2016). More low-cost methods (e.g., runoff or biofiltration systems) have high land requirements, again establishing costly trade-offs with agricultural production. The discharge of untreated processing water that may degrade aquatic ecosystems is a zero-tolerance criterion for the UTZ, Nespresso AAA, and Rainforest Alliance certifications. It is prohibited for 4C farmers after three years and Fairtrade farmers, more vaguely, "must handle waste water from central processing facilities in a manner that does not have a negative impact" (FLO 2011, p. 18).

(40 percent, twelve native species, two strata) and was one of the noncritical criteria, which meant that producers could opt out of it if they fulfilled enough of the other requirements.

[20] First, residual solid matter should be filtered out from the water and the pH level balanced (from an average pH of 4–7), for instance, using limestone. In a second step, the organic matter (in particular sugars) dissolved in the processing water need to be metabolized, for instance, through anaerobic digestion (in biodigestors or anerobic lagoons) or aerobic decomposition in biofiltration wetlands (Rattan *et al.* 2015).

Finally, an intensive use of chemical fertilizers and pesticides can lead to run-off and pollution if rains carry agrochemicals into local waterways (Perfecto *et al.* 1996). This has led environmentalists to recommend 'buffer zones' – zones in which no coffee is grown, and where alternative plants provide a barrier to the waterways – to protect local streams and sources. These buffer zones, however, present real economic dilemmas to producers who give up income by foregoing the possibility of planting coffee in these zones. The use of buffer zones is a noncritical criterion in the 2010 Rainforest Alliance standard and a continuous improvement criterion in all other schemes; they range from stipulating no minimum distance to a minimum distance of 5 m (in the Rainforest Alliance standard).

Ecosystem Protection in Practice

Out of the three countries in our sample, the threat of coffee production to deforestation is highest in Honduras. Here, the comparative advantage in production costs, along with the relative lack of alternative rural employment options, makes coffee an attractive farming option, and has led to steady increases in Honduras' production capacity. Ironically, the considerable outmigration of rural Hondurans to the United States has caused heightened investment in coffee land in Honduras since it is the best way (indeed, one of the only ways) to invest remittances in the country. In 2010, as the US economy crumbled and coffee prices soared, people came back to Honduras to farm their land (field notes, Honduran cooperative, 2016). Yet, this pattern creates a vicious cycle, as the increased output lowered prices in the long run, which has caused even more migration in recent years.

The growth trend in the Honduran coffee sector is reflected in the micro-data, in which around half of all producers – independent of their group – report having expanded their coffee area in recent years. Surprisingly, a substantial share of producers in the groups we have hitherto considered more advanced in their environmental practices – Rainforest Alliance (24 percent) and Fairtrade/organic farmers (32 percent) – report having replaced forest when expanding their coffee field.[21]

[21] To gauge the presence of deforestation, I used a two-part question. First, farmers reported whether they had expanded their coffee area in the last five years and, if so, what that land had been used for previously. The possibility of choosing from a range of answers (coffee, subsistence agriculture, forest, pasture, fallow, or

It is noteworthy that the Fairtrade/organic certification only prohibits the deforestation of protected areas and those that possess HCV. It is thus possible for farmers to assert that the areas did not possess such conservation value, and be in compliance with the standard, while de facto tree cover is being lost. On the other hand, better practices are visible in the UTZ group, which has low rates of replacing forests (7 percent), although they possess as much proportional forested land as the Rainforest Alliance farmers at the time of our survey. The UTZ, Rainforest Alliance, and Fairtrade/organic groups also contain higher shares of producers that planted trees in the past year (47–77 percent) than their respective control groups (24–45 percent). This shows a precarious balancing of environmental and economic concerns that recalls the "lexical ordering of money and responsibility" (Ayres and Braithwaite 1987, p. 27) in which economic subsistence mainly wins out over environmentalist norms. This balance is only moderately changed by private regulatory governance, and where it is possible, deforestation still occurs, although it is unclear whether the deforested areas were of HCV or not.

On the other hand, with the exception of the Fairtrade group, it is rather common to find agroforestry practices[22] on coffee farms, especially at a lower level of shade cover (from 25 to 50 percent). A total of 12 percent of noncertified farmers have agroforestry systems, with rising levels when moving to the 4C (19 percent), UTZ (34 percent), Rainforest Alliance (43 percent), and Fairtrade/organic farmers (57 percent).[23] In Honduras, shade production has long been the norm and technification

other) was designed to inspire confidence and lead to lower social desirability bias than if we had asked "did you deforest recently." It should be noted that the format of the questionnaire made it impossible to differentiate between HCV, primary, and secondary forest, although to our knowledge none of the sampled farmers were directly adjacent to protected areas and no large-scale plantations existed in the vicinity, so that all forest is likely to be natural forest.

[22] Based on an observational walk-through of the farm plots and corroborated by visual evidence, data collectors were asked to log whether the farm showed a significant number of different shade species; whether native shade trees were present; whether the shade trees had multiple strata; and what percentage of the coffee plants (0–25, 25–50, 50–75, or 75–100 percent) were covered by shade. These indicators were then combined into the reported agroforestry indicators.

[23] This result raises the question whether the expansion into forested areas by the producers was in line with a land sharing practice. However, producers that planted coffee on previously forested areas are evenly divided between those with low, medium, and high rates of shade. We can therefore not draw clear conclusions on this question.

proceeded the least of the three case study countries (McCook 2008). In this context, private sustainability standards – particularly Rainforest Alliance and Fairtrade/organic – can contribute to maintaining higher-cost systems and protect them to a certain extent from intensification pressures. Yet, there is a drop-off when I calculate 'intensive' agroforestry in 'agroforestry gardens' where over half of coffee plants are shaded – here, only 13 percent of Rainforest Alliance farmers and 28 percent of Fairtrade/organic farmers qualify, and almost none of the producers in the other groups.

Rainforest Alliance farmers (46 percent) have significantly higher levels of processing water treatment than their own matched controls (19 percent) or the other groups (13–14 percent). Yet, they are still far away from universal implementation. Almost no UTZ farmers (7 percent) report implementing a wastewater treatment system, although they are required to do so according to the UTZ code. It is likely that the financial costs of installing such relatively capital-intensive systems forestall more widespread adoption, even if farmers are willing to implement such practices. Finally, the Rainforest Alliance requirement of a buffer zone of at least 5 m is linked to significant (although not universal) increases in the distance between the cropland and waterways. Around half of other farmers – certified or noncertified – implement a buffer zone of 5 m or more, while almost all Rainforest Alliance (85 percent) and Fairtrade/organic farmers (100 percent) do so.

In Colombia, land holdings are rather static and few producers report having expanded their land. This may also be due to regional characteristics – I focused my analysis on the *eje cafetero*, the traditional coffee-growing area, which showcased the highest density of certification groups of the country. However, the production frontier – and associated land use problems – tends to be further south (in Nariño) and east (in Tolima), where private sustainability standards are comparatively underrepresented (Grabs *et al.* 2016). Hence, most producers fulfill the certification requirements by default. Tree planting is only practiced by 10–20 percent of farmers, with little additionality shown in certified groups. Agroforestry is almost nonexistent, mainly due to the level of shade cover and the types and diversity of trees used. Only around 50 percent of producers show more than 25 percent shade cover. Furthermore, if shade is used, the main production system is in line with the 'shaded monoculture' model, where banana and plantain trees (and occasionally other fruit trees) provide shade and water reservoirs. While this provides limited farm diversification and is preferable to a sun plantation system in terms of climate change resilience, it does not meet a high standard of biodiversity.

Wastewater treatment significantly increases with certification, from only 1 percent of noncertified producers to 27 percent of Fairtrade farmers (+26 percent over matched controls), 32 percent of C.A.F.E. Practices producers (no significant change), 42 percent of Nespresso AAA farmers (no significant change), and 87 percent of Rainforest Alliance/AAA farmers (+30 percent over matched controls). On the other hand, the Rainforest Alliance/AAA group has the lowest implementation rates of the 5 m minimum buffer zone requirement (73 percent) apart from the Fairtrade group (64 percent). Overall, this requirement is fulfilled at higher levels than in the Honduran sample, with over 60 percent in all cases, and up to 97 percent of producers in the noncertified cooperative, respecting a 5 m buffer.

In Costa Rica, finally, coffee producers have little to no dedicated forest area on their farms. Coffee expansion almost never occurs on forest land, most likely because there was little available forest land in these areas to begin with. Rather, the expansion in Costa Rica is mainly driven by the consolidation of existing coffee farms (in around half of the cases), as well as the reversion of pasture or fallow land into coffee lands. The share of farmers planting trees, in contrast, shows large differences between certification groups, with the Rainforest Alliance/AAA farmers (83 percent) showcasing great dedication and high additionality (+28 percent over matched controls). However, the results are more mixed for the Rainforest Alliance/C.A.F.E. (23 percent) and the C.A.F.E. Practices (36 percent) groups, and the noncertified farmers (58 percent) actually perform better than the Fairtrade group (44 percent).

Regarding agroforestry, the results from Costa Rica mirror those in Colombia. Notably, the noncertified farmers show the greatest share – 12 percent – that have implemented limited agroforestry practices. While over 70 percent of the remaining producers use moderate amounts of shade cover, they tend to implement agronomic best practices such as planting the Poró tree (*Erythrina poeppigiana*), a native species of Costa Rica that is nitrogen-fixing and has been traditionally used in Costa Rican shade systems. Its fast growth allows producers to cut its branches back to the trunk during coffee cherry ripening, when larger amounts of sunlight are beneficial to cherry size and sweetness. In the following months, the tree regenerates and will have established enough foliage to protect the plants during flowering and the emergence of new cherries (field notes, Costa Rican extension agent, 2017). The organic material is frequently used for soil cover, although this does not automatically translate into effective soil protection, since only around 20–50 percent of producers show more than 50 percent soil coverage. It is thus an effective system that harnesses some agroecological co-benefits, but is still strongly biased toward agricultural production optimization and is unlikely to provide habitat for a significant amount of wildlife, especially considering the high amount of agrochemical use (with one single producer reporting to use only organic methods) (Caudill *et al.* 2015). Finally, in Costa Rica, due to the centralized processing infrastructure in Costa Rica, the vast majority of farmers sell their coffee in cherry to the cooperative or private processing mill, and are not affected by the wastewater requirement at the farm level. Independent of rule strictness, river protection is practiced across the board, with most farmers using 10 or 20 m buffer zones according to the collected data.

On balance, private sustainability standards seem to have played only a minor role in the prevention of deforestation in this data set. Of the three country cases, the only case where deforestation is a strong concern in coffee production is Honduras – and there, of the farmers that live in higher altitudes where coffee areas border forest, one-quarter to one-third have expanded their coffee farms onto former forestland. In addition, with the exception of the organic standard, these schemes lead to few changes in producers' land sharing practices that would significantly enhance the biodiversity on coffee plantations. Even the more stringent environmental certification schemes show only limited effectiveness. For instance, in the three case study countries, 43, 1, and 3 percent of Rainforest Alliance producers have diverse agroforestry systems with more than 25 percent shade cover; and 13, 0, and 1 percent implemented agroforestry systems with more than 50 percent shade. These results support the reported view that "anything that is not a critical criterion is subject to an economic cost-benefit analysis" (field notes, Honduran extension agent, 2016), with many producers clearly making the calculus that the implementation of diverse agroforestry is too costly when considering the economic benefit of certification. They also buttress the observation by Solér *et al.* (2017, pp. 239–241), who note that "shade-relevant control points in Rainforest Alliance and UTZ certification are open for interpretation and will harbor a wide range of coffee production systems under shade." Bose *et al.* (2016, p. 950), in turn, describe that "94.36% (n = 142) of [their sample of Indian Rainforest Alliance] certified growers said that neither certified buyers nor auditors had actively encouraged shade-grown coffee during initial and follow-up meetings or inspections." Yet, in line with the Honduran results, there is some evidence that traditional agroforestry systems may be maintained when producers receive sufficient premiums as a compensation for their economic trade-offs (Hardt *et al.* 2015; Haggar *et al.* 2017; Takahashi and Todo 2017).

The protection of aquatic ecosystems, finally, shows large differences between countries, with Costa Rican farmers performing better both thanks to their centralized processing infrastructure and through almost universal good river protection practices. In Colombia, the picture is mixed – buffer zone distances are well implemented, while the implementation of wastewater treatment shows the best results in the strict third-party verification system that the Rainforest Alliance/ AAA group is subject to. In Honduras, the implementation of costly compliance criteria such as wastewater treatment systems is limited, likely due to financial constraints. The protection of river banks is also only partially adopted, with the costly option of leaving 5 m of unused land beside the river implemented at significantly higher levels by the Rainforest Alliance and Fairtrade/organic farmers than the rest. These findings partially support, but also considerably attenuate, the positive results by authors such as Rueda and Lambin (2013), Rueda *et al.* (2014), Philpott *et al.* (2007), and Haggar *et al.* (2015, 2017) on land-use change, and terrestrial and aquatic ecosystem protection in Rainforest Alliance and organic farmers. They further align with Kuit *et al.* (2010, 2013, 2016), who only find marginal change in costly practices in 4C- and UTZ-certified farmers.

Section 5.5 shows that private sustainability standards may be successful in enforcing high-cost practices in very select cases – specifically, when rules are binding, and the economic capacity for compliance is present, but producers had hitherto been faced with few external incentives for compliance. For instance, this is the case for the use of minors on coffee farms in Costa Rica (with the partial exception of the Costa Rican Rainforest Alliance/AAA group), and the installation of wastewater treatment systems in select groups in Colombia and Costa Rica. In cases where state action and outreach has been successful, such as regarding labor standards in Colombia, private sustainability standards do not make a big change. Finally, in cases where high economic barriers or adverse incentives prevent best practices – such as the instances of minimum wage payments in Honduras and Costa Rica, or the prevention of deforestation, use of wastewater treatment systems, and use of child labor in Honduras – certifications have a mixed track record. This aligns with my qualitative fieldwork results, where a recurrent response to the inquiry into the most difficult requirements to fulfill was "to pay minimum salary ... and anything that requires much upfront investment." This was because "without the premium there is no money to make these investments," and frequently the premium is paid out late or at lower levels than anticipated (field notes, Honduran extension agents, 2016). Furthermore, the results on minimum wage payments have shown that while private sustainability standards are a product of globalization, their reliance on national labor legislation in fact reinforce the unequal cost structures that producers face, while relying on equal price premiums as incentives. Hence, the promise of private sustainability standards to function as payments for social and ecosystem services remains unfulfilled.

5.6 Aggregating Individual Behavior to Collective Results

In sum, the current evidence base indicates that market-driven regulatory governance in the coffee sector provides the greatest additionality in productivity improvements (in particular, in the Rainforest Alliance, Nespresso AAA, and Starbucks C.A.F.E. Practices programs), as well as select good agricultural practices. Such practices include IPM, the use of organic inputs, the use of PPE, and the maintenance of preexisting diverse agroforestry systems. Other practices show lower levels of additionality. Notably, these include practices that are dependent on local infrastructure or services (e.g., waste management), have high financial outlays (e.g., building agrochemical sheds or water treatment facilities), or constitute large opportunity costs (paying minimum wages, giving up production surface, refraining from coffee expansion, or reverting from a technified to a diversified agroforestry system). Given these results, what are the likely aggregate effects of market-driven regulatory governance on the sustainability of the coffee sector?

This question requires us to once again carefully examine what institutional goals we are actually evaluating (compare Chapter 3). On the one hand, recent industry-led definitions highlight the need to meet future coffee demand sustainably on existing land. For instance, following the Sustainable Coffee Challenge's Sustainability Framework,

sustainable practices will ensure coffee contributes to economic prosperity and improved well-being for the 25 million coffee growers, workers and their families; by implementing sustainable agricultural practices to improve productivity on the existing 10 million hectares of coffee to sustain supply and enable the sector to meet rising consumption and the growing demand for coffee in a socially and environmentally responsible way; without clearing one additional hectare of high conservation value forest or depleting other natural resources for enhanced coffee production. (SCC 2016, p. 17)

Similar definitions have been proposed by the Global Coffee Platform (GCP 2017a) and the International Coffee Organization (ICO 2017d).

On the other hand, earlier multi-stakeholder efforts established the 2001 Conservation Principles for Coffee Production, which aimed to represent "the foundation of any conservation-based certification program" as well as "guide the development of industry sourcing guidelines and codes of conduct" (Conservation International *et al.* 2001, p. 3). The principles focus on aligning coffee production with biodiversity conservation while improving the social and economic livelihoods of producers and provide economic benefits to local communities. They are reprinted in full in Appendix 3. For the purposes of this section, it is instructive to put emphasis on Principle 2 regarding ecosystem and wildlife conservation. It specifies that

coffee production systems maintain and enhance biological diversity and ecosystem functions on farms and surrounding areas ... Where coffee is grown in areas originally covered by forest, a canopy cover of diverse native tree species that conserves local and endemic biodiversity is incorporated into coffee production systems ... Pruning of shade trees preserves their reproductive processes and protects the habitat they provide for plants and animals ... Coffee farms and surrounding areas create a diverse landscape mosaic that serves as wildlife habitat and migration corridors between protected areas. (Conservation International *et al.* 2001, p. 4)

The principles furthermore include the diversification of farms as a key element that may help them achieve sustainable livelihoods.

We can see that two contrasting visions of the end goal of sustainability in the coffee sector exist. In the first, highly professionalized, productive, and efficient farmers maximize returns on their existing coffee land to meet increasing coffee demand. In the second, coffee becomes part of a diversified agroecosystem that allows for the highest possible conservation of biodiversity hot spots and wildlife habitats while still providing livelihood strategies for local residents. The next sections will examine which of these two possible end goals private sustainability standards are able to meet when aggregating their effects.

Market-Driven Regulatory Governance's Contribution to the End Goal of a Resource-Efficient, Productive Coffee Sector

Aggregating the results of both this study and the existing evidence, it appears that select market-driven regulatory governance programs may indeed assist the sector in becoming more productive. Higher yields compared to uncertified farmers or yield increases after certification are noted in Rainforest Alliance, Starbucks C.A.F.E. Practices, and Nespresso AAA farmers, while the evidence on the impact of Fairtrade, UTZ, and 4C participation on productivity is more equivocal. On the other hand, organic certification is almost always accompanied by yield losses.

To assess the wider-reaching implications of this finding, and translate the relative effect of local yield improvements to the absolute effect on global productivity and output, it is instructive to compare and contrast in which country contexts private sustainability standards are the most likely to be adopted. Table 5.2 has been adapted from the State of Sustainable Markets report 2017 (Lernoud *et al.* 2017) and reports the estimated share of private sustainability standard coverage relative to total national coffee area (FAO 2018) of a selection of coffee-producing countries in 2015. For each standard, only area shares of the ten largest contributing countries are reported. Thus, a blank entry in Table 5.2 signifies the production of insignificant volumes as a relative contribution to the world market. It furthermore uses average yield estimates from 2012 (Neumann 2012) and 2017 (GCP 2017b) by country to calculate the average yield change between 2012 and 2017.

Table 5.2 shows that the largest coffee-producing countries are the ones where verification with 4C is the most widespread, and also significant volumes of UTZ coffee are produced. The top three – Brazil, Colombia, and Vietnam – each show between 30 and 40 percent of their total coffee-growing area that falls under the 4C verification scheme. They are also the

Table 5.2 *Percentage of national coffee area under different certification schemes, average yields, and yield changes.*
Source: Neumann (2012), GCP (2017b), Lernoud et al. (2017), FAO (2018)

Country	4C	Fairtrade	Organic	Rainforest Alliance	UTZ	Average yields (lbs/ha), 2017	Average yield change (%), 2012–2017
			National coffee area (%), 2015				
Brazil	33.34	3.31	–	4.17	6.80	3,580	+11.84
Vietnam	28.19	–	–	–	11.08	5,357	+0.99
Colombia	41.60	26.64	–	4.92	6.24	2,016	+63.88
Costa Rica	–	34.22	–	26.41	–	2,632[24]	–
Honduras	14.04	–	6.00	–	12.81	2,400	−0.31
Indonesia	5.96	–	6.04	1.32	1.34	1,543	+64.29
Kenya	7.03	44.60	–	–	8.31	661	+6.32
Uganda	6.27	16.85	–	–	11.66	1,378	−9.41
Ethiopia	1.78	31.80	22.01	6.68	–	860	−35.63
Peru	17.60	42.18	26.12	9.40	–	1,200	−33.78
Tanzania	1.60	75.34	32.17	8.66	–	990	+82.54

[24] Average yields in 2012.

ones that show some of the highest average yields, as well as significant increases (in the cases of Brazil and Colombia) in recent years, although Colombia's improvements are over low baseline levels due to coffee rust outbreaks in 2012. UTZ certification is further found in emerging coffee origins such as Honduras and Uganda, while Fairtrade certification is more variable and dependent on the underlying institutional framework of coffee-producing countries (especially the traditional role of cooperatives), with significant presence in Colombia, Costa Rica, Peru, Kenya, Ethiopia, and Tanzania. Here, as in the case of the Rainforest Alliance, considerable certification presence spans countries with some of the highest (Colombia, Costa Rica) but also lowest (Ethiopia, Tanzania) average yields, indicating that these certified producers are likely to show considerable heterogeneity while competing in the same certified niche market. Finally, it is also apparent from Table 5.2 that countries with large shares of organically certified coffee-growing area – Ethiopia, Peru, and Tanzania – either showed significant decreases in yields in recent years (in the cases of Ethiopia and Peru) or low yield levels in general (Ethiopia, Tanzania), which may attest to the low-input style of agriculture. On the other hand, whether by circumstance or causal effects, those production origins that showed a significant presence of Rainforest Alliance certification and little organic production (Brazil, Colombia, Indonesia, and Costa Rica) all showed yield increases (Brazil, Colombia, Indonesia) or high yield levels in general (Costa Rica).

Market-Driven Regulatory Governance's Contribution to the End Goal of a Coffee Sector That Protects Biodiversity Hot Spots

We have seen that an alternative institutional end goal of market-driven regulatory governance is to guarantee the strongest possible conservation of biodiversity hot spots and wildlife habitats while still providing livelihood strategies for local residents through the production of cash crops. This would be possible through the protection and expansion of traditional agroforestry systems (Gordon *et al.* 2007; Philpott *et al.* 2007, 2008). However, recent developments show opposite global trends. Jha *et al.* (2014) conclude that from 1990 to 2010, global shade coffee cultivation decreased by 20 percent, continuing the decline of this traditional practice that was introduced with the technification wave of coffee in the 1970s. The authors estimate that in

2012, 41 percent of global coffee area was managed with no shade, 35 percent with sparse shade,[25] and only 24 percent with traditional diverse shade[26] (Jha *et al.* 2014).

Table 5.3 shows that most countries that provide 'sustainably certified' coffee showcase either no presence of traditional diversified shade or have suffered significant decreases in such shade cover from 1990 to 2012. Large decreases and low levels of shade are visible even in countries with a strong presence of Rainforest Alliance certification such as Colombia, Costa Rica, El Salvador, and Guatemala. Relatedly, Bosselman (2012) estimates that between 2000 and 2009 Costa Rican coffee-growing regions in a biological corridor experienced a 50 percent loss of shaded coffee and shade trees in the conversion to sun coffee, pasture, or other crops. Interestingly, in line with the present analysis, Honduras stands out as a country that showcases relatively high and increasing levels of diverse traditional shade. Along with Mexico, it is the only country in which shade has expanded over the period under analysis by Jha *et al.* (2014). While Mexico simultaneously has the largest share of national coffee area covered by organic certification, such certification only accounts for 6 percent of Honduras' area.

Jha *et al.* (2014) highlight the perceived increases in yield from shade reduction and shifting economic incentives in value chains as important explanatory factors that may shift farmers' production decisions. Indeed, when comparing Table 5.3 with Table 5.2 (I preserved the ordering of recurring producing countries), the trade-off of yields and traditional shade is immediately apparent. High-yield countries such as Brazil, Vietnam, and Costa Rica show the lowest shares of diverse shade, while Peru, for instance, with a 90 percent incidence of traditional shade, has much lower average yield levels. The aggregate data confirm the results from Section 5.5 that certification schemes may support the maintenance of traditional shade systems, as in the cases of organic certification in Mexico and Peru. However, they are unable to either provide strong pull incentives for the reestablishment of such systems, or to constitute powerful countervailing factors against the

[25] Sparse shade was defined as coffee plantations with a minimal but existing canopy (1–40 percent cover) and usually one or two species of shade trees (all with fewer than ten species).

[26] Traditional diverse shade was defined as coffee plantations with a closed or nearly closed canopy (more than 40 percent cover) and ten or more species of shade trees.

Table 5.3 *Percentage of national coffee area under different certification schemes and under traditional diverse shade.*
Source: Jha et al. (2014), Lernoud et al. (2017), FAO (2018)

Country	National coffee area (%), 2015					Diverse shade (%), 2012	Change in area under diverse shade (%), 1990–2012
	4C	Fairtrade	Organic	Rainforest Alliance	UTZ		
Brazil	33.34	3.31	–	4.17	6.80	0	–
Vietnam	28.19	–	–	–	11.08	5	–
Colombia	41.60	26.64	–	4.92	6.24	30	–14
Costa Rica	–	34.22	–	26.41	–	0	–
El Salvador	2.39	–	–	14.21	–	24	–76
Guatemala	1.81	–	–	8.50	3.10	40	–17
Honduras	14.04	–	6.00	–	12.81	35	+202
India	1.76	–	–	4.70	–	60	+24
Indonesia	5.96	–	6.04	1.32	1.34	25	–
Kenya	7.03	44.60	–	–	8.31	15	–
Mexico	8.84	17.69	38.03	–	–	30	+198
Nicaragua	2.41	51.48	–	–	18.36	25	–39
Peru	17.60	42.18	26.12	9.40	–	90	–
Tanzania	1.60	75.34	32.17	8.66	–	0	–

policies of national coffee institutions who prioritize technification and yield increases.

While this is merely a correlative analysis of standard adoption and yield changes, it points to a salient dilemma. As different standards, with different underlying production systems, become widespread in coffee-producing countries, those standards that underpin and support yield increases – in line with the industry-driven goal of a productive coffee sector – are both targeted at high-yielding origins and support their frontrunner status. Ironically, standards that are not in line with the productivist mind-set may contribute to the marginalization of production origins in the world coffee market, with decreasing relative volumes of such coffees making up the grand total of world consumption. These self-reinforcing dynamics through private sustainability standards may thus contribute to, rather than forestall, the growing concentration of production origins (Verma 2015) and intensification of global production (Jha *et al.* 2014). However, excess reliance on few origins threatens the resilience of the market against climate and currency shocks. This trend thus decreases the overall sustainability of the mainstream market in the long run while nominally contributing to the support of high-yielding, productive origins.

In the definitional debate surrounding 'sustainable coffee', the advocates of a land sparing/sustainable intensification approach seem to have gained the upper hand. Although highlighted as one major aspect of sustainable coffee in the early 2000s, shade production is no longer a defining characteristic of any mainstream certification, making it difficult for conscious consumers in the marketplace to support the production of coffee under agroforestry conditions. On the one hand, this is motivated by the recognition that the ecological conditions of coffee producers around the world are diverse, and that in certain regions (e.g., high-altitude locations with heavy cloud cover, or areas such as the Brazilian *Cerrado* that did not have native forest cover) the use of shade may negatively affect production potential. On the other hand, agroforestry methods have very positive impacts on biodiversity and habitat protection, as well as on farm resilience to climate change and the equilibration of production potential between years. Many overviews of private sustainability standards highlight the loss of shaded coffee and biodiversity in coffee-growing regions as one of the main *raisons d'être* of sustainability standards (Caudill *et al.* 2015; Lernoud *et al.* 2017). It is thus striking that none of the competing standards sees the promotion of shade production as a central part of their mission. In consequence, coffee produced under the rules of market-driven regulatory governance mirrors the traditional production conditions in each origin country (with more traditional shade methods in Honduras, technified shade in Costa Rica, and a mix of technified shade and sun production in Colombia). Few institutional incentives are in place to maintain or reproduce diversified agroforestry systems, even as shade production methods continue to decline around the world (Jha *et al.* 2014). Here, the aggregation of individuals changed by market-driven regulatory governance does not lead to significantly different results than would likely exist in the absence of these programs.

The use of aggregate figures such as these has considerable limitations. To name a few, the average yield data do not come from the same source and were not elaborated with the same methodology, they do not compare the same farmers, and do not control for other variables. Still, the aggregate effect of the introduction of private sustainability standards on the establishment of a productive, resource-efficient, and resilient coffee sector is equivocal, particularly when other country-level institutional characteristics and market dynamics are considered.

Overall, the empirical results of Chapter 5, when seen from this bird's eye perspective, suggest that the effectiveness of certification schemes on changing the sustainability of the coffee sector is limited and needs to be appraised in a differentiated fashion. The next chapter will hone in on aspects of institutional design, fit, and on-the-ground regulatory enforcement strategies to draw out lessons learned on the appropriateness, successes, and drawbacks of different certification schemes' institutional choices.

6 | *Designing Effective Private Institutions*

Certification is being adapted to becoming more of a developmental tool, where non-compliance results in support rather than exclusion ... Rather than an in-out certification, it is seen as being a continuous improvement, learning approach to certification, which is highly embraced by the sector.

(Karin Kreider, Executive Director of the ISEAL
Alliance [ISEAL 2016, 33:00])

If private regulatory governance is to change producers' behavior in the long-term, private regulatory institutions need to be incentive-compatible. This means that regulatory design choices and incentives need to be aligned with boundedly rational microeconomic behavior. As explained in Chapter 2, standard-setters face a design dilemma between regulatory stringency and inclusivity in this regard. On the one hand, institutional rational choice insights on shirking, freeriding, and the danger of underregulation favor precise, objective, and universally applicable rules, such as 'zero tolerance' requirements that differentiate a certain category of goods from others. On the other, the socio-legal literature cautions that too strict rule-setting or enforcement can lead to regulatory unreasonableness, the drop-out of producers from voluntary standards, and suboptimal social outcomes. In such cases, implementing compliance management, rather than compliance enforcement, may result in greater goal attainment and additionality (Bardach and Kagan 1982; Auld *et al.* 2015).

This chapter aims to tease out which approach is more promising in the case of the coffee sector. In a first step, it presents the overall regulatory system put into place by private sustainability standards, as well as how they employ third-party auditors to enforce their rules. It furthermore examines auditors' enforcement attitudes on the ground, which in public policy may range from a strict rule-bound attitude to a persuasive, educating role (Bardach and Kagan 1982; Hawkins 1984). In a second step, it draws on the data presented in Chapter 5 to test whether these choices make a difference for promoting additionality on the ground.

6.1 The Institutional Design Choices of Coffee Standards

Chapter 4 has already covered institutional design choices regarding premium enforcement, showing that the Fairtrade and Fairtrade/organic systems are the only ones that explicitly regulate premium payment and size, while all other standards rely on market-based incentives. This section investigates in greater detail how standards chose to design their rules and compliance enforcement mechanisms.

Stringency versus Inclusivity in Standard-Setting: In-group/Out-group Differentiation versus Continuous Improvement

In a first step, we can roughly distinguish private sustainability standards in coffee that pursue an in-group/out-group approach, aligned with the rationale of protecting significant economic benefits for in-group members, and those that pursue a strategy of continuous improvement, aligned more with the socio-legal insights of incremental compliance management.

Of the standards analyzed in this study, two are mainly in-group/out-group differentiators: the Rainforest Alliance (on the basis of the 2010 Sustainable Agriculture Network [SAN] Sustainable Agriculture Standard)[1] and the organic standard. In the 2010 Rainforest Alliance standard structure, producers had to meet twenty binding criteria as well as 80 percent of the rest of the criteria.[2] This was often prohibitively

---

[1] The 2010 SAN Sustainable Agriculture Standard and 2011 SAN Group Certification Standard were the binding standards at the time of the farm samples and will be the standards principally discussed here. However, as will be explored, in 2017, the Rainforest Alliance published a new standard, based on continuous improvement and binding as of July 1, 2017, in preparation for their merger with UTZ that was announced in June 2017 and legally completed in January 2018. It thus no longer pursues an in-group/out-group differentiation approach.

[2] Due to widespread discontent with the 'one farm fails, the whole group fails' rule in the 2004 group standard, the 2011 group standard loosened this requirement. Instead, it instituted the following rule: "of groups with a size of 17 or more group members, maximum 20% of the sampled farms may score less than 80% of the Sustainable Agriculture Standard but equal or higher than 70%, only if they show full compliance with all its critical criteria" (SAN 2011, p. 7).

difficult for entry-level farmers, as voices from Honduran extension agents depict. One noted that "for 4C, it is easier to get farmers up to the standard thanks to the step by step process; with Rainforest Alliance in turn it is hard to get them to score more than 80 points in the first year of certification." Another explained that "Rainforest Alliance also has a good demand but a low supply because it is so difficult to implement" (field notes, Honduran extension agents, 2016).

The 80 percent criterion leaves some leeway for individual calculations on the trade-off between indicators, which farms keenly exploit. As one exporter described, "anything that is not a critical criterion is subject to an economic cost-benefit analysis: how many points can I sacrifice and still get 80 overall. For example, in Brazil it is almost impossible to have shade cover on mechanized farms, but the recommended 40% shade cover is not a critical criterion, so they give up those points" (interview 21, Honduran exporter 1, 2016). This comment also shows the limits of creating a uniform standard in a globalized market – here, as in the mainstream commodity market, Central American farmers with 5 ha of land on steep slopes again end up competing with industrialized Brazilian farms that may span thousands of hectares.[3]

Organic standards, in turn, also apply a strict in-group/out-group differentiation approach, although on a narrower set of indicators. Here, the binding criterion is the renunciation of any synthetic fertilizers and pesticides, which in practice necessitates far-reaching changes in farm management toward the adoption of integrated pest management (IPM) and other best practices.

On the other hand, in recent years, all standards with the exception of organic certification have moved toward a continuous improvement approach. This approach has been the preferred approach by UTZ and 4C from the beginning. The 2014 UTZ Core Code for Group Certification, for instance, specifies 60 mandatory requirements for year 1 of the certification, increasing to 113 requirements in year 4. The 4C standard uses a traffic light system and moves from less to more stringent enforcement criteria of prohibited

---

[3] We can note that this challenge had been the main rationale for Fairtrade International (FLO) to remain adamant about only allowing smallholder farmer cooperatives to access their standard. Yet, with the split of Fair Trade USA, this differentiating criterion is likely to be watered down, at least in the US market (Renard and Loconto 2013; Jaffee and Howard 2016).

practices over subsequent audits. Fairtrade International (FLO) also adopted this model when it added more individual-level compliance indicators regarding environmental and social practices to their scheme. In the latest development, the 2017 Rainforest Alliance standard moved from a compliance to a continuous improvement framework. It did so in order to "combine . . . a very high level and ambitious standard covering human rights, environmental, and production issues with a scaled implementation approach designed to make it more accessible to the many farmers in the world who are still in the early steps in their journey towards sustainability" (Sustainable Brands 2016).

While the adoption of continuous improvement strategies may have opened access for certification to more producers, the shift in regulatory strategy is likely to have adversely affected the benefits they draw from it. By setting up continuous improvement guidelines, certification organizations created much more diffuse entrance barriers, allowing entry-level (first year) producers to access the same in-group (and, therefore, market for certified products) as more advanced producers that are held to higher standards. This may have contributed to the erosion of price premiums shown in Chapter 4, undermining the incentive structure market-driven governance – according to a logic of control – is based on. In such cases, cooperative – or conciliatory – compliance management (based, for instance, on learning and capacity building) may still be an option (Chayes and Chayes 1995; Downs *et al.* 1996; Young 2011; Bernstein and Cashore 2012). However, as noted by Gunningham and Grabowsky (1998), learning and capacity-building may only persuade producers to adapt win-win practices, and it will be much harder to convince them of practices that represent economic trade-offs and win-lose scenarios.

Finally, the Starbucks C.A.F.E. Practices and Nespresso AAA models have a further distinction. Due to their use as a sourcing management tool, all coffee sold within the model needs to attain minimum quality scores, as evaluated upon delivery. Successful farmers also need to adhere to a limited number of critical requirements, but, thereafter, all further progress is measured in a scoring system where certain points can be awarded in each sustainability category. Many practices are treated cumulatively, where several possible levels of compliance are defined that are each assigned points. Farmers that score beyond a given threshold[4] are given preferential supplier status; but no farmer that complies with the critical criteria is excluded from the scheme neither in the short nor in the long run.

Stringency versus Inclusivity in Enforcement: Certification Body Oversight

The different private sustainability standards also use different strategies to enforce their standards in the field. These can again be roughly divided into those that emphasize stringency or a logic of control, by keeping close oversight over their certification body or requiring third-party accreditation for control bodies, and those that emphasize inclusivity and low-cost mainstreaming, which allow for proxy accreditation or desk oversight of certification bodies in the field.

The organic standards, the Rainforest Alliance, and FLO use the strategy of *accreditation*. It means that certification bodies that make audit decisions have been evaluated on their processes and competencies regarding the relevant standard by national or international accreditation bodies. Certification bodies carrying out audits for the Rainforest Alliance certification, for instance, "must hold a valid ISO 17065:2012 accreditation. Further on, compliance with Rainforest Alliance's additional protocols is required, including but not limited to requirements on audit protocols, auditor competence, and data systems" (Rainforest Alliance 2017b). In 2017, ten certification bodies worldwide were authorized by the Rainforest Alliance, including its own associated RA-Cert. In a possible conflict of interest, RA-Cert provides the Rainforest Alliance standard-setting organization with 23 percent of its revenue from certification fees (Rainforest Alliance 2018b). For organic standards, providing a comprehensive overview is more complex as there exist a multitude of national and private organic standards; however, the procedure is the same. FLO is the only entity that has a strict policy to only allow their own certification body – FLOCERT, which is also ISO 17065 accredited – to administer audits.

---

[4] C.A.F.E. Practices suppliers need to achieve ≥60 percent in each of three categories for preferred and ≥80 percent for strategic partner status. Nespresso AAA suppliers need to achieve ≥33 percent of all criteria for the 'emerging', ≥66 percent for 'high performing', and ≥80 percent of all criteria plus ≥50 percent in each of ten principles for a 'certified' status, in which case they become Rainforest Alliance certified.

This private limited company is an independently governed subsidiary of the nonprofit standard-setter FLO (FLOCERT 2018).

The ISO 17065 standard is an accreditation specifying requirements for any organization that certifies products, processes, and services. It is solely procedural in nature and focuses on issues such as impartiality, liability, financing, confidentiality, and nondiscrimination (ISO 2012). Certification bodies that wish to certify a certain standard apply to accreditation bodies (such as International Organic Accreditation Service [IOAS], Assurance Services International [ASI], or national accreditation bodies) and specify the standard (i.e., organic or the Rainforest Alliance) that they are applying for. Subsequently, they are evaluated both on their procedural capacity (as specified by ISO 17065) as well as their competence and substantive knowledge of the particular product sector and standard. ISO 17065 accreditation is usually limited to the scope of the standard in question – for instance, a certification body would be accredited under ISO 17065 to carry out organic audits (interview 63, ASI, 2017).

In turn, UTZ and 4C use *proxy accreditation*, which means that they accept certification bodies that are accredited with ISO 17065 under other related agricultural standards such as organic or GlobalGAP (since the combination of ISO 17065 + UTZ or ISO 17065 + 4C is not possible). They then approve certification body applications following a desk review of their compliance with additional standard-specific requirements. This leads UTZ to work with nearly sixty UTZ-approved certification bodies, and 4C (through the private assurance service provider Coffee Assurance Services) to work with twenty-five approved verifiers (CAS 2018b; UTZ Certified 2018b).

In the field, proxy accreditation procedures appear to lead to greater competition between certification bodies. This is appreciated by producers, as the following quote from Costa Rica demonstrates: "Verification is often very expensive, particularly if there is no free market for auditing bodies to compete. For instance, for UTZ, auditing bodies such as Mayacert can make competitive offers (US$1,800 for an audit), whereas in monopoly situations like Fairtrade or Rainforest Alliance [where only one certification body is operating in Costa Rica] you need to pay $6,000" (interview 16, Costa Rican processor 2, 2015). However, the strategy of proxy accreditation was seen critically by staff of accreditation bodies, who doubted that quality and competence can be assured to the same extent. They further observed that "in markets where many certification bodies compete, the competitive pressure increases and audits become shorter and shorter" (interview 63, ASI, 2017). Furthermore, they highlighted that proxy accreditation does not allow for an independent third-party verification of substantive knowledge of the standards in question, given that the accreditation had been provided for a different standard (e.g., organic or GlobalGAP) (interview 63, ASI, 2017). On the other hand, the in-house desk review for some standards such as UTZ requires evidence of training sessions or other capacity-building measures.

Starbucks' C.A.F.E. Practices program is administered by the evaluation, certification, and auditing firm Scientific Certification Systems Global Services (SCS). SCS then trains and approves third-party organizations that verify suppliers participating in C.A.F.E. Practices. The verification organization approval procedure resembles proxy accreditation in that SCS directly reviews applications of verification organizations who wish to evaluate C.A.F.E. Practices suppliers. However, no accreditation with any other standard is required as a qualification requirement (SCS 2017). Finally, Nespresso's AAA program, using a continuous improvement methodology, initially does not use third-party audits at all, but is implemented by agronomists hired by Nespresso who apply their 'Tool for the Assessment of Sustainable Quality' (TASQ). This TASQ checklist is first applied once in its entirety to each farmer that enters the program. Thereafter, a simplified version is used to assist farmers in improving the insufficient areas in a step-by-step process. Nespresso AAA is thus the only standard scheme that puts 'boots on the ground' as a central part of its theory of change. In 2012, 25 Nespresso AAA clusters in 8 countries included a total of 52,854 farmers, for which 214 agronomists were responsible (thereby, one agronomist for around 250 farmers) (Nestlé-Nespresso 2013). As a last step, farmers can attain Rainforest Alliance certification, at which point they are first internally reviewed by so-called cluster administrators before Rainforest Alliance auditors verify the provided information.

Stringency versus Inclusivity in Enforcement: Auditor Behavior

While all private sustainability standards highlight the importance of auditors to be impartial, professional and to act with integrity, few specify how much discretion auditors have in making their certification decisions, or which attitude to adopt during the auditing process. One exception is UTZ, which in its 'Guidance Documents on Good Auditing Practices' notes that "there are situations or documents that may be not exactly matching the requirement of the UTZ Code, but are respecting the spirit and the goal of such requirement." It recommends that auditors should "be flexible and open-minded" and "mind the principles of every block in the UTZ Code of Conduct" (UTZ Certified 2017, p. 9). Similarly, with the exception of the critical criteria, during the Rainforest Alliance audits, "auditors may evaluate if specific elements are applicable or not and may adjust scoring accordingly" for every single criterion (SAN 2010, p. 9), delegating considerable responsibility to the auditors.

In accordance with the ISO 17065 standard, the instructions to auditors by the Rainforest Alliance, Starbucks C.A.F.E. Practices, and 4C highlight the need to refrain from providing technical assistance or consultancy services to current or potential certified clients to avoid conflicts of interest. For instance, Starbucks C.A.F.E. Practices is clear that "it is not possible to give any recommendations or consulting with respect to compliance with program requirements" (SCS 2017, p. 32). Similarly, the Rainforest Alliance notes that during the auditing process, "information offered regarding the interpretation of or compliance with the Sustainable Agriculture Standard should be general in nature and not specific to a client's audit findings" (Rainforest Alliance 2015, p. 7). This forecloses the possibility of the auditor helping their clients toward compliance in a more cooperative approach (cf. Braithwaite 1985; Hawkins 1984). On the other hand, it then mentions that "examples of good practices related to the standard, including photographs and descriptions of other clients' compliance efforts, are permitted if presented as examples and not as a recommendation for compliance" (Rainforest Alliance 2015, p. 7) – blurring the line of acceptable regulatory behavior again.

In practice, farmer organization representatives report that both 'legalistic' and more 'reasonable' auditors exist in the field, and that they tend to interpret rules differently. For instance, when enforcing the buffer zones to protect water bodies from pollution, in Honduras, extension agents recounted that "some auditors say it's fine to plant close to the river if you plant living fences and only use organic methods close to the river, while others insist on the 5 meter gap between the edge of the river and planting" (field notes, Honduran extension agents, 2016). Field staff also reported that from their observations, newer auditors and consultants are stricter and apply the standard more to the letter (taking the 'official perspective') than more experienced auditors (who tend to take 'the civilian perspective'). This aligns with the observations of public regulatory enforcement by Hawkins (1984, pp. 40–41) and Bardach and Kagan (1982, p. 129), who note that in their case studies, "officials who had less training were more befuddled by the complexities of the entities they regulate, more legalistic, and more inclined to 'hide behind the code' than more highly trained professional officials; the latter were more likely to espouse a substantive law enforcement style, being attentive to ultimate purpose and conflicting values." Since extension agents knew the rotation of auditors from experience, they could subtly gear their audit toward a more favorable (or 'reasonable' outcome) by virtue of their timing, as this off-hand comment demonstrates: "let's do the audits in July, there are less consultants around then. I don't want to get the lady XY [who had been perceived as unreasonable in the past]" (field notes, Honduran extension agents, 2016).

Farmer representatives also perceived notable differences between standards in the way auditors balanced stringency and inclusivity. One certification coordinator in a Costa Rican processor, who had eighteen years of experience of working with certifications, noted that

the Rainforest Alliance is very expensive, rigid and at times illogical in its specificity, for example when asking for the identification of biological corridors on farms, or different requirements for trees depending on the slope. They do not differentiate between big farms, where these standards make sense, and small ones where they really don't. The Starbucks C.A.F.E. Practices auditor came with a ridiculously large folder of checklists. UTZ used to be the best and most practical, since it was formulated by agronomists and producers in Central America, but they complicated it as well.

In his perspective,

there are just some impossible things – such as having 100% mandatory attendance at meetings when there are old and sick producers that need to send deputies – that can make it impossible to implement the standard to the book. Or the fact that each standard asks for exclusive capacity-building workshops when it would be much more efficient to just do one. The way it is, they are not sustainable. They should coordinate their demands and construct a generic, ISO-type approach. (Interview 16, Costa Rican processor 2, 2015)

Similarly, in a different Costa Rican cooperative, the rigidity of certification requirements were perceived by field staff as "ridiculous" and "not what producers want or need." Standards' tendency to introduce "unfeasible" requirements without giving room for alternatives or meaningful consultation with producers was portrayed as "cultural imperialism" that caused this cooperative to create their own certification model as an alternative (interview 57, Costa Rican cooperative 3, 2017).

The Strategies of Surrogate Enforcers

When examining the enforcement model of market-driven regulatory governance in detail, we can take note of a further complication: in an effort to make certification more accessible, most agricultural standards provide opportunities for the collective certification of groups of smallholder farmers in addition to single-farm certification. This model of group certification was implemented in all analyzed cases in this book. In this case, group members' actions will reflect back on each other and their collective 'sustainable' reputation, and there is a strong need for within-group collaboration and collective action to maintain the access to sustainable markets for all (Rivera *et al.* 2017). In group certifications, farm-level audits are only implemented in a subsample of the entire certified group. For most schemes, the appropriate sample size (which can be adapted subject to risk assessment) is defined as the square root of the number of group members (4C is a notable exception, requiring only 50 percent of the square root). This means that in a certified group of 100 farmers, 90 percent of farmers will not be surveyed by a third-party certification body at the moment of the audit. In a group of 1,000 farmers, only 32 individuals –3 percent of farmers – will be audited. For this reason, 'internal management schemes' become essential for compliance enforcement, and group administrators – cooperatives, traders, nonprofit organizations, and so on – and their field staff assume important regulatory roles, functioning de facto as "surrogate enforcers" (cf. Gunningham and Grabosky 1998) of the standard in their producer group in preparation of the audit. The vast majority of certification group administrators pursue an internal 'pre-audit' that is used to define the final scope (i.e., the identities of the producers) that will apply for the audit. Subsequently, they are responsible for assuring that producers meet their certification responsibilities lest the entire group lose its certification.[5] Many certification schemes explicitly mention this delegation of enforcement responsibility. The Rainforest Alliance, for instance, notes that "the group scheme is based on *delegating* to an Administrator the responsibility of evaluating 100% of the members. For this reason, only a sample of the farms is evaluated ... Therefore, within the SAN group certification framework, evaluation of compliance with the Sustainable Agriculture Standard by each group member farm is the responsibility of the group administrator" and the internal inspection of all group member farms is mandatory for group certification (SAN 2013, p. 5)

Here, a version of the regulatory dilemma between stringency and inclusivity plays out at a lower level. Group administrators want to keep as many farmers in the certification group as possible, but any one farmer that is violating critical requirements jeopardizes the certification status of the entire group. The experiences of one Costa Rican agronomist showcase that in this case, cooperative compliance enforcement focused on an effective and context-appropriate translation of rules-in-the-book to rules-in-practices is frequently the most successful strategy. When asked about her approach to rule enforcement, she underlined the importance of being very delicate and respectful in trying to reform practices that have possibly been passed down from generations. She also highlighted that creativity is often key to encouraging low-cost compliance with the Rainforest Alliance requirements (i.e., using an old barrel, fridge, or washing machine as a storage unit for agrochemicals), since the necessity for high-cost investments will often deter compliance. Additionally, both she and another agronomist mentioned the need to work closely with each farmer's production circumstances, including within their financial means and educational levels (field notes, Costa Rican agronomist, 2015). Such a customized approach, however, presupposes a high requirement of human resources and organizational capacity that needs to be financed somehow – which in the market context is frequently only possible through the price premium.

---

[5] However, some schemes may also be amenable to exceptions in this realm. During field work in Honduras, group administrators noted that "according to the 2011 standard, if producers fail the audit, group administrators can ask for a change of scope, excluding the failures" (field notes, 2016).

On the other hand, in some cases, agronomists also use the 'stick' of the external authority of the certification and its audits to cajole farmers into complying with practices that may be beneficial to them at least in the long term. For instance, one cooperative representative explained that while audits were first seen as cumbersome, they turned out to be a useful way to be shown ways of improvement and were perceived to get easier from year to year. He highlighted that "producers are incentivized to improve their practices through external audits, much more than if cooperative members just give them advice" (field notes, Honduran cooperative, 2016). Similarly, other group coordinators mentioned their satisfaction with certification schemes because it could be used as a tool that made recommendations enforceable and, despite being a voluntary scheme, brings accountability and allows for check-ins of technicians (field notes, Honduran extension agent, 2016). The simple label of 'private regulation' thus belies a complex array of regulatory strategies at multiple levels of the supply chain.

6.2 The Importance of Rule Knowledge

Reflecting on the results presented in Chapter 5, we have found many instances where farmers certified according to private sustainability standards do not show 100 percent compliance even with critical (i.e., nonnegotiable) indicators. Why could this be? Is this due to regulations being impractical, unachievable, or poorly translated into the field? Before turning to rule formulation and stringency, we need to examine one first possibility: maybe farmers in this sample, which are all listed as members of certification groups according to official documents, do not actually realize that they are certified – and have little knowledge of the rules that they are supposed to comply with. This corresponds to Ostrom's *rule cognizance*; that is, whether the rules-in-form specified in standard documents were effectively translated into rules-in-practice recognized and accepted by regulated farmers. The possibility that farmers are confused about their certification group membership is understandable if we remind ourselves of the challenges of producers as boundedly rational actors. Especially in the complex production environment of small-scale farmers, certification is only one of many factors they need to keep in mind, with others including weather, price volatility, pest and disease outbreaks, local input price changes, and exchange rate movements. When deciding where to focus their limited attention and efforts, it might make sense for producers to simply participate in any program offered to them without paying close attention to its name or formal requirements. This, however, may lead to imperfect transmission of rules-in-form into rules-in-practice, and suboptimal implementation results.

Indeed, many farmers in this data set were unable to accurately report which certification schemes they were participating in. The highest shares of accurate responses were found in the Honduran Rainforest Alliance group (78 percent), the Colombian Nespresso AAA group (76 percent), and the Costa Rican Fairtrade farmers (72 percent); on the other side, as few as 7 percent of Honduran UTZ farmers and 3 percent of Colombian 4C farmers self-categorized accurately into the correct certification group. This state of affairs is understandable if certification is considered a low-priority item – 'one more thing' – that boundedly rational farmers with limited cognitive resources have to pay attention to. In many rural settings, a multiplicity of development projects, quality standards, and certification schemes are underway simultaneously (Valkila and Nygren 2010). This reality emerged in qualitative interviews as well, with one Costa Rican mill owner who implements a number of sustainability standards reporting that

the farmers do not come to my door saying 'I want to be Rainforest Alliance-certified. What can you do about it?' For them, it's 'another one? Alright, you take care of filling out the paperwork.' So what I do I fill out? ... We [as processors] need to provide the personal protection equipment, we need to help to make sure they are not keeping insecticides next to the house, we need to do everything. Because it's us [the mill] that loses the certification. (Interview 7, Costa Rican processor 1, 2015)

Yet, this situation simultaneously distances farmers from the private regulatory institution they are purportedly governed by. Considering the low average levels of literacy and education particularly of Honduran and Colombian farmers, it is likely that a majority of these smallholder farmers have never seen the rules-in-form in the form of the standard documents. They are thus reliant on intermediaries – cooperative managers, extension agents, auditors, nongovernmental organization actors, or others – to translate and disseminate the appropriate and applicable rules to them, which may result in losses of information and accuracy.

Although few quantitative studies in the literature to date consider rule cognizance, similar results have been observed in other settings.

Snider *et al.* (2017) find in a Costa Rican survey that only 17 percent of farmers interviewed from cooperatives with collective C.A.F.E. Practices certification – including one of the cooperatives in the present survey – had knowledge of the certification. They find higher recognition of the Fairtrade certification, with 51 percent of farmers being familiar with it, although they did not test specific knowledge of rules related to the certification. This mirrors my results in Honduras and Costa Rica, although not in Colombia, where only 35 percent of Fairtrade farmers correctly self-identified. Similarly, Valkila and Nygren (2010, p. 328) observe that most of the members of the Nicaraguan Fair Trade cooperatives they investigated "demonstrated a relatively poor understanding of what Fair Trade is, not to mention the civic conventions included. At best, they knew that their cooperative was selling coffee to Fair Trade markets; however, most were unaware of the rights and responsibilities that this entailed." This ignorance was mirrored in "limited awareness of the rules set by Fair Trade regarding working conditions on coffee farms" (Valkila and Nygren 2010, pp. 330–331).

Can the lack of rule cognizance explain the limited compliance outcomes, indicating that certification organizations and implementing agents should focus their efforts on greater awareness-raising and training efforts regarding the responsibilities of participating farmers? To understand this question, I test whether certification cognizance – as measured by the proxy of correct self-identification – has a significant effect on rule compliance. I applied within-group t-tests for five indicators that are binding for certification compliance with most private standards: minimum wage payments; respect for the minimum working age; the use of complete protection equipment; guaranteeing potable drinking water; and the prevention of deforestation.

The Honduran sample shows vast differences in the knowledge surrounding certifications. The Rainforest Alliance and Fairtrade groups show between 71 and 87 percent of correct self-identification, the 4C group drops down to 64 percent, and the UTZ group stands out with only 7 percent of farmers that were cognizant of the fact of belonging to the UTZ certification scheme. As noted, it is of course possible that they have participated in trainings and follow best practices without associating it to the UTZ label per se. However, this result shows that the concept of certification – and associated private rule implementation and enforcement – might be more complex in the field than on paper. Certification cognizance is significantly correlated with lower shares of producers that hire minors and those that make efforts to have access to potable water on the farm. Slight increases – although mostly nonsignificant – are also visible among producers that use complete protection equipment. On the other hand, the indicators regarding minimum wage payment and forest replacement are mainly unaffected. This may be due to their higher economic opportunity cost and direct link to farm profitability; conversely, installing a water filter or turning away 10-year-old job seekers may be less central to the business case.

Colombian farmers on average showed lower likelihoods of correctly self-identifying which certification group they were a part of than their Honduran counterparts. While 76 percent knew that they were Nespresso AAA certified, only 58 percent of Rainforest Alliance/AAA, 35 percent of Fairtrade, 11 percent of C.A.F.E. Practices, and 3 percent of 4C producers correctly reported their certification status. This may be due to the stronger presence of cooperative-level and Federación Nacional de Cafeteros de Colombia (FNC) outreach, which initiate a multitude of programs of which certifications are only a small part. Yet, in the Colombian case, farmers are responsible for selling their coffee into particular marketing channels according to the correct certification, especially if a cooperative has several certification groups. Thus, not knowing which certification group one participates in can lead to losses of potential earnings at the time of sale if a farmer chooses to sell his coffee into the mainstream market instead.

When reviewing compliance results by certification cognizance, the only affected variable is the share of producers using complete protection equipment, which is noticeably higher through the board and significantly higher in Nespresso AAA and Fairtrade farmers who self-identify correctly as certified farmers.[6] On the other hand, minimum wage payments and the hiring of minors are universally complied with. It is likely that compliance is due to underlying national or regional institutional characteristics, rather than the private regulation per se. Potable drinking water and forest replacement, finally, show inconclusive associations

---

[6] It should be noted that this variable is subject to desirability bias since we asked farmers to report their behavior; thus, if they know they should be using full protection because they know the standards' rules, these responses may represent either specific rule cognizance or rule compliance. Nevertheless, there is a significant difference in response behavior.

with certification cognizance. However, it can be noted that the highest shares of farmers deforesting land to replace it with coffee occurs among farmers that did not self-identify correctly.

Finally, in Costa Rica, similar to the Colombian sample, around half of the members of higher-quality groups report the correct self-identification in that group when prompted, with higher levels of self-identification in the Fairtrade and noncertified groups. However, there is very little correlation between certification cognizance and rule compliance. As in Colombia, most compliance behavior – no deforestation, the availability of potable water, and no hiring of minors – occurs universally in all farmer groups independently of their knowledge of being governed by an additional private regulatory institution. In cases where universal compliance is not present – minimum wage payments and the use of complete protection equipment – the knowledge of being certified only makes a difference in the Rainforest Alliance/C.A.F.E. group. All others behave equally, with Rainforest Alliance/AAA farmers even showing lower rates of personal protection equipment (PPE) use and fewer C.A.F.E. Practices farmers paying minimum wages if they correctly self-identified their own certification. Here, as in the case of Honduras, it is possible that the economic ability of farmers limits their capacity to comply with additional rules.

While the majority of producers that are subject to private sustainability standards recognize their new status, a significant minority (and, in some certification groups, even most) are unaware of their participation in a certification scheme or confused about which scheme – out of a multiplicity of on-the-ground initiatives – applies to them. Of the limited criteria in certification standards that are nonnegotiable, complete compliance only occurs in situations where the underlying institutional characteristics ensure that all producers – independent of certification scheme – are compliant. If this is not the case, the data show limited compliance, heightened in some but not all cases by rule knowledge, which may be a result either of misunderstanding the requirement, being unwilling to comply, or lacking the financial capacity to do so. Given the greater disconnect between certification cognizance and compliance in cases that constitute high economic opportunity costs, such as paying local minimum wages or expanding coffee production on forestland, it is likely that economic factors play an important role. This will be more formally tested in the next sections.

This section has also shown that changes in nonnegotiable rules *may* affect the strategies that individuals adopt in the cases of behavioral change such as the hiring of minors in Honduras and the use of PPE in Colombia, but that such change is not self-evident. In the next steps, I probe deeper into such institutional design choices and their impact on *outcome additionality* (defined as the difference in behavior between similar certified and noncertified farmers) as my main dependent variable.

6.3 A Meta-analysis of Outcome Additionality

The overview of regulatory design choices in Section 6.1 shows that private sustainability standards are moving increasingly toward more flexible standard-setting and enforcement. Thinking back to the individual requirements introduced in Chapter 5, we can note that it is often those requirements likely to constitute the greatest costs, but also provide the highest ecosystem services – for instance, maintaining on-farm biodiversity, protecting aquatic ecosystems, or safeguarding and connecting conservation landscapes – which are worded and interpreted in the most flexible ways. For instance, they may become part of continuous improvement strategies, show fluid rule interpretation such as the high conservation value concept or the required width of buffer zones, or be phased out completely from private regulation (e.g., the shade coffee requirement). Is this shift in standard-setting something we need to worry about? How much does the stringency of private regulation influence the outcome additionality of market-driven governance?

To answer this question, and test the other hypotheses regarding the impact of different standard design choices specified in Section 2.3, I draw on the results of thirty-two outcome indicators that were presented in Chapter 5. Made up of fifteen socially sustainable practices and seventeen environmentally friendly practices, they are represented in Table 6.1. I further separate them into Tier I, II, and III indicators in line with the explanations in Section 3.5.

For each indicator, I drew on the propensity score matching results of the treatment effect on the treated and calculated the standardized effect size (Cohen's d) of certification for each of the fourteen certification groups under analysis (five groups each in Honduras and Colombia, four in Costa Rica). The standardized effect size is a measure often used

Table 6.1 *Production practices used for meta-analysis*

		Socially sustainable production practices		Environmentally sustainable production practices
Tier I	1	Productivity (in 100 lbs/ha) (as livelihood improvement strategy)	16	Use of organic fertilizer
			17	Synthetic fertilizer efficiency improvement (in bags/100 lbs)
			18	Use of traps for pests (e.g., the coffee berry borer) as IPM method
			19	Collection of cherries postharvest as IPM method
			20	Pesticide efficiency improvement (in liters/100 lbs)
Tier II	2	Elimination of use of highly hazardous pesticides	21	Elimination of the use of herbicides
	3	Elimination of open-air burning of household waste	22	On-farm trash collection
	4	Safe pesticide container disposal	23	Over 50 percent of soil covered with cover crops or mulch
	5	Use of complete PPE	24	Use of erosion barriers and terraces
	6	Existence of orderly agrochemical storage facility	25	Use of windbreaks
	7	Existence of complete first aid kit	26	Planting of trees in last year
	8	Access to potable drinking water	27	Over 25 percent of crops covered by shade trees
	9	Farm diversification (as climate change adaptation method)		
Tier III	10	Increase of workers' wage per day (in US$)	28	Elimination of all synthetic input use
	11	Increase of pickers' wage per day (in US$)	29	Treatment of waste water
	12	Payment of minimum wage for all workers	30	Elimination of deforestation for crop expansion

Table 6.1 (*cont.*)

Socially sustainable production practices		Environmentally sustainable production practices	
13	School attendance of school-age children	31	Implementation of diverse agroforestry with >25 percent shade cover
14	Elimination of school-age children doing dangerous work, for example, applying pesticides	32	Implementation of diverse agroforestry with >50 percent shade cover
15	Elimination of hiring of minors (below 14/15 years of age)		

in meta-analyses. It normalizes the measured effect size by the pooled standard deviations of the treatment and control groups. This allows us to compare indicators measured in different units, and compare effects while accounting for both their size and their statistical significance. It also allows for negative effect sizes.

To test the hypotheses specified in Chapter 2, and reprinted in Table 6.2, I coded whether the criterion was a critical (i.e., compulsory) practice or not in each groups' respective standard (to test H1 and H2); whether an effective training component for the requirement existed (to test H3; as measured in t-tests of within-group improvements in the requirement with training); whether participation in the group led to individualized, significant price premiums paid (above 20 percent of mainstream market price; H4); whether complying with the requirement represented significant upfront investment costs (H5); whether it represented significant and long-lasting opportunity costs regarding yields or net income (H6); whether the certification scheme employed a restrictive (auditor monopoly or strict accreditation) or flexible (proxy accreditation, self-verification, etc.) auditor policy (H7); and whether there was a public regulatory equivalent in the country under analysis (H8 and H9). An overview of this coding exercise can be found in Appendix 4.

For a first overview of differences in the effectiveness of certification on behavior change, I compared the standardized effect size between indicators in Tiers I, II, and III. The results are shown in Figure 6.1.

Table 6.2 *Hypotheses under investigation in the meta-analysis*

Hypotheses under investigation

H1	Critical requirements (those that are mandatory for certification attainment) are **more likely** to show outcome additionality than noncritical requirements because they do not allow for cost-minimizing choices between alternative options and provide clarity on obligations for both auditor and auditee, leading to low amounts of on-the-ground variability.
H2	Critical requirements are **less likely** to show outcome additionality than noncritical requirements because they do not account for producers' capacity to comply and do not give auditors leeway to aid participants toward compliance.
H3	Requirements in groups that had received effective training on the practice in question are **more likely** to show outcome additionality due to participants' improvements in their capacity to comply.
H4	Programs that offer individualized, significant price premiums (>20 percent over noncertified price) to producers are **more likely** to show outcome additionality due to their provision of a financial disincentive for noncompliance.
H5	Requirements that necessitate significant upfront investment costs are **less likely** to show outcome additionality due to limits in regulatees' capacity to comply and their likelihood to opt out of or evade such requirements.
H6	Requirements that represent significant continuous opportunity costs are **less likely** to show outcome additionality due to limits in regulatees' financial capacity to comply and their likelihood to opt out of or evade such requirements.
H7	Programs that only allow for one monopoly auditing organization or that require accreditation to their standard are **more likely** to show outcome additionality than programs that allow for a large group of proxy-accredited or desk-approved auditing organizations due to higher familiarity with the relevant standards and the reduction of adverse incentives and conflicts of interest.
H8	Private regulation requirements that mirror public regulation are **more likely** to show outcome additionality due to the provision of enforcement capability for clear rules on the ground.
H9	Private regulatory requirements that mirror public regulation are **less likely** to show outcome additionality due to regulatory duplication.

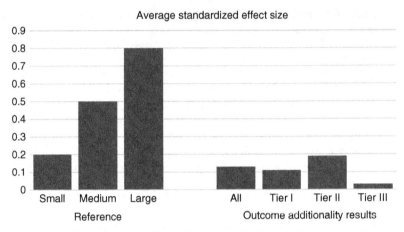

Figure 6.1 Average standardized effect size of indicators by types of practices

As a first result, I find that the average standardized effect size of certification on enhanced sustainable practices, across all thirty-two indicators and all fourteen certification groups, is 0.13. In general, according to Cohen, a standardized effect size of $d = 0.2$ (i.e., an average effect of 0.2 pooled standard deviations) can be considered a 'small' effect size, 0.5 represents a 'medium' effect size, and 0.8 can be considered a 'large' effect size (Walker 2008). Accordingly, the effect of certification in this pool of observations on producer behavior can be considered as very small. When I disaggregate between indicator groups, however, interesting differences emerge. Tier I indicators have an average effect size of 0.11; Tier II indicators show a Cohen's d of 0.19; and Tier III indicators show an average effect size of 0.03. This is a first meta-analytical confirmation of the findings of Chapter 5: indicators in the highest tier of sustainability show the least amount of improvement, while those that are linked to long-term benefits for producers show greater promise. Regarding the Tier I indicators, the mediocre results in improving input efficiency pull the mean effect size downward.

Second, to test my hypotheses quantitatively, I applied a linear regression model with the standardized effect size as outcome variable. I further added country and, in an extended model, certification scheme dummies to account for residual differences. Table 6.3 shows the results for the simple and extended model, using all observations. To test for differentiated effects by type of indicator, I also ran the same

Table 6.3 *Results of meta-analysis of institutional design and outcome additionality*

	Determinants of standardized effect size of certification	
Variables	Model 1	Model 2
Critical requirement	0.23*** (0.08)	0.20*** (0.07)
Effective training	−0.03	−0.04
Investment costs	0.18*** (0.06)	0.18*** (0.05)
Opportunity costs	−0.12** (0.05)	−0.12** (0.05)
Restrictive auditor policy	0.05	0.00
Price premiums	0.14*** (0.05)	0.20* (0.12)
Public equivalent	−0.19** (0.10)	−0.18* (0.09)
Controls		
Honduras	0.13** (0.05)	−0.03
Colombia	−0.03	−0.03
Fairtrade	−	−0.05
Fairtrade/organic	−	0.32* (0.17)
UTZ	−	0.05
4C	−	0.04
Rainforest Alliance	−	0.13
AAA	−	−0.22* (0.12)
Observations	435	435
R^2	0.19	0.23

* = $p < 0.10$; ** = $p < 0.05$; *** = $p < 0.01$; standard errors are added in the parentheses for significant results.

model on the three tiers of practices separately. The results of this analysis are shown in Table 6.4. The results of this analysis are discussed and put into context in Sections 6.4–6.7, as well as Chapter 7.

6.4 The Importance of Binding Rules

As a first observation, the analyses in Tables 6.3 and 6.4 both show that elevating standard requirements to 'critical' status, in which compliance is necessary to achieve and maintain certification, increases the mean effect size of the outcome additionality in certified farmers over matched controls. Table 6.3 shows that when controlling for all other variables

Table 6.4 *Results of meta-analysis of institutional design and outcome additionality, by indicator type*

Determinants of standardized effect size of certification – by indicator type			
Variables	Tier I	Tier II	Tier III
Critical requirement	1.23* (0.69)	0.15** (0.07)	0.21
Effective training	–0.14	–0.04	–0.02
Investment costs	–	0.23*** (0.06)	0.27
Opportunity costs[7]	–	–	–
Restrictive auditor policy	–0.01	–0.01	0.00
Price premiums	–0.09	0.44*** (0.16)	0.01
Public equivalent	–	–0.26 (0.18)	–0.18
Controls			
Honduras	0.14	–0.10	–0.01
Colombia	–0.07	–0.06	0.04
Fairtrade	0.01	–0.09	0.00
Fairtrade/organic	–0.01	0.29	0.31
UTZ	–0.04	0.10	0.04
4C	–0.19	0.11	0.07
Rainforest Alliance	0.17	0.16	0.14
AAA	–0.01	–0.40** (0.17)	–0.03
Observations	84	210	141
R^2	0.31	0.31	0.15

* = p < 0.10; ** = p < 0.05; *** = p < 0.01; standard errors are added in the parentheses for significant results.

and a number of confounding factors, critical requirements have higher standardized effect sizes by around 0.2–0.23 pooled standard deviations. The disaggregated analysis in Table 6.4 shows that this result holds for both Tiers I and II indicators, while there is also a strong, but

---

[7] Since the presence of high opportunity costs determined whether indicators were categorized as Tier I, II, or III indicators, the opportunity cost variable dropped out of the disaggregated analysis. The same is true for investment costs and public equivalent in the case of Tier I indicators.

nonsignificant impact among Tier III indicators of rule stringency on outcome additionality. These results lead me to *accept H1* (critical requirements are more likely to show outcome additionality because they do not allow for cost-minimizing choices between alternative options and provide clarity on obligations for both auditor and auditee). Conversely, they suggest *rejecting H2* (critical requirements are less likely to show outcome additionality because they do not take into account capacity to comply and do not give auditors leeway to aid participants toward compliance). The results also support a more restrictive view of regulation and auditing in the realm of private regulation. They highlight the danger that flexible and discretionary rules may lead to underregulation, regulatory capture, and regulatory ineffectiveness (Bardach and Kagan 1982; Hawkins 1984; Hawkins and Thomas 1989), and empirically confirm the model of boundedly rational producer behavior chosen for this book, wherein producers will prioritize fulfilling binding requirements over continuous or optional ones.

These results are further supported by existing literature. Some of the earliest research on voluntary environmental programs concluded that in the absence of strong institutional pressures such as monitoring and sanctioning for noncompliance, participants selectively prioritized environmental management practices that provided financial benefits and failed to implement more costly practices (Rivera *et al.* 2006; deLeon and Rivera 2009). Darnall and Sides (2008) highlight that specific and challenging goals are likely to lead to greater performance of voluntary environmental programs than moderately or easily attainable goals. Regarding agricultural sustainability certifications, both Blackman and Naranjo (2012) and Ibanez and Blackman (2016) identify well-defined (rather than fuzzy) standards as a hallmark of effective certification programs. Underscoring the importance of the clarity of obligations, Blackman and Naranjo (2012, p. 63) observe that "in general, inspectors enforce prohibitions against negative practices (use of agrochemicals) more stringently than they require the positive ones (soil conservation, etc.)." They suggest that this was because of a lower likelihood of indeterminacy of the prohibition of negative practices, as opposed to judging when positive obligations have been fulfilled. Takahashi and Todo (2017) conclude that rigorous certification criteria and auditing systems may lead to conservation effects, and advocate for strengthening respective environmental regulations.

In addition, Bose *et al.*'s (2016) example of Rainforest Alliance certification in Indian agroforestry systems showcases that flexible regulatory enforcement may lead to motivational crowding-out of prior, stricter views of sustainability. One producer commented on the surprising laxity of the audit as follows:

planters are removing shade trees and planting exotics like silver oak, but RA certification is not preventing this, because shade cover is an optional criterion and not mandatory. When the auditors came I had to specially request them to mark that I was following RA's standards on shade cover (i.e., maintaining 40% shade and 12 tree species per hectare), but the auditor did not know how to measure shade cover or identify tree species to verify that it was, indeed, at least 12 species. I am a nature lover, but what about the hundreds of farmers who are deforesting? (Bose *et al.* 2016, p. 950)

This misalignment between local and international norms of sustainability led to great confusion and disillusionment with certification that had negative spillovers into interest in conservation projects in general, and shade production in particular. For instance, one producer was quoted as saying "if all environment projects are like certification, I am not interested in keeping my shade trees" (Bose *et al.* 2016, p. 953). Here, the low stringency and expectation of the private regulatory system appear to have lowered the intrinsic motivation of producers to maintain their initial high ecological standards in a variation of the 'crowding-out' effect of the introduction of extrinsic rewards (Frey and Jegen 2001).

6.5 The Importance of Effective Training

As second criterion, I analyze whether "requirements in groups that had received effective training on the practice in question are more likely to show outcome additionality due to participants' improvements in their capacity to comply," as hypothesis 3 states. Training in good agricultural practices (GAPs), environmental management, and worker safety may introduce farmers to more efficient and safe ways of managing their farm and has been identified as a key pathway for rural development and the achievement of more sustainable producer livelihoods (Feder *et al.* 2004; Tilman *et al.* 2011). This is recognized by the private governance initiatives: all certifications include the provision of continuous training by group administrators, the cooperative leadership, or company agronomists (e.g., Nespresso AAA) as a central component of their theory of change. UTZ and Starbucks C.A.F.E. Practices have the largest range of suggested training topics, while others are more parsimonious. The Rainforest Alliance, for instance, simply mandates the implementation of a "training program for its group members to comply with Sustainable Agriculture Network standards" (SAN 2011, p. 12). Further, UTZ and Fairtrade make special reference to the participation of women in training activities.

To understand the contribution of training on practice improvements, I started by asking producers whether they had received training in various categories (including GAPs, environmental management, and safe agrochemical use) in the preceding years, and whether they had regularly attended such training and implemented what they had learned on their farms.

In Honduras, the popularity of GAP training and the presence of multiple supporting institutions means that even 74 percent of noncertified farmers report having had access to such training. The UTZ and 4C groups do not show statistically significant higher rates of training access, although the Rainforest Alliance (95 percent) and Fairtrade groups (100 percent) do. The results regarding environmental training are more disparate. While only 25 percent of noncertified farmers had received such capacity building, up to 79 percent of certified farmers had, with Rainforest Alliance (79 percent), UTZ (52 percent), and Fairtrade/organic (56 percent) showing significantly higher rates. The share of access to agrochemical training is also notably higher in the Fairtrade (91 percent) group, with other groups hovering between 50 and 71 percent of producers that recalled such training. Along with Rainforest Alliance farmers (82 percent), the Fairtrade groups (91–100 percent) also show higher shares of farmers that always attend and implement training. On the other hand, in the UTZ, 4C, and noncertified groups almost half of all farmers (59–68 percent) do not attend training sessions regularly and do not implement what the learned on a regular basis. Finally, only 45–57 percent of women[8] regularly attend training activities. This share is only marginally higher in the groups certified with standards that emphasize women's inclusion in training activities.

In Colombia, the greater institutional support structure – as exemplified by strong cooperatives, a strong coffee institution (the FNC), and the presence of multinational traders – has led to a situation defined

---

[8] This includes both female household heads and the wives of male household heads.

by a multiplicity of training efforts. Cooperative staff report that they need to schedule training carefully in order not to overburden produced cers' time (field notes, Colombian extension agents, 2016). This is visible in producers' reported access to GAP training, which is at a very high overall level, although the Fairtrade groups (96 percent) show higher rates than the noncertified farmers (86 percent). Access to environmental training is more variable, with high levels in the uncertified (77 percent) and one Fairtrade cooperative (71 percent). The other cooperative shows low baseline levels of training (18 percent); while the 4C (63 percent) and Nespresso AAA (73 percent) programs allow farmers to get more training in this area, the C.A.F.E. Practices program does not. The provision of agrochemical training shows a significant difference between the Fairtrade cooperatives (86 percent) and the noncertified control group (37 percent), with farmers that had additional certifications showing slight, but not significant, improvements over the Fairtrade baseline. At 80–90 percent, attendance and implementation rates are higher than in the Honduran sample, and do not vary dramatically across certified and noncertified groups. In this sample, women's participation in training is lower than in the Honduran sample (at around 40 percent), particularly in the certified cooperatives – which is ironic given Fairtrade's mandate for gender equity and inclusion.

In Costa Rica, finally, certified and noncertified farmers have similar rates of access to GAP (86–100 percent), environmental (60–80 percent),[9] and agrochemical training (70–96 percent). However, farmers surprisingly show lower attendance and implementation rates (around 50–60 percent) than the Colombian and many Honduran farmers, especially in the certified groups (with the notable exception of the Rainforest Alliance/AAA group). It is possible that in the Costa Rican context, the availability of alternative sources of income makes farmers less reliant on coffee farming and less inclined to invest time on training and practice changes. Interestingly, the noncertified cooperatives show similar implementation rates as the Rainforest Alliance/AAA group (83–86 percent), showing that strong cooperative effects through socialization may equally lead to greater buy-in. The data also show that the

---

[9] With the exception of one cooperative that showed very low levels of environmental training, lowering the mean C.A.F.E. Practices and Rainforest Alliance results.

attendance levels of women is the lowest of the three country cases, although they are slightly higher in the Rainforest Alliance-certified groups, and that few women in this sample either help on the farm or pursue off-farm jobs.[10]

In a second step, we need to recognize that not all training is equal. One expert noted that

you can't really certify without having any sort of training. The problem is that you could have a training event where you put a guy with a loudspeaker in front of a group of 1000 farmers for one hour and they call it a training event. Or you could have a field school program with 20 to 25 farmers, 10 meetings a year, full day, and that would also be training. There is a huge range. (Interview 14, Kuit Consulting, 2015)

To assess whether trainings were *effective* within the certification group, I used a Student's t-test to compare producers in the same certification group that reported receiving relevant training with those that did not.[11]

In the Honduran sample, Rainforest Alliance producers that report receiving environmental training not only report statistically significant higher yields but also show better fertilizer and pesticide efficiency than their peers. This speaks either to the fact that the trainings were highly

---

[10] On balance, I find that the inclusion of women in training activities is highest in the country with the strongest cultural norms of *machismo* and the lowest a priori expectation of gender equality – in Honduras. This may speak to the fact that the increasing professionalization of commodity production in Colombia and Costa Rica favors male over female decision-making. While the overall share of couples reporting joint decision-making over productive decisions is 52 percent in Honduras, it is 42 percent in Colombia and only 18 percent in Costa Rica. What is more, in the Honduran Rainforest Alliance and Fairtrade/ organic groups, this share drops to 29 and 19 percent, respectively, possibly because of the more complicated production rules. This result highlights that gender equality does not necessarily follow from professionalization or certification, and might need to be more strongly regulated by sustainability standards.

[11] I chose this technique given that, as noted, not all training (or service provision in general) is equal. Using regressions, or other forms of inference that would group observations across certification groups, might conflate effective with ineffective trainings and diminish the explanatory power of particular certifications' approaches. Furthermore, using within-group Student's t-test analysis allows us to keep other within-group characteristics constant and focus solely on the additional impact of training provision. It should however be noted that in some cases the relatively small N resulting from restricting the calculation to a single treatment group may lead to an underestimation of the real statistical difference in means.

effective in training them, or that the more efficient and successful farmers also show a higher motivation to attend the environmental trainings.[12] Interestingly, noncertified producers with environmental training show significantly better pesticide efficiency than the rest – almost reaching the average pesticide efficiency of a number of certified groups. Hence, training activities, even outside of the scope of a certification program, may contribute to significant change. Environmental training also contributes to statistically significant higher rates of adoption of IPM techniques such as insect traps in both certified and noncertified producers, with 73–95 percent of trained farmers using such traps compared to around 30 percent of nontrained farmers. The only exceptions are the Fairtrade and Fairtrade/organic groups, where all farmers – trained and nontrained – show very high implementation rates of this practice. Finally, environmental training also increases wastewater treatment significantly from very low levels in all groups, illustrating that capacity building is an important step to improve practices in this case. However, it is likely that the financial costs of installing such relatively capital-intensive systems forestall more widespread adoption even if farmers are willing to implement such practices. On the other hand, agrochemical safety training has no notable effect on any of the worker safety indicators in question – possibly, economic constraints (regarding the acquisition of PPE or the building of appropriate storage facilities) prevent full compliance.

In Colombia, the Rainforest Alliance/AAA, Nespresso AAA, and Starbucks C.A.F.E. Practices groups show significant differences in pesticide efficiency between producers with and without environmental training – in all groups, when producers report having received environmental training, they use 60 percent fewer pesticides per unit of output. The Nespresso AAA, C.A.F.E. Practices, and 4C groups also show significantly fewer farmers using chemical herbicides among those with environmental training. In combination with the Rainforest Alliance data from the Honduran survey, these results suggest that especially for farmers that are moving toward greater

---

[12]   As I am not privy to time series data, it is difficult to draw causal statements from the observed correlations. However, correlation analysis does not show high rates of correlation between indicators that might indicate high producer motivation (e.g., environmental training recall, use of record keeping, use of soil analysis, age, or education) in either of the groups. This leads me to believe that rather than comparing a 'perfectly motivated' producer group with the rest, we are finding different pathways to success for different producers.

professionalization and (possibly) intensification, acquainting them with environmentally beneficial practices may have positive impacts on their input use efficiency. We can again observe the high importance of environmental training for initiating wastewater treatment in the Fairtrade, Nespresso AAA, and Starbucks C.A.F.E. Practices groups, all of which showed around 11–18 percent of implementation by nontrained farmers and around 50 percent by trained farmers. Even the 4C group, which shows lower levels of adoption, moves from 6 percent of producers without environmental training to 17 percent of producers with such training that utilize wastewater treatment systems. In the AAA, 4C, and Fairtrade groups, agrochemical training is significantly correlated with the use of PPE – in each group, 72–82 percent of trained farmers reported using the full protection equipment compared to 6–30 percent of untrained farmers. Further, the 4C and Fairtrade groups also showed significant improvements in the results for agrochemical storage and first aid kit presence when they reported to have received agrochemical training. These training programs seem to have shown particular effectiveness.

On the other hand, in Costa Rica, environmental training is significantly correlated with improved input efficiency in two groups – the Rainforest Alliance/AAA and Fairtrade-certified farmers – although the record for the rest of farmers is more mixed, potentially due to the low implementation rates. The IPM practice of collecting cherries postharvest also increases significantly with training in the Rainforest Alliance/C.A.F.E., C.A.F.E., and Fairtrade groups, roughly doubling in each case. Many other practices, however, show little differences between trained and nontrained farmers.

To gauge the overall contribution of such training activities on the outcome additionality of certified groups over noncertified controls, in the meta-analysis described earlier, I coded for each indicator whether participation in environmental, agrochemical, or recycling training showed significant differences in outcomes in each group according to the performed t-tests. I then tested whether such effective training contributed to the overall outcome additionality in the two models. However, both the aggregated and disaggregated model results in Table 6.3 and 6.4 show no independent impact of such trainings on aggregate improvements of certified farmers over noncertified ones.

Thus, my results lead me to *reject H3* (requirements in groups that had effective training are more likely to show outcome additionality due to participants' improvements in their capacity to comply), since they show no significant coefficients in the comparative analysis. The likely reason is that in many cases, even when training was effective as shown, it was rarely rolled out to sufficient producers to create significant outcome additionality in the overall group. Here, the promise of certification schemes to further cooperative or conciliatory compliance management (Bardach and Kagan 1982) is still unfulfilled. An alternative – and more positive – interpretation is that this result is driven by the fact that trainings are occurring in both certified and noncertified entities (particularly in Colombia and Costa Rica). Hence, the within-group improvements do not drive between-group differences.

In other instances, training and capacity-building have been identified as significant potential pathways toward improvements. Similar to the results in Chapter 5, Rueda and Lambin (2013) find that Rainforest Alliance-certified farmers are significantly more likely to use soil analyses to guide the application of fertilizer on their farms. Using qualitative data, Elder *et al.* (2013) hypothesize that training is responsible for a higher likelihood of Fairtrade-certified farmers to practice agroforestry and apply manure on their coffee plots. Akoyi and Maertens (2017) identify a well-organized private extension system as a major explanatory factor for superior results in land and labor productivity of farmers with combined Rainforest Alliance–UTZ–4C certification. On the other hand, Kuit *et al.* (2016) note that training is not correlated with any improvements in economic or agronomic performance in their sample of 4C farmers, leading to the conclusion that the messages and methods used may require further analysis. Given that my data set identifies effective training outcomes, a combination of increased quality *and* quantity of training is likely necessary to assure that training and capacity building translates into on-the-ground additionality impact.

6.6 The Importance of Financial Incentives and Opportunity Costs

This section first investigates how the market-driven incentives have played out in each of the country settings by comparing the reported average price received by each certification group and delving deeper into local implementation mechanisms that may explain these findings.

It then turns to testing hypotheses 4–6 on the impact of the provision of formal price premiums, upfront, and continuous opportunity costs on certification group behavior.

Interestingly, when calculating the average price attained per pound of coffee in Honduras, we can see that all certified farmer groups report higher prices than the noncertified control group, with price differentials that go beyond the reported official price premiums (US$0.00–0.02 for 4C, US$0.03 for UTZ, US$0.04 for Rainforest Alliance) particularly in the market-based certification groups (see Table 6.5). This has several possible explanations. The most powerful, considering Honduras' decentralized and privatized marketing infrastructure, is that participation in a certified producer group allows farmers more direct access to exporters and lowers their dependence on small-scale *coyote* intermediaries that may give them poor deals or cheat them on coffee weight or quality. Quality and micro-regional differences may also come into play (although both certified and control sampling groups are spread across several larger coffee-producing regions).

Colombian average farm-gate prices, although higher than the noncertified average of Honduran farmers, are not significantly different from the Honduran certified groups (see Table 6.6). Yet, this similarity hides the multiple additional services provided through the cooperatives and

Table 6.5 *Average prices by certification group in Honduras*

Means by group	Rainforest Alliance	FT/organic	Fairtrade	UTZ	4C	Noncertified
Weighted price (US$/lb)	0.92	0.98	0.95	0.84	0.83	0.76

Table 6.6 *Average prices by certification group in Colombia*

Means by group	Rainforest Alliance/ AAA	Nespresso AAA	C.A.F.E. Practices	4C	Fairtrade	Noncertified
Weighted price (US$/lb)	0.87	0.88	0.90	0.94	0.88	0.89

national coffee institution that are cofinanced through coffee earnings and automatically deducted from the export coffee price, which tend to be less present in the Honduran case. There are few differences in average reported prices received by groups certified with additional standards compared to their Fairtrade and noncertified counterparts, showing a limited economic benefit of engaging in costly certification practices. One reason for these results may be the more stringent quality requirements of the Rainforest Alliance, Nespresso AAA, and Starbucks C.A.F.E. Practices certifications in the Colombian case, which means that only a small share of the overall harvest can be sold at the higher price premiums.

In the Costa Rican case, the high-quality focus and the strong institutional marketing infrastructure provides producers with per-unit farmgate prices that lie almost 30 percent above Colombian and 50 percent above Honduran prices (see Table 6.7). Yet, we see inconsistent trends in how certification plays out in these groups, with most differences being driven by cooperative-level differences. Only two cooperatives pay out specific price premiums to farmers that are tied to the specific standard scheme they are in. The first pays Rainforest Alliance/AAA farmers a premium of US$0.25 and Starbucks C.A.F.E. Practices farmers a premium of US$0.13. However, they are only allocated a relatively small quote for this high-end coffee, and most of their coffee is sold at average prices of US$1.16. The second cooperative pays US$0.06/lb for the total volume that Rainforest Alliance/C.A.F.E. Practices-certified farmers sell to the cooperative, despite the fact that not all coffee is sold as Rainforest Alliance-certified product. The cooperative makes up for the difference due to the fact that for the product sold, they receive a premium of US$0.08–0.10/lb (field notes, 2017). The other cooperatives do not make individual-level payouts

Table 6.7 *Average prices by certification group in Costa Rica*

Means by group	Rainforest Alliance/ AAA	Rainforest Alliance/ C.A.F.E.	C.A.F.E. Practices	Fairtrade	Noncertified
Weighted price (US$/lb)	1.35	1.50	1.39	1.25	1.50

related to certifications, stating instead, for instance, that "the premiums we receive for the Rainforest Alliance, C.A.F.E. Practices and Fairtrade coffee are split equally between the producers" (interview 57, Costa Rican cooperative 2, 2017). However, they showcase average farm-gate prices between US$1.34 and US$1.45, with the most advanced cooperative reaching US$1.58/lb (ICAFE 2016).

The reason why most cooperatives do not set individual incentives is not completely clear, but most likely it has to do with the centralized final price-setting mechanism established through the coffee law. This feature of the Costa Rican sector will be further explained in Chapter 7. Whatever the reason, this quirk of the Costa Rican system has interesting implications for behavioral outcomes of producers subject to more stringent production rules.

On the one hand, several cooperative leaders noted that more advanced (e.g., Rainforest Alliance) producers pursued the practices out of conviction, not due to monetary incentives. This might uncover alternative hypotheses to the assumption of boundedly rational profit maximization that lies at the heart of this book. For instance, as argued by Snider *et al.* (2017), who worked with cooperatives in the same regions of Costa Rica as our case study, it is possible that the motivation to pursue sustainable practices does not mainly stem from an economic perspective. Rather, it may come from underlying values such as social capital, a commitment to the common good, and generalized trust (Cohen and Prusak 2001; Pretty and Smith 2004). Such alternative hypotheses could be explored in future research. It would be interesting to determine whether such farmers complete both mandatory and voluntary requirements with the same intensity and motivation, or whether a lexical ordering of money and responsibility continues to hold even in farmers that are exceptionally committed to the provision of public goods.

Alternatively, the nonexistence of a price incentive for certification may lead to lower feelings of buy-in and commitment. Referring back to the results of the previous section, the Costa Rican Rainforest Alliance/AAA group, a certified group that did receive a dedicated price premium through the cooperative structure, had the highest attendance (80 percent) and implementation rates (86 percent) of trainings. Comparing Rainforest Alliance/C.A.F.E. farmers that did receive individualized price premiums with those that did not, training attendance is not higher – quite the opposite, in fact, considering that

44 percent of farmers with premiums responded that they always attended, compared to 58 percent in the other group. However, there are large differences in training implementation: 78 percent responded that they always followed recommendations made in trainings, compared to 33 percent. Farmers with individualized premiums were also more likely to always teach new practices to their workers (80 versus 30 percent). While I cannot completely exclude cooperative effects, these results indicate the possibility that financial incentives increase the willingness of farmers to conform to proposed changes.

Similarly, attendance and implementation rates were highest in the Honduran Rainforest Alliance, Fairtrade, and Fairtrade/organic producers, which are again the only ones to receive substantive price premiums directly linked to certification according to the coding scheme (see Appendix 4). This may speak to the fact that greater resource availability can lead to more in-depth, useful training, or that the price incentives of group membership led to greater buy-in, identification, and motivation of participating farmers. It is important to test whether such price premiums can be systematically linked to outcome additionality.

Tables 6.3 and 6.4 show that the offer of substantive price premiums, defined as price premiums that constitute 20 percent or more of the noncertified price, was correlated with significant differences in standardized effect size. The effect is particularly pronounced in Tier II indicators, where short-term costs need to be incurred to lead to long-term benefits. This leads me to *accept H4* (programs that offer individualized, significant price premiums [>20 percent over noncertified price] to producers are more likely to show outcome additionality due to their provision of a financial disincentive for noncompliance).

As a next factor, I investigate whether upfront investment costs or continuous opportunity costs constitute significant impediments to the generation of outcome additionality by private regulations. Here, I am guided by Gunningham and Grabosky (1998), as well as Rivera *et al.* (2006), both of who underscore that boundedly rational economic actors will be more willing to adopt changes that improve their competitiveness, and will be reluctant to comply with regulations that create sustained financial sacrifice for them.

Interestingly, *H5* ("Requirements that necessitate significant upfront investment costs are less likely to show outcome additionality due to limits in regulatees' capacity to comply and their likelihood to opt out of or evade such requirements") *is rejected* by the meta-analysis. Both regression analyses find that, on the contrary, practices with upfront investment costs show a *better* performance than those without them. Again, this is particularly true for Tier II practices. This result is likely driven by three interrelated factors. First, it shows the information asymmetry at work in making decisions related to certification, where investment decisions – such as building an agrochemical shed or a water treatment plant – are made before the real payoff is known and in expectation of future benefits, while continuous costs are more easily adjusted downward when it becomes apparent that such benefits are not forthcoming. Second, the requirements that require upfront investments are also often the most visible to auditors and the easiest to 'check off' (i.e., whether a first aid kit is present) and might receive overproportional attention for that reason. Third, such requirements are also often reliant on broader institutional support that may even include the provision of public infrastructure (e.g., the provision of potable water), leading to above-average differences in outcomes between certified and noncertified farmers and little within-group variability, since we are measuring the presence or not of such communal institutional support. This would then lead to above-average results in standardized effect size.

On the other hand, private sustainability standards might not provide sufficient incentives to convince farmers to adopt sustainable production practice changes that continuously lower expected net income. In this case, the lexical ordering of money and responsibility might be too strong and the changes in institutional arrangements and incentives not pronounced enough to change mainstream market incentives. Qualitatively, the presence of continuous opportunity costs can explain the low implementation rates of many of the practices described in Section 5.5. For instance, that section highlighted the limited effectiveness of standards in supporting the implementation of biodiverse shade cover, particularly at rates of over 50 percent. To understand whether this can be linked back to their opportunity costs, I decided to use the full sample of producers to test what they are giving up when they opt to produce shade-grown coffee.

Table 6.8 shows that, compared to full sun production, each level of shade produces more severe yield losses, with the worst effects at 75–100 percent of shade (with the exception of Costa Rica, where such production was almost nonexistent). Note that in Colombia and

Table 6.8 *The impact of shade practices on yields (qq/ha)*

Regression results	Honduras	Colombia	Costa Rica
25–50 percent shade	−8.91*** (1.70)	−4.68*** (1.75)	−2.04
50–75 percent shade	−7.25*** (2.37)	−7.00*** (2.57)	−7.01** (2.90)
75–100 percent shade	−21.18*** (2.61)	−12.79*** (4.16)	−4.22
Select control variables[13]			
Female gender	−2.95* (1.69)	−3.35* (1.83)	−3.95** (1.95)
Age	−0.24*** (0.05)	−0.28*** (0.06)	−0.09
Years of schooling	−0.38* (0.20)	−0.12	−0.30
Household size	−0.66** (0.28)	−1.26*** (0.46)	0.44
Coffee area	0.26*** (0.04)	−0.38** (0.18)	0.16
Region (Occidente/ Andes/Tarrazu)	8.31*** (1.36)	3.17* (1.80)	6.28*** (2.02)

$* = p < 0.10$; $** = p < 0.05$; $*** = p < 0.01$; standard errors are added in the parentheses for significant results.

Costa Rica these results reflect the scenario of technified shade, as noted, with full diverse agroforestry systems likely to produce lower yields still. When no strong regulatory requirements mandate such adjustments in exchange for equivalent price premiums, it is understandable that few farmers will voluntarily make such an income sacrifice. Yet, this limits the promise of market-driven regulatory governance in driving deep behavioral changes for biodiversity conservation in cash crop farming.

In addition, one-third of farmers in the Fairtrade/organic group actually did use synthetic inputs – mostly fertilizers, although two also used pesticides (one of which was a World Health Organization 1a highly toxic substance). This includes the producer introduced in

[13] Additional control variables included land tenure, location (distance to school, health service, and markets), altitude, and participation in coffee institutions and other farmer organizations (Instituto Hondureño del Café and Asociación Nacional del Café in Honduras, FNC and Junta Directiva in Colombia, Unión de Pequeños Productores Agropecuarios Costarricenses in Costa Rica).

the opening vignette who explained his rationale by noting that "only using organic fertilizer simply does not produce high enough yields" (field notes, Honduran coffee producer, 2016). This aligns with cooperative leaders' explanation that they switched to organic production "because [they] were told it would pay higher prices" (field notes, Honduran cooperative, 2016). However, yields decreased a lot during the organic transition, with productivity still at lower levels than in the conventional lots (as the data shown in Chapter 5 attest to). In their experience, it was difficult to sell organic Fairtrade coffee at the minimum price since the price premium just about covers the additional costs and lower productivity, meaning that on average the organic producers are on par with conventional producers. Here, the price premium indeed functions as a payment for ecosystem services, but not as the price differentiation tool that motivated their transition in the first place. Thus, reaping the benefits of higher prices with yields that are close to conventional levels becomes more attractive to producers. It is also instructive that almost none of the other producer groups take on the gamble of giving up agrochemicals without this price incentive, highlighting again the high private cost to do so.

This intuition is supported in the meta-analysis of Table 6.3. It tells us that the presence of continuous opportunity costs, all else equal, lowers the standardized effect size of certification by 0.12 standard deviations. Hence, my results allow me to *accept H6* ("Requirements that necessitate significant continuous opportunity costs are less likely to show outcome additionality due to limits in regulatees' financial capacity to comply and their likelihood to opt out of or evade such requirements").

These insights are confirmed by Giuliani *et al.* (2017), who note that coffee farmers participating in in-house certifications show considerable eco-efficiency improvements, according to an 'environmental standard' that focuses on waste management, energy, water, and input use efficiency. However, they show no improvements in social standards such as paying higher salaries, eradicating child labor, or improving the safety conditions of workers. Giuliani *et al.* (2017, p. 307) note that such "heightened attention to social issues may be perceived as costly and delivering very little immediate return." Hence, it is likely to be opposed or delayed, whereas eco-efficiency showcases more immediate rewards in on-farm performance. In analyzing Moroccan fast fashion suppliers, Rossi (2013, p. 231) finds a similar lexical ordering of money and responsibility in small-scale producers' limited capacity to comply. She quotes an interviewee as saying that

firms need to have the means to be compliant. If they cannot cover the expenses, they ask themselves why they are doing it ... If they have to choose between survival and exports, they will choose survival, which means that they would delay the social compliance and maybe not export as much as they would, rather than close the factory because they cannot afford the expenses.

These results speak to the decoupling of standards and practices that constitute continuous costs, as also observed in the horticulture (Ouma 2010), garment (de Neve 2009; Mezzadri 2012), and light manufacturing (Taylor 2011) sectors. Giuliani (2016) and Giuliani *et al.* (2017) further highlight that decoupling is more likely in the absence of rigorous monitoring – leading us to the next factor under analysis.

6.7 The Importance of a Restrictive Auditor Policy

Robust third-party auditing mechanisms are frequently highlighted as a design criterion that may increase the effectiveness of private regulatory programs (Rivera *et al.* 2006; Darnall and Sides 2008; deLeon and Rivera 2009; Blackman and Naranjo 2012; Ibanez and Blackman 2016). The auditing literature, in turn, highlights the conflicts of interest inherent in a for-profit auditing market with high levels of competition (De and Nabar 1991; Jahn *et al.* 2005; Anders *et al.* 2007; Zorn *et al.* 2012). Empirically, Albersmeier *et al.* (2009) observe in a review of auditing scores in the German meat sector the high overall score, low failure levels (only around 2.5 percent of firms fail the audit), and unexplained within-region heterogeneity in auditing results that is likely due to nonconformities in auditing practices. Similarly, Zorn *et al.* (2012) find significant differences in scores across organic auditors that might be due to adverse selection, and highlight that the European organic control system has insufficient information on audit details (including missing definitions of key terms such as 'infringement' and 'irregularity') to adequately perform its monitoring role.

Hence, excessive competition that drives down rates and puts downward pressure on the scrutiny of controls (Zorn *et al.* 2012) may be an important explanatory factor why schemes with more restrictive auditor policies show greater outcome additionality. To address this aspect of effective certification design, the meta-analysis tested for the impact of a more restrictive auditing oversight to avoid the potential conflicts-of-interest and principal-agent problems related to a race-to-the-bottom between auditing firms.

At a first glance, the variable 'restrictive auditor oversight' shows no significant impact on the meta-analysis models in either Tables 6.3 or 6.4. This may be the case because this feature is coded by standard, rather than by individual indicator or group. Thus, it is correlated both with trends in rule stringency, price premiums, and with the certification dummies added to Model 2 of Table 6.3. This correlation is particularly apparent when comparing the Rainforest Alliance and Fairtrade/organic groups to the 4C and company-owned schemes, making it more difficult to isolate the independent effect of restrictive auditor policies. *H7* ("Programs that only allow for one monopoly auditing organization or that require accreditation to their standard are more likely to show outcome additionality than programs that allow for a large group of proxy-accredited or desk-approved auditing organizations due to higher familiarity with the relevant standards and the reduction of adverse incentives and conflicts of interest") is thus *inconclusive*, with qualitative support in favor, but quantitative difficulty in isolating this variable. Still, as a policy prescription, theory and empirics align to recommend greater stringency in vetting and overseeing auditing firms in order to avoid principal-agent dilemmas, adverse selection, and conflicts of interest.

In reviewing the data and integrating it with the existing literature, I was able to draw out a number of general insights on the ideal design of market-driven regulatory governance institutions to attain greater outcome additionality. First, universal and clear compliance rules are more likely to lead to outcome additionality than flexible, continuous arrangements; this is particularly the case when rule-compliant behavior creates long-term opportunity costs. Then, trainings to advance the capacity to comply need to be both effective and widespread to affect significant behavioral change within the certified group. Given that this data is based on self-reported training participation, it is likely that training sessions need to be repeated frequently to enhance uptake and recall among farmers. Furthermore, standards should provide meaningful price premiums to motivate and support standard implementation.

However, further financial support can also come from institutional sources such as cooperatives or processors that provide small-scale farmers with help to afford upfront investment costs. Finally, a strict auditor policy with high degrees of transparency, vetting, and oversight should be considered by private regulatory standard-setters to prevent a race to the bottom and collusion between auditors and auditees.

Having discussed the design characteristics of private governance initiatives in isolation, we now turn to a final important consideration when evaluating polycentric governance regimes: how the different governance elements work in conjunction. Chapter 7 examines the interactions of private governance initiatives with the preexisting public institutional infrastructure present in the three case study countries, and derives insights on public–private interaction by harnessing the cross-case variability.

7 | *Interacting with Public Institutions*

The most important actor [for sectoral sustainability] is the government. The government has certain obligations with regard to infrastructure or education, for instance. In Colombia, the FNC's role in providing these elements has improved the general conditions of coffee growers. Governments have to work together with the industry and us, the retailers.

(Fernando Serpa, Walmart, 2017 World Coffee Producers' Forum)

In early research on private regulation, it was often implicitly assumed that private standards entered a regulatory vacuum left behind by the 'retreat of the state' (Strange 1996) in response to economic globalization and trade liberalization. This notion has been disproven, given that work in multiple sectors and disciplines has shown a complex interplay of public and private institutions at work in the field (Gulbrandsen 2004, 2014; Amengual 2010; Bartley 2011, 2018; Cashore and Stone 2014; Distelhorst *et al.* 2015). It is thus of high importance to examine what existing institutional space private standards enter, and how they work in this preexisting institutional framework. This chapter first presents relevant international and national coffee institutions in the public sphere, before considering various aspects of the interaction between public and private institutions: the importance of country-level institutional support in certification uptake, the fit regarding the local marketing infrastructure, and the effectiveness of standards in enforcing local laws.

7.1 International and National Coffee Institutions

The boom and bust cycles of the coffee market, and related impacts on producers' livelihoods and exporting countries' foreign exchange earnings, have repeatedly attracted the attention of policymakers at both the international and national level.

International Institutional Solutions

Ever since the production of coffee moved from the realms of colonial empires to newly independent nations in the South, stabilizing coffee prices at high levels has been a key policy goal of major coffee-producing countries. One infamous example is that of Brazil, which at the beginning of the twentieth century controlled over three-quarters of global coffee production. Under its valorization strategy, from 1906 onward it started releasing its coffee onto the world market through the centralized Instituto Brasileiro do Café, which also provided a purchase guarantee for local producers. In order to maintain a demand–supply balance at high prices, it stockpiled coffee and on occasion even destroyed it – in the most noteworthy episode, destroying one-third of its harvested coffee crop between 1931 and 1939, corresponding to nearly 80 million bags or three years of global consumption (Luttinger and Dicum 2011). However, in a typical example of an international collective action problem, the initial period of high prices in the early 1900s attracted new actors onto the world coffee stage, notably Colombia. Its aggressive expansionist strategy made it increasingly costly for Brazil to maintain the same price level. After several diplomatic overtures failed, the two countries agreed to a joint price support system in 1936. But again, the actions of external free riders – this time, from Central America, Africa, and Asia – caused increasing costs and lead to the collapse of the bilateral agreement in 1937 (Luttinger and Dicum 2011).

The loss of European markets during World War II and general dissatisfaction with the raging price war between Brazil and Colombia led to a renewed effort at cooperation through the Inter-American Coffee Agreement. This agreement, struck in 1940, included the United States, which collaborated in apportioning its market (at that time, representing 80 percent of world demand) in order to maintain friendly allies in its hemisphere during World War II. After the war, coffee-producing nations heavily exploited this precedent of US trade policy moving away from its free market preference for geopolitical reasons as they lobbied for international cooperation. The issue of commodity price volatility was put on the global agenda in the context of the proposed Havana Charter and the UN Economic and Social Council's 1947 decision to establish the Interim Coordination Committee for International Commodity Agreements (ICCICA)

(Green and Auld 2017). These agreements aimed to stabilize the price of tropical commodities such as coffee, sugar, tin, cocoa, rubber, and wheat by setting export quotas among participating countries and committing importing countries to only source from the pool of participants. From 1964 onward, these initiatives have been coordinated by the United Nations Conference on Trade and Development (Green and Auld 2017).

After a repeat unsuccessful attempt at the cartelization of Latin American producers from 1957 to 1959, which again was undercut by free riders and outsiders from other nations, Colombia and Brazil sought the participation of the United States to support an International Commodity Agreement (ICA) for coffee. The United States agreed, motivated by the perceived importance of stabilizing noncommunist regimes in Latin America and the anticipated threat to Kennedy's Alliance for Progress agenda by low global coffee prices (Luttinger and Dicum 2011). This perception was readily utilized by Latin American politicians, such as Colombian senator Enrique Escovar, who is quoted as saying "pay us good prices for our coffee or – God help us all – the masses will become one great Marxist revolutionary army that will sweep us all into the sea" (Luttinger and Dicum 2011, p. 86). It led to the first ICA of 1962 and the market stabilization efforts described in Chapter 3.

Since the lapse of the ICA's quota system in 1989, no alternative formal institutional framework spanning both producing and consuming countries has attempted to govern prices. From 1992 onward, coffee-producing countries attempted to unilaterally arrive at an export quota system through the Association of Coffee Producing Countries (Rice and McLean 1999). Participating members committed to warehousing 20 percent of their production and releasing these goods on an agreed-upon schedule. However, the retention (rather than destruction) of excess crops did not create sufficiently strong market signals to affect price levels significantly. The unwillingness of some countries (notably Brazil) to fully cooperate with the scheme marked its rapid demise, accelerated by a 1994 weather-related price spike (Rice and McLean 1999). Thereafter, a political and scientific consensus emerged that a return to supply management is unlikely (Muradian and Pelupessy 2005; FNC 2017). The International Coffee Organization (ICO) continues to exist as a gathering forum for country representatives of coffee-producing and consuming countries, and it prepares international statistics and reports on the state of coffee markets. However, it has lost most of its regulatory clout (Ponte 2002).

National Institutional Solutions

Pre-1989, most coffee-producing countries had established dedicated coffee institutions such as Brazil's Instituto Brasileiro do Café, which acted as state-led commodity marketing boards to aggregate supply, overcome producer atomization, and increase the market power of producers. While many such institutions were abolished in the 1990s in the course of market-oriented structural adjustment reforms and neoliberalization, these preexisting structures have provided the foundation for more recent national-level efforts at strengthening producer livelihoods (Talbot 2002; Romero 2012).[1] Such approaches today usually focus on a combination of income, credit, and input support as well as incentives for product differentiation through quality or sustainability characteristics.

Lora (2013) gives an up-to-date overview of the extent of coffee-sector governance in twelve leading coffee producers that account for almost 80 percent of world production. His analysis shows that the common assumption of nonintervention by producing countries highly oversimplifies the current institutional landscape. Out of twelve countries, four set minimum prices for export contracts (Ivory Coast, Costa Rica, Colombia, and Brazil, although Brazil's is a nonenforceable reference price). Six coffee institutions manage specialty coffee certifications; eight keep a register of export contracts; eight offer credit to coffee farmers; nine regulate export-level coffee quality; ten provide extension services and technical assistance by public institutions; ten are involved in international promotion activities; and eleven grant export licenses to exporters. On the flipside, ten of twelve countries impose taxes on coffee processing or exporting, although these contributions frequently fund the public extension or price support activities (Lora 2013).

Coffee farmers are also supported through a variety of other public measures. These include producer income assistance (e.g., in Colombia during the 2012/2013 harvest) (Minagricultura 2016), price stabilization funds (in Brazil, Ivory Coast, Costa Rica, and Mexico) (Lora 2013); and assistance in disease prevention and post-outbreak replanting, such as during the coffee rust outbreaks of 2008–2011 in Colombia and

---

[1] In the process of reorganization, coffee institutions have taken on a variety of formal legal statuses, with many formerly public institutions being given a public-private or private nonprofit status. However, for the purposes of this study, this changed little in their mission and operating procedures and will not be at the focus of analysis in the following sections.

2012–2013 in Central America (FNC 2013; Avelino *et al.* 2015). This rise in producing-country market and sustainability governance activities provides an important underpinning to understand the contributions of private governance initiatives in their relevant country context. In the following, I provide a short overview of the institutional landscape of the three country case studies at the center of this analysis. In a first step, Table 7.1 shows the presence of Lora's (2013) institutional support mechanisms in the three case study countries.

Table 7.1 *Government/regulatory institution involvement in coffee-sector governance. Source: Adapted from Lora (2013)*

Government/regulatory institution involvement in coffee-sector governance	Honduras	Colombia	Costa Rica
Market regulation	No	No	No
Minimum prices	No	Yes	Yes
Export tax	No	Yes	Yes
Other taxes	Yes	No	Yes
Credit provision	Yes	Yes	No
Input provision	Yes	No	No
Extension services	Yes	Yes	Yes
Research and development	Yes	Yes	Yes
Basic off-farm processing	Yes	No	No
Quality control	Yes	Yes	Yes
Inventory management	Yes	Yes	No
Stabilization fund management	No	No	Yes
Export quality control	Yes	Yes	Yes
Certification of specialty coffee	No	Yes	No
International marketing	Yes	Yes	Yes
Domestic marketing	No	Yes	No
Export license provision	Yes	Yes	Yes
Quota and export contract provision	No	No	Yes
Contract ledger maintenance	Yes	Yes	Yes
Total	12	13	12

Honduras: In Honduras, the Instituto Hondureño del Café (IHCAFE) is the coffee institution responsible for implementing national sectoral policies and service provision. Although Lora (2013) characterizes the Honduran institutional landscape as quite strong in international comparison (with governmental or parastatal intervention or regulation in twelve out of nineteen issue areas), local accounts report that IHCAFE is rather ineffective in the provision of extension services, and the institution is seen as politicized and corrupt (Criterio.hn 2016). IHCAFE board members often go on to receiving political appointments, which is why the organization is said to be seen as a stepping-stone for a political career by its leaders (interview 15, Honduran exporter 1, 2015). Of the coffee tax levied on coffee producers (amounting to US$0.135/lb), US$0.09 is redistributed to them at later times of the year in an effort to smooth cash flows and assist with debt repayment. The rest of the contribution is supposed to fund outreach activities, but according to producers there is little evidence of such activities in the field (Criterio.hn 2016; Hondudiario 2017; La Tribuna 2017). This is not surprising given that IHCAFE only employs around 50 extension agents to reach an estimated 100,000 coffee producers (IHCAFE 2011).

In general, governmental institutions, including extension services, were substantially weakened during a period of structural adjustment in the 1990s, which left a patchwork of decentralized public and private initiatives defined by weak leadership and a considerable fragmentation of efforts (USAID *et al.* 2017). Furthermore, there has been evidence of mismanagement of IHCAFE funds. For instance, the head of IHCAFE admitted that money was used to finance the 2013 electoral campaign of conservative president Juan Orlando Hernandez (ConfidencialHN 2016). A new requirement to certify specialty coffees for export is similarly seen more as a rent-seeking racket than a real quality improvement strategy (interview 15, Honduran exporter 1, 2015). Producers do not receive input subsidies from governmental or para-statal sources.

This environment leaves much of the actual coffee production process in private hands, with intermediaries as well as national and international exporters providing crucial processing infrastructure and services, but also holding large amounts of market power over producers. Intermediaries in particular, but also exporters, are known to cheat producers on conversion rates (e.g., from cherry coffee to wet and from wet to dry parchment) and quality assessments in order to push the price down (interview 21, Honduran exporter 1, 2016). Cooperatives in turn have the reputation of suffering from mismanagement problems and not providing sufficient services to their members to warrant participation (field notes, Honduran extension agent, 2016). There is also no cultural tradition of working in groups and under strict rules, which makes it difficult for cooperatives to recruit and retain sufficient members to gain adequate volumes for export (field notes, Honduran cooperative manager, 2016).

Colombia: In stark contrast, the Federación Nacional de Cafeteros de Colombia (FNC) is widely considered as the most powerful coffee institution in the world. Founded in 1928, the FNC has led most of Colombia's coffee-related policy, including the international collaboration attempts detailed earlier, and has acquired a potent role in domestic politics as well. It also officially represents Colombia at the ICO (Luttinger and Dicum 2011).

Inter alia, the FNC guarantees the purchase of all coffee at a local reference price that aims to smoothen global price volatility, provides smallholders with credit, storage facilities, and quality control, leads research and extension services, and supports rural development through education, infrastructure, and value chain development (interview 48, FNC, 2016). It also administrates the National Coffee Fund (Fondo Nacional del Café), which finances these activities through member fees (US$0.06/lb) as well as contributions from the national government and international partners. The fund is also used for income protection-related redistribution measures (Contraloría General 2013). The vast majority of coffee farmers are registered members of the Federación, and it has built up an extensive infrastructure with purchasing stations and extension offices that span the country (interview 48, FNC, 2016).

Historically, the presence of the FNC in rural regions, even those not under control of the central government and in rebel (FARC [Fuerzas Armadas Revolucionarias de Colombia – Ejército del Pueblo]) hands, has led them to take over wider para-statal functions with regards to health and educational infrastructure and service provision. Anecdotally, their willingness to make arrangements with local leaders regarding the distribution of resources gave them a special status and provided immunity as a third party in a tense conflict. This allowed them to act as a 'shadow government' and created considerable loyalty in the rural population (field notes, Colombian extension agent, 2016). In recent years, the state has taken over most of the social welfare functions again, while the FNC tends to focus more narrowly on its mission of producing and marketing coffee. However, in its role as mouthpiece of coffee producers, it still has substantial political influence, since a dissatisfied rural population can create considerable instability for the Colombian central government (field notes, Colombian extension agent, 2016). From time to time, its strong interventionist role (in particular, the purchasing guarantee and price stabilization mechanisms) comes under critique. Most recently, a broad review process in 2013 pitted market liberal reform ideas against the traditional institutional set-up in defining a new "Coffee Competitiveness Strategy for Colombia" (Coffeelands 2015). Nevertheless, the vast majority of structural recommendations were met with widespread opposition and were not followed when the subsequent Coffee Contract (*contrato cafetero*) of 2016 was signed, signaling little likelihood that substantive institutional changes will follow from the report (Diario del Huila 2016).

On the ground, these institutions form part of a tripartite marketing infrastructure, with competition between generally strong cooperatives with varying levels of business expertise (linked to the FNC network) and private exporters, alongside FNC purchasing stations reaching into rural areas that would otherwise have difficult access to market. The purchasing guarantee at a set minimum price, exercised through cooperatives and the FNC, has proven to provide a robust mechanism to set farm-gate price floors. However, this is also subject to producer loyalty: as noted by one cooperative, as soon as they closed down their purchasing station in a distant valley due to the lack of volume received and the pressure of private buyers luring away producers, prices plummeted due to the lack of competition (interview 44, Colombian cooperative 2, 2016).

Costa Rica: Due to the crop's historical significance and the country's social democratic tradition, the coffee sector in Costa Rica is extremely well regulated. The Coffee Law of 1962 (Ley 2762) regulates the production process in minute detail, including quality control at processing, profit margins of mills and exporters, price-setting mechanisms, and even credit provision. Since 1989, the government has only allowed Arabica coffee to be grown in order to protect the Costa Rican reputation for quality (interview 34, ICAFE, 2016). Furthermore, several laws regulate the environmental effects of coffee production and processing, most importantly the water pollution linked to wet milling. Between 1992 and 1998, a program spearheaded by the Instituto del Café de Costa Rica (ICAFE) and the Ministry for Health upgraded wet milling technologies across the country at a cost of over US$100 million (ICAFE 2015b).

The historical focus on wet milling also streamlined the production process, since all coffee cherries are brought to mills, which then leverage their size to sell the green coffee beans to exporters. In 2010, 127 registered coffee mills were distributed across the coffee-growing regions. A majority of them are micro-mills, operated by single farmers or small groups to produce premium quality. Of the larger mills, around 56 percent are operated by cooperatives, while the rest belong to national and multinational corporations. In effect, the 10 percent largest mills process around 70 percent of all coffee (Coricafe 2012). However, this concentration has not led to mills unduly leveraging their market power since it is legally stipulated that mills pass 91 percent of the final sales price, minus processing costs, on to farmers. In this process, a strictly regulated liquidation process allows farmers to get a minimum price upon delivery, followed by tri-semestral payments and a final premium once all processed coffee has been sold to international markets (ICAFE 2015a). This smoothing of cash flows has noticeably benefited farmers' investment possibilities. Additionally, credit is made available through harnessing cooperatives' and producer organizations' economies of scale (ResponsAbility 2013).

ICAFE has traditionally played an important role in the array of the country's institutions, and still administers the complex marketing framework that has emerged from the implementation of Ley 2762. This includes calculating processing costs considered appropriate for mills and, on the basis of this as well as the 9 percent allowable profit, once a year publishing the mandatory price that mills have to pass down to producers in a public document. Mills (both private and cooperative-owned) are obliged to comply with these stipulations and balance their payable accounts through the final liquidation payment, which is paid just before the next harvest starts (interview 7, Costa Rican processor 1, 2015). On the other hand, ICAFE shows less hands-on involvement in providing extension services or input subsidies (which generally happens through cooperative or private mill initiatives), although it actively promotes Costa Rica as premium origin on the international market.

These different approaches to market and price management are evident when comparing farm-gate prices (i.e., prices paid to growers) of the three countries, as done in Figure 7.1. It should be noted that Costa Rica and Honduras fall in the 'Other milds' group, with a slightly lower indicator price than the Colombian price. Colombian farmers

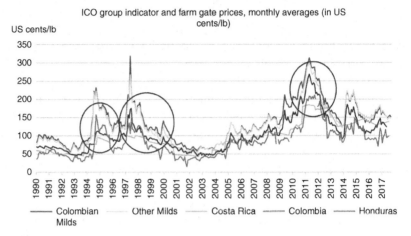

ICO group indicator and farm gate prices, monthly averages (in US cents/lb)

Figure 7.1 ICO group indicator prices and farm-gate prices for Honduras, Colombia, and Costa Rica, monthly averages 1990–2017 (in US cents/lb). Not adjusted for inflation. Source: ICO (personal communication)

consistently receive higher farm-gate prices than the Honduran and Costa Rican producers, even when indicator prices are aligned. This may reflect a combination of a higher level of farm-level processing (with most Colombians selling dry parchment coffee, as opposed to Costa Ricans selling cherry and Hondurans selling wet parchment) and quality, as well as the efficient market access infrastructure and farmer organization provided through the FNC. In turn, the differences between Costa Rica and Honduras, who face the same indicator price, can be mainly explained through their divergences in marketing institutions. Although Costa Rica tends to have a higher country differential due to its higher coffee quality, the main differences visible in Figure 7.1 is that in Honduras' free market environment, the transmission of global prices (and price volatility) to producers is much more immediate. Both price boom and bust cycles are directly passed on to farmers' bottom lines, whereas the managed system of Costa Rica (and, to a lesser extent, that of Colombia) is able to smooth this year-to-year volatility considerably – see, for instance, the boom and bust cycles of 1994–1996, 1997–2000, and 2010–2013 (circles in Figure 7.1). However, Figure 7.1 also shows that national systems are unable to stabilize prices indefinitely, given that producer price levels in all three countries dropped to rock bottom during the coffee crisis of 2000–2002.

7.2 Integration of Private Regulation into Public Institutional Structures and Strategies

How then does the institutional and legal infrastructure at origin influence the adoption and effectiveness of private sustainability standards on the ground? Regarding adoption, we can observe both structural and strategic aspects at play that have to do with the sectoral set-up and the strength of the respective coffee institution in setting incentives and rules regarding production and marketing.

Structural Conditions and Impediments to Private Regulation

The structures that para-statal coffee institutions have set up in marketing coffee at origin differ substantially between the three cases. As explained earlier, and illustrated in Figure 7.1, the Honduran case is the closest to a free market system. Apart from levying the coffee tax and administrating the coffee fund, IHCAFE does not intervene much in the supply chain connecting exporters to farmers on the ground. This allows price swings in both directions to be transmitted to producers in a relatively unmitigated fashion – subject only to the power relations between supply chain actors. This may be why we see a comparatively larger impact of being included in certified value chains on Honduran farmers' final prices. On the other hand, the weak extension infrastructure and the low level of producer organization that stems from a historical and political disregard for producer empowerment means that the avenues to certification, and its potential benefits, tend to be controlled by private actors that make top-down decisions regarding the regions and producer groups they will work with. Individual farmers located in isolated rural areas are thus reliant on the benevolence, and substantial financial assistance, of commercial and not-for-profit actors to access differentiated markets. In the absence of such help, they are exposed to the mainstream market with all its vagaries and volatility.

Colombia's marketing infrastructure provides a number of measures that assist smallholder farmers in their ability to weather difficult market conditions, but without creating structural impediments to the implementation of certification schemes. The FNC's purchasing guarantee creates an effective price floor in rural areas, which however is tied to daily coffee prices in the international coffee market. The strong presence of the FNC in rural regions, including through a dense network of extension assistance, provides a level of baseline support for farmers that allows them to be connected to potential opportunities such as certification. It also offers training on baseline knowledge related to good agricultural practices that puts farmers at a comparative advantage in fulfilling certification requirements. Furthermore, cooperatives have a long history in Colombia and are an essential component of the sector's organization of smallholder producers. The combination of these traits makes the Colombian institutional infrastructure a close-to-ideal framework for the roll-out of private sustainability standards.

Arguably, the most difficult institutional environment for private standards in this three-country comparison is the tight regulation of the coffee sector of Costa Rica. As noted earlier, the Coffee Law empowers ICAFE to review all sales and processing costs and set the legally mandated farm-gate price that mills have to pay out to their producers. To allow this system to work, the Costa Rican coffee sector is highly centralized, with a focus on aggregating coffee in cooperative-owned and private mills that process and dry beans. The mills then announce purchasing prices and volumes to ICAFE and are responsible for the tri-semestral payments. Until recently, this mechanism did not allow mills to make note of price differentiation. Even now, there are only two options: announce a split between lower-lying and higher-lying regions, and a split between 'differentiated', 'ripe', and 'green' coffee. Each of these categories then requires a separate bureaucratic process of detailing sales volumes, prices, and production costs. This makes it excessively difficult to accurately document the small-group differentiation on which sustainability certification relies to pass through volume-based price premiums to the farm-gate price. Our case study shows various ways of making it work in the system: the first cooperative (which engaged in individual incentive-setting) combined the options documented (high/low, differentiated/ripe, etc.) and submitted six different categories of coffee for ICAFE review in 2015/2016, allowing them to further sub-differentiate their product. However, this seems to create a high administrative burden, since none of the other cooperatives used this strategy; rather, most of them submitted two (ripe and green coffee) or three categories at most. The other mill that distributed individual price premiums did so in a way that circumvented the ICAFE system by redistributing the total premium received on the certified coffee in an equitable fashion to all Rainforest Alliance farmers, irrespective of whether their coffee had been sold as certified or conventional coffee. Yet, this practice is slightly unorthodox, as the gained premium will show up in the sales receipts and would artificially inflate the required farm-gate price of noncertified farmers as well if those sales are bundled together for ICAFE review. Individual differentiation in a system designed around collective action is exceedingly difficult.

This barrier also holds for the physical infrastructure present in Costa Rica. The country's tendency of milling coffee cherries jointly in large mills owned by cooperatives or private exporters makes the subdivision of coffees more complicated than in the cases of Honduras or Colombia, where coffees are frequently processed on-farm. Informants often talked about the need to adopt certifications on a whole-cooperative level to make it financially worthwhile and save the costs of separating out smaller volumes that needed to be milled, processed, and dried apart. In other cooperatives, this process was only possible because the decline of coffee volumes farmed in the region meant that there was excess capacity at the mill level. Yet, this of course creates other economic difficulties.

Strategic Conditions and Impediments to Private Regulation

One further complication arises when public institutional goals are in direct conflict with requirements that are or could be incentivized by private certification schemes. As noted earlier, both the Colombian FNC and the Costa Rican ICAFE were created to support the overall development of their countries' respective coffee sectors. This includes both an expansion in financial value and in total production volume (or, in the case of Costa Rica, a battle against shrinking production volumes), and has generally come in the form of advocating for 'technified' production practices that maximize yields over the available production area. This prioritization led to the first wave of deforestation of shade coffee areas in the 1970s in both countries, and the subsequent adoption and dissemination of the best practice of 'technified shade', which allows for optimal production volume, but does not meet biodiversity criteria. Similarly, the planting recommendations of the FNC leave little room for more varied agroforestry schemes. Farmers that choose to pursue traditional, diversified practices thus act against what is perceived as the best institutional and scientific advice in the field.

Mitigating these contradictions somewhat, the FNC has adopted the establishment of Colombia as a sustainable origin as one of its goals and – until shortly – strongly supported the adoption of certification schemes. This included establishing its own certification groups (in which the FNC is the certificate holder) in regions where no fitting cooperative was present (Grabs *et al.* 2016). However, noting that "standards have focused intensively on environmental sustainability, but left economic sustainability issues behind" (Velez 2015), the FNC is currently developing its own, country-wide sustainability project titled 100/100, reclaiming both the definition of sustainability in coffee practices and its enforcement (Velez 2016). It further called for a 'Global Economic Accord' based on farmer profitability (Brown 2015), which culminated in 2017 in the first World Coffee Producers' Forum. At this forum, the low and volatile farm-gate prices, rather than environmental impacts, were put into focus as main impediment to coffee sustainability (Perfect Daily Grind 2017). These events may be seen as signals that the FNC's future focus will come into greater conflict with ambitious private certification schemes.

The Costa Rican ICAFE, in turn, was never closely involved with private certification schemes. Its main policy objective is to create and defend a national coffee brand that rests squarely on the notion of "Costa Rica as a sustainable origin" (field notes, ICAFE, 2016). It uses coffee industry events (in particular, the yearly Semana Internacional del Café, which it hosts) to inform stakeholders about the range of public regulations that are enforced in the country in an effort to convince buyers that all Costa Rican coffee – not just certified batches – can be part of a sustainable purchasing strategy (field notes, ICAFE, 2015). It further aims to integrate the coffee sector in its national climate mitigation policy through initiatives such as the NAMA Café (Nieters *et al.* 2015). In this sense, the dissemination of certification schemes in the Costa Rican coffee sector actually runs counter to the collective goal of ICAFE, given that it creates costs to certified farmers and simultaneously creates – potentially artificial – distinctions to noncertified farmers that are subject to the same level of national legislation.

In addition, ICAFE – as well as FNC – have maintained that a high-quality strategy is more likely to yield premium prices and producer benefits than a focus on sustainability certification alone. In this vein, they have championed quality-improving practices, such as the maintenance of only Arabica (and, in Costa Rica, mainly non-rust resistant Caturra varietals) varietals,[2] high levels of fertilization, and intensive shade management that run counter to progressive environmental practices and forward-looking climate change adaptation. Finally, both coffee institutions and coffee-focused certification schemes have in common that diversification away from coffee is not part of their central mission, making it more difficult for such alternatives to be passed down to the farm level as best practice.

7.3 Private Standards as Complements or Regulatory Duplication

With all that said, does private governance provide additionality above and beyond what national and local institutions are able to provide? A final strength of the cross-sectional survey design pursued in this survey is that it provides us with the possibility of comparing the effectiveness of private regulatory governance across different public institutional settings. This section will discuss the interaction of public and private institutional arrangements in greater detail, first focusing on equivalency at the requirement level, and then moving toward broader interactions and layering (Bartley 2011) of the various institutional contexts and incentives.

The Impact of Equivalence in Requirements

Chapter 2 specified two contrary hypotheses regarding the effectiveness of private regulation in circumstances where it mirrors requirements laid down by local law. On the one hand, it could be that they provide both additional carrots (financial incentives) and sticks (compliance audits) that strengthens the enforcement capacity of local laws on the ground, and act as complements to public regulation. On the other, it could be that their repetition of preexisting laws amount to little more than regulatory duplication, which should lower their additionality in the field.

---

[2] Although recent developments point toward a relaxation of this requirement as countries are contemplating allowing the production of Robusta in lower-lying, geographically defined regions (Portafolio 2017; Pretel 2018).

I tested these two hypotheses in the meta-analysis presented in Chapter 6 by coding the requirements that referred back to national law as separate from those that did not. This includes requirements such as following minimum wage law, local law requiring the minimum working age and approach to child labor, and relevant environmental regulations. For instance, the vast majority of currently existing forest in Costa Rica is under strict legal protection (inscribed in the Ley Forestal No. 7575) characterized by a focus on absolute protection of tree cover. Even private forested land requires permits and an environmental management plan in order to extract wood from it (Solano B. 2015). This legal apparatus seems well enforced, given that experts note the impossibility of even sustainable forestry operations (Solano B. 2015). In consequence, imports of wood from Chile and other Latin American countries have soared (Fallas Villalobos 2014). Here, private regulation on the prohibition of deforestation closely mirrors public legislation.

Both models in Table 6.3 find that where private regulation mirrors existing public law, private regulation is significantly less likely to lead to outcome additionality in my sample. Table 6.4 shows large negative effects for both Tier II and III indicators, although in the disaggregated models the coefficient loses its statistical significance. These results *favor H9* (private regulatory requirements that mirror public regulation are less likely to show outcome additionality due to regulatory duplication) *over H8* (private regulation requirements that mirror public regulation are more likely to show outcome additionality due to the provision of enforcement capability for clear rules on the ground).

When reviewing the compliance results, a further interesting dichotomy emerges that explains the significantly negative influence on outcome additionality of regulatory duplication. On the one hand, in many instances, both certified and noncertified groups respect the respective regulation (for instance, with regard to prohibited pesticides, minimum wage law in the case of Colombia, or the prohibition of deforestation in Costa Rica). However, in cases with significant opportunity costs, neither certified nor noncertified farmers showcase widespread compliance (e.g., in the case for minimum wage payments in Honduras and Costa Rica). Here, the additional enforcement capability provided by private auditors does not appear to significantly spur adoption of practices that lie outside of smallholder producers' financial capacity to comply. This, again, may lead to cases where the only choice of producers is to continue producing in noncompliance of formal public or private requirements, or shut down their operation. This is similar to the situation Rossi (2013) describes in the Moroccan textile industry. A combination of decoupling standards from practice and the likelihood of auditor leniency for strategic or capacity-related reasons might prevent such noncompliance from being detected or raised by third-party auditors. On the other hand, private sustainability standards may be successful in enforcing national laws in select cases – specifically, when the economic capacity for compliance is present, but producers had been faced with few external incentives for compliance hitherto. For instance, this is the case for the employment of minors on coffee farms in Costa Rica (with the partial exception of the Rainforest Alliance/AAA group).

Where country-level institutions provide substantial support to producers through a variety of policy means, it may boost their capacity to comply with public and private regulation, but simultaneously lower the level of differentiation that certified producers achieve in practice. Hence, in cases where state action and outreach has been successful, such as in Colombia, private sustainability standards do not appear to add much beyond replicating existing laws. Newsom *et al.* (2006) similarly find that forest operations in US states with mandatory best management practices need to make fewer changes to qualify for certification than those in states where best management practices is voluntary. Meidinger (2006) notes that, for this reason, certification is more likely to be adopted in jurisdictions with reasonably good governmental standards and enforcement. The next section will discuss this trade-off between compliance capacity and additionality in different institutional contexts in more depth.

Country-Level Implementation Support and Producer Structure

When examining the country dummies in Model 1 of Table 6.3, we find that requirements in Honduras are significantly more likely to showcase outcome additionality than those in Costa Rica, while there is no significant difference to the performance of Colombian certified producers. In the extended model, these effects disappear when adding in certification dummies as well. Yet, the model confirms quantitatively the qualitative insight that Honduran certified groups appear to show-case greater outcome additionality than their Colombian and Costa Rican counterparts. This is likely due to three connected factors. First, the lower overall institutional capacity leaves noncertified Honduran farmers more isolated, less well covered by extension services, and without effective input provision, marketing, and educational infrastructure. Second, our sampling and matching strategies in Colombia and Costa Rica used farmers that were members of cooperatives as baseline observations. Finally, as explained earlier, alternative institutional incentives regarding good agricultural practices may also have come into conflict with incentives provided by private regulatory governance programs.

As noted in earlier sections, although it is a leading coffee-producing country, Honduras suffers from low overall and sector-specific institutional capacity, scoring last in the World Governance Indicators and Social Progress Index presented in Table 1.4, and showing evidence of corruption and mismanagement of funds by the national coffee institution that leaves many coffee producers without effective assistance. Producers in the field complain of nonextant extension services, the nonexistence of input subsidies that they witness in other countries such as Colombia, and a general atmosphere of insecurity that makes it harder to do business (Dietz *et al.* 2018). Most extension services and infrastructure are provided by private actors such as traders, who are likely to favor certified farmers in the dissemination of knowledge on good agricultural practices and opportunities for collective action such as requesting soil analyses and collecting used agrochemical containers. Furthermore, the rules and regulations introduced by private standards are likely to be new information to noncertified farmers, and the incentive for differentiation from a low baseline price may be higher than for farmers in more established origins. On the other hand, in countries with strong and engaged coffee institutions such as the Colombian FNC, who have built up efficient extension services and host regular training sessions, producers are likely to have access to a variety of capacity-building measures, and already universally apply best practices (such as integrated pest management practices) (Rueda and Lambin 2013; Rueda *et al.* 2014).

These results align with the insights of Giuliani *et al.* (2017), who find that the effect of being certified on the pursuit of environmental practices is higher in countries in institutionally weak countries. In contrast, they observe that a country's institutional strength has a direct positive impact on farmers' social conduct. They explain this by referring to the stronger enforcement capacity of such countries, which may generate an overall disincentive for socially harmful practices. This insight, added to this work's evidence base, highlights the commonality of the duplication of private and public regulatory efforts in the sphere of social sustainability (and related lower likelihood of outcome additionality). Environmental sustainable practices, in turn, tend to be less strongly regulated by public agencies and appear to showcase a greater potential to be influenced by private standards.

Giuliani *et al.* (2017) also note that cooperatives are important intermediary organizations for disseminating good agricultural practices, and that in-house certifications show a greater positive impact on environmental practices in farmers that sell to cooperatives than those that sell to private intermediaries. The importance of effective farmer organizations as pathways for behavior change is widely recognized, and one main reason why Fairtrade International insists on restricting its Fairtrade certification to smallholder cooperatives. In other regions, for instance, in Uganda, well-organized contract farming schemes can provide similar functions (e.g., frequent extension visits, quality input delivery, timely and reliable payments) (Akoyi and Maertens 2017). Either way, an underlying insight from the existing literature is that it is difficult to build individual capacity for sustainability practices without previously building up the prerequisite organizational capacity of farmer groups or collectives.

This insight is supported by the results in the present study, in which the sampling strategy in Colombia and Costa Rica focused on farmer cooperatives only. Here, certification turned out to be an uneven predictor of on-the-ground sustainability practices, given that farmers in similar uncertified organizations also pursued a number of capacity-building strategies. These results underscore the multiplicity of functions of sustainability certifications in the marketplace, where they are used by producer organizations in a keen cost–benefit calculation that aims to maximize possible market access benefits. However, due to the market dynamics highlighted in Chapter 4, there is a 'decoupling' of the economic signaling function of private certification schemes and their requirements alongside the 'decoupling' of standards and practice. This dual decoupling explains the uneven additionality results when holding institutional capacity constant.

One further reason may be that, as Snider *et al.* (2017) argue, existing producer cooperatives have more knowledge about their member farmers and may be more likely to closely select farmers that are already compliant with required practices, who – when matched with farmers of similar education levels, farm size, and distance from urban centers – may show limited additionality levels. On the other hand, as one consultant noted,

> with the smaller farmers, it is a lot more challenging for a trader to [select farmers close to the required level of certification], and I work for a number of the traders on things like this. Because it requires a level of detail and a level of data that often even the traders don't have. So for small-scale farmers, it is probably a bit more random within a given region where they decide to operate, and that choice of course can be driven by the supply chain infrastructure they already have in place, or the fact that they see better productivity in such a region, but that is on a fairly generic level. It doesn't drill down, at least in my experience, to a selection of individual small-scale farmers. (Interview 14, Kuit Consulting, 2015)

In such certification groups that have been assembled according to a regional 'blanket inclusion' strategy, outcome additionality may then become more likely.

In sum, Chapter 7 has shown that embedding alternative institutional arrangements such as market-driven regulatory governance schemes into a preexisting, complex web of domestic institutions leads to unpredictable results that tend to water down the effectiveness of the regulatory mechanism. Local-level institutions – both legislative instruments as well as national producer organizations – have a strong impact on farmers' behaviors, both when evaluating compliance and when considering alternative pathways toward viable coffee sectors. In sectors with low institutional capacity and strong a priori presence of private actors, such as Honduras, it is on the other hand more likely that private regulatory mechanisms will lead to behavior change and on-the-ground changes in outcomes. Yet, as noted in Chapter 6, not all standards perform equally, with large differences in their effectiveness that can be systematically linked to their design choices. The next chapter summarizes the overall findings of this book and provides an outlook into the future of implementing and analyzing market-driven regulatory governance.

8 | Conclusions

Sustainability has a price. The costs of sustainability must be shared too.

(Silas Brasileiro, Executive Director of the Brazilian
National Coffee Council, 2017 World
Coffee Producers' Forum)

Sitting at my desk in an office in Germany, the bumpy car ride through the hinterland of Honduras appears more and more like a distant memory. Yet, the questions that ran through my mind as I looked out for sustainably managed coffee farms on the side of the road remain as present as ever. Now that the field notes are assembled, the interviews transcribed, and the data evaluated, do those individual impressions of producers, traders, and roasters hold true? Are there fundamental flaws in the design and execution of market-driven regulatory sustainability schemes in the coffee sector? How effective are they in introducing different incentives and behavioral rules in the field and along the value chain? And can we identify ways forward that will allow them to meet their objectives of changing production practices while redistributing wealth across the value chain?

This chapter first summarizes the main insights of the analysis undertaken in this book, which evaluated and explained the effectiveness of market-driven regulatory sustainability governance. Next, it probes their generalizability for other types of value chains. Finally, I put the book's insights into conversation with recent work in the field of private governance, and suggest implications for research, practitioners, and governments in their quest for paths to more sustainable value chains.

8.1 The Effectiveness of Market-Driven Regulatory Sustainability Governance in the Coffee Sector

In the preceding chapters, I have argued that market-driven regulatory governance encounters an institutional design dilemma when aiming to

Table 8.1 *The institutional design dilemma of market-driven regulatory governance initiatives*

Goals	Persistent market-based incentives	Upscaling and mainstreaming
Optimal design choices		
Standard-setting	Reasonably high entry barriers	Improvement pathways for lower-performing producers
Standard enforcement	Strict in-group/out-group differentiation	Improvements in capacity to comply
	Legalistic compliance enforcement	Cooperative compliance management
Standard coexistence	Single standard/super-seal	'Co-opetition' by segmenting the market and differentiated targeting

scale up and enter the mainstream of global value chains (see Table 8.1). On the one hand, it is crucial to protect the market incentives of participating producers by maintaining relatively strict barriers to entry; on the other, scaling up requires a focus on inclusivity and continuous improvement that is at odds with such strict in-group/out-group differentiation. The trade-offs that standard-setters make in addressing this dilemma critically determines their effectiveness and reach.

Investigating this dilemma in the coffee sector has shown that the expansion of private sustainability standards from niche markets into the mainstream has to a large part eroded their function as signifiers of differentiation that allowed producers to receive significant price premiums in the early 2000s. This is due to a number of interrelated reasons. Most certification organizations have moved toward a continuous improvement approach to regulation, where rules are successively introduced and flexibly interpreted. While this opens up the certification pathway to a greater number of producers, it simultaneously weakens the entry barrier that differentiates participating from nonparticipating farmers. It also allows producers at different levels of implementation (and implementation costs) to compete for the same demand for certified coffee, which puts downward pressure on premiums. Further, the promise that private sustainability schemes could provide increased access to differentiated markets led many producers to attain standard certification without having established firm purchasing commitments by buyers, contributing to an oversupply of certified coffee. The resulting erosion of premium pricing was compounded by coordination problems among producers, information asymmetry on future demand for certified coffee, and time lags between upfront investment costs and possible long-term benefits. On the roasters' side, the fact that different standards were competing for market shares in the sustainable coffee segment allowed buyers to choose options that provided them with low-cost 'sustainable' coffee in high quantities while maintaining their conventional sourcing strategies. As buyers had their pick of certified coffees, mainstream market selection criteria such as improved quality entered negotiations, further weakening the link between sustainable practices and the economic benefits that were supposed to incentivize them.

This pressure has led to a redefinition of the notion of sustainability in coffee production, moving from a civil society-led vision of redistributive justice (as embodied in the Fairtrade standard) and strong environmental and biodiversity protection (as strived for in the organic and Bird Friendly standards) toward a productivist focus on sustainable intensification and a land sparing approach. On the one hand, this shift is visible in the standard documents, which put an increasing focus on productivity improvements (including in the Fairtrade standards), while agroforestry requirements have been rolled back in stringency (particularly in the Rainforest Alliance standard). On the other, the shift toward a more industry-oriented mind set is notable in the discourse regarding sustainability standards. The benefit of price premiums is increasingly downplayed, while 'alternative value creation' such as the move toward more professionalized and productive farms is highlighted. Yet, such an approach contradicts the main motivation of most value chain actors to engage in private sustainability schemes – which is to garner differentiated prices that rise above the mainstream commodity model. Already, the decrease in price premiums has meant that the system barely covers the operational costs of group certification and auditing expenses, with ever smaller margins reaching the farmers that are supposed to change their production practices. Under such conditions, implementing behavioral changes – particularly those that increase farm-level investment or opportunity costs – appears difficult from a micro-institutional rational choice perspective.

This intuition was confirmed by the analysis of the implementation rates and outcome additionality of a wide range of environmental and social sustainability requirements across all seven major private sustainability standards targeting coffee (Fairtrade, Fairtrade/organic, UTZ, Rainforest Alliance, 4C, Starbucks C.A.F.E. Practices, and Nespresso AAA) in three country settings. Chapter 5 showed that changing producer behavior is increasingly difficult as the (opportunity) cost of implementation rises. When reviewing indicators of sustainable intensification, farmers participating in a number of standards – Rainforest Alliance, Starbucks C.A.F.E. Practices, and Nespresso AAA – stand out for showing higher yields than comparable farmers. In some cases (particularly Rainforest Alliance-certified farms), these yields were achieved with similar or lower amounts of chemical fertilizer and pesticide inputs, confirming that sustainable intensification – to an extent – is possible. Regarding requirements that shift time horizons backward, practices that are mandatory, but not excessively costly – such as wearing the appropriate personal protection equipment – see widespread improvements. On the other hand, the flexibility of many environmental rules (i.e., practices that improve soil health or prevent erosion) allows for the interpretation of a wide range of status quo practices as meeting standard requirements, creating only limited practice changes. Practices with high opportunity costs are least likely to be adopted, even if they constitute mandatory rules, and are highly dependent on a supportive institutional context. This holds true both for private standard requirements such as phasing out the use of agrochemicals, as well as requirements that mirror local public regulation such as minimum wage laws. Finally, producers appear locked into their current production systems as regards shade management or sun production, with very few examples of biodiversity-improving agroforestry management emerging in the context of sustainability standard implementation.

Exploring a range of determinants of rule implementation and outcome additionality, Chapter 6 found that knowledge of one's certification group is an imperfect predictor of compliance, with certification cognizance affecting the implementation of only a minority of rules. Those that were perceived as too costly were disregarded even when producers knew that they were certified, and likely were aware that noncompliance could lead to decertification if they were audited.

Further, I found that universal and clear compliance rules are more likely to lead to outcome additionality than flexible, continuous arrangements, particularly when rule-compliant behavior creates long-term opportunity costs, which on its own decreases the likelihood of significant outcome additionality. Price premiums are crucial to motivate producers to adhere to standard requirements – but only a minority of producers in my survey benefit from them. Trainings to advance the capacity to comply need to be both effective and widespread to affect significant behavioral change. It is furthermore likely that training sessions need to be repeated frequently to enhance uptake and recall among farmers. Yet, the data also strengthen Gunningham and Grabosky's (1998) argument that trainings alone are unlikely to convince farmers to move their production practices into a direction that could lead to net yield or income losses, even if such practice changes could have strong beneficial impacts on ecosystems or the long-term health of the local community.

Finally, national-level institutional differences are paramount in shaping the effectiveness of market-driven regulatory governance in the field. Compliance with many indicators represents very different opportunity costs to farmers depending on the public infrastructure (e.g., regarding waste management), legal framework (e.g., regarding minimum wages), and public extension service and support (e.g., regarding capacity-building on sustainable practices and cofunding of sustainability improvements) in place. This explains both the context specificity of previous findings as well as the differential outcomes in this analysis. In many respects, members of the same cooperative or region have shown much greater similarities in practices than members of the same certification scheme.

Aggregating the existing evidence on a sector-wide level, I argue that to date, market-driven regulatory sustainability governance in coffee has been *ineffective at creating alternative institutional arrangements from the conventional market*. Countries with a high level of standard coverage continue to account for an ever-increasing share of global coffee production due to concurrent productivity increases. Simultaneously, biodiversity-friendly coffee production in diverse agroforestry systems is nonexistent or decreasing at rapid rates in these countries. Countries that have widely adapted more stringent environmental standards such as the organic standard have in the past suffered from disease outbreaks that decimated their output volumes, or show extremely low yields, marginalizing them on the mainstream market. Furthermore, the decline of price premiums reoriented producers' focus to either productivity or quality improvements to improve net incomes. Hence, the potential of market-driven regulatory governance to rectify market failures by internalizing social and environmental externalities (i.e., through the establishment of payments for social and ecosystem services through premium payments) has not been realized. Such systems may have provided a first impetus for industry actors to reflect on the definition and operationalization of sustainable coffee production in the wake of the coffee crisis in the early 2000s. Yet, their proposed solution mechanism – market-driven regulatory governance – today only shows *partial goal attainment*; and even this only when allowing for *moving goal posts* toward a definition of sustainable coffee production as intensified production with minimal social and environmental safeguards in place. Yet, they have not managed to address the core problem the industry is grappling with: the fact that many coffee farmers are losing money on their production, leading to a low uptake of farming in the next generation and the specter of a supply shortfall in the next fifty years ahead.

Given that the coffee industry is one of the sectors that have made the greatest strides in developing and adopting market-driven regulatory sustainability governance, this is a discouraging outcome. It also serves as a cautionary tale to other actors and organizations that have tried to copy the initial successes of third-party certifications and multi-stakeholder initiatives in a widening array of commodities and consumption goods. The promise that 'it will be effective as soon as it is taken up by the mainstream' may not necessarily be true. Indeed, the opposite appears to have taken place in the coffee sector. The correspondence between a theory of change and its actual on-the-ground effects thus needs to be carefully assessed on a case-by-case basis. Private governance initiatives, as rapidly as they have developed to serve as 'stopgap measures' for filling the governance gap in globalized marketplaces, are as hard – or even harder – to implement as governmental rules (cf. Auld and Renckens 2018). This state of affairs has implications both for the coffee sector and for the future of the practice and scholarship of market-driven regulatory governance. Before turning to the implications of this research, however, it is necessary to discuss the generalizability of insights from this one (sub)sectoral case study.

8.2 Generalizability of Insights

This book primarily draws on evidence from the implementation of market-driven regulatory governance in three Latin American, Arabica-coffee–producing countries. How far are those insights likely to travel to other coffee-producing origins, other soft commodity sectors, and the broad range of market-driven regulatory governance initiatives?

First, certification schemes have expanded faster in Latin American coffee-producing origins than in Africa or Asia. In 2016, Latin America represented 72 percent of 4C-certified area, 55 percent of Fairtrade, 46 percent of organic, 64 percent of Rainforest Alliance, and 67 percent of UTZ-certified area (Lernoud *et al.* 2018). This is commonly attributed to two reasons: one, the fact that Latin America has a higher level of producer organization, which facilitates certification; and two, that it is the leading Arabica-producing region. As we have seen, Arabica coffee garners a higher price in the world market than Robusta, and is more likely to show high-quality attributes that add to the consumer value proposition and attract "convenient environmentalists" (Delmas and Colgan 2018, p. 199). In consequence, the results presented in this book are likely to represent best-case scenarios of certification implementation in the coffee sector. On the one hand, in regions with fewer institutional support systems and more atomized producers, the implementation of market-driven governance will be highly dependent on the efforts of private traders rolling out certification, as we saw in the case of Honduras. On the other, given the overall lower price profile of Robusta coffee, Robusta-producing origins are likely to derive even fewer price advantages from certification, unless Robusta coffee undergoes its own quality revolution. This means that producers will have a lower financial capacity to comply with the requirements of sustainability standards, and the productivist pressure is likely to be even higher than in the Arabica market. Some first pieces of evidence support this assumption (Kuit *et al.* 2010, 2016; Chiputwa *et al.* 2015).

Existing evidence also suggests that the broad insights of this work – that the institutional design dilemma lowers the likelihood that sustainable production practices with high opportunity costs will be implemented at a higher rate in certified producers as standards scale up their coverage – are likely to hold true across many sectors that use market-driven regulatory governance. This includes, but is not limited to agricultural commodities produced by smallholder producers.

Parallels are most likely to exist in sectors with similar features as coffee. These include a consumer-facing product, a large number of small-scale producers scattered across various emerging economies, and a value chain that is dominated by powerful traders and manufacturers, who have considerable liberty to switch between suppliers. These conditions contribute to the proliferation of standards and the co-opetition between them, which drives one aspect of the institutional design dilemma. In the agricultural realm, some such sectors (e.g., cocoa or tea) have been targeted by the same sustainability standards as coffee, including Fairtrade, Rainforest Alliance, and UTZ, with similar results. For instance, the cocoa sector has an analogous history of certification expansion, standards' alignment with buyers' demands, a decline of price premiums, limited producer benefits and impacts, and the rise of alternative supply chain interventions (Kuit and Waarts 2014; Fountain and Huetz-Adam 2018; Thorlakson 2018). In a striking parallel to my findings, Lemeilleur *et al.* (2015) highlight the productivist mentality behind Rainforest Alliance certification in cocoa, arguing that "certification, proclaimed to be 'in the name of sustainability', is mainly perceived as a productivity-enhancing tool." Trends that link certification mainstreaming to a loss of price premiums, an increasing focus on productivity and quality improvements, and the ultimate use of market-driven governance schemes as a market access barrier have also been identified in tea (Dolan 2010; Cameron 2017).

Other sectors have had a more difficult time linking certified small-scale producers in the Global South to the value chain at scale. This includes agricultural commodities that are intermediate products and produced on both industrial plantations and smallholder farms – such as cotton, soy beans, sugarcane, or palm oil (Lernoud *et al.* 2018) – as well as sectors where production locales span both the Global North and South, such as the forestry and fisheries sectors (Ponte 2012; Moog *et al.* 2015). The exclusionary feature of private sustainability standards in these sectors is a continuous point of contention, and the inclusion of Southern smallholders ranks high on their list of priorities. Current identified barriers to smallholder inclusion – the high costs of certification, insufficient buyer demand, unreliable price premiums, and a lack of producer capacity to fulfill sustainable production requirements – mirror the issues brought up in this book and seem a perpetual concern for market-driven regulatory governance. The story of coffee can provide lessons learned on how to achieve such inclusion while maintaining regulatory effectiveness: namely by providing clear behavioral rules, substantial financial incentives, continuous capacity-building support, and consistent demand for sustainable products.

But we can look beyond agricultural commodities to find parallels that suggest transferable insights. Rather than focusing on agricultural versus other sectors, it is instructive to think about two key features of private governance initiatives: the motivations of producers who participate in private regulation; and their participation in the design of standards and criteria. As has been explored by Potoski and Prakash (2009), under some conditions firms band together and adhere to private regulation (e.g., voluntary environmental programs) to protect a collective reputation (see also Rivera *et al.* 2017). In other cases, they do so to preempt governmental regulation (Abbott and Snidal 2009; deLeon and Rivera 2009). A third variant of private governance aims to solve coordination problems (as opposed to cooperation problems) (Büthe and Mattli 2011). One key feature of many of these previously examined programs is that they are *self-regulatory*: here, the firms that participate in standard-setting and become part of the 'club' are the same firms that have to implement behavioral changes.

Instead, this analysis of *market-driven* regulatory governance focuses on producers (especially those with relatively low technical or financial capacities) that are motivated to adhere to a private regulation in order to gain economic benefits, including market access. The private regulation is often imposed from the outside by other supply chain actors, with producers given little input over the rules they are asked to abide by. In such cases, there is a high risk of buyers imposing such standards to squeeze their suppliers in terms of the conditions and expectations placed on them, and to pass the costs of compliance down to them (Dauvergne and Lister 2013). We are then likely to find similar types of behavior, including a reinterpretation of rules on the ground and selective noncompliance, as in the coffee sector. Indeed, the decoupling literature, which examines when firm-level practices depart from formal labor and environmental standards, includes empirical work in the apparel and footwear (Kim 2013), garment (Mezzadri 2012), and toy manufacturing (Egels-Zandén 2007), as well as coffee (Giuliani *et al.* 2017) sectors.

In this sense, the following insights, which bring the conclusions of this book into conversation with recent work on eco-labels and private governance, should ring true for a range of global value chains.

8.3 'Aiming Big' Requires 'Aiming High' to Be Effective

The ability of private sustainability standards to scale up and expand their coverage quickly has hitherto frequently been seen as a hallmark of success. On the one hand, this is due to the frequent use of standards' global coverage as a proxy for their effectiveness in changing sectoral practices. On the other, such standards are purported to be more credible. In a review of the procedural characteristics of a range of eco-labels, van der Ven (2019) states that standards that 'aim big' – by targeting multinational retailers and aiming for broad market coverage – show greater procedural credibility. He attributes this to three interlinked factors: an increased scrutiny of their procedures by civil society groups due to their association with large brands; a learning effect among standard-setters; and a higher organizational capacity to improve procedural aspects due to a larger staff and budget of standards that 'aim big'. He thus puts forth a 'theory of targets of governance', which claims that standards targeting big retailers are likely to be more trustworthy, while cautioning against smaller labels that evade nongovernmental organizations' (NGOs') critical scrutiny. He also does not find an effect of within-sectoral competition on standards' credibility. Yet, this book shows that van der Ven's (2019) procedural turn of analysis needs to be complemented by a detailed examination both of standards' *content* and their *implementation*. It tells a different story: namely, that standards that aim big need to make compromises in both content and implementation, which limits their effectiveness. While competition indeed leads to their alignment on procedural characteristics, it simultaneously puts downward pressure on certain 'add-on' features that hold the highest opportunity costs (Reinecke *et al.* 2012; Manning and Reinecke 2016; Dietz, Auffenberg, *et al.* 2018a). It also limits the financial capacity standards are able to harness through the marketplace to implement such features, given the dilution of standards' differentiation characteristics.

This story also puts into question van der Ven's (2019) framing of buyers as key targets of private governance. By putting the regulated – that is, producers – at the focus of analysis, this book is able to demonstrate the dilemmas that faces market-driven governance schemes that have to target and appeal to *both* buyers and producers. In this sense, it deepens Ponte's (2012) argument that standards have to simultaneously manage demand-side *and* supply-side (as well as civic) concerns, which are often at odds with each other. It further expands on what Bartley *et al.* (2015, p. 217) call the "contradiction of concentrated retailing." As they write, "while facilitating product certification and conscientious consumption in some ways, the concentrated power of large retailers also puts downwards pressure on prices in global value chains and poses risks for the independence and integrity of certification initiatives." They come to this conclusion by looking at the apparel, furniture, and electronics industries. Seeing a similar pattern emerge in commodity agriculture, with manufacturers such as roasters taking up the role of concentrated veto players (Levy *et al.* 2016), should lead us to hold businesses to a higher standard if they are indeed to be the 'saviors' of the planet (Lenox and Chatterji 2018).

This requires significant innovations in sustainable supply chain management. Rather than using market-driven regulatory governance instrumentally to track their supply and manage reputational risk by passing it on to standard-setting organizations (Dauvergne and Lister 2013; Bartley 2014; Elder *et al.* 2014; Grabs 2018), lead firms should commit to sourcing products from strong standards with a reasonable set of binding rules, and pay stable and high prices corresponding to the local costs of production of such goods. Otherwise, firms are opening themselves up to several areas of mid- and long-term risk. Mid-term, this includes the 'PR disaster' mentioned at the beginning of the book, when consumers realize that a gap exists between their image of certified products and the socioeconomic and environmental reality on the ground. Long-term, and more fatally, it could lead to a supply shortfall as producers exit sectors that are nonprofitable, or adopt intensified practices that do not account for climatic and other types of risks.

Unfortunately, current trends appear to go in an opposite direction, in the coffee sector and elsewhere. To date, market-based regulatory governance initiatives have been frequently called *voluntary* sustainability standards given the third-party, nongovernmental status of standard-setting organizations and the free choice of firms to participate or not in such sustainability certifications. However, as buyer concentration and related power within the supply chain increases, global buyers have an increasing ability to unilaterally impose production standards – along with their costs – onto their suppliers (Gereffi *et al.* 2005; Dauvergne and Lister 2012; Elder *et al.* 2014; Grabs 2017; Grabs and Ponte 2019). The rise of in-house certification, verification and traceability schemes based on the model of Nespresso AAA and Starbucks C.A.F.E. Practices highlights the importance of more closely analyzing the role of new between-actor dynamics in designing, implementing, and enforcing market-driven regulatory governance. As single firms take it upon themselves to define their own sustainable or responsible sourcing standards and to verify that such standards are upheld as an alternative to third-party certification, it will become important to critically evaluate the stringency, coverage, and design characteristics of such initiatives along with their distributive impact. Recall that boundedly rational producers are assumed to opt out of voluntary standards that create increased production costs without related financial benefits unless they have virtually no other access to market. If the current market development continues to move toward the concentration of both buying firms and traders of international commodities, and their development of own-company sourcing standards – as is happening in coffee, but also in other tropical commodities such as cocoa (Fountain and Huetz-Adam 2018) – producers may no longer have a choice of other marketing avenues but to sell to local monopsonies that may squeeze producers even further as a condition to market entry. Such dependency relationships have already been observed in the field (Bitzer *et al.* 2008), but could become exacerbated in this new form of market-driven regulatory governance. Here, deeper analyses of today's global value chain structure and the political economy of global commodity markets may become necessary (Giovannucci and Ponte 2005; Ponte and Gibbon 2005).

8.4 Balancing Collaborative and Confrontational Firm–NGO Interactions

Stroup and Wong (2017) introduce a further constraint to the strategy of aiming big: the authority trap of leading international NGOs. As they note, NGOs tend to gain authority by preferring collaboration to the condemnation of corporate practices. Yet, the resulting private initiatives frequently prove weak or ineffective. Standard-setting organizations in the area of global value chain governance have encountered a similar dilemma. Initially, such NGOs used a range of confrontational means, such as direct targeting, to convert industry actors toward better sourcing practices (Cashore *et al.* 2004; Sasser *et al.* 2006). However, as they have engaged with large supply chain actors, they have increasingly preferred partnership models to confrontational relationships. This follows a general trend among international NGOs toward friendlier engagement with corporations (Spar and La Mure 2003; Soule 2009; Snow and Soule 2010). While select NGOs such as Danwatch still engage in naming-and-shaming campaigns (Hjerl Hansen 2016), the majority of civil society organizations are turning away from contentious confrontations with industry that center on pressuring them to pay higher and fairer prices for sustainable coffee. The latter focus constitutes a typical "problem that require[s] a fundamental redistribution of power" (Bartley 2007, p. 300), where the optimal result is market-driven regulatory governance. Rather, they are pivoting to more collaborative approaches focused on development assistance, where the optimal result is a partnership based on philanthropic donations as a "minimally intrusive way" (Abbott and Snidal 2009, p. 60) of fulfilling stakeholder demands. Direct-impact projects supported by NGOs focus for instance on farmer training in good agricultural practices, gender equality, or climate change resilience (Peyser 2014; Tchibo 2014; JDE 2016).

Not only that, many standard-setting organizations have redefined their mission and theories of change, repositioning their expertise and networks as ideal preconditions to become partners for rural development projects, consultants in sector transformation, and stakeholders in broader public–private partnerships (Grabs 2017; Millard 2017; Fransen 2018). Indeed, Fransen (2018) argues that private standard organizations are taking first steps to pivot entirely away from their original regulatory governance functions toward service-focused roles vis-à-vis large buyer firms with their own corporate sustainability programs. In coffee, for instance, the Rainforest Alliance is rolling out Nestlé's 'Nescafé Better Farming Practices' project to 12,000 farmers in Sumatra (Millard 2016), as well as assisting Caffé Nero's sustainable farming training program in Latin America (Mace 2016). Fairtrade International, in turn, recognized in its 2016/2017 Annual Report that "the [commercial] landscape has changed significantly in recent years, with some companies starting to move away from independent standards and certifications to create their own corporate sustainability schemes" (FLO 2017c). In response, in 2017 it launched an "Offer to Business" under which "Fairtrade will launch new services to companies beyond existing standards and certification such as supply chain management" (FLO 2017c).

Yet, this book allows us to question the wisdom of a movement in this direction. It suggests that the greatest change in practices is likely to occur when *clear rules* are passed down through *continuous capacity-building activities* and incentivized through *higher prices* passed down to producers. This requires civil society actors to take up both collaborative (when supporting capacity building) as well as confrontational, watchdog roles (to oversee rule implementation as well as power abuse in global supply chains). If confrontational NGOs move out of this space, it will in turn lower the reputational risk of companies and allow them greater leeway to shape sustainability governance in their best interest. The importance of a 'radical flank effect' (Burchell and Cook 2013) should thus not be underestimated; and civil society organizations would benefit from coordinating accordingly.

8.5 Supporting Market-Driven Regulatory Governance: The Role of Governments

Similar to Bartley (2018), my analysis shows an intricate web of public and private regulations that affect producer behavior. Some institutions, such as the Colombian Federación Nacional de Cafeteros de Colombia (FNC), explicitly and successfully supported producers to achieve certification as a market access strategy. In other cases, such as under Costa Rica's Coffee Law, existing institutional regulations that aim to smooth price fluctuations and regulate profit margins of intermediaries may actually present obstacles to the passing through of market incentives coming from differentiation strategies. The cross-country comparison thus shows a hitherto underappreciated trade-off between countrywide collective action and supporting the differentiation of select subgroups.

Recently, certification organizations are moving toward considering 'landscape' or 'jurisdictional' approaches to achieve greater coverage at lower costs (UNFSS 2016; Stickler *et al.* 2018). Here, they rely on governments' support in aligning public policies, extension agency work, and broader policies. Such initiatives have interesting antecedents in collective voluntary environmental programs in the tourism sector, as studied by Blackman *et al.* (2014) and Rivera *et al.* (2017), although their larger geographic scope might make them more difficult to implement than the community-level tourism programs. For first-movers, such a jurisdictional approach offers the chance to distinguish an entire region as 'sustainable origin' with third-party backing. Such an approach may overcome the trade-off between supporting within-regional differentiation and holistic improvements. On the other hand, as more regions achieve such a status, its differentiation potential will sink, locking them in the same treadmill of chasing decreasing marginal gains.

As producing countries weigh the potential benefits and drawbacks of differentiation strategies versus collective action, it is instructive to consider lessons from the past. Indeed, a number of producing country actors have recently made efforts to overcome their collective action problem by realigning their political priorities. The first World Coffee Producers' Forum was hosted by the Colombian FNC in Medellin in 2017, and culminated in a statement that called for a study of historical coffee production costs and prices that would "analyse if the international contributions of coffee, both of the New York and London stock exchanges, reflect the reality of physical market, and give alternative solutions to outlined issues in the Forum" such as "very low prices for producers, excessive volatility, and the largest fraction of the value of the coffee supply chain being held by other agents" (Perfect Daily Grind 2017). To industry experts, this forum and its action plan signaled the willingness of coffee-producing countries to reconsider uniting forces, as done in the past (see Section 7.1) – which, considering the increasing concentration of production in a small number of countries, would be difficult, but possible. One idea for such collective action would be for producing countries to work together to establish a new level playing field regarding sustainable practices, establish reasonable supply management systems of such sustainable coffee, and bundle their respective coffees with quality and emotional attributes that would allow them to compete on a differentiated, rather than commodity market. Such an innovation would have the greatest success if taken seriously by buyers and communicated carefully to producers, as explored in the next section.

8.6 United But Separate: Bundling Sustainability, Quality, and Productivity Incentives at the Producer Level

Delmas and Colgan (2018) argue that appealing to consumers that are 'convenient environmentalists' requires firms to bundle sustainable product attributes with attributes such as quality, status, emotion, and money. To a large part, such bundling has already taken place in the sustainable coffee sector. After a period where Fairtrade and organic coffees were known as morally superior, but bad-quality alternatives to conventional goods, requiring a trade-off between sensory and moral preferences, companies trading in certified products started to focus more on the consumer value proposition (Tallontire 2000). Today, certified coffees tend to be more present in higher-quality segments (bundling sustainability and quality) and have engaged in significant storytelling (bundling sustainability with emotion), while mainstreaming has also allowed for the entry of certified goods in discount retailers and the low-end price segment (bundling sustainability and money). This segmented marketing strategy has arguably contributed to the rapid scaling up of certified coffees.

However, this study has also shown that bundling attributes at the consumer end can lead to trade-offs at the producer end, unless incentives are carefully separated. My study has brought forth instances of higher quality being expected at the same time, and for the same price incentive, as compliance with sustainability attributes. This may lead to a conflation of perceived expectations, trade-offs between incompatible production practices, and – notably – the prioritization of the most necessary conditions for market entry, which tends to be quality, over sustainable practices. As companies aim to bundle sustainability with affordable consumer prices, the priority is set on enhancing productivity and lowering production costs, which again may subsume important principles of sustainability. Bundling sustainability, quality, and productivity at the producer level, on the other hand, would require setting clear and separate economic incentives for each of these factors. This would allow producers to fulfill both quality-enhancing and sustainable practices while being compensated for both, as well as factor in trade-offs between conflicting market signals. Further, such market signals should be clear, reliable, and long-term in their design in order to overcome the information asymmetries that producers face when making decisions on upfront investments in the expectation of future trade-offs.

8.7 Implications for Sustainable Consumers

What does this state of affairs mean for sustainably minded consumers who care about biodiversity protection and improvement of smallholder livelihoods? The present evidence suggests that indiscriminately purchasing coffee declared 'sustainable' is a strategy that is ever more tenuously linked to actual improvements on the ground. There are a number of possible avenues forward for consumers.

First, one could envision awareness-raising campaigns targeted at strengthening individual-level purchasing strategies that steer brands toward particular sourcing strategies. From a political consumerism perspective, if the limit of the effectiveness of the current instruments is 'label confusion' in the marketplace and a lack of information on the actual sustainability measures required by different standards (Harbaugh *et al.* 2011), the creation and dissemination of information such as the data presented in this book could allow for fast improvements on the ground. Recommending ethical consumers to only choose products certified with the Smithsonian Migratory Bird Center's Bird Friendly label or the Fairtrade/organic combination, for instance, which in this and other work have been linked to the greatest agroecological benefits, could provide a more clear and streamlined demand incentive for roasting companies to prefer certain (more stringent) schemes over others, as well as greater financial resources to act as payments for social and ecosystem services, as hypothesized earlier. On the other hand, it would require a concerted consumer-level action plan to overcome the market power of retailers at the point of sale, as well as a fast recruitment effort of emerging consumer markets in producing countries as well as Asia to make sure no displacement effects of unsustainable goods into lower-priced markets take place.

A second avenue would be to harness the collective power of consumers in more organized ways and create civil society campaigns that hold roasting companies accountable to specific and measurable sourcing commitments of specific standards. This would prevent buyers from exploiting the market-based pricing system by changing their demands and sourcing strategies flexibly in an effort to minimize added costs, as is currently done. For instance, in direct opposition to the functional theory behind market-driven regulatory governance, the director of sustainability of a large US roaster reported during a 2017 webinar that "we had to differentiate from single certifications; committing to one certification could have skewed demand and prices and the overall goal for our partnerships was to source sustainable coffees without falsely increasing the price paid at origin" (Innovation Forum 2017). Pressuring roasters to make long-term, credible sourcing commitments that they reliably fulfill could overcome the time-based information asymmetry that was at the heart of the decline in price premiums over the last decade, and naming-and-shaming campaigns might exert enough reputational risk for well-known brands to comply with such demands. Yet, the dynamism at the heart of the coffee market, particularly on the roasting level, makes it likely that portfolios are spun off, tainted brands are spun off, and new companies with a 'blank slate' appear on the scene (Grabs 2018). In such cases, enforcing temporal accountability and long-term commitments becomes much more challenging, and possibly even meaningless if companies who made such commitments cease to exist in their same form.

A final possibility for demand-side action is to take a closer look at the central tenet of strong sustainable development, which aims to embed a functioning social and economic system inside recognized planetary boundaries. If we truly value the importance of the subtropical forests and ecosystems that currently occupy the land that coffee production might move into when climate change makes existing coffeelands unsuitable, we might start to question the assumption of a 25 percent demand increase in the next decade (Verma 2015; ICO 2017b) in greater depth. After all, coffee has traditionally been a luxury good and has little nutritional value or importance for food security. Thus, limiting ourselves to a more conscious consumption of fewer but better cups of coffee – for which we are willing to pay substantially higher prices to farmers – might be a way to achieve economic, social, and environmental sustainability on a larger scale through the mainstream market. While abrupt demand decreases might in the short run lead to oversupply and price dips that would need to be managed through institutional safeguards, in the long run it would discourage crop expansion into ecologically sensitive land. It would also encourage farmers to diversify their holdings by adding other crops to their current agroecosystem and possibly even moving from farming into alternative sources of income generation. This has happened endogenously in Costa Rica, the country where our surveyed coffee farmers have the highest standard of living and a large share of others have become 'weekend farmers' that use their holdings as a supplementary, rather than their primary source of income. From a meta-perspective, while acknowledging the need for immediate improvements in producer livelihoods, it is sobering to keep in mind that for farms under a certain minimum size – according to interviewed experts, between 5 and 10 hectares – it will be difficult for any type of coffee production to be economically sustainable, given the need to generate enough returns for forward-looking investments as well as cover family expenses. In cases where farms are smaller than this, the most sustainable long-term scenario for a smallholder coffee farmer might indeed be to *get out of coffee* – even if this is seldom mentioned in the industry discourse.

Ultimately, the research for this book taught me that making supply chains sustainable will require the combination of public and private efforts, consumer and producer choices, economic incentives and intrinsic motivations, and changes in both individual agency and systemic constraints. However, what is increasingly clear to all actors involved is that the current economic model of commodity production is not able to support truly sustainable practices on the ground, neither in socioeconomic nor in environmental terms. How to share the costs of sustainable production equitably and fairly in a world with limited planetary boundaries and a growing population with ever-increasing consumption demands will be a critical topic of research for many years to come.

8.8 Making the 'Effectiveness' Turn with a New Theoretical Framework

Finally, analyses of these and other questions may benefit from applying new theoretical frameworks to market-driven regulatory governance such as the micro-institutional rational choice framework presented in this study. Its ability to analytically connect the constitutional, collective choice, and operational level of action; to differentiate between rules-in-form and rules-in-practice; to acknowledge the existence of simultaneous, conflicting, and overlapping institutional arrangements; and to put the targeted individual – whether it is a farmer or producing firm – in the middle of the examination of market-driven regulatory governance makes this framework a useful and to date underused approach to studying private governance. Future research may focus more strongly on the interactions on different levels of action, for instance, feedback processes between the collective-choice and operational levels or determinants of rule-making decisions based on constitutional level choices, alongside cross-sectoral analyses of differences in public or market institutional frameworks that may influence the effectiveness of market-driven regulatory governance in improving the environmental and social impacts of global production and consumption.

Indeed, I would contend that the micro-institutional rational choice framework as presented here has the potential to travel far beyond analyses of private regulatory governance and be useful for any governance or regulatory analysis that is concerned with how effective different types of governance approaches are in solving the problems they were established to address. As global challenges such as ecosystem degradation, climate change, or resource scarcity increase in their urgency and severity of implications if left unaddressed, it is of growing relevance for political science scholars to closely tie their institutional analyses and policy advice to on-the-ground impacts that different types of regulatory solutions may have. As discussed in Chapter 2, this is however a highly complicated endeavor, and is becoming ever more challenging as the global governance arena becomes more and more polycentric. Today, multilateral, national, and regional policy solutions coexist with mechanisms originating in business and civil society communities, leading to complex horizontal and vertical institutional interplay (Young 2002). The micro-institutional rational choice framework with its focus on rules-in-practice and incentive mechanisms provides a clarifying lens to confront this complexity and evaluate on-the-ground effects of polycentric regimes. In allowing for simultaneous institutional arrangements, it is well equipped to handle polycentricity (and, in fact, was developed explicitly with polycentricity in mind). It is further able to link these effects to design choices – both of rules and of rule-making institutions – in a clear and theoretically consistent way that opens up many avenues of future research. It is my hope that future political science and governance research will be increasingly concerned with linking institutions to their problem-solving potential and on-the-ground outcomes in the physical world, and may find it helpful to use and adapt the proposed theoretical framework to do so. After all, as the opening quote of this book aptly stated, if all the institutions and governance arrangements we study do not lead us to greater environmental protection and social equity, what is the point?

Appendix 1

Overview of Qualitative Interviews

Nr.	Date	Organization	Type
1	13.08.2015	Roaster 1	Roaster
2	19.08.2015	INCAE Business School	Researcher
3	06.11.2015	Importer-affiliated NGO	NGO
4	12.11.2015	Cambridge University	Researcher
5	17.11.2015	Fair Trade USA/Coffee Kids	NGO
6	18.11.2015	Centre for Agriculture and Bioscience International/ Coffee & Climate	NGO
7	19.11.2015	Costa Rican processor 1	Producer organization
8	23.11.2015	Importer 1	Trader
9	24.11.2015	Multinational exporter 1	Trader
10	25.11.2015	Importer 2	Trader
11	26.11.2015	Roaster 2	Roaster
12	30.11.2015	ANACAFE	Institution
13	02.12.2015	Costa Rican cooperative 1	Producer organization
14	07.12.2015	Kuit Consulting	Researcher
15	08.12.2015	Honduran exporter 1	Trader
16	08.12.2015	Honduran exporter 2	Trader
17	10.12.2015	Costa Rican processor 2	Producer organization
18	06.01.2016	Colombian cooperative 1	Producer organization
19	13.01.2016	Roaster 2	Roaster
20	14.01.2016	Roaster 3	Roaster
21	21.01.2016	Honduran exporter 1	Trader
22	25.01.2016	Universidad de los Andes	Researcher
23	05.03.2016	Multinational exporter 1	Trader
24	06.03.2016	Roaster 4	Roaster
25	14.03.2016	Roaster 2	Roaster
26	11.05.2016	UNDP	Institution
27	11.05.2016	Colombian exporter 1	Trader

(*cont.*)

Nr.	Date	Organization	Type
28	18.05.2016	Promoción de Café de Colombia	Institution
29	03.06.2016	Importer 3	Trader
30	07.06.2016	Roaster 5	Roaster
31	08.06.2016	Federación Nacional de Cafeteros de Colombia/ Coffee Institute	Institution
32	10.06.2016	Federación Nacional de Cafeteros de Colombia	Institution
33	14.06.2016	Colombian exporter 2	Trader
34	20.06.2016	ICAFE	Institution
35	27.06.2016	Plataforma de Comercio Sostenible de Colombia	Institution
36	27.06.2016	Roaster 5	Roaster
37	28.06.2016	Brazilian exporter 1	Trader
38	29.06.2016	Roaster 6	Roaster
39	06.07.2016	Colombian exporter 3	Trader
40	10.07.2016	Roaster 7	Roaster
41	17.07.2016	Multinational exporter 2	Trader
42	18.07.2016	Multinational input trader 1	Trader
43	01.08.2016	Colombian cooperative 1	Producer organization
44	09.08.2016	Colombian cooperative 2	Producer organization
45	15.08.2016	Colombian exporter 3	Trader
46	15.08.2016	Universidad de los Andes	Researcher
47	16.08.2016	Promoción de Café de Colombia	Institution
48	16.08.2016	Federación Nacional de Cafeteros de Colombia	Institution
49	16.08.2016	Colombian exporter 3	Trader
50	05.09.2016	Cambridge University	Researcher
51	01.10.2016	Roaster 8	Roaster
52	10.10.2016	Costa Rican exporter 3	Trader
53	08.11.2016	Enveritas	NGO
54	09.11.2016	Roaster 1	Roaster
55	15.01.2017	Catholic Relief Services	NGO
56	17.01.2017	Costa Rican cooperative 2	Producer organization
57	25.01.2017	Costa Rican cooperative 3	Producer organization

(*cont.*)

Nr.	Date	Organization	Type
58	25.01.2017	Costa Rican cooperative 1	Producer organization
59	16.03.2017	Costa Rican cooperative 4	Producer organization
60	15.05.2017	Coffee Assurance Services	NGO
61	18.05.2017	Fairtrade Labelling Organizations International	NGO
62	04.07.2017	Global GAP	NGO
63	05.07.2017	Assurance Services International	NGO
64	13.11.2017	International Coffee Organization	Institution
65	23.11.2017	Roaster 9	Roaster
66	04.05.2018	Roaster 3	Roaster

Appendix 2

Propensity Score Matching Analysis and Covariates

To calculate the additionality of practices, I used a combination of propensity score matching and linear/logit regression techniques. Propensity score matching is a pseudo-experimental impact evaluation technique that uses statistical methods to construct the counterfactual outcome – what would have happened to certified producers had they not been certified – and calculates the impact of certification (τ) as the difference between a certified farm's outcome and its counterfactual:

$$\tau_i = Y_i(1) - Y_i(0), \tag{1}$$

where the potential outcomes are defined as $Y_i(D_i)$ for each individual i; i = 1, ..., N; N denotes the total population; and the treatment indicator D_i equals 1 if individual i is certified and 0 otherwise (Caliendo and Kopeinig 2008). The total impact of certification can then be approximated by calculating the average treatment effect on the treated (ATET), that is, the difference between expected outcome values with and without certification for those who actually participated in a certification group (Caliendo and Kopeinig 2008):

$$\tau_{ATET} = E(\tau \,|\, D = 1) = E[Y(1) \,|\, D = 1] - E[Y(0) \,|\, D = 1]. \tag{2}$$

Since participation in a certain certification program is rarely a random outcome, the main challenge when using matching techniques lies in the identification of comparable noncertified farms. Usually, this is done by identifying characteristics that could have influenced a household's participation in the certification process such as education levels, farm size, gender of the household head, and region. However, as one adds matching covariates, it becomes increasingly difficult to guarantee a precise match in all characteristics. Using the propensity score – the likelihood to be certified, given the set of underlying covariates – allows this matching problem to be reduced to one single dimension (Heckman *et al.* 1998). The ATET is then calculated by taking the mean of the difference in outcomes between treated individuals and their matched controls based on the propensity score.

For the logit model, my explanatory variables include farm size (either total size or coffee area, depending on respective better fit), farmer's gender, farmer's age, farmer's level of education, household size, land tenure, association membership status, location information (time to school, clinic, and market), altitude, and region (where applicable). These variables were informed by theory as well as a literature review of publications that had previously used propensity score matching (PSM) or other impact evaluation techniques in evaluating coffee certifications (Arnould *et al.* 2009; Bolwig *et al.* 2009; Ruben *et al.* 2009; Kamau *et al.* 2010; Kuit *et al.* 2010, 2013, 2016; Barham *et al.* 2011; Beuchelt and Zeller 2011; Ruben and Zuniga 2011; Blackman and Naranjo 2012; Jena *et al.* 2012; van Rijn *et al.* 2012; Ruben and Fort 2012; Elder *et al.* 2013; Rueda and Lambin 2013). The logit model was estimated for each certified group separately and covariates were dropped if they were collinear or had adverse effects on the explanatory power of the logit model. In a next step, I calculated the propensity score for each subgroup of certified and possible controls and checked that the balancing property was satisfied. If it was not, I exchanged interchangeable variables (e.g., total area and coffee area) or dropped variables with low predictive power (e.g., one of the distance estimators) and reestimated the propensity score. The final matching covariates for each certified group are listed later.

For the propensity score matching model, I used logit models with two nearest neighbors and caliper sizes of 0.2–0.3 in the propensity score matching algorithm, and report Abadie–Imbens robust standard errors. I also applied sensitivity analyses that included changing model type (probit vs. logit), the number of nearest neighbors (1 vs. 2 vs. 5), and adding covariates. None of the sensitivity analyses showed significant differences from the main results, which is why I focus on reporting results from the main model specification as described earlier.

To further test the robustness of our results, I also used regression analysis.[1] Here, I used the following specification:

$$Y_i = \alpha_0 + \beta X_i + \gamma T_i + \varepsilon_i, \tag{3}$$

where Y_i is the outcome variable of farm i, X_i is a vector of control variables, T_i is the treatment variable (certification with the respective standard), ε_i the idiosyncratic error term, and α_0, β, and γ parameters to be estimated, with γ consisting the reported effect of certification, when controlling for all other covariates. I used a linear regression model and ordinary least squares with heteroscedasticity-robust standard errors for continuous variables and logit estimation for binary ones. For the logit results, I report the average marginal effect and the associated Delta-method standard error. I use the same covariates in the regression models as for the matching analyses, but add land tenure, distance to school, and distance to health clinic in those cases where they were dropped from the PSM analysis to provide a better comparability of regression results.

The two methods are combined to add robustness to the results, but in theory they broadly identify the same variable: the additional effect on the outcome in question that can be attributed to participation in the respective certification scheme while keeping all other covariates equal.[2] The true effect of certification participation is likely to lie within the range established by the two results, with findings considered more robust the higher the results' significance and the closer the two procedures' results align.

---

[1] After reviewing the literature, I decided against weighting the regression by the propensity scores due to its likelihood to increase the random error in the estimates and to bias the estimated standard errors downward, and the possibility that weighting could increase the bias in estimated causal parameters (Freedman and Berk 2008).

[2] To be precise, they report outcomes that are subtly different. In the results of my propensity score matching analysis, I report the ATET, that is, the effect is calculated by approximating what would have happened if certified producers had not been certified. The regression methods by definition use the entire sample to calculate inference; their results are thus closer to the average treatment effect, where the effect also takes into consideration what would have happened if noncertified farmers had been certified. For the purposes of impact evaluation, it is however more precise to calculate the ATET through propensity score matching since selection effects might make it unlikely that untreated individuals would have been treated; thus, I report the ATET as my main result and supplement the regression results as a robustness test.

Table A2.1 *Covariates for propensity score matching of Honduran certification groups*

Covariates used in PSM analysis	Rainforest Alliance	UTZ	Fairtrade conventional	Fairtrade/ organic	4C
Gender	x	x	x	x	x
Age	x	x	x	x	x
Literacy		x			
Years of schooling	x		x	x	x
Household size	x	x			x
Land tenure	x	x	x	x	
Time to clinic	x				
Time to school	x		x	x	
Time to market				x	
Total area	x	x	x		
Coffee area				x	x
Instituto Hondureño del Café membership	x	x			x
Asociación Hondureña de Productores de Café membership	x		x	x	
Asociación Nacional del Café membership					x
Own coffee mill			x		
Region dummy (Occidente)	x	x	x	x	x

Table A2.2 *Covariates for propensity score matching of Colombian certification groups*

Covariates used in PSM analysis	Rainforest Alliance/ AAA	Nespresso AAA	C.A.F.E. Practices	4C	Fairtrade
Gender	x	x	x		x
Age	x	x	x	x	x
Literacy					
Years of schooling	x	x	x	x	x
Household size	x	x	x	x	x

Table A2.2 (*cont.*)

Covariates used in PSM analysis	Rainforest Alliance/ AAA	Nespresso AAA	C.A.F.E. Practices	4C	Fairtrade
Land tenure	x	x	x		x
Time to clinic	x	x	x	x	x
Time to school	x	x	x	x	x
Time to market		x	x	x	x
Total area	x			x	x
Coffee area		x	x		
Federación Nacional de Cafeteros de Colombia membership	x	x	x	x	x
Junta membership	x	x	x	x	x
Own coffee mill		x			x
Altitude	x	x	x		x
Region dummy (Andes)		x	x		

Table A2.3 *Covariates for propensity score matching of Costa Rican certification groups*

Covariates used in PSM analysis	Rainforest Alliance/ AAA	Rainforest Alliance/ C.A.F.E. Practices	C.A.F.E. Practices	Fairtrade
Gender	x	x	x	x
Age	x	x	x	x
Years of schooling	x	x	x	x
Household size	x	x	x	x
Land tenure	x	x	x	x
Time to clinic	x	x	x	x
Time to school		x	x	x
Time to market	x		x	
Total area				x
Coffee area	x	x	x	x
Unión de Pequeños Productores Agropecuarios Costarricenses membership	x	x	x	x
Fairtrade dummy		x		

Appendix 3

Conservation Principles for Coffee Production

Revised Version, April 4, 2001
Conservation International
Consumer's Choice Council
Rainforest Alliance
Smithsonian Migratory Bird Center
Summit Foundation

The following Conservation Principles for Coffee Production apply to farms and processing facilities in all coffee-growing regions of the world and should be the foundation of any conservation-based certification program. In addition, they can be used to guide the development of industry sourcing guidelines and codes of conduct, changes in government or financial sector policy to encourage sustainable agriculture, and modernization of technical assistance programs. It is also recognized that coffee quality is fundamental to market value. A complementary emphasis is required through all stages of the coffee value chain to ensure delivery to the consumer of a high quality product.

In many cases, these Principles require collaboration between producers, communities and local and national governments. Specific applications of these Conservation Principles will vary by region in accordance with their climates, ecological variables, traditions and cultures. However, programs that aim to improve coffee production systems must at least address and monitor progress in accordance with the following Conservation Principles to ensure that there is a real conservation benefit.

1. SUSTAINABLE LIVELIHOODS: Coffee production systems and commercialization should improve the social and economic livelihoods of producers and provide economic benefits to local communities.

- Coffee producers are empowered to access markets and to develop long-term trading relationships with buyers.
- Equitable prices for producers are a primary consideration in all marketing agreements.
- Coffee producers are encouraged to diversify their sources of income through the development of on-farm and/or community-based alternatives to coffee production.
- Coffee producers should apply long-term management plans that guide farm production activities and that are periodically revised to address the environmental and social impacts of production, as determined by ongoing monitoring and audits.
- Communities are directly involved, from the beginning, in a participatory process of management planning, monitoring and implementation.
- Co-operatives work to ensure that the basic rights and needs of their members are met and are committed to continual improvement over time.
- Coffee farms that employ workers conform to local laws and applicable international conventions related to workers' rights and benefits and are in a process of continual improvement over time.
- Wages and benefits meet or exceed the minimum required under local and national laws.
- Working conditions meet or exceed applicable laws and regulations related to health and safety of workers.
- Workers and their families, including seasonal workers, are provided with access to potable water, sanitary facilities, adequate housing, education and training, transportation, and health services.
- Workers' rights to organize and negotiate freely with their employers are guaranteed in accordance with local laws and international obligations.

2. ECOSYSTEM AND WILDLIFE CONSERVATION: Coffee production systems maintain and enhance biological diversity and ecosystem functions on farms and surrounding areas.

- There is no disturbance of intact natural forest.
- Rare, threatened or endangered species and habitats are protected, including adequate measures to restrict hunting and commercial collection of threatened flora and fauna.

- Where coffee is grown in areas originally covered by forest, a canopy cover of diverse native tree species that conserves local and endemic biodiversity is incorporated into coffee production systems.
- Pruning of shade trees preserves their reproductive processes and protects the habitat they provide for plants and animals.
- Areas of high ecological value located on and around coffee farms and producer communities, including wetlands and native forests, are protected.
- Coffee farms and surrounding areas create a diverse landscape mosaic that serves as wildlife habitat and migration corridors between protected areas.
- Land restoration programs using native species are implemented on areas degraded by unsustainable cropping, grazing or extractive practices.

3. SOIL CONSERVATION: Farm management practices control erosion and conserve or enhance soil structure and fertility.

- Most soil nutrients are supplied by on-farm sources, by means such as organic fertilizers, cover crops, mulch and compost.
- Environmentally appropriate measures are taken to control erosion and build soil quality, particularly on sloped terrain or adjacent to water courses and wetland areas.

4. WATER CONSERVATION AND PROTECTION: Coffee production systems reduce water use to the greatest extent possible and prevent pollution of all water sources.

- All existing sources of contamination are eliminated and potential sources are managed, to prevent pollution of water resources.
- Vegetative buffer zones are in place adjacent to all water sources.
- The volume of water used in wet processing and on farms is continually reduced through the application of more efficient technologies and recycling of water.
- No alteration of the course or hydrology of streams or other surface water occurs.

5. ENERGY CONSERVATION: Energy is used efficiently at all stages of the coffee production system, and renewable sources of energy are used whenever possible.

- Efforts are made to reduce the use of non-renewable energy sources such as petroleum-based fuels and to incorporate renewable sources of energy such as solar drying.
- Firewood comes from well-managed sources that avoid degradation of natural forest and that employ environmental safeguards.

6. WASTE MANAGEMENT: Waste and coffee by-products are managed to minimize environmental impacts by applying the principles of reduction, reuse and recycling.

- Measures are taken to continually reduce the overall quantity of waste produced on the farm.
- All organic farm by-products and domestic waste, including coffee pulp and parchment, are composted and reused in the coffee production system.
- Recycling of inorganic waste is encouraged. Inorganic waste that is not recycled, including chemicals and other toxic materials, is not burned and is properly managed, using landfills if available.

7. PEST AND DISEASE MANAGEMENT: Coffee production systems strive to eliminate all inputs of chemical pesticides, fungicides, herbicides and synthetic fertilizers.

- Farms are certified organic or are demonstrating increasing reductions in the toxicity and quantity of synthetic agrochemicals being applied, leading to the elimination of agrochemical use.
- Organic management techniques are employed, including biological, cultural and mechanical pest and disease controls. Monitoring programs are in place to assist in the application of non-chemical preventive controls.
- Synthetic agrochemicals are used only in extreme cases when necessary to avert severe crop loss and substantial economic failure.
- No agrochemicals that are banned for agricultural use in their country of use, country of origin or by international agreement are stored or used on the farm.
- Effective measures are taken to ensure the health and safety of farm workers who may handle or be exposed to agrochemicals, including the provision of education, protective clothing and access to adequate medical treatment.

- All farm inputs are applied in a selective, targeted manner in order to minimize drift to neighboring fields, polluted run-off or ground-water contamination.

Glossary:

Agrochemicals: Synthetic substances used to control competition from other organisms (e.g., pesticides and herbicides), and to provide crops with the nutrients necessary to compensate for lack of soil fertility (fertilizers).

Areas of high ecological value: Those areas that possess one or more of the following attributes:

- areas containing globally, regionally or nationally significant concentrations of biodiversity;
- areas that are in or contain rare, threatened or endangered ecosystems;
- areas that provide basic services of nature (e.g., watershed protection or erosion control) in critical situations;
- areas fundamental to meeting the basic needs of local communities (e.g., subsistence or health);
- areas critical to local communities' traditional cultural identity (areas of significance identified in cooperation with such local communities).

Biological Diversity: The variability among living organisms from all sources including, inter alia, terrestrial, marine and other aquatic ecosystems and the ecological complexes of which they are a part; this includes diversity within species, between species and of ecosystems.

Buffer zones: In protecting critical ecological areas, the buffer is an area of forest land that reduces the impacts of adjacent activities on the critical area. In managing biosphere reserves, it is a portion or edge of a protected area that has land-use controls that only allow activities compatible with the objectives of the protected area.

Canopy cover: The multiple storeys of foliage in a stand of trees or shrubs, in particular the uppermost continuous layer of branches and foliage.

Degraded land: Land that has suffered damage to its natural composition, structures and functions to such an extent that the structures required for future ecological processes are no longer present.

Economic failure: In the context of this document, a substantial loss of crops due to factors external to the management practices of the farm, resulting in severe negative economic repercussions and potential bankruptcy to the farm or cooperative.

Ecosystem: A community of plants, animals, and their physical environments, functioning together as an interdependent unit.

Endangered species: Any species which is in danger of extinction throughout all or a significant portion of its range.

Landscape Mosaic: The pattern of different ages and types of ecosystems distributed across the landscape.

Local laws: Includes all legal norms given by organisms of government whose jurisdiction is less than the national level, such as departmental and municipal laws, as well as customary norms.

Long-term: The time-scale manifested by the objectives of the management plan and the commitment to maintain a viable ecological system. The length of time will vary according to ecological conditions, and will be a function of how long it takes a given ecosystem to recover its natural structure and composition following disturbance.

Natural: Areas where many of the principal characteristics and key elements of native ecosystems such as complexity, structure and diversity are present.

Organic: An integrated system of farming based on ecological principles, that replenishes and maintains long-term soil fertility by optimizing conditions for biological activity within the soil, rather than through the application of agrochemicals.

Renewable sources of energy: Any resource that provides energy and is capable of indefinite renewal on a human-based time scale.

Restoration: A process of returning ecosystems or habitats to their native structure and species composition.

Threatened species: Any species that is endangered or is likely to become endangered within the foreseeable future throughout all or a significant portion of its range.

Appendix 4

Overview of Meta-analysis Coding Matrices

Table A4.1 *Coding of indicator-specific criteria*

Indicators included in the meta-analysis	Public equivalent			Investment and opportunity costs		Mandatory/critical in private sustainability standard						
Socially sustainable production practices	Honduras	Colombia	Costa Rica	Investment costs	Opportunity costs	FT/ Fairtrade	organic	UTZ	4C	Rainforest Alliance	AAA	C.A.F.E.
1 Productivity (in 100 lbs/hectare) (as livelihood improvement strategy)												
2 Elimination of use of highly hazardous pesticides	x (Rainforest Alliance, 4C)					x	x	x	x	x	x	x
3 Elimination of open-air burning of household waste				x			x					
4 Safe pesticide container disposal								x				
5 Use of complete personal protection equipment				x				x		x	x	
6 Existence of orderly agrochemical storage facility				x				x				

#	Indicator													
7	Existence of complete first aid kit			x			x							
8	Access to potable drinking water			x			x	x	x					
9	Farm diversification (as climate change adaptation method)								x					
10	Increase of workers' wage per day (in US$) to minimum wage	x	x	x	x	x	x		x	x	x	x	x	x
11	Increase of pickers' wage per day (in US $) to minimum wage	x	x	x	x	x	x		x		x	x	x	
12	Payment of minimum wage for all workers	x	x	x	x	x	x		x		x	x	x	x
13	School attendance of school-age children	x	x		x	x	x				x	x		x
14	Elimination of school-age children doing dangerous work (e.g., applying pesticides)	x	x	x	x	x	x		x		x	x	x	x

Table A4.1 (*cont.*)

Indicators included in the meta-analysis	Public equivalent			Investment and opportunity costs		Mandatory/critical in private sustainability standard						
	Honduras	Colombia	Costa Rica	Investment costs	Opportunity costs	FT/ Fairtrade	organic	UTZ	4C	Rainforest Alliance	AAA	C.A.F.E.
Socially sustainable production practices												
15 Elimination of hiring of minors (below 14/15 years of age)	x	x	x		x	x	x	x	x	x	x	x
Environmentally sustainable production practices												
16 Use of organic fertilizer							x					
17 Synthetic fertilizer efficiency improvement (in bags/100 lbs)							x					
18 Use of traps for pests (e.g., the coffee berry borer) as integrated pest management (IPM) method												

19 Collection of cherries postharvest as IPM method		
20 Pesticide efficiency improvement (in liters/100 lbs)	x	
21 Elimination of the use of herbicides	x	
22 On-farm trash collection		
23 Over 50 percent of soil covered with cover crops or mulch		
24 Use of erosion barriers and terraces		
25 Use of windbreaks		
26 Planting of trees in last year		
27 Over 25 percent of crops covered by shade trees		x
28 Elimination of all synthetic input use	x	x

Table A4.1 (*cont.*)

Indicators included in the meta-analysis	Public equivalent			Investment and opportunity costs		Mandatory/critical in private sustainability standard					
Socially sustainable production practices	Honduras	Colombia	Costa Rica	Investment costs	Opportunity costs	FT/Fairtrade organic	UTZ	4C	Rainforest Alliance	AAA	C.A.F.E.
29 Treatment of waste water				x		x	x			x	
30 Elimination of deforestation for crop expansion			x		x				x	x	x
31 Implementation of diverse agroforestry with >25 percent shade cover					x						
32 Implementation of diverse agroforestry with >50 percent shade cover					x						

Table A4.2 *Coding of program-specific criteria*

Program-specific indicators	Restrictive auditor policy	Substantive price premium		
		Honduras	Colombia	Costa Rica
Fairtrade	x (monopoly through Fairtrade International certification)	x		
Fairtrade/organic	x (monopoly for Fairtrade; accreditation for organic)	x		
UTZ	No – proxy accreditation			
4C	No – proxy accreditation			
Rainforest Alliance	x (accreditation)	x	x	x
Nespresso AAA	No – internal verification		x	x
Starbucks C.A.F. E. Practices	No – verification by internally approved entities			

References

Abbott, K. W., and Snidal, D. (2001). International 'standards' and international governance. *Journal of European Public Policy* 8(3):345–370. https://doi.org/10.1080/13501760110056013.

Abbott, K. W., and Snidal, D. (2009). The governance triangle: Regulatory standards institutions and the shadow of the state. In: Mattli, W., and Woods, N. (eds.). *The Politics of Global Regulation*. Princeton, NJ: Princeton University Press, pp. 44–88.

Akoyi, K. T., and Maertens, M. (2017). Walk the talk: Private sustainability standards in the Ugandan coffee sector. *The Journal of Development Studies* 54(10):1792–1818. https://doi.org/10.1080/00220388.2017.1327663.

Albersmeier, F., Schulze, H., Jahn, G., and Spiller, A. (2009). The reliability of third-party certification in the food chain: From checklists to risk-oriented auditing. *Food Control* 20(10):927–935. https://doi.org/10.1016/j.foodcont.2009.01.010.

Altieri, M. (1995). *Agroecology: The Science of Sustainable Agriculture*. Boca Raton, FL: CRC Press.

Amengual, M. (2010). Complementary labor regulation: The uncoordinated combination of state and private regulators in the Dominican Republic. *World Development* 38(3):405–414.

Anders, S. M., Souza Monteiro, D. M., and Rouviere, E. (2007). Objectiveness in the market for third-party certification: Does market structure matter? 105th Seminar, March 8–10, Bologna, European Association of Agricultural Economists.

Anderson, C., Pimbert, M., and Kiss, C. (2015). *Building, Defending and Strengthening Agroecology: A Global Struggle for Food Sovereignty*. Wageningen: ILEIA, Centre for Learning on Sustainable Agriculture.

Aravind, D., and Christmann, P. (2011). Decoupling of standard implementation from certification: Does quality of ISO 14001 implementation affect facilities' environmental performance? *Business Ethics Quarterly* 21(1):73–102.

Arcuri, A. (2015). The transformation of organic regulation: The ambiguous effects of publicization. *Regulation & Governance* 9(2):144–159. https://doi.org/10.1111/rego.12066.

Arnould, E., Plastina, A., and Ball, D. (2009). Does fair trade deliver on its core value proposition? Effects on income, educational attainment and health in three countries. *Journal of Public Policy and Marketing* 28 (9):186–201. https://doi.org/10.1509/jppm.28.2.186.

Aronne, E. (2017). Agricultura descarta eliminar el uso de pesticida denominado Paraquat en producción piñera. *Monumental*. Available at: www.monumen tal.co.cr/2017/06/25/agricultura-descarta-eliminar-el-uso-de-pesticida-deno minado-paraquat-en-produccion-pinera/ (accessed: November 5, 2017).

Auld, G. (2010). Assessing certification as governance: Effects and broader consequences for coffee. *The Journal of Environment & Development* 19 (2):215–241.

Auld, G. (2014). *Constructing Private Governance: The Rise and Evolution of Forest, Coffee, and Fisheries Certification*. New Haven, CT: Yale University Press.

Auld, G., Balboa, C., Bernstein, S., and Cashore, B. (2009). The emergence of non-state market-driven (NSMD) global environmental governance: A cross-sectoral analysis. In: Delmas, M. A., and Young, O. R. (eds.). *Governance for the Environment: New Perspectives*. Cambridge: Cambridge University Press, pp. 183–218.

Auld, G., Bernstein, S., and Cashore, B. (2008). The new corporate social responsibility. *Annual Review of Environment and Resources* 33(1):413–435.

Auld, G., and Renckens, S. (2018). *Micro-Level Interactions in the Compliance Processes of Transnational Private Governance*. Toronto: TBGI Project Working Paper No. 25.

Auld, G., Renckens, S., and Cashore, B. (2015). Transnational private governance between the logics of empowerment and control. *Regulation & Governance* 9(2):108–124. https://doi.org/10.1111/rego.12075.

Avelino, J., Cristancho, M., Georgiou, S., *et al.* (2015). The coffee rust crises in Colombia and Central America (2008–2013): Impacts, plausible causes and proposed solutions. *Food Security* 7(2):303–321. https://doi.org/10 .1007/s12571-015-0446-9.

Awoke, A., Beyene, A., Kloos, H., Goethals, P. L. M., and Triest, L. (2016). River water pollution status and water policy scenario in Ethiopia: Raising awareness for better implementation in developing countries. *Environmental Management* 58(4):694–706. https://doi.org/10.1007/s00267-016-0734-y.

Ayres, I., and Braithwaite, J. (1987). *Responsive Regulation: Transcending the Deregulation Debate*. New York: Oxford University Press.

Bacon, C. M. (2010). Who decides what is fair in fair trade? The agri-environmental governance of standards, access and price. *Journal of Peasant Studies* 37(1):111–147.

Balmford, A., Green, R. E., and Scharlemann, J. P. W. (2005). Sparing land for nature: Exploring the potential impact of changes in agricultural yield on the area needed for crop production. *Global Change Biology* **11** (10):1594–1605. https://doi.org/10.1111/j.1365-2486.2005.001035.x.

Bamber, P., Guinn, A., and Gereffi, G. (2014). *Burundi in the Coffee Global Value*. Durham, NC: Center on Globalization, Governance & Competitiveness, Duke University.

Bardach, E., and Kagan, R. A. (1982). *Going by the Book: The Problem of Regulatory Unreasonableness*. Philadelphia: Temple University Press.

Barham, B. L., Callenes, M., Gitter, S., Lewis, J., and Weber, J. (2011). Fair trade/organic coffee, rural livelihoods, and the "agrarian question": Southern Mexican coffee families in transition. *World Development* **39** (1):134–145. https://doi.org/10.1016/j.worlddev.2010.08.005.

Barham, B. L., and Weber, J. G. (2012). The economic sustainability of certified coffee: Recent evidence from Mexico and Peru. *World Development* **40**(6):1269–1279. https://doi.org/10.1016/j.worlddev.2011.11.005.

Barrett, H. R., Browne, A. W., Harris, P. J. C., and Cadoret, K. (2002). Organic certification and the UK market: Organic imports from developing countries. *Food Policy* **27**(4):301–318. https://doi.org/10.1016/S0306-9192(02)00036-2.

Bartley, T. (2007). Institutional emergence in an era of globalization: The rise of transnational private regulation of labor and environmental conditions. *American Journal of Sociology* **113**(2):297–351.

Bartley, T. (2011). Transnational governance as the layering of rules: Intersections of public and private standards. *Theoretical Inquiries in Law* **12**(2):517–542.

Bartley, T. (2014). Transnational governance and the re-centered state: Sustainability or legality? *Regulation & Governance* **8**:93–109. https://doi.org/10.1111/rego.12051.

Bartley, T. (2018). *Rules without Rights: Land, Labor, and Private Authority in the Global Economy*. Oxford, New York: Oxford University Press.

Bartley, T., Koos, S., Samel, H., Setrini, G., and Summers, N. (2015). *Looking behind the Label: Global Industries and the Conscientious Consumer*. Bloomington: Indiana University Press.

Bennett, E. A. (2017). Who governs socially-oriented voluntary sustainability standards? Not the producers of certified products. *World Development* **91**:53–69. https://doi.org/10.1016/j.worlddev.2016.10.010.

Bernauer, T. (1995). The effect of international environmental institutions: How we might learn more. *International Organization* **49**(2):351–377. https://doi.org/10.1017/S0020818300028423.

Bernstein, H., and Campling, L. (2006). Commodity studies and commodity fetishism II: 'Profits with principles'? *Journal of Agrarian Change* **6** (3):414–447. https://doi.org/10.1111/j.1471-0366.2006.00128.x.

Bernstein, S., and Cashore, B. (2007). Can non-state global governance be legitimate? An analytical framework. *Regulation & Governance* 1 (4):347–371. https://doi.org/10.1111/j.1748-5991.2007.00021.x.

Bernstein, S., and Cashore, B. (2012). Complex global governance and domestic policies: Four pathways of influence. *International Affairs* 88 (3):585–604. https://doi.org/10.1111/j.1468-2346.2012.01090.x.

Beuchelt, T. D., and Zeller, M. (2011). Profits and poverty: Certification's troubled link for Nicaragua's organic and Fairtrade coffee producers. *Ecological Economics* 70(7):1316–1324. https://doi.org/10.1016/j .ecolecon.2011.01.005.

Beyene, A., Yemane, D., Addis, T., Assayie, A. A., and Triest, L. (2014). Experimental evaluation of anaerobic digestion for coffee wastewater treatment and its biomethane recovery potential. *International Journal of Environmental Science and Technology* 11(7):1881–1886. https://doi .org/10.1007/s13762-013-0339-4.

Bird, K., and Hughes, D. R. (1997). Ethical consumerism: The case of "fairly-traded" coffee. *Business Ethics: A European Review* 6(3):159–167. https:// doi.org/10.1111/1467-8608.00063.

Bitzer, V., Francken, M., and Glasbergen, P. (2008). Intersectoral partnerships for a sustainable coffee chain: Really addressing sustainability or just picking (coffee) cherries? *Global Environmental Change* 18(2):271–284. https://doi .org/10.1016/j.gloenvcha.2008.01.002.

Bitzer, V., Glasbergen, P., and Arts, B. (2013). Exploring the potential of intersectoral partnerships to improve the position of farmers in global agrifood chains: Findings from the coffee sector in Peru. *Agriculture and Human Values* 30:5–20. https://doi.org/10.1007/s10460-012-9372-z.

Black, J. (2008). Constructing and contesting legitimacy and accountability in polycentric regulatory regimes. *Regulation & Governance* 2 (2):137–164. https://doi.org/10.1111/j.1748-5991.2008.00034.x.

Blackman, A., and Naranjo, M. (2012). Does eco-certification have environmental benefits? Organic coffee in Costa Rica. *Ecological Economics* 83:58–66. https://doi.org/10.1016/j.ecolecon.2012.08.001.

Blackman, A., Naranjo, M. A., Robalino, J., Alpízar, F., and Rivera, J. (2014). Does tourism eco-certification pay? Costa Rica's Blue Flag program. *World Development* 58:41–52. https://doi.org/10.1016/j .worlddev.2013.12.002.

Blackman, A., and Rivera, J. (2011). Producer-level benefits of sustainability certification. *Conservation Biology* 25(6):1176–1185. https://doi.org/10 .1111/j.1523-1739.2011.01774.x.

Blanco Sepúlveda, R., and Aguilar Carrillo, A. (2015). Soil erosion and erosion thresholds in an agroforestry system of coffee (*Coffea arabica*) and mixed shade trees (*Inga* spp and *Musa* spp) in Northern Nicaragua.

Agriculture, Ecosystems & Environment **210**:25–35. https://doi.org/10.1016/j.agee.2015.04.032.

Blavet, D., De Noni, G., Le Bissonnais, Y., *et al.* (2009). Effect of land use and management on the early stages of soil water erosion in French Mediterranean vineyards. *Soil and Tillage Research* **106**(1):124–136. https://doi.org/10.1016/j.still.2009.04.010.

Bloomfield, M. J. (2012). Is forest certification a hegemonic force? The FSC and its challengers. *Journal of Environment and Development* **21**(4):391–413. https://doi.org/10.1177/1070496512449822.

Bolwig, S., Gibbon, P., and Jones, S. A. M. (2009). The economics of smallholder organic contract farming in tropical Africa. *World Development* **37**(6):1094–1104. https://doi.org/10.1016/j.worlddev.2008.09.012.

Borkhataria, R., Collazo, J. A., Groom, M. J., and Jordan-Garcia, A. (2012). Shade-grown coffee in Puerto Rico: Opportunities to preserve biodiversity while reinvigorating a struggling agricultural commodity. *Agriculture, Ecosystems & Environment* **149**:164–170. https://doi.org/10.1016/j.agee.2010.12.023.

Borlaug, N. E. (2000). Ending world hunger. The promise of biotechnology and the threat of antiscience zealotry. *Plant Physiology* **124**(2):487–490. https://doi.org/10.1104/pp.124.2.487.

Bose, A., Vira, B., and Garcia, C. (2016). Does environmental certification in coffee promote 'business as usual'? A case study from the Western Ghats, India. *Ambio* **45**(8):946–955. https://doi.org/10.1007/s13280-016-0796-3.

Bosselmann, A. S. (2012). Mediating factors of land use change among coffee farmers in a biological corridor. *Ecological Economics* **80**:79–88. https://doi.org/10.1016/j.ecolecon.2012.05.007.

Braithwaite, J. (1985). *To Punish or Persuade: Enforcement of Coal Mine Safety*. Albany: State University of New York Press.

Bravo, J. (2015). Costa Rica necesita recolectores nicaragüenses para el café. *La Prensa*. Available at: www.laprensa.com.ni/2015/09/26/nacionales/1909047-costa-rica-necesita-recolectores-nicaraguenses-para-el-cafe (accessed: May 4, 2018).

Bravo, J. (2016). Costa Rica necesita 70 mil cortadores de café. *La Prensa*. Available at: www.laprensa.com.ni/2016/10/17/economia/2118377-costa-rica-necesita-70-mil-cortadores-de-cafe (accessed: January 29, 2018).

Bray, J. G., and Neilson, J. (2017). Reviewing the impacts of coffee certification programmes on smallholder livelihoods. *International Journal of Biodiversity Science, Ecosystem Services & Management* **13**(1):216–232.

Breitmeier, H., Underdal, A., and Young, O.R. (2011). The effectiveness of international environmental regimes: Comparing and contrasting findings from quantitative research. *International Studies Review* 13(4):579–605. https://doi.org/10.1111/j.1468-2486.2011.01045.x.

Brown, E., Dudley, N., Lindhe, A., *et al.* (2013). *Common Guidance for the Identification of High Conservation Values*. Oxford: HCV Resource Network.

Brown, N. (2015). Colombia's FNC to present global economic accord based on farmer profitability. *Daily Coffee News by Roast Magazine*. Available at: http://dailycoffeenews.com/2015/11/25/colombias-fnc-to-present-global-eco nomic-accord-based-on-farmer-profitability/ (accessed: November 3, 2016).

Bunn, C., Läderach, P., Rivera, O. O., and Kirschke, D. (2015). A bitter cup: Climate change profile of global production of Arabica and Robusta coffee. *Climatic Change* 129(1–2):89–101. https://doi.org/10.1007/s105 84-014-1306-x.

Burchell, J., and Cook, J. (2013). Sleeping with the enemy? Strategic transformations in business–NGO relationships through stakeholder dialogue. *Journal of Business Ethics* 113(3):505–518. https://doi.org/10 .1007/s10551-012-1319-1.

Büthe, T., and Mattli, W. (2011). *The New Global Rulers: The Privatization of Regulation in the World Economy*. Princeton, NJ: Princeton University Press.

Buttel, F. H. (2000). Ecological modernization as social theory. *Geoforum* 31(1):57–65. https://doi.org/10.1016/S0016-7185(99)00044-5.

Byerlee, D., Stevenson, J., and Villoria, N. (2014). Does intensification slow crop land expansion or encourage deforestation? *Global Food Security* 3 (2):92–98. https://doi.org/10.1016/j.gfs.2014.04.001.

Calegari, M. J., Schatzberg, J. W., and Sevcik, G. R. (1998). Experimental evidence of differential auditor pricing and reporting strategies. *The Accounting Review* 73(2):255–275.

Caliendo, M., and Kopeinig, S. (2008). Some practical guidance for the implementation of propensity score matching. *Journal of Economic Surveys* 22(1):31–72. https://doi.org/10.1111/j.1467-6419.2007.00527.x.

Cameron, B. (2017). *Brewing a Sustainable Future: Certifying Kenya's Smallholder Tea Farmers, 2007–2017*. Princeton, NJ: Princeton University.

Carter, D. P., Scott, T. A., and Mahallati, N. (2018). Balancing barriers to entry and administrative burden in voluntary regulation. *Perspectives on Public Management and Governance* 1(3):207–221. https://doi.org/10 .1093/ppmgov/gvx005.

CAS (2018a). CAS | Coffee Assurance Services. *Coffee Assurance Services*. Available at: http://cas-veri.com/ (accessed: March 9, 2018).

CAS (2018b). *4C List of Approved Verifiers*. Bonn: Coffee Assurance Services.

Casabé, N., Piola, L., Fuchs, J., *et al.* (2007). Ecotoxicological assessment of the effects of glyphosate and chlorpyrifos in an Argentine soya field. *Journal of Soils and Sediments* 7(4):232–239. https://doi.org/10.1065/js s2007.04.224.

Cashore, B. (2002). Legitimacy and the privatization of environmental governance: How non-state market-driven (NSMD) governance systems gain rule-making authority. *Governance* 15(4):503–529. https://doi.org/ 10.1111/1468-0491.00199.

Cashore, B., Auld, G., Bernstein, S., and McDermott, C. (2007). Can non-state governance 'ratchet up' global environmental standards? Lessons from the forest sector. *Review of European Community & International Environmental Law* 16(2):158–172. https://doi.org/10.1111/j.1467-9388 .2007.00560.x.

Cashore, B., Auld, G., and Newsom, D. (2004). *Governing through Markets: Forest Certification and the Emergence of Non-State Authority.* New Haven, CT: Yale University Press.

Cashore, B., Elliott, C., Pohnan, E., Stone, M., and Jodoin, S. (2015). Achieving sustainability through market mechanisms. In: Panwar, R., Kozak, R., and Hansen, E. (eds.). *Forests, Business and Sustainability.* Abingdon: Routledge.

Cashore, B., and Stone, M. W. (2014). Does California need Delaware? Explaining Indonesian, Chinese, and United States support for legality compliance of internationally traded products. *Regulation & Governance* 8(1):49–73. https://doi.org/10.1111/rego.12053.

Caudill, S. A., DeClerck, F. J. A., and Husband, T. P. (2015). Connecting sustainable agriculture and wildlife conservation: Does shade coffee provide habitat for mammals? *Agriculture, Ecosystems & Environment* 199:85–93. https://doi.org/10.1016/j.agee.2014.08.023.

Ceddia, M. G., Sedlacek, S., Bardsley, N. O., and Gomez-y-Paloma, S. (2013). Sustainable agricultural intensification or Jevons paradox? The role of public governance in tropical South America. *Global Environmental Change* 23(5):1052–1063. https://doi.org/10.1016/j .gloenvcha.2013.07.005.

Chamlee, V. (2016). Starbucks hopes to win over coffee snobs with more fancy coffee shops. *Eater.* Available at: www.eater.com/coffee-tea/2016/10/20/1 3345778/starbucks-reserve-coffee-bars (accessed: October 27, 2016).

Chayes, A., and Chayes, A. H. (1995). *The New Sovereignty.* Cambridge, MA: Harvard University Press.

Chiputwa, B., Spielman, D. J., and Qaim, M. (2015). Food standards, certification, and poverty among coffee farmers in Uganda. *World Development* 66:400–412. https://doi.org/10.1016/j.worlddev.2014.09.006.

CIMS (2013). *Securing the Long-Term Sustainable Future of Coffee Supply in Colombia*. Alajuela: CIMS.

Coffee & Climate (2015). *Climate Change Adaptation in Coffee Production*. Hamburg: Initiative for Coffee & Climate.

Coffee & Climate (2017). C&c tools. *Coffee & Climate Toolbox*. Available at: http://toolbox.coffeeandclimate.org/ (accessed: January 6, 2020).

Coffeelands (2015). FNC reacts to the Misión Cafetera report. *Coffeelands*. Available at: https://coffeelands.crs.org/2015/05/the-fnc-reacts-to-recommendations-for-reform/ (accessed: December 15, 2017).

Cohen, D., and Prusak, L. (2001). *In Good Company: How Social Capital Makes Organizations Work*. Boston: Harvard Business Review Press.

Cohen, L. (2015). Factbox: With dealmaking, JAB holding expands its coffee empire. *Reuters*. Available at: www.reuters.com/article/us-keurig-green-m-a-jab-factbox-idUSKBN0TQ1ZI20151208 (accessed: October 20, 2016).

Cohen, L. (2016). Sucafina-backed coffee trader enters U.S. to tap specialty market. *Reuters*. Available at: www.reuters.com/article/coffee-sucafina-usa-idUSL1N14P14I20160105 (accessed: October 28, 2016).

ConfidencialHN (2016). Lo Último: Presidente de Cafetaleros Admite Uso de Fondos Para Campaña de JOH. *ConfidencialHN*. Available at: https://confidencialhn.com/lo-ultimo-presidente-de-cafetaleros-admite-uso-de-fondos-para-campana-de-joh/ (accessed: January 6, 2020).

Conservation International (2016). *Coffee in the Twenty First Century: Will Climate Change and Increased Demand Lead to New Deforestation?* Arlington, VA: Conservation International.

Conservation International, Consumer's Choice Council, Rainforest Alliance, Smithsonian Migratory Bird Center, and Summit Foundation (2001). *Conservation Principles for Coffee Production*. Available at: http://courses.washington.edu/kvcfr/readings/week10/KVogt%20certification/Conservation%20Prction-Final.pdf (accessed: November 13, 2019).

Contraloría General (2013). *Informe Final de Auditoria Programa de Proteccion Al Ingreso Cafetero (AIC-PIC) Fondo Nacional Del Cafe Federación Nacional de Cafeteros de Colombia (Octubre a Diciembre 2012 – Enero a Julio 2013)*. Bogota: Contraloría General de la República.

Coricafe (2012). *Costa Rica: In Depth Coffee Report. Coffee Industry Structure*. Alejuela: Coricafe.

COSA (2018). COSA indicators – master list. *COSA – Committee on Sustainability Assessment*. Available at: https://data.thecosa.org/indicators-master-list/ (accessed: April 21, 2018).

Craves, J. (2017). The New Rainforest Alliance shade requirements. *Coffee & Conservation*. Available at: www.coffeehabitat.com/2017/02/new-rainforest-alliance-shade-requirements/ (accessed: September 19, 2017).

Creswell, J. W., and Clark, V. L. P. (2007). *Designing and Conducting Mixed Methods Research*. Thousand Oaks, CA: SAGE.

Criterio.hn (2016). Cafetaleros no saben que hacen con los fondos que le quitan a cada productor. *Criterio.hn*. Available at: https://criterio.hn/cafeta leros-no-saben-hacen-los-fondos-le-quitan-productor/ (accessed: January 6, 2020).

Cutler, A. C. (2017). Private transnational governance in global value chains: Contract as a neglected dimension. In: Cutler, A. C. and Dietz, T. (eds.). *The Politics of Private Transnational Governance by Contract*. Abingdon, New York: Politics of Transnational Law, pp. 79–96.

Damalas, C. A., and Koutroubas, S. D. (2016). Farmers' exposure to pesticides: Toxicity types and ways of prevention. *Toxics* 4(1):1. https://doi.org/10.3390/toxics4010001.

DaMatta, F. M. (2004). Ecophysiological constraints on the production of shaded and unshaded coffee: A review. *Field Crops Research* 86 (2):99–114. https://doi.org/10.1016/j.fcr.2003.09.001.

Darnall, N., and Sides, S. (2008). Assessing the performance of voluntary environmental programs: Does certification matter? *Policy Studies Journal* 36(1):95–117.

Dauvergne, P., and Lister, J. (2010). The power of big box retail in global environmental governance: Bringing commodity chains back into IR. *Millennium* 39(1):145–160. https://doi.org/10.1177/0305829810371018.

Dauvergne, P., and Lister, J. (2012). Big brand sustainability: Governance prospects and environmental limits. *Global Environmental Change* 22 (1):36–45.

Dauvergne, P., and Lister, J. (2013). *Eco-Business: A Big-Brand Takeover of Sustainability*. Cambridge, MA: MIT Press.

De, S., and Nabar, P. (1991). Economic implications of imperfect quality certification. *Economics Letters* 37(4):333–337. https://doi.org/10.1016/0165-1765(91)90067-U.

de Beenhouwer, M., Aerts, R., and Honnay, O. (2013). A global meta-analysis of the biodiversity and ecosystem service benefits of coffee and cacao agroforestry. *Agriculture, Ecosystems & Environment* 175:1–7. https://doi.org/10.1016/j.agee.2013.05.003.

de Janvry, A., McIntosh, C., and Sadoulet, E. (2015). Fair trade and free entry: Can a disequilibrium market serve as a development tool? *The Review of Economics and Statistics* 97(3):567–573. https://doi.org/10.1162/REST_a_00512.

de Neve, G. (2009). Power, inequality and corporate social responsibility: The politics of ethical compliance in the South Indian garment industry. *Economic and Political Weekly* 44(22):63–72.

DeFries, R. S., Fanzo, J., Mondal, P., Remans, R., and Wood, S. A. (2017). Is voluntary certification of tropical agricultural commodities achieving sustainability goals for small-scale producers? A review of the evidence. *Environmental Research Letters* 12(3):033001.

deLeon, P., and Rivera, J. E. (eds.) (2009). *Voluntary Environmental Programs: A Policy Perspective*. Lanham, MD: Rowman & Littlefield.

Delmas, M. A., and Colgan, D. (2018). *The Green Bundle: Pairing the Market with the Planet*. Stanford, CA: Stanford University Press.

Delmas, M. A., and Grant, L. E. (2014). Eco-labeling strategies and price-premium: The wine industry puzzle. *Business & Society* 53 (1):6–44. https://doi.org/10.1177/0007650310362254.

Diario del Huila (2016). Nuevo contrato cafetero vs la Misión del Café. *Diario del Huila*. Available at: www.diariodelhuila.com/economia/nuevo-contrato-cafetero-vs-la-mision-del-cafe-cdgint20160629121825128 (accessed: December 15, 2017).

Dietz, T., and Auffenberg, J. (2014). *The Efficacy of Private Voluntary Certification Schemes: A Governance Costs Approach*. Bremen: Center for Transnational Studies (ZenTra) of the Universities of Bremen and Oldenburg.

Dietz, T., Auffenberg, J., Estrella Chong, A., Grabs, J., and Kilian, B. (2018). The Voluntary Coffee Standard Index (VOCSI). Developing a composite index to assess and compare the strength of mainstream voluntary sustainability standards in the global coffee industry. *Ecological Economics* 150:72–87. https://doi.org/10.1016/j.ecolecon.2018.03.026.

Dingwerth, K., and Pattberg, P. (2009). World politics and organizational fields: The case of transnational sustainability governance. *European Journal of International Relations* 15(4):707–743. https://doi.org/10 .1177/1354066109345056.

Distelhorst, G., Locke, R. M., Pal, T., and Samel, H. (2015). Production goes global, compliance stays local: Private regulation in the global electronics industry. *Regulation & Governance* 9(3):224–242. https://doi.org/10.1111/r ego.12096.

Dolan, C. S. (2010). Virtual moralities: The mainstreaming of Fairtrade in Kenyan tea fields. *Geoforum* 41(1):33–43. https://doi.org/10.1016/j .geoforum.2009.01.002.

Downs, G. W., Rocke, D. M., and Barsoom, P. N. (1996). Is the good news about compliance good news about cooperation? *International Organization* 50(3):379–406. https://doi.org/10.1017/S0020818300033427.

Driver, C. S. (1989). Regulatory precision. In: Hawkins, K., and Thomas, J. N. (eds.). *Making Regulatory Policy*. Pittsburgh: University of Pittsburgh Press, pp. 199–232.

Duru, M., Therond, O., and Fares, M. (2015). Designing agroecological transitions: A review. *Agronomy for Sustainable Development* **35** (4):1237–1257. https://doi.org/10.1007/s13593-015-0318-x.

Egels-Zandén, N. (2007). Suppliers' compliance with MNCs' codes of conduct: Behind the scenes at Chinese toy suppliers. *Journal of Business Ethics* **75**(1):45–62. https://doi.org/10.1007/s10551-006-9237-8.

Elder, S. D., Lister, J., and Dauvergne, P. (2014). Big retail and sustainable coffee: A new development studies research agenda. *Progress in Development Studies* **1**:77–90.

Elder, S. D., Zerriffi, H., and Le Billon, P. (2013). Is Fairtrade certification greening agricultural practices? An analysis of Fairtrade environmental standards in Rwanda. *Journal of Rural Studies* **32**:264–274. https://doi .org/10.1016/j.jrurstud.2013.07.009.

Elkington, J. (1997). *Cannibals with Forks: Triple Bottom Line of 21st Century Business*. Oxford: Capstone Publishing Ltd.

Espach, R. (2006). When is sustainable forestry sustainable? The Forest Stewardship Council in Argentina and Brazil. *Global Environmental Politics* **6**(2):55–84.

Fairtrade Foundation (2012). *Fairtrade and Coffee. Commodity Briefing*. London: Fairtrade Foundation.

Fallas Villalobos, C. (2014). Madera chilena se arraiga en Costa Rica. *El Financiero, Grupo Nación*. Available at: www.elfinancierocr.com/nego cios/madera-chilena-se-arraiga-en-costa-rica/E4NBH7PJVBHDNGHM M5AQ7HEQVE/story/ (accessed: February 21, 2018).

FAO (2018). FAOSTAT – crops. *FAOSTAT*. Available at: www.fao.org/fa ostat/en/#data/QC (accessed: March 15, 2018).

Feder, G., Murgai, R., and Quizon, J. B. (2004). The acquisition and diffusion of knowledge: The case of pest management training in farmer field schools, Indonesia. *Journal of Agricultural Economics* **55** (2):221–243. https://doi.org/10.1111/j.1477-9552.2004.tb00094.x.

Fickling, D. (2016). Hedge funds on caffeine high hanker for a double shot. *Bloomberg Gadfly*. Available at: www.bloomberg.com/gadfly/articles/20 16-10-31/coffee-buzz (accessed: November 2, 2016).

Financial Times (2016). Gourmet coffee boom perks elude growers. *Financial Times*. Available at: www.ft.com/content/7cfe9990-289f-11e6- 8b18-91555f2f4fde (accessed: December 21, 2017).

Fischer, E. F., and Victor, B. (2014). High-end coffee and smallholder growers in Guatemala. *Latin American Research Review* **49**(1): 155–177.

Fitter, R., and Kaplinsky, R. (2001). Who gains from product rents as the coffee market becomes more differentiated? A value chain analysis. *IDS Bulletin* **32**(3):69–82.

FLO (2011). *Fairtrade Standard for Small Producer Organizations. Current Version: 01.05.2011.* Bonn: Fairtrade Labelling Organizations International.

FLO (2015). *Fairtrade Theory of Change.* Bonn: Fairtrade Labelling Organizations International.

FLO (2017a). *Creating Innovations, Scaling up Impact: Annual Report 2016–2017.* Bonn: Fairtrade Labelling Organizations International.

FLO (2017b). Becoming a Fairtrade producer. *Fairtrade International (FLO).* Available at: https://web.archive.org/web/20190503175848/www .fairtrade.net/producers/becoming-a-fairtrade-producer.html (accessed: January 6, 2020).

FLO (2017c). *Building the Fairtrade of the Future: Creating Innovations, Scaling up Impact: Annual Report 2016–2017.* Bonn: Fairtrade Labelling Organizations International.

FLO (2018a). Minimum price and premium information. *Fairtrade International (FLO).* Available at: www.fairtrade.net/standards/price-and-premium-info.html (accessed: May 1, 2018).

FLO (2018b). Fairtrade International (FLO): Annual reports. *Fairtrade International (FLO).* Available at: www.fairtrade.net/search/library?fm a=&fmb=annualReport (accessed: January 6, 2020).

FLO (2018c). Aims of Fairtrade standards. *Fairtrade International (FLO).* Available at: www.fairtrade.net/standard/aims (accessed: January 6, 2020).

FLOCERT (2018). Quality and appeals. *FLOCERT.* Available at: www .flocert.net/about-flocert/vision-values/quality-and-appeals/ (accessed: May 3, 2018).

FNC (2013). Colombia, better prepared against the coffee leaf rust than its neighbors in Central America. *Cafe de Colombia.* Available at: www .cafedecolombia.com/bb-fnc-en/index.php/comments/colombia_better_ prepared_against_the_coffee_leaf_rust_than_its_neighbors_in/ (accessed: November 1, 2016).

FNC (2017). Informe sobre el primer foro mundial de países productores de café. Medellín (Colombia) Julio de 2017. *Ensayos sobre Economía Cafetera* 32:19–33.

Fountain, A., and Huetz-Adam, F. (2018). *Cocoa Barometer 2018.* Oxford, The Hague, Utrecht: Oxfam/Hivos/Solidaridad.

Fransen, L. (2011). Why do private governance organizations not converge? A political–institutional analysis of transnational labor standards regulation. *Governance* 24(2):359–387.

Fransen, L. (2012). Multi-stakeholder governance and voluntary programme interactions: Legitimation politics in the institutional design of Corporate Social Responsibility. *Socio-Economic Review* 10(1):163–192.

Fransen, L. (2015). The politics of meta-governance in transnational private sustainability governance. *Policy Sciences* **48**(3):293–317. https://doi.org/10.1007/s11077-015-9219-8.

Fransen, L. (2018). Beyond regulatory governance? On the evolutionary trajectory of transnational private sustainability governance. *Ecological Economics* **146**:772–777. https://doi.org/10.1016/j.ecolecon.2018.01.005.

Fransen, L., and Burgoon, B. (2012). A market for worker rights: Explaining business support for international private labour regulation. *Review of International Political Economy* **19**(2):236–266. https://doi.org/10.1080/09692290.2011.552788.

Freedman, D. A., and Berk, R. A. (2008). Weighting regressions by propensity scores. *Evaluation Review* **32**(4):392–409. https://doi.org/10.1177/0193841X08317586.

Frey, B. S., and Jegen, R. (2001). Motivation crowding theory. *Journal of Economic Surveys* **15**(5):589–611. https://doi.org/10.1111/1467-6419.00150.

Fridell, G. (2007). *Fair Trade Coffee: The Prospects and Pitfalls of Market-Driven Social Justice*. Toronto: University of Toronto Press.

Gabriel, D., Carver, S. J., Durham, H., *et al.* (2009). The spatial aggregation of organic farming in England and its underlying environmental correlates. *Journal of Applied Ecology* **46**(2):323–333. https://doi.org/10.1111/j.1365-2664.2009.01624.x.

Garcia-Johnson, R. (2003). US certification initiatives in the coffee industry: The battle for just remuneration. In: Frynas, J. G., and Pegg, S. (eds.). *Transnational Corporations and Human Rights*. London: Palgrave Macmillan, pp. 137–161.

Garnett, T., Appleby, M. C., Balmford, A., *et al.* (2013). Sustainable intensification in agriculture: Premises and policies. *Science* **341**(6141):33–34. https://doi.org/10.1126/science.1234485.

Garry, V. F. (2004). Pesticides and children. *Toxicology and Applied Pharmacology* **198**(2):152–163. https://doi.org/10.1016/j.taap.2003.11.027.

Gaveau, D. L. A., Linkie, M., Suyadi, Levang, P., and Leader-Williams, N. (2009). Three decades of deforestation in southwest Sumatra: Effects of coffee prices, law enforcement and rural poverty. *Biological Conservation* **142**(3):597–605. https://doi.org/10.1016/j.biocon.2008.11.024.

GCP (2015). *4C Association Annual Report 2015: Evolving toward a Sustainable Future*. Geneva: Global Coffee Platform.

GCP (2017a). 17 million farmers, 2 billion cups drunk each day: Why coffee sustainability matters – The Global Coffee Platform. *Global Coffee Platform*. Available at: www.globalcoffeeplatform.org/latest/2017/17-million-farmers-2-billion-cups-drunk-each-day-why-coffee-sustainability-matters (accessed: October 12, 2017).

GCP (2017b). A quick scan on improving the economic viability of coffee farming. *Global Coffee Platform*. Available at: www.globalcoffeeplatform.o rg/resources/a-quick-scan-on-improving-the-economic-viability-of-coffee-far ming (accessed: March 15, 2018).

Gereffi, G., Humphrey, J., and Sturgeon, T. (2005). The governance of global value chains. *Review of International Political Economy* 12(1):78–104. https://doi.org/10.1080/09692290500049805.

Gibson, R. B. (2006). Beyond the pillars: Sustainability assessment as a framework for effective integration of social, economic and ecological considerations in significant decision-making. *Journal of Environmental Assessment Policy and Management* 08(03):259–280. https://doi.org/10 .1142/S1464333206002517.

Giovannucci, D., and Ponte, S. (2005). Standards as a new form of social contract? Sustainability initiatives in the coffee industry. *Food Policy* 30 (3):284–301. https://doi.org/10.1016/j.foodpol.2005.05.007.

Giuliani, E. (2016). Human rights and corporate social responsibility in developing countries' industrial clusters. *Journal of Business Ethics* 133 (1):39–54. https://doi.org/10.1007/s10551-014-2375-5.

Giuliani, E., Ciravegna, L., Vezzulli, A., and Kilian, B. (2017). Decoupling standards from practice: The impact of in-house certifications on coffee farms' environmental and social conduct. *World Development* 96:294–314.

Glaser, B., and Strauss, A. (2000). *The Discovery of Grounded Theory: Strategies for Qualitative Research*. New Brunswick, NJ: Routledge.

Gliessman, S. R. (2015). *Agroecology: The Ecology of Sustainable Food Systems*. Boca Raton, FL: CRC Press.

Gordon, C., Manson, R., Sundberg, J., and Cruz-Angón, A. (2007). Biodiversity, profitability, and vegetation structure in a Mexican coffee agroecosystem. *Agriculture, Ecosystems & Environment* 118(1):256–266. https://doi.org/10.1016/j.agee.2006.05.023.

Gowdy, J. M., and Walton, M. (2010). Sustainability concepts in ecological economics. In: Majumdar, M., Wills, I., Sgro, P. M., and Gowdy, J. M. (eds.). *Fundamental Economics – Volume II*. Paris: EOLSS Publications, pp. 396–407.

Grabosky, P. (1991). Professional advisers and white collar illegality: Towards explaining and excusing professional failure. *The University of New South Wales Law Journal* 13(1):73.

Grabosky, P. (1995). Using non-governmental resources to foster regulatory compliance. *Governance* 8(4):527–550. https://doi.org/10 .1111/j.1468-0491.1995.tb00226.x.

Grabs, J. (2017). *The Rise of Buyer-Driven Sustainability Governance: Emerging Trends in the Global Coffee Sector*. Rochester, NY: Social Science Research Network.

Grabs, J. (2018). Assessing the institutionalization of private sustainability governance in a changing coffee sector. *Regulation & Governance*. https://doi.org/10.1111/rego.12212.

Grabs, J., Kilian, B., Hernández, D. C., and Dietz, T. (2016). Understanding coffee certification dynamics: A spatial analysis of voluntary sustainability standard proliferation. *International Food and Agribusiness Management Review* 19(3): 31–56.

Grabs, J., and Ponte, S. (2019). The evolution of power in the global coffee value chain and production network. *Journal of Economic Geography* 19 (4): 803–828. https://doi.org/10.1093/jeg/lbz008.

Granovetter, M. (1985). Economic action and social structure: The problem of embeddedness. *American Journal of Sociology* 91(3):481–510. https://doi.org/10.1086/228311.

Graz, J.-C., and Nölke, A. (2012). Introduction: Beyond the fragmented debate on transnational private governance. In: Graz, J.-C., and Nölke, A. (eds.). *Transnational Private Governance and Its Limits*. London: Routledge, pp. 1–26.

Green, J. F. (2010). Private standards in the climate regime: The greenhouse gas protocol. *Business and Politics* 12(3):1–37. https://doi.org/10.2202/1469-3569.1318.

Green, J. F., and Auld, G. (2017). Unbundling the regime complex: The effects of private authority. *Transnational Environmental Law* 6 (2):259–284. https://doi.org/10.1017/S2047102516000121.

Green, R. E., Cornell, S. J., Scharlemann, J. P. W., and Balmford, A. (2005). Farming and the fate of wild nature. *Science* 307(5709):550–555. https://doi.org/10.1126/science.1106049.

Gresser, C., and Tickell, S. (2002). *Mugged: Poverty in Your Coffee Cup*. Oxford: Oxfam.

Gretler, C. (2015). Nestle to lose single-serve coffee crown as JAB Snags Keurig. *Bloomberg.com*. Available at: www.bloomberg.com/news/articles/2015-12-08/nestle-to-lose-single-serve-coffee-crown-as-reimanns-snag-keurig (accessed: November 22, 2016).

Guhl, A. (2009). *Evaluación de La Cobertura Boscosa En El Municipio de Aratoca (Santander). Bosque, Café Con Sombrío y Certificación Rainforest Alliance*. Bogota: CIDER – Universidad de los Andes.

Gulbrandsen, L. H. (2004). Overlapping public and private governance: Can forest certification fill the gaps in the global forest regime? *Global Environmental Politics* 4(2):75–99.

Gulbrandsen, L. H. (2005). The effectiveness of non-state governance schemes: A comparative study of forest certification in Norway and Sweden. *International Environmental Agreements: Politics, Law and Economics* 5 (2):125–149.

Gulbrandsen, L. H. (2009). The emergence and effectiveness of the Marine Stewardship Council. *Marine Policy* 33(4):654–660.

Gulbrandsen, L. H. (2014). Dynamic governance interactions: Evolutionary effects of state responses to non-state certification programs. *Regulation & Governance* 8(1):74–92.

Gunningham, N., and Grabosky, P. (eds.) (1998). *Smart Regulation: Designing Environmental Policy.* Oxford, New York: Clarendon Press.

Guthman, J. (2004). Back to the land: The paradox of organic food standards. *Environment and Planning A* 36(3):511–528. https://doi.org/10.1068/a36104.

Guthman, J. (2007). The Polanyian way? Voluntary food labels as neoliberal governance. *Antipode* 39(3):456–478. https://doi.org/10.1111/j.1467-8330.2007.00535.x.

Guyton, K. Z., Loomis, D., Grosse, Y., *et al.* (2015). Carcinogenicity of tetrachlorvinphos, parathion, malathion, diazinon, and glyphosate. *The Lancet Oncology* 16(5):490–491. https://doi.org/10.1016/S1470-2045(15)70134-8.

Haggar, J., Asigbaase, M., Bonilla, G., Pico, J., and Quilo, A. (2015). Tree diversity on sustainably certified and conventional coffee farms in Central America. *Biodiversity and Conservation* 24(5):1175–1194.

Haggar, J., Barrios, M., Bolaños, M., *et al.* (2011). Coffee agroecosystem performance under full sun, shade, conventional and organic management regimes in Central America. *Agroforestry Systems* 82(3):285–301. https://doi.org/10.1007/s10457-011-9392-5.

Haggar, J., Soto, G., Casanoves, F., and de Melo Virginio, E. (2017). Environmental-economic benefits and trade-offs on sustainably certified coffee farms. *Ecological Indicators* 79:330–337. https://doi.org/10.1016/j.ecolind.2017.04.023.

Harbaugh, R., Maxwell, J. W., and Roussillon, B. (2011). Label confusion: The Groucho effect of uncertain standards. *Management Science* 57(9):1512–1527. https://doi.org/10.1287/mnsc.1110.1412.

Hardin, G. (1968). The tragedy of the commons. *Science* 162(3859):1243–1248. https://doi.org/10.1126/science.162.3859.1243.

Hardt, E., Borgomeo, E., dos Santos, R. F., *et al.* (2015). Does certification improve biodiversity conservation in Brazilian coffee farms? *Forest Ecology and Management* 357:181–194. https://doi.org/10.1016/j.foreco.2015.08.021.

Hawkins, K. (1984). *Environment and Enforcement: Regulation and the Social Definition of Pollution.* Oxford, New York: Clarendon Press.

Hawkins, K., and Thomas, J. N. (1989). *Making Regulatory Policy.* Pittsburgh: University of Pittsburgh Press.

Heckman, J. J., Ichimura, H., and Todd, P. (1998). Matching as an econometric evaluation estimator. *The Review of Economic Studies* **65** (2):261–294. https://doi.org/10.1111/1467-937X.00044.

Helm, C., and Sprinz, D. (2000). Measuring the effectiveness of international environmental regimes. *Journal of Conflict Resolution* **44**(5):630–652. https://doi.org/10.1177/0022002700044005004.

Hjerl Hansen, J. (2016). Bitter coffee: Slavery-like working conditions and deadly pesticides on Brazilian coffee plantations. *Danwatch*. Available at: www.ituc-csi.org/IMG/pdf/danwatch-bitter-coffee-march-2016.pdf (accessed: November 13, 2019).

Hondudiario (2017). "Secuestrada la caficultura en Honduras", denuncian productores de café. *Hondudiario*. Available at: http://hondudiario.com/2017/08/01/secuestrada-la-caficultura-en-honduras-denuncian-produc tores-de-cafe/ (accessed: December 15, 2017).

Hughell, D., and Newsom, D. (2013). *Impacts of Rainforest Alliance Certification on Coffee Farms in Colombia*. New York: Rainforest Alliance.

Hylander, K., Nemomissa, S., Delrue, J., and Enkosa, W. (2013). Effects of coffee management on deforestation rates and forest integrity. *Conservation Biology* **27**(5):1031–1040. https://doi.org/10.1111/cobi.12079.

Ibanez, M., and Blackman, A. (2016). Is eco-certification a win–win for developing country agriculture? Organic coffee certification in Colombia. *World Development* **82**:14–27. https://doi.org/10.1016/j.worlddev.2016.01.004.

ICAFE (2015a). Proceso de liquidación. *ICAFE*. Available at: www.icafe.cr/nuestro-cafe/proceso-de-liquidacion/ (accessed: November 14, 2019).

ICAFE (2015b). El café sostenible de Costa Rica. *ICAFE*. Available at: www.icafe.cr/nuestro-cafe/el-mejor-cafe-del-mundo/ (accessed: November 14, 2019).

ICAFE (2016). *Precio de Liquidación Final Cosecha 2015–2016*. San Jose: Instituto del Café de Costa Rica.

ICO (2014). *World Coffee Trade (1963–2013): A Review of the Markets, Challenges and Opportunities Facing the Sector*. London: International Coffee Organization.

ICO (2015). *Coffee in China*. London: International Coffee Organization.

ICO (2016). *Assessing the Economic Sustainability of Coffee Growing*. London: International Coffee Organization.

ICO (2017a). *World Coffee Consumption*. London: International Coffee Organization.

ICO (2017b). *Total Production by All Exporting Countries*. London: International Coffee Organization.

ICO (2017c). Frequently asked questions. *ICO*. Available at: www.ico.org /show_faq.asp?show=8 (accessed: December 13, 2017).

ICO (2017d). Developing a sustainable coffee economy. *ICO*. Available at: www.ico.org/sustaindev_e.asp (accessed: October 12, 2017).

ICO (2019a). *Total Production by All Exporting Countries*. London: International Coffee Organization.

ICO (2019b). *World Coffee Consumption*. London: International Coffee Organization.

ICO (2019c). *Indicator Prices – Monthly Averages*. London: International Coffee Organization.

IHCAFE (2011). *Instituto Hondureño del Café – Informe Anual Cosecha 2010–11*. Tegucigalpa: IHCAFE.

ILO (2018). Ratifications of C138 – Minimum age convention, 1973 (No. 138). *NORMLEX Information System on International Labour Standards*. Available at: www.ilo.org/dyn/normlex/en/f?p=1000:11300:0::NO:11300: P11300_INSTRUMENT_ID:312283 (accessed: May 4, 2018).

Index Mundi (2015). Green coffee Arabica production by country. Available at: www.indexmundi.com/agriculture/?commodity=green-coffee&graph =arabica-production (accessed: January 6, 2020).

INE (2017). Hogares en condición de pobreza 2016. *Instituto Nacional de Estadística Honduras*. Available at: www.ine.gob.hn/V3/2016/07/04/bole tin-pobreza-en-los-hogares-junio-2016/ (accessed: January 6, 2020).

Informa-Tico (2017). Costa Rica: Ambientalistas piden la prohibición del paraquat, agroveneno ilegal en 40 países. *NODAL*. Available at: www .nodal.am/2017/08/costa-rica-ambientalistas-piden-la-prohibicion-del-par aquat-agroveneno-ilegal-40-paises/ (accessed: November 5, 2017).

Ingenbleek, P., and Meulenberg, M. (2006). The battle between "good" and "better": A strategic marketing perspective on codes of conduct for sustainable agriculture. *Agribusiness* 22(4):451–473. https://doi.org/10 .1002/agr.20097.

Ingenbleek, P., and Reinders, M. (2013). The development of a market for sustainable coffee in the Netherlands: Rethinking the contribution of fair trade. *Journal of Business Ethics* 113(3):461–474. https://doi.org/10.1007 /s10551-012-1316-4.

Innovation Forum (2017). How innovative sustainable business tools track progress and measure impact. *Innovation Forum*. Available at: https://innova tion-forum.co.uk/analysis.php?s=how-innovative-sustainable-business-tools-track-progress-and-measure-impact (accessed: March 1, 2018).

ISEAL (2016). *Top Trends in Sustainability Standards*. Webinar series. Available at: https://vimeo.com/173491599 (accessed: January 6, 2020).

ISEAL Alliance (2011). *Joint Statement Fairtrade, SAN/Rainforest Alliance & UTZ CERTIFIED*. Berne: ISEAL Alliance.

ISO (2012). *ISO/IEC 17065:2012 – Conformity Assessment – Requirements for Bodies Certifying Products, Processes and Services*. Geneva: International Organization for Standardization.

ITC (2011a). *The Coffee Exporter's Guide – Third Edition*. Geneva: International Trade Centre.

ITC (2011b). *The Impacts of Private Standards on Producers in Developing Countries: Literature Review Series on the Impacts of Private Standards – Part II*. Geneva: International Trade Centre.

Jaffee, D., and Howard, P.H. (2016). Who's the fairest of them all? The fractured landscape of U.S. fair trade certification. *Agriculture and Human Values* 33(4):813–826. https://doi.org/10.1007/s10460-015-9663-2.

Jahn, G., Schramm, M., and Spiller, A. (2005). The reliability of certification: Quality labels as a consumer policy tool. *Journal of Consumer Policy* 28 (1):53–73. https://doi.org/10.1007/s10603-004-7298-6.

JDE (2016). At the source. *Jacobs Douwe Egberts Corporate Responsibility*. Available at: https://web.archive.org/web/20180814181827/www .jacobsdouweegberts.com/CR/source/ (accessed: January 6, 2020).

Jena, P. R., Chichaibelu, B. B., Stellmacher, T., and Grote, U. (2012). The impact of coffee certification on small-scale producers' livelihoods: A case study from the Jimma Zone, Ethiopia. *Agricultural Economics* 43 (4):429–440. https://doi.org/10.1111/j.1574-0862.2012.00594.x.

Jha, S., Bacon, C. M., Philpott, S. M., *et al.* (2014). Shade coffee: Update on a disappearing refuge for biodiversity. *BioScience* 64(5):416–428. https:// doi.org/10.1093/biosci/biu038.

Jurjonas, M., Crossman, K., Solomon, J., and Baez, W.L. (2016). Potential links between certified organic coffee and deforestation in a protected area in Chiapas, Mexico. *World Development* 78:13–21. https://doi.org/10 .1016/j.worlddev.2015.10.030.

Kahneman, D. (2013). *Thinking, Fast and Slow*. New York: Farrar, Straus and Giroux.

Kamau, M. W., Fort, R., Mose, L., and Ruben, R. (2010). The impact of certification on smallholder coffee farmers in Kenya: The case of 'UTZ' certification program. Joint 3rd African Association of Agricultural Economists (AAAE) and 48th Agricultural Economists Association of South Africa (AEASA) Conference, September 19–23, Cape Town.

Kim, J. Y. (2013). The politics of code enforcement and implementation in Vietnam's apparel and footwear factories. *World Development* 45:286–295. https://doi.org/10.1016/j.worlddev.2012.12.004.

Kiser, L. L., and Ostrom, E. (1982). The Three Worlds of Action: A metatheoretical synthesis of institutional approaches. In: Ostrom, E. (ed.). *Strategies in Political Inquiry*. Beverly Hills, CA: Sage, pp. 179–222.

Kiser, L. L., and Ostrom, E. (2000). The three worlds of action: A metatheoretical synthesis of institutional approaches. In: McGinnis, M. D. (ed.). *Polycentric Games and Institutions. Readings from the Workshop in Political Theory and Policy Analysis*. Ann Arbor: University of Michigan Press, pp. 56–88.

Kolk, A. (2005). Corporate social responsibility in the coffee sector: The dynamics of MNC responses and code development. *European Management Journal* 23(2):228–236. https://doi.org/10.1016/j .emj.2005.02.003.

Kolk, A. (2013). Mainstreaming sustainable coffee. *Sustainable Development* 21(5):324–337. https://doi.org/10.1177/1745691612459060.

Konradsen, F., van der Hoek, W., Cole, D. C., *et al.* (2003). Reducing acute poisoning in developing countries – options for restricting the availability of pesticides. *Toxicology* 192(2):249–261. https://doi.org/10.1016/S030 0-483X(03)00339-1.

Kraft, K. (2015). Perspectives on PRM, part 1: Ed Canty – "risk management is everyone's business." *Coffeelands*. Available at: http://coffeelands .crs.org/2015/09/perspectives-on-prm-part-1-ed-canty-risk-management- is-everyones-business/ (accessed: October 28, 2016).

Kuhlman, T., and Farrington, J. (2010). What is sustainability? *Sustainability* 2(11):3436–3448. https://doi.org/10.3390/su2113436.

Kuit, M., Guinée, L., Van Anh, P., Jansen, D., and van Rijn, F. (2016). *4C Impact Study Phase 2: Estimating the Impact of Implementation of the 4C Entry Level Standard in Uganda and Vietnam*. Wageningen: Kuit Consultancy.

Kuit, M., van Rijn, F., and Jansen, D. (2010). *Assessing 4C Implementation among Small-Scale Producers. An Evaluation of the Effects of 4C Implementation in Vietnam, Uganda and Nicaragua*. Wageningen: Kuit Consultancy.

Kuit, M., van Rijn, F., Vu, T. M. T., and Pham, V. A. (2013). *The Sustainable Coffee Conundrum*. Wageningen: Kuit Consultancy/Wageningen University and Research.

Kuit, M., and Waarts, Y. (2014). *Small-Scale Farmers, Certification Schemes and Private Standards: Is There a Business Case? Costs and Benefits of Certification and Verification Systems for Small-Scale Farmers in Cocoa, Coffee, Cotton, Fruit and Vegetable Sectors*. Wageningen: Technical Centre for Agricultural and Rural Cooperation ACP-EU (CTA).

La Tribuna (2017). Productores protestan por corrupción en Ihcafé. *Diario La Tribuna Honduras.* Available at: www.latribuna.hn/2017/08/01/pro ductores-protestan-corrupcion-ihcafe/ (accessed: December 15, 2017).

Läderach, P., Ramirez–Villegas, J., Navarro-Racines, C., *et al.* (2017). Climate change adaptation of coffee production in space and time. *Climatic Change* 141(1):47–62. https://doi.org/10.1007/s10584-016-1788-9.

Lambin, E. F., Meyfroidt, P., Rueda, X., *et al.* (2014). Effectiveness and synergies of policy instruments for land use governance in tropical regions. *Global Environmental Change* 28:129–140. https://doi.org/10 .1016/j.gloenvcha.2014.06.007.

Lampkin, N. H., Pearce, B. D., Leake, A. R., *et al.* (2015). *The Role of Agroecology in Sustainable Intensification.* Report for the Land Use Policy Group. Newbury: Organic Research Centre, Elm Farm and Game & Wildlife Conservation Trust.

Lemeilleur, S., N' Dao, Y., and Ruf, F. (2015). The productivist rationality behind a sustainable certification process: evidence from the Rainforest Alliance in the Ivorian cocoa sector. *International Journal of Sustainable Development* 18(4):310. https://doi.org/10.1504/IJSD .2015.072661.

Lenox, M., and Chatterji, A. (2018). *Can Business Save the Earth? Innovating Our Way to Sustainability.* Stanford, CA: Stanford Business Books.

Lenox, M., and Nash, J. (2003). Industry self-regulation and adverse selection: A comparison across four trade association programs. *Business Strategy and the Environment* 12(6):343–356. https://doi.org/10.1002/bse.380.

Lernoud, J., Potts, J., Sampson, G., *et al.* (2017). *The State of Sustainable Markets: Statistics and Emerging Trends 2017.* Geneva: International Trade Centre.

Lernoud, J., Potts, J., Sampson, G., *et al.* (2018). *The State of Sustainable Markets: Statistics and Emerging Trends 2018.* Geneva: International Trade Centre.

LeSage, C. (2015). *Honduras. Production Growth and Outlook.* Herradura: SINTERCAFE.

Levy, D., Reinecke, J., and Manning, S. (2016). The political dynamics of sustainable coffee: Contested value regimes and the transformation of sustainability. *Journal of Management Studies* 53(3):364–401.

Lewin, B., Giovannucci, D., and Varangis, P. (2004). *Coffee Markets: New Paradigms in Global Supply and Demand.* Washington, DC: The World Bank.

López-Bravo, D. F., de M. Virginio-Filho, E., and Avelino, J. (2012). Shade is conducive to coffee rust as compared to full sun exposure under standardized fruit load conditions. *Crop Protection* 38(Supplement C):21–29. https://doi.org/10.1016/j.cropro.2012.03.011.

Lora, E. (2013). *Las políticas y las instituciones cafeteras alrededor del mundo. Misión de Estudios Para La Competitividad de La Caficultura En Colombia.* Bogota: Universidad del Rosario.

Luttinger, N., and Dicum, G. (2011). *The Coffee Book: Anatomy of an Industry from Crop to the Last Drop.* New York: The New Press.

Mace, M. (2016). Caffé Nero triples sustainable farming training scheme. *edie .net.* Available at: www.edie.net/news/7/Caff–Nero-triples-sustainable-farming-training-scheme-commitment–/ (accessed: November 3, 2016).

Makkawi, B., and Schick, A. (2003). Are auditors sensitive enough to fraud? *Managerial Auditing Journal* 18(6/7):591–598. https://doi.org/10.1108 /02686900310482722.

Manning, S., Boons, F., Von Hagen, O., and Reinecke, J. (2012). National contexts matter: The co-evolution of sustainability standards in global value chains. *Ecological Economics* 83:197–209.

Manning, S., and Reinecke, J. (2016). A modular governance architecture in-the-making: How transnational standard-setters govern sustainability transitions. *Research Policy* 45(3):618–633. https://doi.org/10.1016/j .respol.2015.11.007.

Margolis, H. (1991). Self-interest and social motivation. In: Earley, J. E. (ed.). *Individuality and Cooperative Action.* Washington, DC: Georgetown University Press, pp. 129–136.

Mariño, Y. A., Pérez, M.-E., Gallardo, F., *et al.* (2016). Sun vs. shade affects infestation, total population and sex ratio of the coffee berry borer (*Hypothenemus hampei*) in Puerto Rico. *Agriculture, Ecosystems & Environment* 222:258–266. https://doi.org/10.1016/j.agee.2015.12.031.

Marks, A. R., Harley, K., Bradman, A., *et al.* (2010). Organophosphate pesticide exposure and attention in young Mexican-American children: The CHAMACOS study. *Environmental Health Perspectives* 118 (12):1768–1774. https://doi.org/10.1289/ehp.1002056.

Marx, A. (2008). Limits to non-state market regulation: A qualitative comparative analysis of the international sport footwear industry and the Fair Labor Association. *Regulation & Governance* 2(2):253–273. https://doi.org/10.1111/j.1748-5991.2008.00037.x.

Marx, A., and Cuypers, D. (2010). Forest certification as a global environmental governance tool: What is the macro-effectiveness of the Forest Stewardship Council? *Regulation & Governance* 4(4):408–434.

McCook, S. (2008). Chronicle of a plague foretold: Crop epidemics and the environmental history of coffee in the Americas. *Varia Historia* 24 (39):87–111. https://doi.org/10.1590/S0104-87752008000100005.

McGinnis, M. D. (2011). An introduction to IAD and the language of the Ostrom workshop: A simple guide to a complex framework. *Policy Studies Journal* **39**(1):169–183. https://doi.org/10.1111/j.1541-0072 .2010.00401.x.

Mebratu, D. (1998). Sustainability and sustainable development: Historical and conceptual review. *Environmental Impact Assessment Review* **18** (6):493–520. https://doi.org/10.1016/S0195-9255(98)00019-5.

Meidinger, E. (2003). Forest certification as environmental law making by global civil society. In: Meidinger, E., Elliott, C. and Oesten, G. (eds.). *Social and Political Dimensions of Forest Certification*. Rochester, NY: Social Science Research Network.

Meidinger, E. (2006). The administrative law of global private-public regulation: The case of forestry. *European Journal of International Law* **17**(1):47–87. https://doi.org/10.1093/ejil/chi168.

Meyfroidt, P., Vu, T. P., and Hoang, V. A. (2013). Trajectories of deforestation, coffee expansion and displacement of shifting cultivation in the Central Highlands of Vietnam. *Global Environmental Change* **23** (5):1187–1198. https://doi.org/10.1016/j.gloenvcha.2013.04.005.

Mezzadri, A. (2012). Reflections on globalisation and labour standards in the Indian garment industry: Codes of conduct versus 'codes of practice' imposed by the firm. *Global Labour Journal* **3**(1). https://doi.org/10 .15173/glj.v3i1.1112.

Miles, E. L., Andresen, S., Carlin, E. M., *et al.* (eds.) (2002). *Environmental Regime Effectiveness: Confronting Theory with Evidence*. Cambridge, MA: MIT Press.

Milford, A. (2004). *Coffee, Co-operatives and Competition: The Impact of Fair Trade*. Bergen: CMI Report R 2004: 6.

Milford, A. B. (2014). Co-operative or coyote? Producers' choice between intermediary purchasers and Fairtrade and organic co-operatives in Chiapas. *Agriculture and Human Values* **31**(4):577–591. https://doi.org/ 10.1007/s10460-014-9502-x.

Millard, E. (2016). Smallholder inclusion in company supply chains: Top five success factors. *Eco-Business*. Available at: www.eco-business.com/opinion/ smallholder-inclusion-in-company-supply-chains-top-five-success-factors/ (accessed: November 3, 2016).

Millard, E. (2017). Still brewing: Fostering sustainable coffee production. *World Development Perspectives* **7–8**:32–42. https://doi.org/10.1016/j .wdp.2017.11.004.

Minagricultura (2016). Programas de extensión cafetera. *Ministerio de Agricultura y Desarrollo Rural*. Available at: www.minagricultura.gov.c o/atencion-ciudadano/preguntas-frecuentes/Paginas/Caficultores.aspx (accessed: October 31, 2016).

Mitchell, R. B. (2002). A quantitative approach to evaluating international environmental regimes. *Global Environmental Politics* 2(4):58–83. https://doi.org/10.1162/152638002320980623.

Mitchell, R. B. (2006). Problem structure, institutional design, and the relative effectiveness of international environmental agreements. *Global Environmental Politics* 6(3):72–89. https://doi.org/10.1162/glep .2006.6.3.72.

Mitiku, F., de Mey, Y., Nyssen, J., and Maertens, M. (2017). Do private sustainability standards contribute to income growth and poverty alleviation? A comparison of different coffee certification schemes in Ethiopia. *Sustainability* 9(2):246. https://doi.org/10.3390/su9020246.

Mitiku, F., Nyssen, J., and Maertens, M. (2018). Certification of semi-forest coffee as a land-sharing strategy in Ethiopia. *Ecological Economics* 145:194–204. https://doi.org/10.1016/j.ecolecon.2017.09.008.

Mittermeier, R., Myers, N., Thomsen, J., da Fonseca, G., and Olivieri, S. (1998). Biodiversity hotspots and major tropical wilderness areas: Approaches to setting conservation priorities. *Conservation Biology* 12 (3):516–520. https://doi.org/10.1046/j.1523-1739.1998.012003516.x.

Montagnon, C. (2017). *Coffee Production Costs and Farm Profitability: Strategic Literature Review*. Santa Ana: Specialty Coffee Association.

Moog, S., Spicer, A., and Böhm, S. (2015). The politics of multi-stakeholder initiatives: The crisis of the Forest Stewardship Council. *Journal of Business Ethics* 128(3):469–493.

Morgan, A. (2017). *The New Rainforest Alliance: Innovation, Impact & Efficiency*. Herradura: SINTERCAFE.

Moser, R., Raffaelli, R., and Thilmany, D. D. (2011). Consumer preferences for fruit and vegetables with credence-based attributes: A review. *International Food and Agribusiness Management Review* 14(2):121–142.

MSI Integrity (2013). *2013 MSI Evaluation Report: Common Code for the Coffee Community (4C)*. Boston: MSI Integrity.

MTSS (2018). *Persona Adolescente Trabajadora*. San Jose: Ministerio de Trabajo y Seguridad Social de Costa Rica.

Muradian, R., and Pelupessy, W. (2005). Governing the coffee chain: The role of voluntary regulatory systems. *World Development* 33 (12):2029–2044. https://doi.org/10.1016/j.worlddev.2005.06.007.

Mutersbaugh, T. (2005). Fighting standards with standards: Harmonization, rents, and social accountability in certified agrofood networks. *Environment and Planning A* 37(11):2033–2051. https://doi.org/10.1068/a37369.

Myers, J. P., Antoniou, M. N., Blumberg, B., *et al.* (2016). Concerns over use of glyphosate-based herbicides and risks associated with exposures: a consensus statement. *Environmental Health* 15:19. https://doi.org/10 .1186/s12940-016-0117-0.

Myers, N., Mittermeier, R. A., Mittermeier, C. G., da Fonseca, G. A. B., and Kent, J. (2000). Biodiversity hotspots for conservation priorities. *Nature* 403(6772):853–858. https://doi.org/10.1038/35002501.

Nestlé (2016). Full-year 2015: 4.2% organic growth, trading operating profit margin up 10 basis points in constant currencies. *Nestlé*. Available at: www.nestle.com/media/pressreleases/allpressreleases/full-year-results-2015 (accessed: November 22, 2016).

Nestlé-Nespresso (2013). *History of the Nespresso AAA Sustainable Quality Program*. Lausanne: Nestlé-Nespresso.

Nestlé-Nespresso (2018). *Nespresso* AAA Sustainable Quality™ Program: A triple-win collaboration between Nespresso and the Rainforest Alliance. *Nestlé-Nespresso*. Available at: www.nestle-nespresso.com/newsandfeatures/nespresso-aaa-sustainable-quality-tm-program-a-triple-win-collaboration-between-nespresso-and-the-rainforest-alliance (accessed: March 9, 2018).

Neumann, D. (2012). *The World of Coffee in 2017*. Herradura: SINTERCAFE.

Newman, S. (2009). Financialization and changes in the social relations along commodity chains: The case of coffee. *Review of Radical Political Economics* 41(4):539–559. https://doi.org/10.1177/0486613409341454.

Newsom, D., Bahn, V., and Cashore, B. (2006). Does forest certification matter? An analysis of operation-level changes required during the SmartWood certification process in the United States. *Forest Policy and Economics* 9(3):197–208. https://doi.org/10.1016/j.forpol.2005.06.007.

Nieters, A., Grabs, J., Jimenez, G., and Alpizar, W. (2015). *NAMA Café Costa Rica – A Tool for Low-Carbon Development*. Berlin: NAMA Facility/GIZ Costa Rica.

Nisen, M. (2014). America loves K-cups, but instant coffee rules the world. *Quartz*. Available at: http://qz.com/207354/america-loves-k-cups-but-instant-coffee-rules-the-world/ (accessed October 27, 2016).

North, D. C. (1990). *Institutions, Institutional Change and Economic Performance*. Cambridge: Cambridge University Press.

O'Brien, T. G., and Kinnaird, M. F. (2003). Caffeine and conservation. *Science* 300(5619):587–587. https://doi.org/10.1126/science.1082328.

Ostrom, E. (1990). *Governing the Commons: The Evolution of Institutions for Collective Action*. Cambridge, New York: Cambridge University Press.

Ostrom, E. (1998). A behavioral approach to the rational choice theory of collective action: Presidential address, American Political Science Association, 1997. *The American Political Science Review* 92(1):1–22. https://doi.org/10.2307/2585925.

Ostrom, E. (2005). *Understanding Institutional Diversity*. Princeton, NJ: Princeton University Press.

Ostrom, V. (1999). Artisanship and artifact. In: McGinnis, M. D. (ed.). *Polycentric Games and Institutions: Readings from the Workshop in Political Theory and Policy Analysis.* Ann Arbor: University of Michigan Press, pp. 377–393.

Ostrom, V., and Ostrom, E. (1971). Public choice: A different approach to the study of public administration. *Public Administration Review* 31 (2):203–216. https://doi.org/10.2307/974676.

Ouma, S. (2010). Global standards, local realities: Private agrifood governance and the restructuring of the Kenyan horticulture industry. *Economic Geography* 86(2):197–222. https://doi.org/10.1111/j.1944-82 87.2009.01065.x.

Ovando Palacio, V. H. (2016). El Camino Del Cafe. Available at: https://web .archive.org/web/20160901191418/www.goear.com/cooperandes (accessed: January 6, 2020).

Paiement, P. (2016). ISEAL Alliance and the administrative governance of transnational sustainability standards. *Tilburg Law Review* 21 (2):144–168. https://doi.org/10.1163/22112596-02102004.

Panhuysen, S., and Pierrot, J. (2018). *Coffee Barometer 2018.* The Hague: Hivos.

Pattberg, P. (2005a). The institutionalization of private governance: How business and nonprofit organizations agree on transnational rules. *Governance* 18(4):589–610.

Pattberg, P. (2005b). The Forest Stewardship Council: Risk and potential of private forest governance. *The Journal of Environment & Development* 14(3):356–374.

Pedini, S., Santucci, F. M., and Silvestre, A. L. (2017). Fair trade minimum price: A comparative analysis for the arabica coffee market. *British Journal of Economics, Management & Trade* 17(1):1–15.

Perfect Daily Grind (2017). World coffee producers forum outlines aims for coffee industry. *Perfect Daily Grind.* Available at: www.perfectdailygrind .com/2017/07/world-coffee-producers-forum-outlines-aims-coffee-indus try/ (accessed: August 1, 2017).

Perfecto, I., Rice, R. A., Greenberg, R., and van der Voort, M. E. (1996). Shade coffee: A disappearing refuge for biodiversity. *BioScience* 46 (8):598–608. https://doi.org/10.2307/1312989.

Perfecto, I., and Vandermeer, J. (2008). Biodiversity conservation in tropical agroecosystems: a new conservation paradigm. *Annals of the New York Academy of Sciences* 1134:173–200. https://doi.org/10.1196/annals .1439.011.

Perfecto, I., and Vandermeer, J. (2010). The agroecological matrix as alternative to the land-sparing/agriculture intensification model. *Proceedings of the National Academy of Sciences* 107(13):5786–5791. https://doi.org/10.1073 /pnas.0905455107.

Perfecto, I., Vandermeer, J., Mas, A., and Pinto, L. S. (2005). Biodiversity, yield, and shade coffee certification. *Ecological Economics* **54** (4):435–446. https://doi.org/10.1016/j.ecolecon.2004.10.009.

Petrokovsky, G., and Jennings, S. (2018). *The Effectiveness of Standards in Driving Adoption of Sustainability Practices: A State of Knowledge Review.* Oxford: ISEAL Alliance and 3Keel LLP.

Peyser, R. (2014). 2020: How Keurig Green Mountain plans to improve the livelihoods of one million people in its supply chain. *CSR Wire.* Available at: www.csrwire.com/blog/posts/1277–2020-how-keurig-green-moun tain-plans-to-improve-the-livelihoods-of-one-million-people-in-its-supply -chain (accessed: November 3, 2016).

Phalan, B., Onial, M., Balmford, A., and Green, R. E. (2011). Reconciling food production and biodiversity conservation: Land sharing and land sparing compared. *Science* **333**(6047):1289–1291. https://doi.org/10 .1126/science.1208742.

Philpott, S. M., Arendt, W. J., Armbrecht, I., *et al.* (2008). Biodiversity loss in Latin American coffee landscapes: review of the evidence on ants, birds, and trees. *Conservation Biology: The Journal of the Society for Conservation Biology* **22**(5):1093–1105. https://doi.org/10.1111/j.1523-1739.2008.01029.x.

Philpott, S. M., Bichier, P., Rice, R., and Greenberg, R. (2007). Field-testing ecological and economic benefits of coffee certification programs. *Conservation Biology: The Journal of the Society for Conservation Biology* **21**(4):975–985. https://doi.org/10.1111/j.1523-1739.2007.00728.x.

Pierce, B., and Sweeney, B. (2004). Cost–quality conflict in audit firms: An empirical investigation. *European Accounting Review* **13**(3):415–441. https://doi.org/10.1080/0963818042000216794.

Pierrot, J. (2016). *Trends in Certified Coffees.* San Jose: SINTERCAFE.

Pimm, S., and Raven, P. (2000). Extinction by numbers. *Nature* **403**:843–845.

Ponte, S. (2002). The 'latte revolution'? Regulation, markets and consumption in the global coffee chain. *World Development* **30** (7):1099–1122. https://doi.org/10.1016/S0305-750X(02)00032-3.

Ponte, S. (2008). Greener than thou: The political economy of fish ecolabeling and its local manifestations in South Africa. *World Development* **36**(1):159–175. https://doi.org/10.1016/j .worlddev.2007.02.014.

Ponte, S. (2012). The Marine Stewardship Council (MSC) and the making of a market for 'sustainable fish'. *Journal of Agrarian Change* **12** (2–3):300–315. https://doi.org/10.1111/j.1471-0366.2011.00345.x.

Ponte, S., and Gibbon, P. (2005). Quality standards, conventions and the governance of global value chains. *Economy and Society* **34**(1):1–31. https:// doi.org/10.1080/0308514042000329315.

Pope, J., Annandale, D., and Morrison-Saunders, A. (2004). Conceptualising sustainability assessment. *Environmental Impact Assessment Review* **24** (6):595–616. https://doi.org/10.1016/j.eiar.2004.03.001.

Portafolio (2017). El café robusta seduce a los productores colombianos. *Portafolio.co*. Available at: www.portafolio.co/negocios/cafe-robusta-seria-sembrado-en-colombia-504327 (accessed: May 2, 2018).

Porter, M. E., Stern, S., and Green, M. (2015). *2015 Social Progress Index*. Washington, DC: Social Progress Imperative.

Potoski, M., and Prakash, A. (2009). *Voluntary Programs: A Club Theory Perspective*. Cambridge, MA: MIT Press.

Potts, J., Lynch, M., Wilkings, A., *et al.* (2014). *The State of Sustainability Initiatives Review. Standards and the Green Economy*. Winnipeg: International Institute for Sustainable Development.

Prakash, A., and Potoski, M. (2007). Collective action through voluntary environmental programs: A club theory perspective. *Policy Studies Journal* 35(4):773–792. https://doi.org/10.1111/j.1541-0072.2007.00247.x.

Pretel, E. A. (2018). Exclusive: Costa Rica to lift 30-year ban on planting robusta coffee trees. *Reuters*. Available at: www.reuters.com/article/us-costa-rica-coffee-exclusive/exclusive-costa-rica-to-lift-30-year-ban-on-planting-robusta-coffee-trees-idUSKBN1FT2UH (accessed: May 2, 2018).

Pretty, J., and Smith, D. (2004). Social capital in biodiversity conservation and management. *Conservation Biology* 18(3):631–638. https://doi.org/10.1111/j.1523-1739.2004.00126.x.

Rahn, E., Läderach, P., Baca, M., *et al.* (2014). Climate change adaptation, mitigation and livelihood benefits in coffee production: Where are the synergies? *Mitigation and Adaptation Strategies for Global Change* **19** (8):1119–1137. https://doi.org/10.1007/s11027-013-9467-x.

Rainforest Alliance (2010). A number of ways to measure progress. *The Frog Blog*. Available at: https://web.archive.org/web/20131205230720/https://thefrogblog.org/2010/10/01/a-number-of-ways-to-measure-progress/ (accessed: January 6, 2020).

Rainforest Alliance (2015). *Rainforest Alliance Accreditation Requirements for Certification Bodies*. New York: The Rainforest Alliance.

Rainforest Alliance (2017a). Sustainable agriculture certification. *Rainforest Alliance | Agriculture Certification*. Available at: www.rainforest-alliance.org/business/sas/ (accessed: March 9, 2018).

Rainforest Alliance (2017b). Authorization of certification bodies. *Rainforest Alliance*. Available at: www.rainforest-alliance.org/business/sas/governance/accreditation-certification-bodies/ (accessed: February 11, 2018).

Rainforest Alliance (2018a). Q&A on the Rainforest Alliance-UTZ merger. *Rainforest Alliance*. Available at: www.rainforest-alliance.org/faqs/rainforest-utz-merger (accessed: August 14, 2018).

Rainforest Alliance (2018b). *2017 Annual Report*. New York: Rainforest Alliance.

Ramos-Scharrón, C. E., and Thomaz, E. L. (2017). Runoff development and soil erosion in a wet tropical montane setting under coffee cultivation. *Land Degradation & Development* 28(3):936–945. https://doi.org/10 .1002/ldr.2567.

Rao, P., Gentry, A. L., Quandt, S. A., *et al.* (2006). Pesticide safety behaviors in Latino farmworker family households. *American Journal of Industrial Medicine* 49(4):271–280. https://doi.org/10.1002/ajim.20277.

Rattan, S., Parande, A. K., Nagaraju, V. D., and Ghiwari, G. K. (2015). A comprehensive review on utilization of wastewater from coffee processing. *Environmental Science and Pollution Research* 22 (9):6461–6472. https://doi.org/10.1007/s11356-015-4079-5.

Rauh, V. A., Garcia, W. E., Whyatt, R. M., *et al.* (2015). Prenatal exposure to the organophosphate pesticide chlorpyrifos and childhood tremor. *Neurotoxicology* 51:80–86. https://doi.org/10.1016/j .neuro.2015.09.004.

Rauh, V. A., Garfinkel, R., Perera, F. P., *et al.* (2006). Impact of prenatal chlorpyrifos exposure on neurodevelopment in the first 3 years of life among inner-city children. *Pediatrics* 118(6):e1845–e1859. https://doi .org/10.1542/peds.2006-0338.

Raynolds, L. T. (2009). Mainstreaming fair trade coffee: From partnership to traceability. *World Development* 37(6):1083–1093. https://doi.org/10 .1016/j.worlddev.2008.10.001.

Raynolds, L. T., Murray, D., and Heller, A. (2007). Regulating sustainability in the coffee sector: A comparative analysis of third-party environmental and social certification initiatives. *Agriculture and Human Values* 24 (2):147–163. https://doi.org/10.1007/s10460-006-9047-8.

Raynolds, L. T., Murray, D., and Taylor, P. L. (2004). Fair trade coffee: Building producer capacity via global networks. *Journal of International Development* 16:1109–1121. https://doi.org/10.1002/jid.1136.

Reichman, N. (1992). Moving backstage: Uncovering the role of compliance practices in shaping regulatory policy. In: Schlegel, K. and Weisburd, D. (eds.). *White-Collar Crime Reconsidered*. Boston: Northeastern University Press.

Reinecke, J. (2010). Beyond a subjective theory of value and towards a 'fair price': An organizational perspective on Fairtrade minimum price setting. *Organization* 17(5):563–581. https://doi.org/10.1177/1350508410372622.

Reinecke, J., Manning, S., and von Hagen, O. (2012). The emergence of a standards market: Multiplicity of sustainability standards in the global coffee industry. *Organization Studies* 33(5–6):791–814. https://doi.org/10 .1177/0170840612443629.

Renard, M.-C. (2003). Fair trade: Quality, market and conventions. *Journal of Rural Studies* 19(1):87–96. https://doi.org/10.1016/S0743-0167(02)00051-7.

Renard, M. C., and Loconto, A. (2013). Competing logics in the further standardization of fair trade: ISEAL and the Símbolo de Pequeños Productores. *International Journal of Sociology of Agriculture and Food* 20 (1):51–68.

ResponsAbility (2013). *Fair Trade Coffee from Costa Rica: A Smallholder Success Story. Key Findings.* Zurich: ResponsAbility.

Rice, P. D., and McLean, J. (1999). *Sustainable Coffee at the Crossroads.* Washington, DC: The Consumer's Choice Council.

Rising, J., Simmons, J., Brahm, M., and Sachs, J. (2016). *The Impacts of Climate Change on Coffee: Trouble Brewing.* New York: The Earth Institute, Columbia University.

Rivera, J. (2002). Assessing a voluntary environmental initiative in the developing world: The Costa Rican Certification for Sustainable Tourism. *Policy Sciences* 35(4):333–360. https://doi.org/10.1023 /A:1021371011105.

Rivera, J., de Leon, P., and Koerber, C. (2006). Is greener whiter yet? The Sustainable Slopes program after five years. *Policy Studies Journal* 34 (2):195–221.

Rivera, J., Naranjo, M. A., Robalino, J., Alpizar, F., and Blackman, A. (2017). Local community characteristics and cooperation for shared green reputation. *Policy Studies Journal* 45(4):613–632. https://doi.org/10.1111/psj.12156.

Rivera, J., and Roeschmann, J. (2019). Price-premium effects of business and community green certifications: The case of the Costa Rican hotel industry. *Business Strategy & Development* 2(2):117–126. https://doi .org/10.1002/bsd2.47.

Roldán-Pérez, A., Gonzalez-Perez, M.-A., Pham, T. H., and Dao, N. T. (2009). *Coffee, Cooperation and Competition: A Comparative Study of Colombia and Vietnam.* Geneva: UNCTAD Virtual Institute.

Romero, F. R. (2012). La política comparada de la comercialización internacional del café entre los sectores cafeteros de Colombia y Costa Rica. *InterSedes* 13(26).

Rossi, A. (2013). Does economic upgrading lead to social upgrading in global production networks? Evidence from Morocco. *World Development* 46:223–233. https://doi.org/10.1016/j.worlddev.2013.02.002.

Ruben, R., and Fort, R. (2012). The impact of fair trade certification for coffee farmers in Peru. *World Development* 40(3):570–582. https://doi .org/10.1016/j.worlddev.2011.07.030.

Ruben, R., Fort, R., and Zúñiga-Arias, G. (2009). Measuring the impact of fair trade on development. *Development in Practice* 19(6):777–788. https://doi .org/10.1080/09614520903027049.

Ruben, R., and Zuniga, G. (2011). How standards compete: comparative impact of coffee certification schemes in Northern Nicaragua. *Supply Chain Management: An International Journal* 16(2):98–109. https://doi .org/10.1108/13598541111115356.

Rueda, X., and Lambin, E. (2013). Responding to globalization: Impacts of certification on Colombian small-scale coffee growers. *Ecology and Society* 18(3). https://doi.org/10.5751/ES-05595-180321.

Rueda, X., Thomas, N. E., and Lambin, E. F. (2014). Eco-certification and coffee cultivation enhance tree cover and forest connectivity in the Colombian coffee landscapes. *Regional Environmental Change* 15 (1):25–33. https://doi.org/10.1007/s10113-014-0607-y.

Sabatier, P., Poulenard, J., Fanget, B., *et al.* (2014). Long-term relationships among pesticide applications, mobility, and soil erosion in a vineyard watershed. *Proceedings of the National Academy of Sciences* 111 (44):15647–15652. https://doi.org/10.1073/pnas.1411512111.

SAN (2009). *Guía de Interpretación – Indicadores Para La Producción Sostenible de Café En Honduras.* San Jose: Sustainable Agriculture Network.

SAN (2010). *Sustainable Agriculture Standard. July 2010 (Version 3).* San Jose: Sustainable Agriculture Network.

SAN (2011). *SAN Group Certification Standard. March 2011.* San Jose: Sustainable Agriculture Network.

SAN (2012). *Indicadores Locales Para La Producción Sostenible de Café En Colombia.* San Jose: Sustainable Agriculture Network.

SAN (2013). *General Interpretation Guide – Group Certification Standard. March 2013.* San Jose: Sustainable Agriculture Network.

SAN (2014). *General Interpretation Guide – Sustainable Agriculture Standard. July 2014.* San Jose: Sustainable Agriculture Network.

SAN (2017). *Sustainable Agriculture Standard. For Farms' and Producer Groups' Crop and Cattle Production. July 2017.* San Jose: Sustainable Agriculture Network.

Sánchez Hernández, L., Espindola Rafael, V., van Rikxoort, H., and Cipriani, G. (2016). *Manual Para La Construcción de Sistemas de Tratamiento de Aguas Residuales En Beneficios Pequeños de Café.* Amsterdam: UTZ Certified.

Sasser, E. N., Prakash, A., Cashore, B., and Auld, G. (2006). Direct targeting as an NGO political strategy: Examining private authority regimes in the forestry sector. *Business and Politics* 8(3):1–32. https://doi.org/10.2202/ 1469-3569.1163.

SCAA (2016). *A Blueprint for Farmworker Inclusion.* Santa Ana: Specialty Coffee Association of America.

SCC (2016). *Sustainability Framework – Draft for Consultation*. Sustainable Coffee Challenge.

Schlesinger, P., Brenes, C. L. M., Jones, K. W., and Vierling, L. A. (2017). The Trifinio Region: A case study of transboundary forest change in Central America. *Journal of Land Use Science* 12(1):36–54. https://doi.org/10.1080/1747423X.2016.1261948.

Schreiner, M. (2010). *Honduras 2007 Progress out of Poverty Index® (PPI®): Design Memo*. Kansas City: Progress out of Poverty/Innovations for Poverty Action.

SCS (2017). *Starbucks Coffee Company C.A.F.E. Practices Verifier and Inspector Operations Manual*. Emeryville, CA: SCS Global Services.

Shepsle, K. A. (1989). Studying institutions: Some lessons from the rational choice approach. *Journal of Theoretical Politics* 1(2):131–147. https://doi.org/10.1177/0951692889001002002.

Simon, H. A. (1972). Theories of bounded rationality. In: McGuire, C. B. and Radner, R. (eds.). *Decision and Organization*. Amsterdam: North–Holland Publishing Company.

Simon, H. A. (1978). Rationality as process and as product of thought. *The American Economic Review* 68(2):1–16.

Simon, H. A. (1990). Bounded rationality. In: Eatwell, J., Milgate, M., and Newman, P. (eds.). *Utility and Probability*. London: Palgrave Macmillan, pp. 15–18.

Simonneau, M. (2013). Reunión de la Red Café de CLAC en San Salvador. *Progreso Network*. Available at: http://progresonetwork.ning.com/profiles/blogs/reunion-de-la-red-cafe-de-clac-en-san-salvador (accessed: May 2, 2018).

Sizer, N., and de Freitas, A. (2016). The biggest crisis is also the greatest opportunity. *GreenBiz*. Available at: www.greenbiz.com/article/biggest-crisis-also-greatest-opportunity (accessed: December 21, 2017).

Smithsonian Institute (2017). Bird friendly coffee farms. *Smithsonian's National Zoo & Conservation Biology Institute*. Available at: https://nationalzoo.si.edu/migratory-birds/bird-friendly-coffee-farms (accessed: September 14, 2017).

Snider, A., Gallegos, A. A., Gutiérrez, I., and Sibelet, N. (2017). Social capital and sustainable coffee certifications in Costa Rica. *Human Ecology* 45 (2):235–249. https://doi.org/10.1007/s10745-017-9896-3.

Snider, A., Gutiérrez, I., Sibelet, N., and Faure, G. (2017). Small farmer cooperatives and voluntary coffee certifications: Rewarding progressive farmers of engendering widespread change in Costa Rica? *Food Policy* 69:231–242. https://doi.org/10.1016/j.foodpol.2017.04.009.

Snow, D. A., and Soule, S. A. (2010). *A Primer on Social Movements*. New York: W. W. Norton & Company.

Solano B., A. (2015). En Costa Rica aprovechar la madera del bosque es una utopía. *La Nación, Grupo Nación*. Available at: www.nacion.com/ciencia/m edio-ambiente/en-costa-rica-aprovechar-la-madera-del-bosque-es-una-utopia /2RE44V72LFGOVEIDYMFX6H7KM4/story/ (accessed: February 21, 2018).

Solér, C., Sandström, C., and Skoog, H. (2017). How can high-biodiversity coffee make it to the mainstream market? The performativity of voluntary sustainability standards and outcomes for coffee diversification. *Environmental Management* 59(2):230–248. https://doi.org/10.1007/s0026 7-016-0786-z.

Soto-Pinto, L., Perfecto, I., Castillo-Hernandez, J., and Caballero-Nieto, J. (2000). Shade effect on coffee production at the northern Tzeltal zone of the state of Chiapas, Mexico. *Agriculture, Ecosystems & Environment* 80 (1):61–69. https://doi.org/10.1016/S0167-8809(00)00134-1.

Soule, S. A. (2009). *Contention and Corporate Social Responsibility*. Cambridge: Cambridge University Press.

Spar, D. L., and La Mure, L. T. (2003). The power of activism: Assessing the impact of NGOs on global business. *California Management Review* 45 (3):78–101. https://doi.org/10.2307/41166177.

Starbucks (2014). *C.A.F.E. Practices Smallholder Scorecard*. Seattle: Starbucks Coffee Company.

Starbucks (2018). Responsibly grown and fair trade coffee. *Starbucks Coffee Company*. Available at: www.starbucks.ca/responsibility/sourcing/coffee (accessed: March 9, 2018).

Statista (2016). Gross margin of Keurig Green Mountain's single-serve cup packs worldwide from 2010 to 2015. *Statista*. Available at: www .statista.com/statistics/326520/keurig-green-mountain-gross-margin-of-por tion-packs-worldwide/ (accessed: November 22, 2016).

Steemers, S. (2016). *Coffee Sustainability Catalogue 2016. A Collective Review of Work Being Done to Make Coffee Sustainable*. Bonn: Global Coffee Platform, IDH Sustainable Trade Initiative, Specialty Coffee Association of America, Sustainable Coffee Challenge.

Steering Committee of the State-of-Knowledge Assessment of Standards and Certification (2012). *Toward Sustainability: The Roles and Limitations of Certification*. Washington, DC: RESOLVE, Inc.

Stickler, C., Duchelle, A., Ardila, J. P., et al. (2018). *The State of Jurisdictional Sustainability: Synthesis for Practitioners and Policymakers*. San Francisco: Earth Innovation Institute.

Strange, S. (1996). *The Retreat of the State: The Diffusion of Power in the World Economy*. Cambridge: Cambridge University Press.

Stroup, S. S., and Wong, W. H. (2017). *The Authority Trap: Strategic Choices of International NGOs*. Ithaca, NY: Cornell University Press.

Sustainable Brands (2016). SAN, Rainforest Alliance update certification with focus on climate-smart ag, curbing deforestation. *sustainablebrands .com*. Available at: www.sustainablebrands.com/news_and_views/sup ply_chain/sustainable_brands/san_rainforest_alliance_update_certifica tion_focus (accessed: December 21, 2017).

Takahashi, R., and Todo, Y. (2017). Coffee certification and forest quality: Evidence from a wild coffee forest in Ethiopia. *World Development* 92:158–166. https://doi.org/10.1016/j.worlddev.2016.12.001.

Talbot, J. (2002). Information, finance, and the new international inequality: the case of coffee. *Journal of World-Systems Research* 8(2):214–250.

Tallontire, A. (2000). Partnerships in fair trade: Reflections from a case study of Café Direct. *Development in Practice* 10(2):166–177. https://doi.org/10 .1080/09614520050010205.

Tashakkori, A., and Teddlie, C. (1998). *Mixed Methodology: Combining Qualitative and Quantitative Approaches – First Edition*. Thousand Oaks, CA: Sage Publications.

Taylor, M. (2011). Race you to the bottom … and back again? The uneven development of labour codes of conduct. *New Political Economy* 16 (4):445–462. https://doi.org/10.1080/13563467.2011.519023.

Tchibo (2014). Joining forces: Helping coffee farmers with the transition. *Tchibo Sustainability Report 2014*. Available at: www.tchibo-sustainability.com/serv let/content/1104614/-/home/coffee-vc/220-the-sustainable-development-of- the-coffee-sector/tchibo-joint-forces.html (accessed: November 2, 2016).

Teketay, D. (1999). History, botany and ecological requirements of coffee. *Walia* 20:28–50.

Thaler, R. H., and Sunstein, C. R. (2009). *Nudge: Improving Decisions about Health, Wealth, and Happiness*. New York: Penguin Books.

The J. M. Smucker Company (2016). The J. M. Smucker Company announces fiscal 2016 fourth quarter results and fiscal 2017 outlook. *PR Newswire*. Available at: www.prnewswire.com/news-releases/the-j-m-smucker- company-announces-fiscal-2016-fourth-quarter-results-and-fiscal-2017-ou tlook-300282311.html (accessed: November 22, 2016).

Thorlakson, T. (2018). A move beyond sustainability certification: The evolution of the chocolate industry's sustainable sourcing practices. *Business Strategy and the Environment* 27(8):1653–1665. https://doi.org /10.1002/bse.2230.

Tilman, D., Balzer, C., Hill, J., and Befort, B. L. (2011). Global food demand and the sustainable intensification of agriculture. *Proceedings of the National Academy of Sciences* 108(50):20260–20264. https://doi.org/10 .1073/pnas.1116437108.

Tucker, C. M. (2008). *Changing Forests: Collective Action, Common Property, and Coffee in Honduras*. Berlin: Springer Science & Business Media.

Underdal, A. (2002). One question, two answers. In: Miles, E. L., Underdal, A., Andresen, S., *et al.* (eds.). *Environmental Regime Effectiveness: Confronting Theory with Evidence.* Cambridge, MA: MIT Press.

UNDP (2017). Human Development Index (HDI). *Human Development Reports.* Available at: http://hdr.undp.org/en/content/human-development-index-hdi (accessed: February 22, 2017).

UNFSS (2016). *Meeting Sustainability Goals: Voluntary Sustainability Standards and the Role of the Government.* Geneva: United Nations Forum on Sustainability Standards.

US Bureau of Labor Statistics (2019). Bureau of Labor Statistics Data. *US Bureau of Labor Statistics.* Available at: https://data.bls.gov/pdq/Survey OutputServlet (accessed: July 17, 2017).

USAID, digitalGreen, CARE and IFPRI (2017). *Honduras: Evaluación a Fondo de Los Servicios de Extensión y Asesoramiento.* Washington, DC: Feed the Future.

USDA FAS (2016). *Honduras Coffee Annual 2016.* Washington, DC: United States Department of Agriculture, Foreign Agricultural Service.

UTZ (2017). *Coffee Statistics Report 2016.* Amsterdam: UTZ.

UTZ Certified (2014a). *Core Code of Conduct Version 1.0. For Group and Multi-Group Certification.* Amsterdam: UTZ Certified.

UTZ Certified (2014b). *Code of Conduct Coffee Module Version 1.0.* Amsterdam: UTZ Certified.

UTZ Certified (2016a). Interactive map. *UTZ Certified.* Available at: www .utzcertified.org/en/products/interactivemap (accessed: October 20, 2016).

UTZ Certified (2016b). *UTZ Impact Report March 2016.* Amsterdam: UTZ Certified.

UTZ Certified (2017). *UTZ Guidance Document Good Auditing Practices.* Amsterdam: UTZ Certified.

UTZ Certified (2018a). UTZ – The label and program for sustainable farming. *UTZ.* Available at: https://utz.org/ (accessed: March 9, 2018).

UTZ Certified (2018b). Certification bodies. *UTZ.* Available at: https://utz .org/who-we-work-with/certification-bodies/ (accessed: May 3, 2018).

Valkila, J., and Nygren, A. (2010). Impacts of fair trade certification on coffee farmers, cooperatives, and laborers in Nicaragua. *Agriculture and Human Values* 27(3):321–333. https://doi.org/10.1007/s10460-009-920 8-7.

van der Ven, H. (2014). Socializing the C-Suite: Why some big-box retailers are "greener" than others. *Business and Politics* 16(1):31–63.

van der Ven, H. (2019). *Beyond Greenwash: Explaining Credibility in Transnational Eco-Labeling.* New York: Oxford University Press.

van Rijn, F., Burger, K., and den Belder, E. (2012). Impact assessment in the sustainable livelihood framework. *Development in Practice* **22** (7):1019–1035. https://doi.org/10.1080/09614524.2012.696586.

van Rijsbergen, B., Elbers, W., Ruben, R., and Njuguna, S. N. (2016). The ambivalent impact of coffee certification on farmers' welfare: A matched panel approach for cooperatives in central Kenya. *World Development* 77:277–292. https://doi.org/10.1016/j.worlddev.2015.08.021.

Vandermeer, J., and Perfecto, I. (2012). Syndromes of production in agriculture: Prospects for social-ecological regime change. *Ecology and Society* **17**(4):39. https://doi.org/10.5751/ES-04813-170439.

Velez, R. (2015). *The Dilemma of Economic Sustainability*. Herradura: SINTERCAFE.

Velez, R. (2016). FNC's 100/100 initiative for Colombian coffee. *The First Pull*. Available at: https://nationalcoffeeblog.org/2016/08/01/fncs-10010 0-initiative-for-colombian-coffee/ (accessed: November 1, 2016).

Vellema, W., Buritica Casanova, A., Gonzalez, C., and D'Haese, M. (2015). The effect of specialty coffee certification on household livelihood strategies and specialisation. *Food Policy* 57:13–25. https://doi.org/10 .1016/j.foodpol.2015.07.003.

Verbruggen, P. (2013). Gorillas in the closet? Public and private actors in the enforcement of transnational private regulation. *Regulation & Governance* **7**(4):512–532.

Verma, V. (2015). *Securing Our Future Coffee Supply Chain – A Global View*. Herradura: SINTERCAFE.

Viederman, S. (1994). Five capitals and three pillars of sustainability. *The Newsletter of PEGS* **4**(1):5–12.

Vogel, D. (2009). The private regulation of global corporate conduct. In: Mattli, W., and Woods, N. (eds.). *The Politics of Global Regulation*. Princeton, NJ: Princeton University Press, pp. 151–188.

WageIndicator (2018a). Salario mínimo, por rama actividad económica. *T usalario.Org/Honduras*. Available at: https://tusalario.org/honduras/sal ario/salario-minimo (accessed: November 14, 2019).

WageIndicator (2018b). Salario mínimo, subsidio de transporte. *Tusalario .Org/Colombia*. Available at: https://tusalario.org/colombia/tusalario/sal ario-minimo (accessed: November 14, 2019).

WageIndicator (2018c). Salario mínimo, en nivel de Habilidad. *Tusalario .Org/Costa Rica*. Available at: https://tusalario.org/costarica/tu-salario/sal ario-minimo (accessed: November 14, 2019).

Walker, I. (2008). Null hypothesis testing and effect sizes. *Statistics for Psychology*. Available at: http://staff.bath.ac.uk/pssiw/stats2/page2/pag e14/page14.html (accessed: February 18, 2019).

Williamson, O. E. (1975). *Markets and Hierarchies, Analysis and Antitrust Implications*. New York: Free Press.

Wilson, A. P., and Wilson, N. L. W. (2014). The economics of quality in the specialty coffee industry: Insights from the Cup of Excellence auction programs. *Agricultural Economics* 45:91–105. https://doi.org/10.1111/agec.12132.

Wirth, F. F., Stanton, J. L., and Wiley, J. B. (2011). The relative importance of search versus credence product attributes: Organic and locally grown. *Agricultural and Resource Economics Review* 40(1):48–62. https://doi.org/10.1017/S1068280500004512.

World Bank (2017). Worldwide governance indicators. *World Bank Databank*. Available at: http://databank.worldbank.org/data/reports.aspx?source=worldwide-governance-indicators (accessed: October 25, 2017).

World Commission on Environment and Development (1987). *Our Common Future*. Oxford: Oxford University Press.

Yarbrough, B. V., and Yarbrough, R. M. (1990). International institutions and the new economics of organization. *International Organization* 44 (2):235–259. https://doi.org/10.1017/S0020818300035268.

York, R., and Rosa, E. A. (2003). Key challenges to ecological modernization theory: Institutional efficacy, case study evidence, units of analysis, and the pace of eco-efficiency. *Organization & Environment* 16(3):273–288. https://doi.org/10.1177/1086026603256299.

Young, O. R. (ed.) (1999). *The Effectiveness of International Environmental Regimes. Causal Connections and Behavioral Mechanisms*. Cambridge, MA: MIT Press.

Young, O. R. (2001). Inferences and indices: Evaluating the effectiveness of international environmental regimes. *Global Environmental Politics* 1 (1):99–121. https://doi.org/10.1162/152638001570651.

Young, O. R. (2002). *The Institutional Dimensions of Environmental Change: Fit, Interplay, and Scale*. Cambridge, MA: MIT Press.

Young, O. R. (2011). Effectiveness of international environmental regimes: Existing knowledge, cutting-edge themes, and research strategies. *Proceedings of the National Academy of Sciences* 108 (50):19853–19860.

Young, O. R., and Levy, M. A. (1999). The effectiveness of international environmental regimes. In: Young, O. R. (ed.). *The Effectiveness of International Environmental Regimes. Causal Connections and Behavioral Mechanisms*. Cambridge, MA: MIT Press, pp. 1–32.

Zamora, M. (2013). Column: Independent smallholder farmers are the silent majority. *Daily Coffee News by Roast Magazine*. Available at: http://dail

ycoffeenews.com/2013/06/14/column-independent-smallholder-farmers-are-the-silent-majority/ (accessed: August 9, 2017).

Zorn, A., Lippert, C., and Dabbert, S. (2012). Supervising a system of approved private control bodies for certification: The case of organic farming in Germany. *Food Control* 25(2):525–532. https://doi.org/10.1016/j.foodcont.2011.11.013.

Index

Printed in the United States
by Baker & Taylor Publisher Services